Financial Innovation and Risk Sharing

Financial Innovation and Risk Sharing

Franklin Allen and Douglas Gale

The MIT Press
Cambridge, Massachusetts
London, England

This book was set in Times Roman by Asco Trade Typesetting Ltd., Hong Kong and was printed and bound in the United States of America.

Library of Congress Cataloging-in-Publication Data

Allen, Franklin, 1956–
  Financial innovation and risk sharing / Franklin Allen and Douglas Gale.
     p.   cm.
  Includes bibliographical references and index.
  ISBN 0-262-01141-7
  1. Financial engineering. 2. Risk assessment. I. Gale, Douglas. II. Title.
HG176.7.A44   1994
332—dc20
                                                                      93-51058
                                                                          CIP

Contents

Preface

For several years we have been working on problems related to financial innovation, an area of economics that is attracting increasing interest. Our research began with a simple question that one or the other of us posed as we sat outside the Wharton School in Philadelphia one summer: What would a model of general equilibrium with incomplete markets look like if one tried to make the market structure endogenous? That question eventually led to our paper "Optimal Security Design" (reprinted here as chapter 6), in which we proposed a theory of competitive equilibrium for an economy in which firms can issue new securities. The paper attempted to answer the counterparts of the classical questions concerning existence and efficiency of equilibrium, the optimal form and number of securities, and so on, when the market structure was endogenous. Although the setting was highly stylized, it allowed us to pose some important questions about the impact of one type of financial innovation—issuing new securities—on economic welfare.

That exercise showed us that one could extend the classical theory to deal with this richer set of questions; but, in the end, we concluded the Walrasian framework was not really satisfactory for addressing issues related to financial innovation. This first became clear while we were working on "Optimal Security Design." We discovered that a price-taking equilibrium of the kind described in the paper would not exist if short sales were allowed. If there are no limits on short sales, there can be no incentive ex post to introduce a new set of securities, because this would imply an arbitrage opportunity. On the other hand, if these securities are not issued, there may be an incentive to innovate ex ante. Since prices do not change when the securities are introduced (that is what price taking means), these two conditions are incompatible, so no equilibrium exists. The problem is that price taking is not an appropriate assumption in this context. An attempt to cope with this difficulty led to "Arbitrage, Short Sales, and Financial Innovation" (reprinted here as chapter 7), in which we analyzed a model of imperfectly competitive firms issuing securities to a competitive securities market. Even when the number of potential innovators becomes very large, the classical condition for perfect competition, equilibrium requires a degree of monopoly power to provide an incentive to innovate.

Another outgrowth of "Optimal Security Design" was the paper on "Incomplete Markets and the Incentives to Set Up an Options Exchange" (reprinted here as chapter 8). In the first paper, new securities are issued by firms, whose motive is to increase their market value by "splitting" their income stream into a number of different claims, which are then sold to different "clienteles." The incentive for firms to innovate in this way is quite different from the incentive of the organizers of a securities exchange, say, who make money from commissions on the volume of trade. In "Incomplete Markets and the Incentives to Set Up an Options Exchange" we analyzed a number of examples of bad incentives, mainly externalities that arise from the general-equilibrium effects of setting up a new market, which lead to market failure. For example, opening an options market will typically have an effect on the price of the underlying stock, but there is no reason why the exchange organizers should take this into account. This kind of general-equilibrium effect may be quite common when new markets are set up, but as far as we know these effects have not been systematically studied from the point of view of their impact on economic welfare.

By this point, we were beginning to see interesting applications and extensions in a number of areas, and we decided to pursue some of these questions independently. In "The Efficient Design of Public Debt" (reprinted as chapter 9), Gale applied some of our ideas on security design to the specialized but important setting of government securities. In "Standard Securities" (reprinted here as chapter 10), Gale investigated the private gains from standardization of securities and showed that these might give financial innovators an incentive to choose the same type of security, even if this were not socially optimal. In "The Changing Nature of Debt and Equity: A Financial Perspective" (reprinted here as chapter 11), Allen reviewed a large body of literature related to the optimal design of securities.

In addressing these separate but related questions, we began to develop a coherent point of view. We were far from having a comprehensive theory of financial innovation, but we had produced a number of worthwhile insights. We also felt that what we had learned was greater than the sum of our papers. At this point the idea of writing a book occurred to us. There was a need for a book addressed to graduate students and researchers who were interested in working in this area and wanted a compact reference for some of the source materials. At the same time, we did not feel that the subject was mature enough for a full-blown text. There were few papers addressing the topics we were mainly interested in, and we were certainly not ready to write the last word on the subject. This suggested a novel approach.

The formula we adopted for the book is a compromise between the possibly premature desire to write a text and the unattractive alternative of simply reprinting our previously published papers. It reflects the way many graduate courses are taught. In the classroom, the professor offers examples, comments, heuristics, and sketches and generally tries to draw the subject together and give the student some perspective, without proving every theorem or discussing every detail of the literature. The students are left to read the literature when they have the time and inclination, sometimes after the course has ended.

Our idea was to begin the book with a lengthy introduction, five chapters as it turned out, in which we would attempt to draw together our ideas, provide some important background material, relate our work to the literature, and make suggestions for future work. This part of the book is written so that a graduate student can sit down and read it straight through. It can also be used as a minitext for a graduate course in the economics of financial innovation. The second part of the book consists of the reprinted papers mentioned earlier. They are intended as a resource that the student/researcher can dip into once he or she has mastered the material in the first part.

The content of the book reflects our interests in two ways. First, we have focused on risk sharing as a motive for innovation. As we point out in part I, risk sharing is a very broad phenomenon touching all kinds of economic activities. Consequently, financial innovation, as we use the term, covers a wider class of problems than one might think. Institutions as diverse as the social security system, monetary and fiscal policy, the family, and the United Way all represent ways of sharing risks. So do more traditional examples such as insurance companies, stock exchanges, financial intermediaries, and options markets. Although our formal models deal mainly with the latter, we are interested in the various ways in which societies deal with risk, and that general perspective has influenced our choice of problems, models, and questions.

Second, we are mainly interested in analyzing the impact of decisions about financial innovation on economic welfare. The question on which we focus throughout is whether market institutions provide efficient ways of sharing risk. From this perspective, the markets and securities that we do not observe are just as important as the ones that we do observe. Rather than simply describing the financial instruments and institutions that are "out there," most of the book looks at the incentives for providing different risk-sharing opportunities and analyzes the efficiency of market solutions in the context of stylized theoretical models. We do this to clarify the principles involved, to provide a foundation for future applied work, and to give some insight to those who are interested in changing the current state of affairs.

Inevitably this focus gives less attention to other topics and approaches. This is not to suggest that they are unimportant. This is a new area of research, and *an awful lot* remains to be done. In part I, particularly in chapter 5, we discuss other approaches and a number of topics that have not been studied and try to indicate how they relate to our work. Although we suggest some topics for future research, we are not trying to define the field. If this book serves to introduce students and researchers to some of the questions and ideas we have found interesting and thereby promotes work on financial innovation, it will have served its purpose.

Over the years we have accumulated debts to many people who read our work, discussed it with us, or listened to us present it in seminars. They made many valuable comments. Their names are listed in notes to the papers reprinted here as chapters 6 through 11. We also want to mention those who read the first five chapters and made many detailed suggestions to improve the content, exposition, and coverage, especially Darrell Duffie, Matthew Jackson, David Hirshleifer, and a number of anonymous reviewers, as well as our graduate students Saumya Banerjee, Adam Dunsby, Francisco Gonzalez, José Marin, and Jason Zhang. We offer our grateful thanks to all of them.

Finally, financial support from the NSF is gladly acknowledged.

I FINANCIAL INNOVATION: AN OVERVIEW

1 Introduction

1.1 What is Finance?

The world has been transformed by the frantic pace of financial innovation in the 1970s and 1980s. Contemplating the revolution that has occurred, it is easy to conclude that we live in a high-tech world of effectively complete markets, in which any contingent claim can be synthesized and any risk can be hedged. And this claim is not implausible if we focus our attention exclusively on the financial world of Wall Street or the City of London.

But if we look at the world outside these confines, the picture is rather different. Consider the risks faced by the typical worker. Many large corporations traditionally practiced policies of lifetime employment for their workers. In the United States IBM and Kodak, for example, were renowned for this. In western Europe many large firms also followed this practice, and in Japan there were very few that did not. Although the rights were usually implicit and were not contractually guaranteed, employees working for these firms were secure in the knowledge that they would not be fired, and the benefits provided by the company were not at risk. In the United States these benefits include health and disability insurance, which are crucial to the employee's welfare. One of the most important changes in the financial markets in the United States and United Kingdom that occurred in the 1970s and 1980s was the development of a market for corporate control. This had important effects on the implicit contracts guaranteeing lifetime employment. It is no longer the case that people can feel secure that they will not be fired. Any firm that retains workers who are not productively employed is likely to be taken over. As a result, firms such as IBM and Kodak have abandoned their unstated lifetime employment policies. Moreover, there is very little that their employees can do to offset the risks arising from such reversals in corporate policy. Insurance against unemployment cannot be purchased on the private market. For these individuals, existing outside the financial world of Wall Street and the City of London, markets are now less complete than they were before: risks that could previously be shared with the employer can now no longer be hedged.

In order to evaluate the efficiency of risk sharing in the economy, it is necessary to consider this larger picture. Much of our interest in risk sharing lies in the part of the economy that lies outside what we normally think of as the "financial markets." The typical worker in the United States now has available financial services and instruments, from NOW accounts to mutual index funds to commodity futures, that were not available twenty years ago. At the same time, if we look at an average worker's assets, we still find a striking lack of diversification and important unhedged risks.

• A very large part of an individual's wealth is tied up in a single asset, his or her home.

• Investments in securities are held in the form of pension plans or mutual funds. Although mutual funds offer the advantages of professional management and diversification, it is not clear the average investor is achieving an optimal portfolio this way. The investor's control over these funds and access to information are both limited, so however sophisticated the fund managers may be, we may doubt whether the investor is achieving optimal risk sharing.

• The U.S. wage earner is largely unprotected against income risk, except to the extent that he or she has self-insured through asset accumulation.

• Health insurance, a bulwark against a major risk, is uncertain since it may be discontinued as a result of unemployment.

• Inflation also poses major risks to the investor's financial security. Traditional hedges against inflation—stocks and real estate—provide partial insurance at best, and expose the individual to the uncertain reaction of asset prices.

Incompleteness of markets is not something that affects only private individuals with limited wealth. If one considers the position of nonfinancial companies, one finds again that markets are effectively incomplete. If they are big enough, firms can hedge risks on commodity prices, interest rates, exchange rates, and so on, but many other risks cannot be shifted. Macroeconomic and sector-specific shocks typically cannot be hedged. Even if firms had access to sophisticated instruments that would allow them to hedge these risks in principle, one wonders whether the information exists that would permit them to make an optimal decision. In any case, what firms are observed to do in practice often seems to fall short of what the theoretical optimum would require.

There is no doubt that within the financial community itself a revolution has taken place. The enormously increased sophistication of financial markets generates benefits that can be shared with the rest of the economy in the form of better services and lower costs. Nonetheless, the revolution is circumscribed. The direct benefits of financial innovation have largely been limited to the financial community. For example, interest rate futures allow investors holding mortgage-backed securities to hedge their interest rate risk (principally generated by the call feature of mortgages). Swaps allow firms to achieve the benefits of "interest arbitrage," either by borrowing where they have a comparative advantage or by signaling their risk class. In both cases the innovation solves a financial problem, narrowly defined, but does not touch the wider risks faced by firms and individuals.

There is another point important for the reader to bear in mind when evaluating the efficiency of risk sharing in the economy, and that is that every economy deals with risk in a different way. The United States and the United Kingdom are unusual in making heavy use of securities and financial markets. Other countries rely more heavily on intermediaries such as banks. In addition, the United States is almost unique in the West in placing a heavy responsibility on the individual. Even there the government plays a significant risk-sharing role through social security, medicare, medicaid, and other programs. The countries of western Europe make much greater use of institutions of the welfare state, which is after all a risk-sharing institution. Any attempt to evaluate the performance of the market must take into account these alternatives.

The reader should now have a sense of what interests us in the process of financial innovation. We think of the *financial* part of the economy as including any activity that helps firms and individuals share risks and smooth fluctuations in income and expenditures. As soon as one thinks about the risks faced by individuals and firms, it is clear that risk sharing and intertemporal smoothing are important determinants of welfare and, equally, that these opportunities are limited. We believe that the lack of opportunities for risk sharing is a major constraint on the welfare of people living in developed countries, especially in the United States. In the countries of western Europe and in the United States, the welfare of the average person is indisputably high. If these economies have a failing, it is not insufficient production of goods, but rather maldistribution of resources—that is, poverty, and a great deal of uncertainty that prevents people with a reasonable standard of living from enjoying the security of knowing that it will continue into the future. These problems are not distinct, since a person who lives in poverty today may have had a good income yesterday, but may have lost it because of some uninsurable event.

In fact, from some points of view (e.g., the Rawlsian "initial position"), all bad outcomes are the result of suboptimal risk sharing. Thus we think of any activity as financial if it provides opportunities to individuals and firms, and we think of risk sharing as playing a central role in the economic allocative process.

The *theory of financial innovation* deals with the provision of opportunities for risk sharing or intertemporal smoothing, and, for the economist, it is natural not only to ask how innovation comes about but also whether the market is doing a good job at providing the institutions and instruments that are needed. The questions we are led to ask include the following:

- What are the incentives for innovation?
- How does institutional structure affect the incentives to innovate?
- How does industrial organization affect innovative performance?
- Do markets work well?
- Can regulation improve welfare?
- Is there a role for government provision?

From this perspective, the topic of financial innovation is a very broad one. It requires nothing less than a positive theory of endogenous market structure (i.e., which markets, institutions, and instruments will be introduced and which will not) together with an analysis of the welfare economics of existing market structures.

Partly because of the breadth of the topic, and partly because we want to focus on issues of efficiency and welfare, there are important aspects of financial innovation that we do not deal with or touch on only briefly. What follows is a brief account of some of these topics.

1.2 Financial Innovation in the 1970s and 1980s

The topicality of financial innovation is liable to mislead the reader. For the specialist in financial markets, the sheer magnitude of financial innovation in the last twenty years and the dollar volume of trade in the new exchanges and instruments justify focusing on the empirical details of recent innovations. We are not primarily concerned with explaining why there was so much innovation in the last two decades. As we shall see, innovation has been taking place, although at a much slower pace, for thousands of years. The introduction of personal loans in ancient Greece was probably a more significant innovation than the invention of interest rate swaps. We are interested in the innovative process in general, rather than one particular episode of innovation in one particular sector of the economy. From this point of view, too, we should be just as concerned with "the dog that didn't bark"—that is, the security or institution that did not get introduced, as with the one that did. If one accepts that innovation is not necessarily efficient, it follows that welfare-improving securities and institutions may not be provided by the market, or else their advent may be long delayed because no one has the right incentives to innovate.

Another corollary of our basic approach is that we are more concerned with modeling processes in terms of rational maximizing behavior than mapping the details of particular current innovations. This may seem an antiempirical stance, but it makes perfect sense in terms of our desire to evaluate the working of the market. Our interest is with the basic principles that govern innovation and determine whether the innovation process is efficient or inefficient. From the point of view of understanding the incentives to innovate and whether the market can be expected in all circumstances to do a good job, the crucial element is to get the principles straight. The facts surrounding each particular example of innovation are relatively straightforward and may not require theoretical analysis. Similarly, the details that are important to a financial specialist are not essential at the level of analysis we are considering.

1.3   The Theory of Corporate Control

These arguments do not mean that we are unaware of the value of other approaches. Risk sharing is only one function of financial instruments and institutions. Another function has been highlighted by the literature on corporate governance. Shares offer the holder the residual rights of ownership; bonds offer the holder the right to assume ownership in certain events—for example, if the issuer defaults. The allocation and transfer of ownership rights have important implications for the efficient (or inefficient) operation of corporations. The design of securities as well as the behavior of financial institutions can be examined from the point of view of the efficient control of the corporation. This is an important aspect both of corporate finance and of the kind of welfare economics that we are attempting here. Our excuses for putting these issues on one side are the usual ones: that we can only hope to deal with a narrower range of issues, and that progress in this area requires some division of labor.

1.4   Information

Another branch of literature that is very important to understanding why we observe the financial institutions and instruments we do deals with incomplete information, specifically with problems of moral hazard and adverse selection. These problems undoubtedly explain why individuals and firms find it impossible to hedge many risks that are important to them. They may also provide a quite general explanation of why the market is leery of many financial innovations until it has some experience of how they perform over a number of years. These issues are very important to understanding the design of financial instruments and the process of financial innovation. We have done some work in this area, but it is at a very early stage. Unfortunately, a full treatment of the issues associated with incomplete information is beyond the scope of this work.

Despite the importance of incomplete information in many financial problems, we believe that much useful work can be done under the assumption of complete information. Moreover, there is a strong argument for avoiding models with incomplete information. It is well known that models with incomplete information are often beset by intractable theoretical problems, which force us to select among multiple equilibria or deal with the notorious sensitivity of the results to the fine details of the modeling. In addition, it is usually difficult to implement these models empirically, because so many of the crucial variables are unobservable. All this suggests that it is practical to begin with the case of complete information.

1.5   The Research Agenda

The first part of this book provides an overview and synthesis of our approach to financial innovation; the second part describes our approach in depth. In the next chapter we begin our overview by taking a look at the history of innovation, both in terms of financial institutions and financial instruments. This survey provides both a motivation for our own approach and an illustration of the need for complementary approaches. We do not make any exclusive claims for our contribution; we simply want to place it in perspective.

One thing that becomes very clear from our survey is that there are distinct types of innovations, distinct types of innovators, and distinct motives for innovation. Among the innovators we find governments, firms, banks and other intermediaries, and exchanges. Among the motives for innovation we find:

• The desire to make markets more complete, for example, to hedge some risk that was previously uninsurable or to reduce the cost of achieving some degree of insurance

• The desire to avoid or circumvent government regulations and taxation

• The desire to reduce transaction costs or increase liquidity

• The desire to reduce agency costs between different security holders

• The desire to change prices of assets that are being held

There are many types of innovations, literally too numerous to mention, and they can be classified in different ways. For example, we could distinguish innovations by the type of innovator or by the motive for innovation. Typically these will be related. So we must distinguish issuers of new securities, who benefit by reducing the cost of capital or the cost of insurance, from the operators of a new exchange, who benefit from the fees and commissions earned by traders. Firms may issue a new security because it increases the value of the firm, or a bank may introduce a new account or financial service to reduce transaction costs.

Alternatively, one can distinguish innovations by what they accomplish: some innovations reduce the transaction costs of doing what could previously be accomplished in the market at greater cost, as in the case of index funds, financial futures, swaps, and so forth. Some divide up the dividend streams of existing securities, as in the case of bond strips or different classes of shares. Some involve side bets on macroeconomic variables, such as interest rate futures and individual stocks.

All of these taxonomies have some value, but since there are so many ways of slicing up the same cake, they threaten to become obstacles to understanding the principles at work behind the process of innovation. This is especially true if one is tempted to focus on the innovations of the 1970s and 1980s, but these are not the central focus of our research. They are at best illustrations of innovations that can occur; the innovations that had already occurred or have not yet occurred or may never occur are just as important. And more important than all these details are the principles that underlie them. We identify the following as being theoretically important:

1. Institutional settings matter. Different types of innovators will have different incentives to innovate, and the incentives determine the type and amount of innovation that will occur.

2. Externalities abound, and, to the extent that costs are not internalized or benefits not captured, we should not expect innovation to be efficient.

3. Free rider problems arise because of the difficulty of "patenting" and the ease of "reverse engineering." This would tend to reduce the degree of innovation, in general, but there may be cases when too much innovation occurs, for example, because the innovator finds she has market power that allows her to extract "rents."

4. Information about new products is critical to the success of innovations. Without information the product will not be used or will be used suboptimally, but information is costly. Overcoming market resistance may be critical to the introduction of a new product or to the determination of whether a new product is needed. Despite the huge volume of innovation, it has been confined to a relatively narrow part of the economy, and information may be one of the reasons.

As we review examples of financial innovation in chapter 2, the reader will see illustrations of the types of innovation, the types of innovators, and the types of motives for innovation. Chapter 3 outlines the relationship between industrial organization approaches to innovation and theories of financial innovation. The principles of financial innovation mentioned above are considered in chapter 4. Finally, in chapter 5, part I of the book concludes with a discussion of other approaches to financial innovation and an agenda for future research.

2 History and Institutions

2.1 Traditional Financial Instruments and Institutions

Financial innovation has been occurring for several thousand years. The most primitive type of financial agreement we know of is a loan from one person to another. There is evidence that loans were used in many early civilizations. It is a natural development of risk sharing and intertemporal smoothing arrangements between families and friends. More sophisticated financial arrangements were developed in Babylonia and Assyria: there were at least two banking firms in the Mesopotamian Valley several thousand years B.C., and *drafts*, which were drawn on one place and payable in another, were widely used.[1] In other ancient civilizations, banking practices developed to an even greater extent. In ancient Greece, bankers accepted *deposits* and lent money; they also changed money and arranged for payments to be made in other cities through correspondents.[2] Bank deposits and bankers' *acceptances*[3] were the first two financial instruments and were in use from a very early date.

During the Dark Ages financial arrangements returned to a primitive state. It was not until the commercial practices of the city-states of northern Italy became relatively sophisticated that bank deposits and bankers' acceptances were rediscovered in the thirteenth century. As trade and commerce in Europe grew, these instruments came to be more and more widely used.

Two other financial instruments have been of great importance historically. *Equities* and *bonds* were both developed during the sixteenth century. Equities were issued by joint stock companies,[4] the first of which was the Russia Company, founded in 1553.[5] Joint stock companies combined the features of two important medieval institutions, trading partnerships and corporations. A trading partnership consisted of a group of people who pursued a business or trading venture together. Often all the partners were actively engaged in the organization. However, there could also be "sleeping partners" who provided financing for the firm and shared in the profits, but who were not actively involved in its day-to-day operations. The important feature of corporations, such as universities and boroughs, was that they had an existence which was separate from their owners. This feature was embodied in joint stock companies and distinguished them from partnerships. This separate legal existence allowed companies to hold property and undertake contracts on their own behalf. The defining characteristics of joint stock companies meant that in addition to providing a stream of income, equities also allowed their owners some control over the running of the firm that issued them.

Bonds were developed during the same period. A *bond* is essentially a formalized, transferable loan. A loan is a private arrangement between two or more parties, whereas a bond is a negotiable instrument. The first true bond was the "Grand Parti," issued by the French government in 1555.[6] Bonds were also issued by firms from an early date; for example, the Dutch East India Company had bonds outstanding in the seventeenth century.[7]

In addition to equities and bonds, other types of securities were developed at an early date. *Convertible securities* have a long history. In continental Europe in the sixteenth century, a number of equity issues forced the equityholders to convert their shares into debt if the equityholders broke certain regulations. In the seventeenth century, a number of English firms undertook conversions to benefit particular shareholders. For example, in 1631 King Charles I was allowed to convert his shares in the New River Company into debt when the company did not do as well as expected. In 1724 stockholders in the York Buildings Company converted half their shares into debt that had equal priority with the firm's existing debt.[8] Over the following years, the rights of conversion came to be specified more carefully at the date of issue, and the use of convertible securities gradually expanded.

Preferred stock is another security that was issued by firms at a relatively early date and has survived to the present day.[9] Some of the original English joint-stock companies gave preferences to certain classes of their stock in the mid-sixteenth century.[10] However, it was not until the late eighteenth century that preferred stock was widely used, first by canal companies and then in the nineteenth century by railway companies.[11] In the English railway mania of the 1840s, in particular, preferred stock was issued in large quantities. The main reason for the popularity of preferred stock was the regulation that required companies in England to restrict their total loans to a third or less of their share capital.[12] The proportion of total railway issues consisting of preference shares grew from 4 percent in 1845 to 66 percent in 1849.[13] In the United States, preferred stock came to be used when industrial combinations appeared in the late 1880s and when the railroads were reorganized in the mid-1890s.[14]

Preferred and convertible shares were not the only types of securities developed in the sixteenth and seventeenth centuries. Other securities were introduced at this time but have not proved as durable. For example, in 1693 the English government issued a *tontine*. This was a hybrid between a bond and a life annuity. The total amount paid each year by the borrower was fixed. Each lender nominated a holder of the security, who initially received an amount proportional to the sum lent. As the nominees died, their share of the fixed total payment was divided among the survivors. After all the nominees died, the government's liability ended.[15] Other types of innovation relied more directly on investors' desire for risk taking. In 1694 a lottery loan known as "the Million Adventure" was issued. In this case £1 million was raised with lenders being guaranteed a return of 10 percent for sixteen years with no repayment of principal at the end. In addition there was a lottery with prize winners being allocated part of a £40,000 annual amount, which was also paid for sixteen years.[16] These and other securities developed during the period were used in various forms for many years but, unlike equities, bonds, convertibles, and preferred stock, have not lasted to the present day.

As the number of joint-stock companies grew, the amount of equities outstanding increased steadily. Companies began to issue bonds as well as shares, so that the total value of securities grew significantly. In addition to the securities issued by firms, governments' need for finance led to a significant expansion in the amount of public debt. As the total amount outstanding became larger, secondary trading became commonplace, and financial markets became more organized. There was a considerable amount of trading of securities in Antwerp and Amsterdam in the sixteenth century, and in 1611 the Amsterdam Bourse was opened. De la Vega (1688) provides a colorful account of the operation of this market and some of his experiences trading on it. Amsterdam was the most important exchange internationally for many years before London and subsequently New York took its place. Dealings in securities in London were not centralized until relatively late. The purpose-built stock exchange was not opened until 1802. Prior to this, the trading of securities mainly took place in coffee houses. The New York Stock and Exchange Board, which was the forerunner of the current New York Stock Exchange, was founded in 1817. Before that transactions were conducted in the streets.

The development of organized secondary markets for securities led to sophisticated trading practices which in turn spurred financial innovation. De la Vega (1688) reports that *options* and *futures*, or "time bargains" as they were known, were used on the Amsterdam exchange soon after it was founded. Options and futures were also extensively used in London by the end of the seventeenth century.[17]

At the beginning of the eighteenth century, the operation of European stock markets was severely disrupted by bouts of speculation. The most famous of these, perhaps, was the South Sea Bubble of 1720. The price of the South Sea Company's stock rose from 131 percent of par at the beginning of February to 950 percent by June 23 and then fell back to 200 percent by the end of the year.[18] This speculation led to the so-called Bubble Act, which made it illegal to form a company without a charter. It also prohibited companies from pursuing any line of business other than the one specified when their charter[19] was issued. The result of this legislation was a severe restriction on the issuing of equities for the next hundred years or so. Although the stocks of existing firms were still traded, there was very little expansion in the number of firms. However, the security markets continued to do well. Government debt expanded because forty-five of the years between 1739 and 1815 were years of war, and there were heavy financing needs. Government bonds came to dominate the market.[20] To raise the large sums required, the government developed a number of innovative securities. For example, for loans during the American Revolutionary War, lenders received a perpetuity, an annuity, and a lottery. In 1779 for every £100 invested, a lender received £100 par value of 3 percent Consols, (i.e., perpetuities) and either an annuity of £3 15s. for twenty-nine years or a life annuity. In addition, if £1,000 was invested, seven tickets in a lottery could be purchased for a further £10.[21]

In the nineteenth century the development of the canals and railways led to the repeal of the Bubble Act, and corporate securities again came to predominate in the London market. In 1860 British government securities amounted to more than 50 percent of the total value of all securities, but by 1914 they had fallen to less than 5 percent of the total.[22] During this period the main innovations were concerned with different types of equity and preferred stock. The majority of English corporations had at least two types of equity, and a significant number had more than this.[23]

In the last half of the nineteenth century and the first half of the twentieth century, the New York market grew in importance. The bonds issued during the Civil War and the active trade in them during the following decades had much to do with this change. In addition, the vast scale of the railroads in the United States and their need for capital led to a large expansion in securities traded.[24] During the First World War, New York finally replaced London as the most important financial market. A number of innovations occurred in the United States during this period. The first, *income bonds*, were issued by the Chesapeake and Ohio Canal Company in 1848. What distinguishes income bonds from ordinary bonds is that interest is paid only if accounting earnings exceed a certain level. They were not used frequently until the railroad reorganizations of the 1880s and 1890s.[25] Tufano (1991) documents how a number of other financing techniques also resulted from railroad reorganizations during the late nineteenth and early twentieth centuries. For example, *car trust certificates*, where the seller of the equipment held title to railroad cars in exchange for what was essentially a lease payment, came to be fairly widely used after their introduction in 1868.[26]

After the Civil War the market for *commercial paper* started to develop. This allowed corporations with a strong financial position to borrow short term in the markets more cheaply than they could borrow at a bank.[27] Another innovation that occurred at the beginning of the twentieth century was the use of *warrants*. These were usually issued with bonds or stocks and essentially consisted of an option which allowed the holder to buy stock at a predetermined amount for a limited amount of time. They were first used when the American Power and Light Company made an issue of 6 percent notes in 1911. After that they were used sporadically until 1925 when their popularity increased rapidly and they came to be widely used.[28]

Another important innovation in the United States during the nineteenth century was the development of commodity futures exchanges in Chicago and New York. These exchanges were not the first historical instances of futures trading. For example, there is evidence that contracts for the future delivery of rice were traded in Japan in the seventeenth and eighteenth centuries.[29] However, modern methods of futures trading were developed in Chicago. By the 1840s Chicago had developed as the commercial center for the midwestern farm states of Illinois, Indiana, Michigan, and Wisconsin. The trading of agricultural products had became chaotic and inefficient, and in response to this a group of merchants established the Chicago Board of Trade (CBOT) in 1848. At the beginning it concentrated on standardizing the quantities and qualities of the grain being traded. However, contracts for the future delivery of grain, which were then called *to-arrive contracts*, soon began to be traded. These allowed producers and processors to share the risk of fluctuations in prices. In

1865 the CBOT established its general rules which formed the foundation of trading practices. These principles were widely imitated by later futures exchanges. In addition to standardizing the quantities and qualities traded, buyers and sellers were required to make payments to the exchange to ensure they fulfilled their obligations. The ability to offset contracts was also adopted. This meant that traders did not necessarily have to deliver or take delivery of the grain; they could eliminate this obligation by selling contracts if they had previously bought or vice versa.[30]

In 1870 the New York Cotton Exchange was founded, and cotton futures began to be traded. In 1874 the Chicago Produce Exchange was founded for the trading of perishable agricultural products such as butter, eggs, and poultry. In 1889 some of the dealers withdrew to found the Chicago Butter and Egg Board, and in 1919 this was reorganized for futures trading in agricultural products, and the name was changed to the Chicago Mercantile Exchange (CME).[31]

By the 1930s, what might be called the traditional financial instruments had all been developed. A summary of these instruments and their characteristics is given in table 2.1.

Table 2.1
Traditional financial instruments

Issuer	Instrument	Characteristics
Firms	Equity	Equityholders are the owners of the firm and are responsible for conducting its affairs
	Bonds	A long-term obligation by the firm to make a series of fixed payments
	Convertibles	A bond that can be swapped for equity at a prespecified ratio or vice versa
	Preferred stock	A hybrid security that combines features of debt and equity
	Commercial paper	A short-term debt security issued by firms that can be easily traded
	Warrants	A long-term call option on a firm's stock issued by the firm
Banks	Deposits	Funds deposited at a bank available on demand or with some delay
	Acceptances	A written promise to pay a given sum at a prespecified date
Exchanges	Commodity futures	Contracts for the future delivery of a commodity
Governments	Bonds	A long-term obligation
	Notes	An intermediate obligation
	Bills	A short-term obligation

2.2 Recent Innovations

The Great Depression and the Second World War and its aftermath ushered in a period in which the set of financial instruments in common use remained relatively stable. In the 1960s, however, a limited amount of innovation began to occur. In 1963 the *Eurobond market*[32] came into existence with a $15 million issue for the Italian company Autostrade. Its development was spurred by the United States's Interest Equalization Tax of the same year, which temporarily excluded most foreign borrowers from U.S. markets.[33] In the currency markets, *parallel loans, back-to-back loans*, and then *currency swaps*[34] were used to get around U.K. exchange controls. The other major development in the 1960s was the founding of the Government National Mortgage Association (GNMA or "Ginnie Mae"), which was the beginning of *securitized mortgages*.

In the 1970s the pace of innovation quickened with the introduction of a number of important new instruments. The first *floating-rate instrument* was issued in 1970 in the Euromarkets. In 1972 the International Monetary Market, which is a division of the CME, started the trading of *financial futures on foreign exchange*. In 1973 the Chicago Board Options Exchange (CBOE) was set up, and this enabled standardized *options* to be traded. *Financial futures on interest rates* were introduced by the CBOT in 1975 with a contract based on GNMA mortgage-backed certificates, by the CME in 1976 with a T-bill futures contract, and by the CBOT in 1977 with a Treasury bond futures contract. In 1982 *financial futures on stock market indices* were initiated. The Kansas City Board of Trade introduced a contract based on the Value Line Stock Index, the CME offered one based on the S&P 500, and the New York Futures Exchange had one based on the New York Stock Exchange Composite Index.[35] The rate of innovation increased in subsequent years. Not only did the number of instruments rise dramatically, but the volume of trade in these markets did also.

The new instruments and markets can be divided into the categories shown in table 2.2. The categories are based on the organization or entity that has been primarily associated with the innovation. For example, the most important type of securitized loans are mortgage-backed securities, which are mainly issued by government agencies, so securitized loans are included in the government category. The classification in table 2.2 includes the major categories of innovation. More detailed surveys of recent

Table 2.2
Recent financial innovations

Main Issuer	Instrument	Characteristics
Firms	Floating-rate debt	The interest rate on the debt is based on LIBOR or the T-bill rate
	Floating-rate preferred	A substitute for money market funds that captures the dividends-received deduction for firms
	Zero coupons	Bonds where there is one payment at the terminal date
	Primes and scores	Equity is split into a prime component that has dividend and capital gains up to a stated price and a score component that has capital gains above this
	Synthetics	Securities that allow combinations of assets to be obtained with low transaction costs
	Poison pill securities	Securities that make takeovers more difficult by granting holders special rights if there is an acquisition bid for issuer
Banks	Swaps	Transactions in which different streams of income are exchanged
Exchanges	Financial futures	Contracts for the future delivery of currencies, securities, or an amount of money based on an index
	Options	The right to buy or sell a security on or before a specified date
Governments	Securitized loans	Pools of mortgages or other types of loans that are publicly traded
	Index-linked securites	Bonds where the payment is linked to an inflation index or a commodity price

innovations are contained in Walmsley (1988, 1991) and Finnerty (1988, 1993). We turn next to a more detailed discussion of the various instruments in table 2.2. These descriptions draw heavily from Walmsley (1988) which contains an excellent history of the development of financial markets since the 1960s.

Firms

Floating-rate Debt   Floating-rate notes were first issued in the Euromarket in 1970 by Ente Nazional per L'Energia Elettrica (ENEL). The rate on these notes was linked to the *London interbank offered rate* (LIBOR) which is the effective borrowing cost for banks in London. Pepsico issued a similar security the following month. However, they remained a novelty until the mid-1970s, when their use in the Euromarket began to expand rapidly. By 1985 the market had grown to $46.8 billion. Floating-rate notes were first issued in the United States in 1974. They were not widely used until the early 1980s. However, even then their use was small relative to the Euromarket, with $11.2 billion being issued in 1985.[36]

A number of variants on floating-rate notes have been issued. In addition to LIBOR various other indexes such as the 91-day T-bill rate have been used. In the mid-1980s securities with various "caps" were introduced. For example, a February 1985 issue for the Kingdom of Denmark had a variable rate with a minimum and a maximum coupon. Floating-rate notes have been issued in many currencies. In addition, some have been redeemable in multiple currencies, and some have been convertible into other currencies.

A number of issues of floating rate notes have been perpetual, that is, there is no redemption date. In the United States, the IRS requires that a security have a redemption date in order for it to qualify as debt and for the interest payments to be tax deductible for corporate income tax purposes. In order to get around this feature of the tax code, U.S. perpetual floating-rate notes are "puttable" so that they can be redeemed at the option of the noteholder. In the Euromarket, however, a number of non-puttable perpetuals have been issued.

Although floating-rate securities have not proved particularly popular in the United States, they have been widely used in the municipal bond market. In the mid-1980s the growth of tax-exempt money market funds created a demand for short-term municipal paper. However, the supply of this paper was relatively small. To satisfy the demand, investment banks created municipal bonds on which the interest rate varied weekly or less. In order to satisfy SEC requirements that the funds hold short-term instruments, the bonds were puttable so that the investors could demand the principal at short notice.

With standard, variable-rate securities, the coupon rate varies with interest rates so that the principal value remains constant. A number of securities have been designed with rather different features to allow them to be used as hedging instruments. For example, in February 1986 the Student Loan Marketing Association (SLMA or "Sallie Mae") issued a "reverse" or "bull" floater on which the coupon rate was (17.2% − LIBOR). The negative correlation of this coupon with short-term interest rates meant it could be combined with standard bonds to give relatively risk-free yields.[37]

Floating-rate Preferred Floating-rate preferred is preferred stock on which the dividend rate fluctuates in line with interest rates. It is designed to be held by corporations, since it enables them to claim the IRC section 246(c) dividends-received deduction.[38] The first instrument of this type was adjustable rate preferred stock. This had the feature that the dividend yield payable changed quarterly and was reset according to a formula relating it to money market yields. Unfortunately, it turned out that this mechanism for resetting the yield did not result in the stability in market value that was desired.[39] This problem led to the development of Dutch auction rate preferred stock (DARPS). In this case the interest rate was set more frequently, usually every forty-nine days. This allowed it to meet the forty-six-day holding requirement of IRC section 246(c). In addition the interest rate was determined in a Dutch auction which allowed for adjustments in interest rates as well as changes in risk premia. This security proved very successful initially although its popularity has declined in recent years.[40]

Zero Coupons Most bonds involve a periodic coupon payment and a repayment of principal at maturity. In the 1960s a number of states such as Michigan and Minnesota pioneered the use of zero-coupon bonds where the only payment was the terminal one with a number of small issues. In June 1966, BP Tanker-Eriksberg also issued a zero-coupon bond. However, these were isolated events, and it was not until after April 1981 when J. C. Penney made a public issue of zero coupons in the United States that they gained significant popularity.[41]

Zero coupons came to be widely used in the early 1980s because of a tax loophole. Corporations were allowed to deduct annually an amount equal to the original discount on the bonds divided by the number of years to maturity. This rule ignored the fact that interest is compounded on zero-coupon bonds and therefore allocated too much interest to the initial periods. When interest rates are low the difference is fairly small, but when interest rates are high, as they were in the early 1980s, the potential tax savings are significant.[42]

Although the loophole was quickly closed when firms started to take advantage of it on a large scale, the market for zero coupons nevertheless continued as their payment characteristics were found to be desirable to investors because of the lack of reinvestment risk, and some tax advantages remained for Japanese investors. A change in rules for holding U.S.

government securities meant that it was simpler for investment banks to "strip" U.S. Treasury bonds and issue separate securities representing the interest stream and the principal. Initial issues such as Treasury Investment Growth Receipts (TIGRs) and Certificates of Accrual on Treasury Securities (CATS) became so popular that the market grew from $2.51 billion in 1982 when they were first introduced to $44.6 billion in 1984.[43] As a result of the popularity of stripped securities, the Treasury introduced Separate Trading of Registered Interest and Principal of Securities (STRIPS) in February 1985. This permitted separate ownership of principal and interest directly and ensured the continued popularity of zero-coupon securities.

Primes and Scores   The first example of primes and scores was the Americus Trust offered to owners of common stock of AT&T in October 1983. This consists of a trust where shares in the company were deposited, and for each underlying share the trust issues a prime and a score security, which are listed separately on the American Stock Exchange. The prime component receives the voting rights, the dividend income from the underlying stock, and capital appreciation up to a prespecified price, which was usually 20–25 percent above the stock price at the time of the creation of the trust; the score component receives the capital appreciation above this prespecified price. The trust lasts for five years and can have up to 5 percent of a corporation's equity. At any time before the expiration of the trust, a prime and a score can be traded in for a unit of stock without cost. At the end of five years the trust is dissolved, and any remaining primes and scores are turned back into equity. In March 1986 the IRS implemented changes in the tax code, which made trusts created after that date subject to a separate corporate income tax. This effectively prevented the creation of further trusts. However, before that date Americus trusts for twenty-seven U.S. corporations including firms such as Exxon, DuPont, American Home Products, and Bristol-Myers were created.[44]

Synthetics   *Synthetics* are securities that combine a bond with something else such as a different currency, a warrant, or an index. They mimic assets or combinations of assets that cannot be obtained directly or that can only be obtained with significant transaction costs. Many synthetics involve transactions in more than one currency so that payoffs are linked to exchange rates at particular dates. Other synthetics are combinations of bonds and options on stock exchange indexes.

The prime examples of currency-based synthetics are dual-currency bonds and "heaven and hell" bonds. *Dual-currency bonds* were initiated in the Euromarkets in 1981. They consist of bonds issued in one currency, but either the coupon or the principal repayment or both are in a different currency. *Heaven and hell bonds* are a development of dual-currency bonds in which the repayment is an explicit function of a particular exchange rate. For example, in the first bond of this type, which was an issue for IBM in 1985, redemption was at par if the yen-U.S.$ exchange rate at maturity was 169. If it was above (below) 169, redemption was also above (below) par according to a simple linear formula.[45] Other types of synthetic bond, which depend on exchange rates in more complex ways, have also been issued. These synthetics allow exchange rate risks to be hedged directly without the necessity of transacting in foreign exchange markets. In many cases the maturities of the bonds are such that it would not be possible to hedge the associated risk directly.

Another important synthetic security is the "bull and bear" bond. The first example of this bond was issued by Swedish Export Kredit in June 1986. It consisted of a yen bond in which the redemption price depended on the level of the Tokyo Exchange Nikkei index at the maturity date. If the index is at 26,067, the redemption is at par. For every 100 points above this, up to a cap of 28,461, the redemption price is increased by 0.4425 percent. Similarly, for every 100 points below, down to a floor of 16,979, the redemption price is reduced by 0.4425 percent.[46] Thus, bull and bear bonds are combinations of a bond and call and put options on stock exchange indexes.

Poison Pill Securities   One of the most important developments in the financial markets in the United States and United Kingdom since the Second World War has been the development of a market for corporate control where hostile bids are commonplace.[47] In response to these bids, a number of antitakeover techniques have been developed. Initially these typically involved *charter amendments*. One example of these amendments is supermajority voting provisions, which require, for example, that 80 percent of shareholders must approve a merger. Another is staggered terms for directors, which can delay the effective transfer of control for a number of years.[48]

An important characteristic of charter amendments is that shareholder approval is required. In 1982 an alternative antitakeover defense was developed to protect the El Paso Company from a raid. This involved issuing what have come to be known as *poison pill securities*. There are a number of variants of these: preferred stock plans, flip-over plans, back-end plans, and voting plans.[49]

Prior to 1984, preferred stock plans were used exclusively. With these, the potential target issues a dividend of convertible preferred stock to its shareholders which grants them certain rights if an acquiring party purchases a large position (30 percent in one plan) in the firm; these rights can be waived at the discretion of the target's board of directors. The preferred stockholders can require the outside party to redeem the preferred stock at the highest price paid for common or preferred stock in the past year. If there is a merger, the acquiring firm must exchange the preferred stock for equivalent securities that it must issue. These preferred stock plans made it more difficult for raiders to acquire firms by removing an incentive for shareholders to bid early on because they can always be sure of getting the highest price paid.

The first flip-over plan was used by Crown Zellerbach in July 1984. The first step is the issue of a common stock dividend consisting of a special form of "right." This gives the holder the right to purchase common stock at an exercise price well above its current market price. They can be exercised starting ten days after an outside party obtains or bids for a substantial amount (e.g., 20 percent) of the target firm's stock for up to ten years. Ordinarily nobody would wish to exercise these rights because the exercise price is well above any likely market price. However, their special feature is that if there is a merger, they "flip over" and allow the holder to buy shares in the merged firm at a substantial discount. This makes hostile mergers extremely costly; friendly mergers are still possible because the rights can be repurchased by the issuing firm for a nominal fee unless they have been triggered. One way of avoiding the defensive features of these flip-over plans was not to merge the company and to transfer the assets instead. This loophole led to the adoption of a "flip-in" clause, which allowed rightsholders, other than the large blockholder, to purchase target shares at a substantial discount if the acquirer transferred assets at less than could be obtained from a third party.

Jerrico used the first back-end plan in October 1984. When acquiring a target, firms often make a "two-tier bid" in which they initially pay a high price for a majority of shares and then use their voting power to force a merger at a lower price, so the remaining shareholders do worse than those who initially tender. This structure provides an incentive for shareholders to tender. Back-end plans are like flip-over plans except the rights issued put a minimum on the amount acquirers must pay in the second part of a two-tier offer.

ASARCO was the first firm to use a voting plan in April 1985. This involved paying a dividend of preferred stock. If an outside party acquired a large block (e.g., 20 percent or more), anybody other than the large blockholder would acquire supervoting rights which would swamp the large blockholder's voting ability. However, ASARCO'S plan was invalidated by a court ruling, so this type of plan has not been widely used.

Banks

Swaps The first swaps occurred in the 1960s and were currency swaps. They arose from a desire by firms to avoid U.K. exchange controls. For example, a U.K. multinational might have excess funds in the United Kingdom that it wished to invest in its U.S. subsidiary. However, because of exchange controls it could not simply move the money from the United Kingdom to the United States. If a counterparty with the opposite needs could be found, the problem could be overcome using *parallel loans.* Suppose this counterparty were an American firm. It would lend a dollar amount to the British firm's subsidiary in the United States. In return the British firm would lend an equivalent amount of sterling in the United Kingdom to the U.S. firm's subsidiary. With a *back-to-back* loan the transaction had the same form except the U.K. and U.S. parent firms dealt directly with each other rather than through their subsidiaries. The main problem with both of these arrangements was that if one party defaulted, it was not clear what obligation the other party had to repay its loan. To overcome this deficiency, *currency swaps* were developed. Initially the American firm would transfer a dollar amount to the British firm, in exchange for which the British firm would make available an equivalent amount in sterling to the U.S. firm. For the duration of the swap, the British firm would pay a dollar rate of interest, and the American firm would pay a sterling rate of interest. At the the end of the agreement, they would pay back the original amounts to each other.[50]

The working of a currency swap is illustrated in figure 2.1. Suppose a U.K. firm called BRIT and a U.S. firm called Americana undertake a swap agreement. BRIT, which has large pound reserves, wants dollar funds; Americana has large dollar reserves and wants pounds. To eliminate exchange rate risk, they undertake a five-year swap. BRIT makes £1 million

		£1 million	
Beginning of agreement	BRIT	———————————————	Americana
		$1.5 million	

		0.07 × £1 million = £70,000	
Each year for five years	BRIT	———————————————	Americana
		0.05 × $1.5 million = $75,000	

		£1 million	
End of agreement	BRIT	———————————————	Americana
		$1.5 million	

Figure 2.1
The operation of a currency swap

available to Americana, which in turn makes $1.5 million available to BRIT. Suppose the five-year pound interest rate they use is 7 percent, while the five-year dollar rate they use is 5 percent. During the agreement Americana pays BRIT 0.07 × £1 million = £70,000, while BRIT pays Americana 0.05 × $1.5 million = $75,000. At the end of the agreement Americana repays the £1 million, and BRIT repays the $1.5 million. In practice, payments are usually netted off so that, depending on the exchange rate at the time, there is only one payment between the parties.[51]

As capital markets became more international, the use of currency swaps expanded. The market began to become an important one in terms of volume when the World Bank became actively involved in it in the early 1980s. In 1981 it undertook a widely publicized swap with IBM that helped to legitimize the technique.[52] The bank reported that in 1983 the use of currency swaps allowed it to lower its average cost of borrowing from about 10 percent to around 8.9 percent.[53] The involvement of the World Bank in the market encouraged other participants, and currency swaps linked to new issues grew from $1 billion in 1981 to $1,155 billion by the end of 1990.[54]

The techniques used for currency swaps were adapted in 1981 for swapping adjustable rate and fixed rate loans.[55] In contrast to currency swaps, principal payments are not made in full: the principal payments as well as the interim payments are netted out. Interest rate swaps grew even more rapidly than currency swaps. The size of the market as measured by the notional principal went from zero before 1981 to $2.3 trillion by the end of 1990.[56]

A number of explanations have been given for the widespread use of currency and interest rate swaps. Price and Henderson (1984) suggested that they are arbitrages based on capital market imperfections. Felgram (1987) has argued that the differentials between firms with good credit ratings and those with poor credit ratings are less in adjustable rate markets than in fixed rate markets. The firm with a good credit rating borrows at a fixed rate, and the firm with a poor rating borrows at an adjustable rate. With the help of an intermediary, which is usually a commercial bank, they swap the interest streams on the loans. The risk of default by either party on the interest streams is borne by the intermediating bank. The loan differential in the two markets is such that it appears all three parties may benefit provided the true risk borne by the intermediating bank is not too large. The reason for the difference between fixed rate markets and variable rate markets is usually not explained in these models. However, Titman (1990) has shown how asymmetric information can be used to explain the loan differentials and how swaps help overcome these asymmetries. Firms that expect their credit quality to improve borrow short term and hedge the risk of interest rate changes with swaps.

In addition to currency and interest rate swaps, many other types of swaps have been undertaken.[57] One example is commodity swaps. These exchange a fixed stream of payments for one which is contingent on a commodity price. These swaps are primarily available for gold, silver, and crude oil. Other commodities such as copper, aluminum, nickel, zinc, and jet fuel can also be swapped, but the markets for these are much thinner. Commodity swaps are typically arranged by international banks. They are used by producing countries and firms to hedge the medium- and long-term risks associated with commodity price changes. As yet, the commodity swap market is small relative to the currency and interest rate swap markets with a total of $10 billion of transactions by the end of 1989.[58]

Swaps, particularly interest rate swaps, have been one of the most successful financial innovations of the 1980s. In many cases swaps allow a reduction in transaction costs compared to other methods of achieving the same outcome. The reallocation of risk these arrangements allow is also important. However, the difficulty of estimating the precise nature of risk borne by intermediating banks in interest rate swaps makes it difficult to ensure that the banks are in fact better off. Given the short time swaps have existed and the lack of experience with defaults, there may be disagreement on the likelihood of default so that the risk is not being properly priced in these transactions.

Exchanges

Financial Futures   As with options, tailor-made financial futures have a long history, but standardized financial futures contracts are of relatively recent origin. They started with the introduction of foreign currency futures at the International Monetary Market (part of the CME) in Chicago in May 1972. This was followed in October 1975 by the CBOT offering a futures contract on GNMA mortgage-backed certificates. However, the contracts that were the most successful and brought significant attention to the markets were the IMM's ninety-one-day T-bill contract introduced in January 1976 and the CBOT's Treasury bond contract introduced in August 1977. The volume of transactions in these grew quickly, with the annual volume in the latter, for example, growing from $2.6 billion in 1978 to $67.9 billion in 1991.[59]

It is not just in the United States that financial futures markets have developed. The two most important foreign markets are the London International Financial Futures Exchange, which was started in September 1982, and the Tokyo Futures Exchange, which opened in October 1985. Both of these markets have been successful, and the Tokyo market in particular has grown very quickly. The French financial futures market, the MATIF (*Marché à Terme des Instruments Financiers*), which was established in 1986, has also proved to be very successful.

In addition to futures on U.S. Treasury securities, stock index futures contracts have been particularly successful. The first of these, which was based on the Valueline Average, was introduced by the Kansas City Board of Trade in February 1982. It was quickly followed in April of the same year by a CME contract based on the S&P 500 stock index and in May by a New York Futures Exchange contract based on the New York Stock Exchange index. By June 1983 the volume in these three futures contracts on a share equivalent basis exceeded that on the New York Stock Exchange, and this has been a regular occurrence since then.[60]

One important feature of financial futures which has contributed to their success is that they permit investors to obtain high leverage. For example, if people wish to borrow to take a stock position, it is typically necessary for them to put up margin of 50 percent of the amount borrowed, and they must pay interest on the remaining 50 percent. In contrast, in futures markets, margins are typically set in dollar terms and are usually less than 10 percent of the face value of securities. Also, there is no need to pay interest on the remainder.[61]

Options   As previously mentioned, options and futures have been used from a very early date. These instruments were tailor made and depended on the characteristics a particular investor demanded. As a result, there were no secondary markets on which such options could be traded. In 1973 the CBOE introduced standardized options, and this allowed an active secondary market to be viable. The CBOE was immediately successful, and by 1984 it had become the second largest securities market in the world, second only to the New York Stock Exchange.

The success of the CBOE led a number of other U.S. and international exchanges to introduce options markets. These included the American Stock Exchange, the Philadelphia Stock Exchange, the European Options Exchange in Amsterdam, and the London Stock Exchange.

Initially the options traded on exchanges were all options on stocks. In the early 1980s options on other instruments were introduced. The first was an options contract on Treasury bond futures which was started by the CBOT in October 1982. Subsequently options on other debt instruments were initiated, including options on specific Treasury bonds, notes, and bills. In December 1982 the Philadelphia Stock Exchange introduced currency options, and this was followed by a number of other exchanges. Options on indexes began in March 1983, when the CBOE offered an option on the S&P 100 index. This and other index options have proved very successful and are widely used.

In addition to standardized options, a number of option-related instruments have also been developed in recent years. These include caps and floors, which are privately negotiated options on interest rates or interest rate indices. Other securities in which options are embedded in the security, such as callable bonds, have also become popular. Finally, warrants on bonds (as opposed to equity) have come to be fairly widely used.

Governments

Securitized Loans   One of the most important developments in recent decades has been the market for mortgage-backed securities. This dates back to the 1950s at least, but it was not until the 1970s that it became an important market in terms of the volume outstanding. The event that transformed the market was the development of "pass-through" securities. These were introduced in 1970 by GNMA. Prior to that date sales of mortgages involved sales of "whole loans." This required the cumbersome process of transferring legal title to the buyer for each loan. The innovation of pass-through securities was that they represented a share in a pool of mortgages that could be freely traded without transfer of title of individual mortgages. The payments on the mortgages are pooled together and paid out to the owners of the securities. The bank that collects the payments and deals with other administrative aspects of the loan earns a fee for undertaking these tasks.

The GNMA's securitization of mortgages was followed by the Federal National Mortgage Association (FNMA or "Fannie Mae") and the Federal Home Loan Mortgage Corporation (FHLMC or "Freddie Mac"). The total amount of securities issued by these three went from $0.3 billion in 1970 to a total of around $1 trillion by the end of 1989.[62] In addition to the securities issued by government agencies, there has also been a growing amount of securitization by private issuers. From a $150 million issue by Bank of America in 1977, this market grew to $5.6 billion in 1986.[63]

After pass-through securities the next major innovation was the development of "pay-through" securities. One of the major uncertainties with pass-through securities was the prepayment risk borne by securityholders. For example, when interest rates fall, many mortgageholders refinance and pay off their mortgages. With pass-through securities this risk is borne equally by all securityholders. With pay-through securities such as collateralized mortgage obligations (CMOs), the mortgage pool is split into a number of securities with different risk characteristics. The tranches differ in the amount of prepayment risk. Prepayments would be allocated to the "fast pay" tranche first, the "medium pay" tranche when that was finished, and a "slow pay" tranche when that was exhausted.[64] Issuers have found that different types of investors had different preferences for these securities. Thus, the fast pay securities tend to be bought by banks and thrift institutions, the medium pay securities by pension funds, commercial banks, and life insurance companies, and slow pay securities mainly by pension funds.[65]

CMOs were developed by the FHLMC in 1983. They were subsequently issued by many other institutions including investment banks, thrifts, and builders. By the end of 1991, there had been 3,548 issues for a total of $701 billion.[66] Other refinements to the pay-through principle have been made. Following the Real Estate Mortgage Investment Corporation provisions in the 1986 Tax Reform Act, stripping of mortgage-backed securities became possible so that principal and interest components could trade separately.

The development of the mortgage-backed securities markets has been followed by the securitization of many other types of loans. These include commercial mortgages, bank loans, automobile loans, and credit card receivables. Overall, the move toward securitization of loans has been one of the major types of financial innovation in recent years. This has been primarily a U.S. phenomenon. There are examples of securitization in other countries, but it has not occurred to anything like the extent it has in the United States.

One interesting feature of many securitizations is what is known as "credit enhancement." Investors are often reluctant to invest in a new security because they are unfamiliar with its features and are unsure about the risks involved. Issuers have sought to remove these barriers by having banks or insurance companies guarantee the securities they are supplying. Such guarantees considerably enhance the ease with which securities can be sold and their subsequent liquidity. The use of credit enhancement expanded rapidly during the early 1980s and by the mid-1980s was widely used in some markets. For example, in the second quarter of 1985, 53.9 percent of issues in the U.S. housing bond market used credit enhancement.[67]

Index-linked Securities   Many years ago the existence of hyperinflation led a number of governments, including Argentina, Brazil, and Israel, to issue bonds linked to the consumer price index or some other measure of inflation. In 1975 the U.K. government linked some types of national saving to an inflation index. The availability of inflation-protected instruments gradually increased until in March 1982 index-linked U.K. government bonds were freely available.

Other bonds have been linked to commodities. Various French governments have issued bonds whose redemption price is tied to the price of gold. A number of private issuers have also used commodity-related bonds. For example, the Sunshine Mining Company issued bonds that were indexed to the price of silver in April 1980, and Refinement International issued gold-indexed bonds in February 1981. Other bonds have been linked to oil, Treasury bond yields, and various other indexes.

The categories listed in table 2.2 do not cover all new securities. As with innovations in previous centuries, not all innovations have been widely imitated. For example, with its acquisition of Electronic Data Systems Corporation, General Motors issued E class shares in 1984. The novel feature of these shares was that their performance was tied to the performance of the subsidiary. The success of these E shares led General Motors to issue similar H class shares when it subsequently acquired the Hughes Aircraft Corporation. However, this type of security has not been widely adopted. Other securities have filled a limited niche. Master Limited Partnerships (MLPs) were designed to have the legal form of a partnership so that corporate taxes could be avoided, but to be publicly traded like a corporation. The first MLP, created for Apache Petroleum in 1981, converted thirty-three oil and gas limited partnerships into one tradeable entity.[68] In addition to the oil and gas industry, MLPs have also been used in the real estate industry. Since their introduction up to the end of 1991, there have been 114 MLP issues with a total value of $9.1 billion.[69] For a more comprehensive listing of modern securities, see Walmsley (1988) and Finnerty (1993).

2.3 The Empirical Effects of Recent Innovation

The examples in the previous section show that there has been extensive financial innovation in recent years. An important question concerns the effects these innovations have had on existing markets. Unfortunately, there has been relatively little study of the detailed impacts of innovations.

One exception is a careful study by Jarrow and O'Hara (1989) of primes and scores where the equity of a company is split into two components. As mentioned, the prime component receives the dividends and income up to a prespecified price, while the score component receives the capital appreciation above this price. Jarrow and O'Hara found that the sum of the values of the prime and score components exceeded the value of the equity. In other words, splitting the equity into two parts created value for shareholders. Limitations on short sales prevented this difference in value from being arbitraged away.

In chapter 4 (section 4.2) we describe a theory of security design in which firms split their income stream in order to increase their value. Short sale constraints prevent arbitrage possibilities. The primes and scores case analyzed by Jarrow and O'Hara provides an interesting illustration of how the splitting of an income stream can create value.

The financial innovation that has perhaps received the most attention is the options markets: there is now a considerable literature on the effect of introducing options. Early studies found little evidence of any changes in the return or volatility of underlying stocks (Trennepohl and Dukes 1979; Klemkosky and Maness 1980; Whiteside, Dukes, and Dunne 1983). However, the results in these papers were based on small samples. A subsequent study by Conrad (1989), using a larger sample, found that introducing an option had a significant effect on the stock's price and volatility. Using data for the period from 1974 to 1980, from the CBOE and the American Options Exchange, she found that:

• The price of the underlying stock is increased by around 2 percent, and this effect appears to be permanent.

• The variance of returns falls.

• The systematic risk (i.e., the beta) is unaffected.

Somewhat surprisingly, these effects occurred just before the listing date and not at the announcement date. The price increase was found to be positively related to opening-day trading volume in the option. Moreover, the effects were found to be constant over the 1974–1980 period.

Detemple and Jorion (1990) considered a large sample of option introductions from the period 1973–1986. Their results confirm Conrad's findings that there is an increase in price, a reduction in the volatility of the underlying stock, and no effect on the systematic risk. In addition they identified a number of other effects on the underlying stock:

• The average price increase of the underlying stock is around 3 percent.

• Delisting an option has the opposite effects to listing, that is, the stock price falls and volatility increases.

• Price and volatility effects become insignificant after 1982.

The third result has been confirmed by Kim and Young (1991).

In addition to the effects on the underlying stock, Detemple and Jorion (1990) looked at the effects of option introduction on the market as a whole and on an index of the industry the underlying stock is in (but excluding the stock itself). They found:

• For each of the fifty-three days on which batches of options were introduced, the market index increases by about 1 percent, and this is statistically significant.

• The variance of the market return decreases.

• The industry index increases by about 1.5 percent, which is more than the market as a whole but less than the stock itself.

Figure 2.2 illustrates these movements in the price of the optioned stock, the industry index, and the market index.

These empirical findings raise a number of questions. The first is why is it that the introduction of options increases the value of the underlying securities and other stocks. Detemple and Selden (1991) present a simple mean-variance example with a risky asset and a safe asset and incomplete markets, where introducing an option raises the value of the risky asset. The basic intuition of the result is that introducing the option allows the risk associated with the stock to be better shared. As a result, the demand

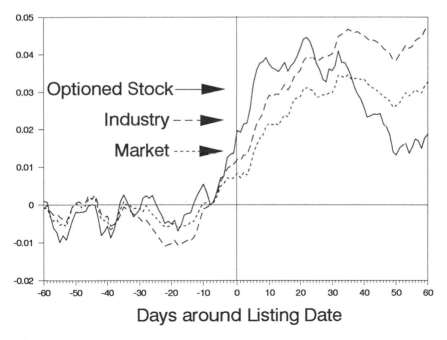

Figure 2.2
Effects of issuing options on the optioned stocks, their industry and the market.

for the risky asset increases, and its price increases. When there are many risky assets, a similar argument can presumably be made. In this case the improvement in risk-sharing possibilities will help to make all assets more attractive, and their prices will all increase. It is important to stress that this argument will not always hold. In fact, an example is presented in chapter 8 where the introduction of an option lowers the value of the underlying firm. However, the argument provides an explanation of why the introduction of options may have had the effect observed by Conrad (1989), Detemple and Jorion (1990), and others.

One implication of Detemple and Jorion's (1990) results concerns the overall effect the introduction of options and the improvement in risk-sharing opportunities has had on the value of the market. They analyze the introduction of three hundred options, but since these were typically introduced in batches, there were only fifty-three days on which introductions occurred. On each of these fifty-three days their results indicate the market rises by approximately 1 percent. Based on this finding, one could argue that the total increase in the value of the market due to innovations in the option market may be as high as $(1.01)^{53} - 1 = 69$ percent, or roughly two-thirds.

Another important question is why has there been a decline in the price and volatility impacts of listing options. One possibility is that the size of the firm on whose stock the option is listed is important in determining the price and volatility impacts. In fact, there was a significant difference in the size of firms on whose stock options were listed before and after 1982. Prior to 1982 the average value of newly "optioned" firms was 0.44 percent of the market, compared to 0.10 percent for those "optioned" after 1982. Another possibility is that the market was sufficiently complete during the latter period that the new options were essentially redundant instruments. In a theoretical investigation, Detemple and Jorion (1988) present conditions under which the price effect of a new option is small when an option on a market index already exists. They suggest that the introduction of index options in 1982 had made markets close to complete, thereby eliminating the price and volatility impacts of new options.

All the above studies were concerned with the introduction of options in the United States. Watt, Yadav, and Draper (1992) investigate the effect of options introduction in the United Kingdom for the period 1978–1989. In contrast to the U.S. results, they found that introducing options only had a temporary effect. In particular, there were positive excess returns on the underlying stocks on the ten days preceding introduction and negative excess returns on the ten days following introduction. They suggest that this temporary effect may be due to the fact that liquidity suppliers charge a premium for their services as the market adjusts to hedging-related demands of dealers, but that this effect is only temporary. They do not suggest an explanation for the difference between the U.S. and U.K. markets.

In sections 4.3 and 4.5 we outline a theory of innovation in which the introduction of new securities leads to important price effects. The empirical evidence concerning the effect of options introduction in the United States provides an important motivation for the study of this type of model. One interesting feature of the evidence is that changes mainly occurred at the date of introduction of the options, not at the announcement date. This is consistent with their being caused by general equilibrium effects which are more difficult to predict than partial equilibrium effects.[70] The disappearance of such effects is consistent with learning about the effects over time and anticipation of announcements of new listings.

Other investigations of financial innovation have focused on products introduced by investment banks. Kanemasu, Litzenberger, and Rolfo (1986) considered the profitability of the unbundling of Treasury securities into principal and interest that occurred in the mid-1980s. Their results indicate that stripping securities allowed the banks significant initial profits. As more investment banks started stripping bonds, their profits were reduced.

Tufano (1989) used a database of fifty-eight financial innovations introduced by investment banks between 1974 and 1986. The new products ranged from mortgage-backed securities to floating-rate notes to commodity-indexed instruments. The cost of developing these ranged from $50,000 to $5 million. His results can be summarized as follows:

• Innovating banks do not charge higher prices for the period before imitation removes their monopoly of the innovation.

• In the long run, innovating banks charge less than rivals offering imitative products.

• Banks that introduce an innovative product subsequently obtain a larger market share than imitators.

In contrast to the results of Kanemasu, Litzenberger, and Rolfo (1986) on the stripping of government bonds, the incentives for innovation are not from increased initial profits. One explanation is that larger market share enables firms to make larger profits because of economies of scale. In section 4.4 we develop a model of competition between investment banks and investigate the role of increasing market share as an incentive to innovate. Another explanation is that price changes, of the type identified in the options-introduction literature, create an incentive for the innovator to introduce a new security because it increases the value of assets the innovator already holds. This motive is essentially the same as the one discussed in section 4.3.

2.4 Discussion

The history of financial innovation and the evidence of its impact demonstrate that it is an important phenomenon. Although it has occurred for many centuries, it appears that the rate of innovation, as measured by the number of new instruments, and the success of these innovations, as measured by the volume traded, have been relatively high since 1970. The development of options and financial futures markets in the 1970s led to a significant change in the way that financial risk could be hedged. In the 1980s the development of new types of financial instruments has been even more significant. The markets for securitized loans and swaps, particularly those for interest rate swaps, have grown enormously. As mentioned in section 2.2, between 1973 and 1989 the amount of Ginnie Mae, Freddie Mac, and Fannie Mae mortgage-backed securities outstanding grew from zero to around $1 trillion. Similarly, between 1981 and the end of 1990, the volume of interest rate swaps denominated in U.S. dollars grew from zero to around $2.3 trillion. In addition to these enormous volumes of new securities, the evidence on the impact of introducing options suggests this may have increased the value of stocks on the NYSE and AMEX exchanges by around two-thirds between 1973 and 1986. These magnitudes show how important financial innovation has been in the last twenty years.

Innovation has not been restricted to any particular type of issuer. Individuals, intermediaries such as banks and exchanges, corporations, and governments have all been important innovators at different stages. The earliest financial arrangements were contracts for borrowing between individuals, which were motivated by gains from trade; they presumably were a natural development of risk-sharing arrangements between families and friends. As these arrangements became frequently used, banks came into existence. The first standardized financial arrangements, which were bank deposits and banker's acceptances, were invented in ancient times and rediscovered in the thirteenth century. During the sixteenth century the ever-increasing need for funds by governments led to the development of bonds which were held by many people. At about the same time, corporations developed from partnerships and corporate equity, and debt also started to be widely held. Over the next three hundred years or so, stock exchanges where these securities could be traded came into existence in many countries. These significantly increased liquidity and reduced transaction costs. A number of other types of security, such as convertibles, preferred stock, and options, were also developed during this period. In recent years organized options and futures markets have come into existence, often with exchange sponsorship. The mortgage-backed security markets were initiated by government agencies. The swap markets were developed primarily by banks without exchange or government sponsorship. Clearly there have been many and various agents of innovation.

In order to understand the reasons for innovation we need to consider the benefits financial innovations have provided to innovators and others. These include the following:

- Increasing risk-sharing opportunities
- Avoiding regulations and taxes
- Reducing transaction costs and increasing liquidity
- Reducing agency costs
- Capturing temporary profits
- Changing prices

Van Horne (1985) suggests that a primary motivation for innovation is to increase risk-sharing opportunities by moving toward more complete markets. Options, financial futures, floating-rate notes, and swaps are illustrations of this category of innovation. The importance of these markets in terms of the volumes traded suggests that this is a very important benefit of innovation.

Miller (1986) argues that innovation and in particular recent innovation has been a response to government regulation and taxes. Even in the middle of the nineteenth century, the popularity of preferred stock in England arose from the fact that corporations were prohibited from borrowing more than a third of their total share capital. More recently the development of the Euromarkets in the 1960s was spurred significantly by the U.S. Interest Equalization Tax, which excluded most foreign issuers from the U.S. market. In the early 1980s, the existence of a tax loophole led to the development of the market for zero coupon bonds. Other examples mentioned above also illustrate the fact that government regulations and taxes have been important stimulants to innovation.

The role of transaction cost savings and improvements in liquidity have been pointed to by Merton (1990) and others as important benefits of financial innovation. Commercial paper, options, financial futures, mortgage-backed securities, swaps, and synthetics are all examples of securities whose success was due in large part to reductions in overall transaction costs and improved liquidity.

In attributing financial innovations to reductions in transaction costs, it is important to distinguish between immediate and underlying causes. For example, options and futures markets were undoubtedly successful because they substantially lowered traders' transaction costs. However, the real motivation for trading in these markets is to hedge or share risks. Lowering transaction costs is the immediate cause of the innovation, but improving risk sharing is the underlying cause of the innovation.

One should also distinguish between the conditions which cause the initial innovation and those which sustain it. For example, we have seen that the popularity of zero-coupon bonds was greatly enhanced by a loophole in the tax code, but the market continued to grow even after the tax loophole was closed. Another example is provided by the introduction of money market mutual funds and money market accounts in the 1970s, which was prompted by a combination of high interest rates in the U.S. money market and regulations which prevented commercial banks from paying competitive interest rates on their deposits. But these innovations are still used in the more recent low-interest environment of the 1990s. There appears to be a kind of hysteresis in the innovative process, possibly related to the information investors acquire from their initial experience with a new security.

Another factor stressed by Merton (1990) is the role of agency costs. Jensen and Meckling (1976) argued that the firm could be thought of as a set of contracts between different parties with different interests. According to this view, the form of securities issued is crucial in regulating the relationship between different groups. For example, if a firm has a large amount of debt outstanding, the equityholders only earn a return if there is a high payoff; this means they (or managers acting on their behalf) have an incentive to undertake risky projects which have some probability of a high payoff irrespective of the expected payoff. A number of authors including Green (1984) and Barnea, Haugen, and Senbet (1985) have argued that convertibles and warrants and other forms of traditional security allow these adverse incentives to be mitigated by allowing bondholders to share in any high payoffs the firm may receive. More recent examples of innovations concerned with agency costs are those to do with corporate control. Many innovations that come under the category of poison pill securities have been designed to discourage takeovers and allow incumbent managers to remain in control.

Silber (1981) has suggested that the search for temporary monopoly profits in an oligopolistic market structure stimulates financial innovation. He provides evidence that the introduction of futures contracts in the period 1960–1980 can be explained by a model of this sort.

The work of Conrad (1989) and Detemple and Jorion (1990) on the introduction of options demonstrates that the price changes associated with financial innovation can be substantial. These effects were felt by a wide range of investors. In many cases, the fact that there are substantial price effects can provide incentives to innovate. For example, given that warrants are similar to options, introducing a warrant may increase the value of the issuing firm by a significant amount. An investment bank may be able to earn a return on an innovation if it increases the value of securities held by the bank. There are many other situations where an issuer will have an incentive to introduce a warrant or other type of new security if this affects the value of the issuer's assets.

There are clearly many benefits from innovation and hence many reasons for innovation. In analyzing recent innovations it is important to understand which of these motives have been most important for recent innovations and why there has been so much innovation since 1970. Walmsley (1988) has pointed to the adoption of flexible exchange rates by the major economies in the mid-1970s and the New Economic Policy adopted by the U.S. Federal Reserve in October 1979, which increased the volatility of interest rates. He argues that the increased risk associated with these two developments led individuals and firms to demand better ways to hedge risk. This demand was crucial, according to Walmsley, for the success of many of the innovations that have improved risk-sharing possibilities. Walmsley also stresses the importance of new technologies, in particular computers. The complexity of many financial innovations is such that they only become practicable if investors have computers available. Without this change in technology, pricing and assessment of the securities can be very haphazard, and this can make investors reluctant to invest in them.

There are many other factors that have contributed to the surge in financial innovation. Financial flows between countries have grown enormously, and this has been an important stimulus to innovation. One cause of increased capital flows is found in the oil price shocks of the 1970s, which greatly increased the funds the oil-producing countries had available to invest in international capital markets. Other causes were the growth in world trade and the relaxation of exchange controls in many countries. These increased flows have led to the development of a global market. The deregulation of financial markets in the United States and other countries has been another important reason for recent innovation. Many of the instruments that have been developed would not have been possible under old regulations.

Financial innovation has changed the world in which we live and work. The observation that the introduction of options markets may have increased the value of stocks on the NYSE and AMEX by as much as two-thirds gives some idea of the potential impact of financial innovation. The fact that mortgage-backed securities and swaps now involve trillions of dollars shows how fundamentally the financial transactions of individuals and firms have changed within a short period of time because of financial innovation. In making plans now, industrial companies and financial institutions must take account of the possibility that financial innovation will significantly alter the environment in which they operate before their plans are carried out. Prior to 1970, innovation was a slow process, and there was stability for long periods of time. Agents may have been justified in ignoring it. Now, however, financial innovation is a fact of life and must be incorporated into every economic agent's decision making.

The remaining chapters of part I deal with theory. In chapter 4 we present a synthesis of our approach to financial innovation, and in chapter 5 we consider other approaches and suggest directions for future research.

Before doing that, however, we review in chapter 3 what the industrial organization literature has to say about innovation.

Notes

1. Chatfield (1977), p. 5.

2. Chatfield (1977), p. 10.

3. This is a written promise by a bank to pay a given sum at a specified date.

4. These were the antecedents of corporations. There are a number of differences between joint-stock companies and corporations. Joint stock companies have greater flexibility of purpose compared to corporations which usually start with a clearly defined purpose. Also, in joint-stock companies the governing board is self-perpetuating, whereas in corporations the directors are elected by shareholders. See Dewing (1934), pp. 35–37, and Dewing (1955), pp. 24–27.

5. Morgan and Thomas (1969), p. 12.

6. Walmsley (1988), p. 3.

7. Kellenbenz (1957), p. xv.

8. Dewing (1934), pp. 376–377.

9. This combines a number of features of debt and equity. The payment is fixed similarly to debt, but if it is omitted, the firm does not go bankrupt similarly to equity. It is senior to equity but junior to debt in liquidation.

10. See Dewing (1934), p. 135.

11. Morgan and Thomas (1969), p. 104.

12. See Morgan and Thomas (1969), p. 104.

13. Walmsley (1988), p. 3.

14. Dewing (1934), p. 136.

15. Morgan and Thomas (1969), p. 19.

16. Morgan and Thomas (1969), p. 20.

17. Morgan and Thomas (1969), p. 20.

18. Neal (1990), p. 111.

19. The legal document creating the company and setting out its purposes.

20. Morgan and Thomas (1969), p. 43.

21. Morgan and Thomas (1969), p. 45.

22. Morgan and Thomas (1969), p. 113.

23. Dewing (1934), p. 135.

24. Baskin (1988), pp. 207–208.

25. Dewing (1934), p. 317.

26. Tufano (1991), pp. 18–19.

27. Guthmann and Dougall (1962), pp. 465–466.

28. Dewing (1934), pp. 309–400.

29. Duffie (1989), p. 3.

30. Duffie (1989), pp. 3–4 and Schwarz, Hill, and Schneeweis (1986), pp. 3–4.

31. Duffie (1989), p. 3 and Hull (1991), p. 3.

32. The Eurobond market was originally the market for dollar bonds in Europe. It subsequently came to encompass the market for bonds in a number of other currencies. Securities are usually listed on the London and Luxembourg Stock Exchanges. Trades are settled through two interlinked settlement systems, Cedel and Euroclear. Chapter 17 of Walmsley (1991) contains a description of the institutional details of the Euromarkets.

33. See chapter 2 of Hayes and Hubbard (1990).

34. An example of a parallel loan is when a U.K. firm lends to a U.S. firm's British subsidiary, and in return the U.S. firm lends to the U.K. firm's American subsidiary. With a back-to-back loan the parent firms deal directly. In a currency swap the repayment obligations are formally linked so that if one party defaults the other is not obligated to repay.

35. Walmsley (1991), pp. 19–25, and Schwarz, Hill, and Schneeweis (1986), pp. 10–13.

36. Walmsley (1988), pp. 187–188 and Walmsley (1991), p. 23 and 48–49.

37. Walmsley (1988), p. 195.

38. This allows either 70 percent of dividends from other firms to be excluded for corporate income tax purposes if less than 20 percent of the paying firm is owned by the receiving corporation or 80 percent if more than this is owned.

39. See Winger et al. (1986).

40. See Alderson, Brown, and Lummer (1987) and Fraser and Alderson (1993).

41. Walmsley (1991), p. 70.

42. See Fisher, Brick, and Ng (1983) and Yawitz and Maloney (1983).

43. Walmsley (1988), p. 214.

44. See Jarrow and O'Hara (1989) and Finnerty (1993).

45. Walmsley (1988), p. 278.

46. Walmsley (1988), p. 299.

47. See Walter and Smith (1990), pp. 126–127.

48. See DeAngelo and Rice (1983), Linn and McConnell (1983), and Jarrell and Poulsen (1987) for a description of these antitakeover techniques and an analysis of their effects.

49. For a full description of these plans see Malatesta and Walkling (1988) and Ryngaert (1988).

50. See Marshall and Kapner (1990) for a full description of the institutional details of swaps.

51. Walmsley (1991), pp. 104–107.

52. Walmsley (1991), p. 34.

53. Walmsley (1988), p. 125.

54. See Walmsley (1988), p. 125; see also International Swap Dealers Association Market Survey (1992).

55. Walmsley (1988), p. 127.

56. International Swap Dealers Association Market Survey (1992).

57. See Abken (1991) for an account of these other swap types.

58. See Abken (1991), pp. 24–26, and Masuoka (1991), p. 16, for an account of commodity swaps.

59. Private communication from the Chicago Board of Trade.

60. Walmsley (1988), p. 119.

61. Walmsley (1988), pp. 106–7, and Schwarz, Hill, and Schneeweis (1986), p. 165.

62. Walmsley (1988), p. 248, and Litan (1991), p. 14.

63. Walmsley (1988), p. 249.

64. The structure of actual CMOs is fairly complex. For a full description see Spratlin and Vianna (1986).

65. Walmsley (1988), pp. 257–258.

66. Finnerty (1993), p. 29.

67. Walmsley (1988), p. 245.

68. Walmsley (1991), p. 60.

69. Finnerty (1993), p. 38.

70. We are grateful to Matt Jackson for suggesting this point.

3 Industrial Organization Approaches to Innovation

Although the study of financial innovation is at an early stage, industrial organization theorists have made an extensive study of innovation in the context of manufacturing processes and products.[1] Before describing our approach to the analysis of financial innovation, it may be helpful to review what the industrial organization literature has to say. Many of the issues that arise in the study of innovation in industry, problems of imitation, intellectual property rights, asymmetric information and so forth have their counterparts in the context of financial innovation. But although there are many parallels, most of the approaches that have proved useful for analyzing financial innovation do not seem to have played an important role in the industrial organization literature.

3.1 Industrial Organization Theories

Four areas have received wide attention.[2]

1. Market structure
2. Patents
3. Network externalities
4. Profitable speculation opportunities

Each area will be considered in turn.

Market Structure

Schumpeter argued that under a perfectly competitive market structure the cost savings or other benefits of innovation would not accrue to the innovator, but would be immediately competed away by rival firms. As a result, competitive firms would not be willing to expend resources to innovate. In contrast, under a monopolistic market structure a firm will have a greater incentive to innovate, since it will be able to recoup any cost savings by maintaining the price of its product, and product improvements will allow it to increase the price. In both cases, increases in profits compensate for expenditures on innovation.

Although monopoly increases the incentives to innovate, it does not provide incentives that are socially optimal. To see this, consider the situation shown in figure 3.1, where the industry has constant marginal costs. Suppose an innovation results in a reduction in marginal cost. The in-

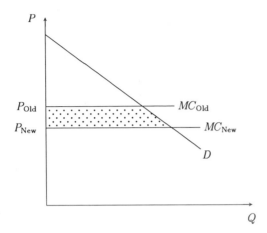

Figure 3.1
Innovation in an ideal world

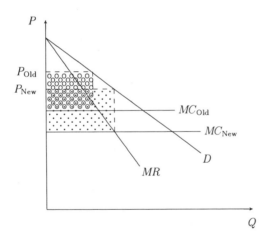

Figure 3.2
Innovation with a monopoly

crease in welfare each period is equal to the shaded area. In an ideal world, the new price would be set equal to the new marginal cost to ensure an efficient allocation of resources. To provide efficient incentives to innovate, the innovating firm would be paid an amount equal to the shaded area for each period the technology is in use. The payment would be financed by a lump sum tax levied on consumers. In contrast, if the industry is a monopoly, the reduction in costs will typically lead to an increase in profits, as shown in figure 3.2. However, price will not be equal to marginal cost, and the size of the increase in profits will usually not be the same as the shaded area in figure 3.1, so the incentive to innovate will not be efficient. For example, the cost of an innovation may be less than the social benefit, so innovation is socially optimal, but the monopolist's increase in profits may be less than the cost, so the innovation is not undertaken.

Scherer (1967) and Kamien and Schwartz (1978) have argued that in oligopolistic industries firms compete by innovating. Firms can gain a temporary advantage by developing a new product, and this allows an increase in their profits until such time as their competitors can imitate the innovation.

Patents

The failure of competitive markets to provide efficient incentives to innovate provides some justification for a system of patents, under which innovating firms are given a monopoly for a period of time. Arrow (1962) showed that when a single firm is awarded an unlimited patent, the incentives to innovate are not the same as the incentives in an ideal world. To see this, consider a competitive industry in which a product is sold at a price p_{old}, equal to marginal cost. A new process is then discovered and patented. The owner of the patent is effectively a monopolist as long as she sets her price below p_{old}. The new price cannot be greater than p_{old} because of potential competition from the old technology. If the price p_m at which marginal revenue is equal to marginal cost is greater than p_{old}, the patent holder will set the new price equal to p_{old}. Her profits each period are equal to the shaded area in figure 3.3a. If p_m is below p_{old}, then p_m will be the new price, as shown in figure 3.3b, and profits each period will again be given by the shaded area. The incentive to innovate in this case is clearly less than in an ideal world since the patent holder is unable to capture the entire increase in consumer surplus.

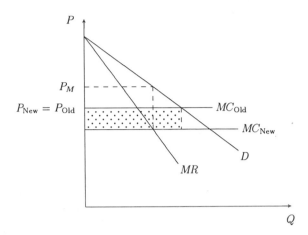

Figure 3.3a
Innovation with a patent when price stays constant

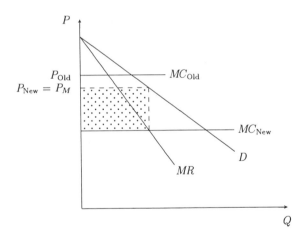

Figure 3.3b
Innovation with a patent when price is reduced

It can be seen from the example of figure 3.3 that the profits from innovation depend crucially on the initial market structure of the industry. If a firm has a monopoly, it has less incentive to innovate than a firm in a perfectly competitive industry in the sense that there will be some innovations that a competitive firm is willing to undertake which a monopolist is not. The reason is that the perfectly competitive firm not only captures the benefit of reducing cost or improving its product but it also gains market power by becoming a temporary monopolist. This is the *replacement effect* identified by Arrow (1962).

Market structure can influence innovation in other ways. For example, Gilbert and Newbery (1982) have pointed out that an incumbent monopolist may have a greater incentive to acquire a new technology than a potential entrant. The reason is that the profits from remaining a monopolist are usually higher than the profits the potential entrant could make by entering and sharing the market with the incumbent. Also, monopolists may find it worthwhile to prevent entry by acquiring patents on new technologies even if they do not intend to use them because this can ensure their monopoly profits continue.

Another important assumption underlying the example of figure 3.3 is that the timing of the innovation is exogenous. In many cases a number of firms compete to innovate first and acquire the sole rights to the patent. The literature on patent races has considered a number of different issues. One is whether firms have the correct incentives in terms of the risk of the R&D strategy they pursue. The "winner take all" aspect of patents means competing firms have an incentive to adopt strategies that are too risky.[3] Another issue is whether monopolists have an advantage over potential entrants. Part of the literature is concerned with "memoryless" models where the probability of a discovery per unit time depends on the current level of R&D expenditure, rather than on the cumulative history.[4] In the case of innovations that are significant enough to allow the entrant to take the place of the monopolist, the replacement effect means the entrant has a bigger incentive than the incumbent; the monopolist is already earning profits, whereas the entrant is not. If the innovation is relatively small, the innovating entrant would have to share the market; therefore, the incumbent monopolist has a greater incentive to innovate because the profits in a monopoly are higher than in a duopoly. Unlike the memoryless models, some models of patent races assume that the probability of discovery per unit time depends on accumulated experience.[5] In this type of model, the first mover usually has a distinct advantage. An exception occurs when information lags prevent the leader's knowing what the follower is doing. In this and other cases, the follower may "leapfrog" the leader.

Network Externalities

With many technologies, an important characteristic of innovation is the existence of network externalities. Positive network externalities occur when each user benefits from the increase in the total number of users. One example is provided by computer programs, which are better supported the greater the total number of users. Another would be video recorder systems; the greater the number of people who have a particular system, the greater the number of videotapes of that type there will be available for rent.

Network models can be divided into two categories, those concerned with the demand side and those concerned with the supply side.[6] On the demand side, the main problem is lack of coordination: consumers must guess which type of network will be adopted. Farrell and Saloner (1985) have identified two types of inefficiency in this context. The first is *excess inertia*, where users all wait to adopt a new technology because others are waiting. The second is *excess momentum*, where consumers adopt an inferior technology because they expect everybody else to do the same. On the supply side, Katz and Shapiro (1985, 1986a, 1986b) have considered the incentives firms have to adopt compatible networks. Among other things, they show that smaller firms have more incentive to become compatible than larger firms. However, the incentives to make compatible products are not socially efficient. In general, it may be better for the government or industry committees to develop standards to overcome some of the coordination problems.

Profitable Speculation Opportunities

Hirshleifer (1971) points out one way in which firms can profit from innovations in the absence of a monopolistic market structure or a patent system. He argues that in many cases innovations change relative prices, and this creates an opportunity for the innovator to profit by making appropriate investments. The example he cites is Eli Whitney's invention of the cotton gin. Although there was a patent on the cotton gin, Whitney was not very successful in enforcing it. Hirshleifer suggests an alternative way in which Whitney might have profited from his invention. Since the cost savings associated with the gin increased the value of cotton-producing land, Whitney could have captured some of the rents generated by his invention by speculating on the price of land. There are, of course, a number of problems with this idea. Wealth constraints and the risk involved in making the necessary long-term investments appear to limit its practical applicability. These problems are somewhat alleviated if an innovator can make investments in the stock and options markets. These markets provide opportunities for hedging risk and allow the speculator to buy on margin.

Vila (1987) has investigated the operation of financial markets when an innovator has the opportunity to speculate. A necessary condition for profitable speculation is the existence of "noise" (as in Grossman and Stiglitz 1980); otherwise the innovator's trades reveal his information, and he cannot make a profit. However, the presence of noise means the innovator bears risk and will only be able to take limited positions. Vila also points out that the ability to speculate on stock price changes can provide bad incentives as well as good ones; he quotes the example of the individual who was prosecuted for buying put options on SmithKline Beckman in 1985 and poisoning one of their main products, Contac, in the hope of causing a fall in the stock price.

Although regarded by many as an interesting idea, Hirshleifer's suggestion has not received a great deal of attention in the industrial organization literature. For example, in his extensive discussion of innovation, Tirole (1988) does not mention Hirshleifer's contribution.

Innovation and Welfare

Most of the work on innovation has been concerned with analyzing the incentives to innovate provided by existing institutions. Much of this work analyzes the operation of the patent system. It has been widely recognized that the patent system is far from ideal. The problems of imitation and "inventing around" patents mean that in many cases patents do not provide very good protection of property rights. To the extent that good protection of property rights is provided, it results in the innovator being granted a monopoly, with all its associated distortions. There are a number of alternatives to patents. General tax subsidies on R&D expenditures and regulation, such as emission controls and mileage limits in the automobile industry, are examples of policies which stimulate innovation. The procurement system used by the Defense Department for developing new weapons systems and the peer review system used by the NSF for sponsoring pure scientific research and by agencies such as NASA are other examples where the government provides direct support. These types of policy have been considered on a case-by-case basis; there has been very little global welfare analysis of the optimal set of policies for providing socially efficient incentives for innovation. This lack of a global welfare analysis is a serious deficiency of the literature.

Another deficiency of the literature is the focus on ex post efficiency. The presumption underlying much of the discussion of patents and the other innovation literature is that if an innovator does not acquire the total surplus from his innovation, there is an efficency loss since in some cases an innovation would not be undertaken even though the benefits outweigh the costs. However, if innovators were to acquire the entire benefits of their innovations, the distribution of wealth would often be bizarre; a few individuals would obtain very large payoffs, while the majority would not obtain anything. If there were complete information about who was going to innovate, then lump sum taxes could be used to redistribute the gains from innovation. In practice, there is clearly very incomplete information on who will innovate and how much effort is required to innovate. Behind the Rawlsian veil of ignorance, before people know whether or not they are going to innovate, they may wish to sign a social contract in which the benefits of innovation are shared more widely. Ex post, there will be less innovation because innovators do not capture the full marginal benefit, but many more people will be better off. Ex ante, it is possible that everybody will be better off from sharing the gains to innovation in this way. This suggests that simply viewing incentives to innovate in an ex post way has some important limitations. However, this ex ante view of innovation has received little attention in the industrial organization literature, and thus the standard ex post view will be used.

3.2   Applications to Financial Innovation

Although the industrial organization literature has explored many of the basic theoretical problems of innovation, the differences between the financial world and the world of manufacturing industry limit the usefulness of some of these models in helping us understand financial innovation. Schumpeterian analyses, which focus on the importance of monopolistic market structures for providing incentives to innovate, have limited applicability since most financial markets are highly competitive. An exception is in the area of competition by exchanges. As mentioned in chapter 2, Silber (1981) has suggested that competition between futures exchanges can be regarded as being like that in an oligopolistic industry where firms try to gain a temporary advantage by innovating. Anderson and Harris (1986) have argued that in this context, delays before imitation can occur are plausible because of regulatory lags. Among other things, they show that this can lead to significant first-mover advantages with the initial innovator gaining a permanent monopoly or a larger share than subsequent imitators. However, in most other financial contexts, imitation of innovations is usually fairly easy, so the innovator does not even achieve a temporary monopoly. Short sales, when feasible, effectively constitute issuing an imitative product. As Tufano (1989) has indicated, direct imitation can be achieved by reverse engineering: "taking the product apart" is typically straightforward, and only a small amount of time is needed to accomplish this. Indeed, one of the peculiarities of many financial products is that the buyer needs to understand how they work; it is not possible simply to sell a "black box." For example, if investors are buying a new security, they will need to know its characteristics in order to be able to combine it efficiently with the other securities in their portfolios. There are examples of innovations that can be kept proprietary, such as a reputable mutual fund with a new trading strategy which is not revealed to investors, but these are relatively rare. Thus a Schumpeterian analysis based on market structure has limited applicability in the context of financial innovation.

Another important difference between innovation in an industrial context and in a financial context concerns the possibility of obtaining a patent. Although recent court decisions based on a broad interpretation of the patent and copyright laws mean that some protection has been accorded to financial innovations, Petruzzi, Del Valle, and Judlowe (1988) argue that most financial products cannot be patented. An example of the type of protection that can be obtained is Merrill Lynch's patent on its Cash Management Account process. The crucial factor in the success of this patent application was the fact that the product made use of a computer for its implementation. However, there are only a few situations where patents are a realistic possibility, so the opportunities for applying the theory of patents to the financial context are limited.

Network externalities do occur in financial markets. For example, stock markets can be thought of as networks. The New York Stock exchange has a very different trading system from the NASDAQ exchange, and the liquidity of a stock depends on the size and the nature of the network it is traded on. This liquidity factor seems to be particularly important in futures markets. If an existing contract is already widely used to hedge a risk, a new contract may be unsuccessful even if it is superior in other ways. Working (1953) quotes the example of Pacific Northwest Wheat. This is a soft wheat whose price is only loosely related to that of hard wheats, which are the basis of markets in Kansas City and Chicago. In order to provide a means of hedging the risk associated with this soft wheat, the Chicago Board of Trade introduced a Pacific Northwest wheat contract. However, it was not successful because a critical mass of hedgers was unwilling to switch from the liquid hard wheat markets even though they provided an imperfect hedge. Black (1986) gives further evidence that the existence of a liquid contract that provides reasonably good hedging opportunities preempts the development of new contracts. Cuny (1993) has provided a theoretical analysis of the importance of liquidity in the innovation of futures contracts. Among other things, he shows that there can be important inefficiencies resulting from coordination problems.

Another situation in which networks are important is when investment banks make issues of securities and sell them to networks of investors or when brokers sell stocks in the secondary markets through their network of customers. Gehrig (1992) has considered a model where financial intermediaries such as brokers compete through distribution networks. It is shown that an equilibrium with a few intermediaries exists that is nevertheless competitive in the sense that spreads tend to zero and equilibrium prices converge to marginal cost as the size of the economy becomes large.

Although there has been some work in the area of financial innovation that is related to the analysis of network externalities in industrial organization, this has been relatively limited. Many of the issues highlighted in the industrial organization literature on coordination problems and competition between networks arise in financial markets. The analysis of networks in this context is a promising area for future research.

Hirshleifer's (1971) suggestion that speculation on the price changes caused by successful innovation can provide incentives for innovation has not received much attention in the industrial organization literature. Presumably, this is because of the practical difficulties in implementing such a strategy. However, in the context of financial innovation, the idea has greater potential for application, because the effects of financial innovation occur much more quickly. Also, as discussed in section 2.3, the introduction of options has had significant effects on other security prices. This makes it easier to design strategies to profit from price changes with relatively little risk.

In the United States and many other countries, governments play an extensive role in regulating financial markets. In most cases this regulation is far more extensive than regulation in other types of markets. This suggests another need for a global welfare analysis of financial innovation. A primary focus of our analysis of financial innovation is the welfare aspect.

3.3 Our Approach to Financial Innovation

An important incentive to innovate may be provided by changes in the value of pre-existing assets. This incentive effect is related to the one identified by Hirshleifer (1971) but does not involve the practical difficulties of speculation in financial markets. As an illustration, consider the case of Kodak. The company had developed sophisticated film and film-processing techniques. One way to increase the value of these assets was to expand the market for film by making cameras much easier to use. They therefore developed popular, lightweight, easy-to-use cameras and greatly increased the value of their existing business. This incentive to innovate appears to be fairly important in practice. Much of the innovation in the automobile and other consumer durable industries does not rely on patents for ensuring profitability. However, if a firm did not undertake any innovation, it would quickly lose market share, and the value of the firm would fall.

In the theory of financial innovation we are about to describe, the idea that firms innovate to maximize their value turns out to be an important one. It is the effect on firm value that provides the incentive for innovation. A firm's basic resource is the stream of cash flows it receives. The financial problem it faces is to split this stream of cash flows to maximize value. In chapter 6 owners of firms split up the stream of cash flows and sell each part to the investors that value it most, taking prices of income streams in different states of the world as given. In chapter 7 the owners of firms are able to affect prices, but again they choose the securities to issue to maximize firm value.

One aspect of financial innovation that does not have a direct counterpart in the industrial organization literature is the risk-sharing benefits of innovation. In the case of options and futures exchanges, for example, the main benefit to developing new products is the fees that investors are willing to pay to use the new instruments to hedge the risk that they face. A model of this type is developed in chapter 8.

Although there are some overlaps between the industrial organization literature and theories that are useful for analyzing financial innovation, they seem to be fairly limited. The ideas that have received the most attention in the industrial organization literature do not really apply in financial markets. Hirshleifer's idea that innovators should speculate and the related idea that firms should innovate to maximize the value of assets that are already held have not received much attention in the industrial organization literature, but have important implications for financial innovation.

Notes

1. For an excellent account of this literature see Tirole (1988), chapter 10.

2. An area that has, as yet, received little attention is research joint ventures. Katz (1986) shows that firms have an incentive to share the costs and knowledge created by research projects. Bhattacharya, Glazer, and Sappington (1990) analyze the optimal level of knowledge sharing and show how this can be implemented. These analyses appear to have little application to financial innovation.

3. See Dasgupta and Stiglitz (1980) and Klette and de Meza (1986).

4. See Reinganum (1984) for a survey of this literature.

5. See Fudenberg et al. (1983) and Harris and Vickers (1985).

6. For surveys of this area see Besen and Johnson (1986) and Besen and Saloner (1987).

4 An Outline of Our Theory

It is clear that technological innovation has had an enormous impact on people's welfare in the advanced countries of the world. The development of the railways and other basic industries in the nineteenth century has been followed by the development of consumer industries such as automobiles and electrical goods in the twentieth century, and the average person's level of consumption has increased dramatically. Innovations in medical technologies together with this increase in living standards have led to much longer life expectancies. Not surprisingly, the economic analysis of technological innovation has received a considerable amount of attention as the literature review in the previous chapter indicates.

Financial innovation has also been crucial to the increase in living standards in this period. In the ancient world, the existence of banks assisted the development of more sophisticated business and trading practices. In the Middle Ages, these practices died out, and economic activity returned to a very low level. For example, trade was limited because of the lack of an easy means of payment. Without banker's acceptances, goods had to be paid for by barter or by precious metals that were difficult and dangerous to transport. It was only with the rediscovery of banking techniques in northern Italy, in the thirteenth century, that trade began to expand and the associated benefits could be obtained.

During this period the scale of business operations was small because borrowing possibilities were limited. The size of an organization was constrained by the wealth a small number of people could amass. It was not until the development of the joint-stock company, or in other words the financial innovation of equity, that larger scale organizations could be created. Companies such as the East India Company and the Hudson Bay Company played an important role in the development of the British Empire and the economic advancement of the United Kingdom.

The development of bonds also had an important impact, particularly on the activities of governments. Prior to the existence of markets for bonds, governments' ability to finance wars was limited because they had to borrow from banks or a small number of individuals. The military success of the British during the eighteenth and nineteenth centuries can at least partly be ascribed to the relative ease of access to funds that the London financial markets allowed.

The repeal of the South Sea Act at the beginning of the nineteenth century allowed the resources needed for the development of the canals and railways in Britain to be mobilized using equity, debt, and preferred stock. The unrestricted use of these financial instruments allowed the scale of business organizations to expand dramatically during this period. The development of the country's infrastructure had important impacts on the viability of other industries.

In the United States, the commodity futures markets that developed in Chicago allowed the risk associated with agricultural products to be spread widely and were a significant factor in the agricultural development of the Midwest during the latter half of the nineteenth century. The other financial innovations that occurred during this period allowed the development of the railroads and helped to pave the way for the dramatic increase in industrial activity that occurred in the early twentieth century. It is difficult to imagine that the major economic advances pioneered by U.S. corporations would have been possible without the development of equity, debt, and the other traditional financing instruments that were used.

Since the Second World War there has again been a dramatic increase in standards of living. One of the most important factors in this has been an enormous expansion in the amount of trade. The financial innovations associated with the development of the Euromarkets have been a significant contributing factor to these changes. The increased ability to raise funds and share risks has greatly expanded the activities that firms are willing to undertake. Similarly, the development of markets for financial futures, options, and mortgage-backed securities in the United States has significantly changed the ability of firms and individuals to hedge risks and has increased the range of activities they are willing to undertake. The change in the nature of equity securities associated with the development of an active market for corporate control has changed the conduct of business.

The former Soviet Union provides an interesting illustration of the role of financial innovation. Although technologically advanced in many ways, its economic system was unable to provide a high standard of living to its citizens because it was economically unsophisticated. There are many reasons for the backwardness of the economic institutions of the Soviet Union. The lack of private ownership, the lack of free markets, and the lack of accounting and other information systems played a major part. To a large extent, the source of underdevelopment can be seen as a lack of financial institutions, broadly defined, and the information and incentives they provided.

Clearly it is important to understand the processes of financial innovation. The history outlined in chapter 2 raises many theoretical questions. On the positive side, what are the causes of innovation? Is there one primary cause or several? Do they operate independently or interact? How does market structure influence innovation? How does the nature of the institutions that are responsible for innovation determine the form and impact of innovation? On the welfare side, we have seen that the potential redistributive effect of innovation can be enormous. In addition, we should be concerned with welfare gains from innovation. How big are the gains (or losses), and how are they shared? What effect does market structure have on welfare? Are regulation and intervention needed?

This is a big topic, and there are many ways of organizing it. In our own research, represented by the papers in this collection, we have mainly chosen to focus on the risk-sharing problem as an analytical framework in which to study the various aspects of financial innovation. There is no doubt that risk and the need for risk sharing, whether in the form of insurance or diversification, are important factors in everyone's life. Despite the large increase in the share of economic activity controlled by the government, the majority of people in most advanced economies work for privately owned businesses. The risk these people face is intimately connected to the activities of the firm they work for. If the firm goes bankrupt, they will lose their jobs and the benefits they receive from their firms. In Europe these may include pension rights; in Japan, in addition, cheap housing and food; and in the United States, health benefits. Even if a person's job is secure, the value of his or her pension plan may be subject to considerable risk. Extensive private ownership of homes has also exposed people directly to risk. There is no one who is not faced with some event whose occurrence would dramatically change his or her welfare. Whatever the source of risk, the welfare of the individual depends heavily on the possibility of hedging this risk. In addition the ability of firms to undertake risky projects and develop new production techniques depends on their ability to spread risk.

Equally clearly, the institutional structure is such that many if not most of the risks that matter cannot be shared. Individuals are still exposed to risks such as bankruptcy, job loss, and fluctuating home prices, in spite of the enormous amount of financial innovation that has occurred in the last twenty years. Many firms cannot finance the projects that they would like to because they are unable to spread the risk and arrange the necessary financing. There are well-known reasons having to do with moral hazard and adverse selection why these opportunities for risk sharing have not been exploited. But as long as they are not, there is the possibility that some financial innovation may improve welfare.

In the classical world of Arrow, Debreu, and McKenzie, these problems do not arise. Every agent's actions, such as the effort expended on different activities, can be observed, and everybody has equal access to this information. All risks are represented by uncertainty about the true state of nature. Since all contingent contracts can be traded, individuals can achieve whatever insurance they want by trading commodities for delivery contingent on states of nature. Furthermore, the equilibrium allocation of risk is Pareto efficient, so there is no scope for welfare-improving financial innovation. Clearly, this is not the world in which we live. One way of capturing the difference is to assume incomplete markets—that is, to assume that some contracts or securities cannot be traded. Financial innovation, then, consists of introducing the missing contracts or securities. By framing the questions this way, we can link our results with the classical theorems of welfare economics, which provide a natural benchmark. We can also analyze the welfare impact of innovation, since we have a well-specified model of the economy, including a complete specification of all economic agents' attitudes to risk. From this point of view, the study of financial innovation is a natural extension of both the classical theory of general equilibrium and the classical theory of welfare economics.

It is also clear that there is much that escapes our net. As stated earlier, the reason that risk sharing is incomplete often has to do with moral hazard or adverse selection. These are problems that do not fit easily in the classical general equilibrium paradigm. More generally, a lot of financial innovation may be dealing with informational problems that do not arise in the classical framework. Some of these issues can be dealt with after a fashion in our framework (see chapter 10, "Standard Securities"), but there is much modern literature that cannot be dealt with. Other approaches to financial innovation such as those based on transaction costs (e.g., Merton 1989 and Ross 1989) and the literature on the governance of firms (e.g., Grossman and Hart 1988 and Harris and Raviv 1988) are discussed in chapter 11. These are obviously important issues. They cannot be decisively separated from the risk-sharing issues that are our main concern, and at some stage they must be dealt with by any serious theory. Our decision to leave them aside for now does not represent an ideological position but simply a practical strategy of dealing with the simplest issues first and trying to understand one piece of the problem before trying to understand the whole, even though we accept that the piece we are studying (risk sharing under complete information) cannot be fully understood in isolation.

In this chapter we explore some of the ideas that are developed in greater detail in later chapters. We start by reviewing the role of securities in achieving an optimal allocation of risk sharing.

4.1 Security Design and Risk Sharing

A Simple Risk-sharing Problem

We can illustrate the basic ideas with a series of simple examples. To focus on risk sharing, we start by eliminating many factors and then reintroduce them as we consider progressively more complicated models. Initially there are two dates and a single good. Risk is introduced in the simplest way possible by assuming individuals' incomes are uncertain. At a later stage, firms will be included. These firms will be assumed to choose their financial structure to maximize their value. Markets are incomplete because there is a cost to issuing securities. A firm's value may be increased by paying this cost, splitting its income stream, and marketing the different pieces to investors with different marginal valuations.

We start with the simplest possible risk-sharing scenario, without any firms.

(A.1) There are two dates $t = 1, 2$ with a single consumption good at each date. The consumption good serves as numeraire.

(A.2) There is a finite set of states of nature $\Omega = (\omega_0, \omega_1, \ldots, \omega_w)$ which occur with probabilities $\mu_0, \mu_1, \ldots, \mu_w$. There is a common information structure. At the first date, agents have no information about the state of nature. At the second date, they observe the true state.

Investors are assumed to be risk averse and interested in consumption at both dates.

(A.3) There is a countable set of *investors*. There is a finite set K of *types* of investors. K is also used to denote the number of types. The cross-sectional distribution of investor types is denoted by $v =$

$(v_1, \ldots, v_K)$, that is, the proportion of investors who are of type k is $v_k > 0$.

(A.4)   Investors have von Neumann–Morgenstern utility functions $U_k(c_1, c_2) = c_1 + V_k(c_2)$ where c_t is consumption at date t and $U_k: \mathbb{R}^2 \to \mathbb{R}$, so consumption can be negative. U_k is continuous, differentiable once, strictly increasing and strictly concave.

It is assumed that c_t can be positive or negative to avoid the complications associated with bankruptcy and the corresponding boundary constraints. This also allows investors' initial incomes to be normalized to zero. The low utility associated with negative consumption can be taken as a proxy for the costs of bankruptcy.[1]

(A.5)   Investors' incomes at date 1 are normalized to zero. Each investor has a random income $Y_k(\omega)$ in state ω at date 2.

(A.6)   There is no storage or investment technology for transforming consumption at date 1 into consumption at date 2.

We assume initially there is no possibility for investors to insure their incomes directly, that is, there are no institutions which would allow them to do this. We shall shortly introduce securities and show how they allow risk to be shared and welfare to be improved. Before doing this, however, it is useful to start by characterizing the Pareto optimal allocation of resources. Suppose a central planner (or government) can reallocate resources.

(A.7)   The planner can transfer resources directly between people at each date. A positive transfer represents a subsidy and a negative transfer a tax. At date 1 the transfer for group k is τ_k. At date 2 the transfer for group k is $\tau_k(\omega)$ in state ω. It is necessary that transfers balance at every date and in every state so

$$\sum_{k \in K} \tau_k = 0; \tag{4.1}$$

$$\sum_{k \in K} \tau_k(\omega) = 0 \quad \forall \omega \in \Omega. \tag{4.2}$$

The planner's problem is to ensure a Pareto optimal allocation of resources. She can do this by maximizing the expected utility of one type, say $k = k_0$, holding the expected utilities of the other groups, all $k \neq k_0$, constant in the usual way. (Recall that their incomes at dates 1 and 2 are zero and $Y_k(\omega)$, respectively.)

$$\underset{\tau_k,\,\tau_k(\omega)}{\text{Max}} \qquad EU_{k_0}(\tau_{k_0}, Y_{k_0}(\omega) + \tau_{k_0}(\omega))$$

subject to $\qquad EU_k(\tau_k, Y_k(\omega) + \tau_k(\omega)) \geq \overline{U}_k, \quad \forall k \neq k_0,$

and the constraints 4.1 and 4.2 (where $\overline{U}_k$ is the level of utility type k's attain in the allocation).

At a Pareto optimum, the first-order conditions imply that marginal rates of substitution are equated:

$$\frac{\partial U_{k_0}/\partial c_2(\omega)}{\partial U_{k_0}/\partial c_1} = \frac{\partial U_k/\partial c_2(\omega)}{\partial U_k/\partial c_1} \, \forall k \neq k_0. \tag{4.3}$$

In this allocation, risk sharing occurs through transfers from those individuals with relatively high incomes to those with relatively low incomes. This implies that each individual's consumption in a particular state depends on the total income in that state. As aggregate income fluctuates across the different states, everybody's consumption moves in the same direction. As a result, total income is a sufficient statistic for individual consumption.

The Leading Example

For concreteness and to avoid unnecessary technicalities, we use an example, which we refer to as the leading example, to explore the requirements of optimal risk sharing here and in later sections. There are assumed to be two states of nature $\Omega = \{\omega_0, \omega_1\}$. The states are equally likely, so $\mu_0 = \mu_1 = 0.5$.

There are two types of investor, so $K = \{k_0, k_1\}$, and they are equally distributed in the population, so $v_0 = v_1 = 1/2$. Each type has the same utility function,

$$U_k(c_1, c_2) = c_1 + V(c_2), \forall k \in K, \tag{4.4}$$

where V is continuous, differentiable once, strictly increasing, and strictly concave. Assuming that investors are risk neutral at date 1 implies that utility is "transferable": one unit of consumption at date 1 generates one unit of utility for everybody. This assumption simplifies the welfare analysis because it allows us to measure welfare gains and losses in terms of consumer's surplus.

The difference between the two types of investor arises from their random future incomes.

$$Y_{k_0} = \begin{cases} 5 & \text{if } \omega = \omega_0 \\ 10 & \text{if } \omega = \omega_1 \end{cases}; \qquad Y_{k_1} = \begin{cases} 10 & \text{if } \omega = \omega_0 \\ 5 & \text{if } \omega = \omega_1 \end{cases}. \qquad (4.5)$$

Clearly both types of investor can benefit from sharing the risks of their individual income fluctuations. It follows from expression 4.3 that marginal rates of substitution must be equated. Since $\partial U_k / \partial c_1 = 1$ for $k = k_0, k_1$, this is equivalent to equating marginal utilities of consumption at date 2 in each state:

$$V'(Y_{k_0}(\omega) + \tau_{k_0}(\omega)) = V'(Y_{k_1}(\omega) + \tau_{k_1}(\omega)), \forall \omega \in \Omega. \qquad (4.6)$$

In state ω_0 type k_0's receive 5, while type k_1's receive 10. Since both have the same utility function, equating marginal utilities means they both consume 7.5. This requires a transfer of 2.5 from type k_1 to type k_0 so $\tau_{k_0}(\omega_0) = 2.5$ and $\tau_{k_1}(\omega_0) = -2.5$. Similarly in state ω_1, except the transfer is in the opposite direction, so $\tau_{k_0}(\omega_1) = -2.5$ and $\tau_{k_1}(\omega_1) = 2.5$. The result that everybody consumes 7.5 in both states depends crucially on the assumption of common utility functions and constant aggregate income across states, of course.

The planner can also transfer consumption at date 1. Since both types are risk neutral at the first date, the amount of the transfer will be determined by the reservation level of utilities $\overline{U}_k$ the planner chooses.

Securities and Risk Sharing

In the absence of securities there would be no possibility of trade. There is only a single good at each date, so, in the absence of transfers, each agent is forced to consume her endowment. The expected utility of type k is

$$EU_k^* = EU_k(0, Y_k(\omega)).$$

Because the endowment is random, each person bears some risk. Since individuals are risk averse, they would be better off if they could share this risk. The autarkic equilibrium will be optimal in special cases, for example, when individuals have identical utility functions and endowments, but typically there will exist gains from trade, that is, from sharing risks. One way for investors to share risk and improve their welfare is by trading securities. In effect, trading appropriately designed securities is a substitute for insurance.

We can illustrate the role of securities in providing insurance by looking at the leading example. Suppose there is a security S with payoffs $(1, 0)$ in states $\{\omega_0, \omega_1\}$. The security is in zero net supply and is issued at date 0 in exchange for the consumption good.

In equilibrium two conditions must be satisfied:

- Every investor maximizes his expected utility
- Markets clear.

Suppose the security trades at price p_S at date 1. The demand of a type-k investor, S_k, is given by the solution to

$$\underset{S_k}{\text{Max}} \quad -p_S S_k + EV(Y_k(\omega) + S_k).$$

The first-order condition, which in this case is necessary and sufficient for an optimum, is

$$p_S = \frac{1}{2} V'(Y_k(\omega_0) + S_k), \text{ for each } k,$$

and the market-clearing condition is

$$S_{k_0} + S_{k_1} = 0.$$

Trading security S allows the two types to share risk and equate marginal utilities of income in state ω_0. For the numerical parameters of the leading example $S_{k_0} = 2.5$, $S_{k_1} = -2.5$, and $p_S = V'(7.5)$.

If a security similar to S but with payoffs $(0, 1)$ were introduced, then risk sharing would be improved in state ω_1. Securities of this type, which pay off in only one state, are known as *Arrow securities*. If there is an Arrow security for each state, then markets are complete, condition (3) will be satisfied in equilibrium, and the allocation of resources will be efficient. If there are too few securities or securities have not been chosen appropriately, markets will be "incomplete," and an efficient allocation of risk will not be achieved. For example, if a security with payoffs $(1, 0.5)$ were introduced and this was the only security, it can readily be seen that the investors will trade the security, but the efficient allocation of consumption will not be attained.

Optimal Security Design

Although a complete set of Arrow securities is sufficient for optimal risk sharing, it is not necessary. In the simple example under consideration, it is possible to choose a single security that allows efficient risk sharing, simply by setting the payoffs equal to the optimal transfers defined by expression 4.6. In particular, suppose in the leading example a security with price p_f has payoffs $f(\omega)$ where

$$f(\omega) = \tau_{k_0}(\omega),$$

that is, its payoffs are $(2.5, -2.5)$. Each investor's decision solves

$$\underset{Q_k}{\text{Max}} - p_f Q_k + EV(Y_k(\omega) + \tau_{k_0}(\omega)Q_k),$$

which gives the (necessary and sufficient) first-order condition

$$p_f = E\tau_{k_0}(\omega)V'(Y_k(\omega) + \tau_{k_0}(\omega)Q_k). \tag{4.7}$$

In the case where

$$Q_{k_0} = 1 \text{ and } Q_{k_1} = -1,$$

and p_f is chosen to satisfy condition 4.7, both types of investor are maximizing expected utility, and the market for security S clears, so that both of the conditions for an equilibrium are satisfied. This equilibrium supports Pareto-optimal risk sharing, since expression 4.6 is satisfied. No investor could be made better off without the other being worse off. The levels of utility achieved are

$$EU_{k_0}^{**} = -p_f + EV(Y_{k_0}(\omega) + f(\omega)),$$

$$EU_{k_1}^{**} = p_f + EV(Y_{k_1}(\omega) - f(\omega)).$$

We have seen how an appropriately designed security can lead to an efficient allocation of resources. Of course, the exercise cannot be taken too seriously, because several features of the example are clearly very special. One of the most important is the presence of only two types of investor, so that an efficient allocation can be achieved with one security. If there are K types of investor and short sales of securities are allowed, no more than $K - 1$ securities are needed, in general. In a later section we derive an upper bound on the number of securities needed for efficient risk sharing when no short sales are allowed.

The basic point remains, however. When markets are incomplete, there are unexploited gains from sharing risks. Introducing securities enables agents to share these risks and capture some of these gains. When markets are complete, new securities are redundant. When markets are incomplete, security design matters because it affects the opportunities for risk sharing. In simple examples, it is obvious what optimal securities look like. In more general contexts, the security design problem is obscure. But it is clear that optimal securities can depend on the parameters of the model in more or less complex ways. Designing securities more cleverly or adding new securities can make a contribution to economic welfare.

4.2 A Competitive Theory of Innovation

In this section we generalize the model of section 4.1 by introducing firms. A closely related model is considered in greater depth in chapter 6.

Assumptions A.1–A.6 are unchanged. The initial focus is on the operation of the market rather than efficiency, so assumption A.7 is dispensed with for the moment. There are now firms which issue securities.

(A.8)   There is a countable number of *firms* indexed by $n = 1, 2, \ldots, \infty$. Firms have identical random future incomes represented by a nonnegative random variable $Z(\omega)$. For simplicity, there is one firm per investor.

Each firm can issue securities, which are claims against its own future income.

(A.9)   A *security* is a promise by a firm to deliver an amount $f(\omega)$ of the consumption good contingent on the state of nature revealed at date 2.

Later we shall be interested in more specialized securities, but to begin with we assume that general securities are traded. A firm's *financial structure* describes the claims outstanding against the firm.

(A.10)   Each firm chooses a financial structure F consisting of a finite set of securities $f(\omega)$. Securities are assumed to have nonnegative values and to exhaust the returns to the firm in each state.

If F is a financial structure and Z is the return to the underlying firm, then

$$\sum_{f \in F} f(\omega) = Z(\omega), \forall \omega \in \Omega.$$

Suppose that the firm wants to issue unlevered equity only. Then the financial structure consists of a single security $F = \{f_0\}$, where f_0 is defined by $f(\omega) = Z(\omega)$. If the firm wants to issue debt and equity, on the other hand, the financial structure is $F = \{f_1, f_2\}$, where

$$f_1(\omega) = \min\{Z(\omega), R\} \text{ and } f_2(\omega) = \max\{Z(\omega) - R, 0\}, \forall \omega \in \Omega.$$

Here the face value of the debt is R.

Other standard securities such as convertible debt, warrants, options, and so forth, can easily be described in this framework.

In a competitive economy, the objective of the firm is to maximize market value. Rather than deriving this feature of equilibrium, we impose it by assuming the firm's owner wants to liquidate her equity in the firm at the first date.

(A.11)   Each firm is initially owned by a risk-neutral entrepreneur who only wants to consume at date 1.

The effect of assumption A.11 is to ensure that the entrepreneur will want to maximize the firm's value at the first date. The assumption of value maximization may not be appropriate in some circumstances. The problem is that the firm's choice of securities to issue has two effects on the welfare of its owners: it changes their initial wealth, and it may change their hedging opportunities by changing the set of securities available for them to hold. Shareholders will want management to take both factors into account when deciding which securities to issue. If hedging considerations are sufficiently important, they may not want to maximize the value of the firm. However, Hart (1979) has provided an argument to show that, under certain circumstances, value maximization will be the appropriate objective in a competitive economy. Either the firm's shares are identical to many other firms, in which case they are redundant, or they must form a negligible part of a typical investor's portfolio. Otherwise, there would be excess demand since the firm itself is negligible in a competitive economy. Thus the securities issued by the firm will have a negligible effect on the welfare of a shareholder, except to the extent that they change the value of the shareholder's initial portfolio. Thus, shareholders will all agree that the firm should maximize value. As long as we are implicitly assuming that the economy is competitive, there is no loss of generality in assuming that the entrepreneur wants to maximize the value of his firm. However, as we shall see in section 4.3, when there are short sales the economy will not be perfectly competitive, even if there is a large number of firms.

The Firm's Decision

In order to maximize her consumption at date 1, the entrepreneur will want to sell her equity in the firm. When markets are complete, the value of the firm is independent of how it is sold. When markets are incomplete, it may be possible to increase the value of the firm by issuing a variety of securities. In incomplete markets the entrepreneur has an incentive to create new securities, that is, to innovate.

(A.12)   There is a finite number of financial structures, denoted by $\{F_i: i = 1, 2, \ldots, I\}$. I is also used to denote the *set* $\{1, 2, \ldots, I\}$. The set of tradeable securities is denoted $F = \cup\{F_i: i \in I\}$.

Since securities are non-negative and the security $f = 0$ can be eliminated without loss of generality, we can safely assume that $f > 0$ for any security f in F_i. For the purpose of establishing existence and (constrained) efficiency, it is sufficient to consider economies in which the number of available financial structures is finite. When it comes to characterizing optimal securities, however, it is convenient to have a richer set of structures. In particular, it is convenient to be able to vary structures continuously. The model is extended to deal with this case later.

An important assumption of the model that leads to markets being incomplete is that issuing a security is costly.

(A.13)   The cost of issuing securities is represented by a *cost function* $C: I \to \mathbb{R}_+$. The cost of issuing the securities in the ith structure is denoted by $C(i)$ or C_i. Costs are measured in terms of the consumption good at date 1 and are paid by the entrepreneurs.

A *price system* is a function p defined on F to $\mathbb{R}_+$, with the interpretation that $p(f)$ is the price of security f, measured in terms of the numeraire good at date 0.

Let P denote the set of price functions. For any price system p in P, define the *market value* of a firm with financial structure F_i to be

$$MV_i(p) = \sum_{f \in F_i} p(f).$$

The *net market value* of a firm with the financial structure F_i is defined to be $NMV_i(p) = MV_i(p) - C_i$. The entrepreneur's problem is to choose a financial structure to maximize net market value.

A numerical example may clarify some of these concepts. Suppose there are two states $\{\omega_0, \omega_1\}$, payoffs $Z(\omega_0) = 2$ and $Z(\omega_1) = 1$, and two possible face values of debt $R = 1$ and $R = 1.5$. The simplest financial structure consists of unlevered equity $F_1 = \{f_0\}$, where $f_0 = (2, 1)$. If the firm issues debt with a face value of $R = 1$, the financial structure $F_2 = \{f_1, f_2\}$ consists of debt and levered equity with payoffs $f_1 = (1, 1)$ and $f_2 = (1, 0)$. If $R = 1.5$ then we have a financial structure $F_3 = \{f_3, f_4\}$ with payoffs $f_3 = (1.5, 1)$ and $f_4 = (0.5, 0)$. With unlevered equity and two types of debt and levered equity, there are three possible financial structures ($I = 3$):

$$F_1 = \{(2, 1)\},$$
$$F_2 = \{(1, 1), (1,0)\},$$
$$F_3 = \{(1.5, 1), (0.5, 0)\}.$$

The set of potential tradeable securities is $F = [(2, 1), (1, 1), (1, 0), (1.5, 1), (0.5, 0)]$.

The cost of a particular financial structure is the cost of issuing the associated securities. If the cost of issuing the unlevered equity in F_1 is 0.1, then $C_1 = 0.1$. Suppose the costs of issuing the securities in F_2 and F_3 are $C_2 = 0.2$ and $C_3 = 0.25$, respectively.

The market value of a firm is simply the sum of the market values of the claims it issues. Suppose the prices of securities are given by $p(f_0) = 1.8$, $p(f_1) = 1.6$, and $p(f_2) = 0.5$. Then the market value of a firm that chooses the financial structure F_1 is $MV_1(p) = 1.8$, and the market value of a firm that chooses F_2 is $MV_2(p) = 1.6 + 0.5 = 2.1$. The net market value must take account of the costs of issuing securities, however. For example, $NMV_1(p) = 1.8 - 0.1 = 1.7$ and $NMV_2(p) = 2.1 - 0.2 = 1.9$.

The Investor's Decision

In this section we assume that investors cannot sell short the securities issued by firms; the transaction costs of doing this are prohibitive. In section 4.3 the effect of relaxing this assumption is considered at length.

(A.14) No short sales of the securities issued by firms are possible.

Given this, a *portfolio* is a function $d: F \to \mathbb{R}_+$ where $d(f)$ is the quantity of security f in the portfolio. Let D denote the set of portfolios. For any d in D, let $W(d)$ denote the random future income generated by the portfolio, that is,

$$W(d) = \sum_{f \in F} d(f)f.$$

For example, suppose there are two states $\{\omega_0, \omega_1\}$ and three securities $f_0 = (2, 1)$, $f_1 = (1, 1)$, and $f_2 = (1, 0)$. If $d(f_0) = 0.6$, $d(f_1) = 1.1$, and $d(f_2) = 0.9$, then the portfolio payoffs in the two states are

$$W(d) = (0.6 \times 2 + 1.1 \times 1 + 0.9 \times 1, 0.6 \times 1 + 1.1 \times 1 + 0.9 \times 0)$$

$$= (4.2, 1.7).$$

It is useful to represent investors' preferences with an indirect utility function that expresses expected utility as a function of the portfolio choice. For an investor of type k, define an *indirect utility function* $u_k: \mathbb{R} \times D \to \mathbb{R}$ by putting

$$u_k(c, d) = E[U_k(c, W(d) + Y_k)], \forall (c, d) \in \mathbb{R} \times D,$$

where c is first-period consumption, d is the portfolio, $W(d)$ is the income from this portfolio, and Y_k is the other random income. Under the maintained assumptions, it can be shown u_k is continuous, differentiable once, concave,[2] and strictly increasing.

The investor chooses a first-period consumption level c and a portfolio d to maximize her expected utility $u_k(c, d)$ subject to the budget constraint $c + p \cdot d = 0$.

Equilibrium

Three conditions define an equilibrium:

1. Firms choose financial structures that maximize their net value.

2. Investors maximize their utility.

3. Markets clear.

In order to describe these formally it is necessary to develop notation for the choices of financial structure that firms make and the consumption and portfolio choices that investors make. The choices of financial structures by firms can be represented by the *cross-sectional distribution*[3] α where α_i is the proportion of firms with the financial structure F_i. Formally, let $\Delta(I)$ denote the set of cross-sectional distributions on I, that is, $\Delta(I) = \{\alpha \in \mathbb{R}^I | \alpha_i \geq 0 \text{ and } \sum \alpha_i = 1\}$. The choices made by investors can be represented by an array $x = \{x_k\}_{k \in K}$ such that $x_k = (c_k, d_k) \in \mathbb{R} \times D$ for every k in K. An *allocation* is an ordered pair $(\alpha, x) \in \Delta(I) \times (\mathbb{R} \times D)^K$. Let $\mathscr{A}$ denote the set of allocations.

An allocation (α, x) is *attainable* if and only if

$$\sum_{k \in K} d_k(f)v_k = \alpha_i, \forall i \in I, \forall f \in F_i.$$

This condition ensures the security markets clear; individuals' total demand for a particular security must equal the amount supplied by firms. Walras's law ensures the market for consumption also clears. Let $\hat{\mathscr{A}}$ denote the set of attainable allocations.

An *equilibrium* is an ordered triple (p, α, x) consisting of a price system p in P and an attainable allocation (α, x) in $\hat{\mathscr{A}}$, satisfying the following conditions:

(E.1) $\alpha_i > 0$ only if $NMV_i(p)$ is maximum;

(E.2) x_k maximizes $u_k(x)$ subject to $x \in \mathbb{R} \times D$ and $c + p \cdot d = 0$, for every k in K.

Condition E.1 ensures that firms are choosing their financial structure to maximize their value, and condition E.2 ensures consumers are maximizing their expected utility. An illustration of equilibrium in the context of the leading example is given below. Before developing this, however, it is helpful to consider the incentives firms have to use securities that are costly to issue.

The Incentive to Innovate

Choosing a complex financial structure can increase market value when markets are incomplete and agents have different marginal valuations of the securities issued. As discussed in section 3.3, the incentive to innovate is provided by the desire of the initial owners of the firm to maximize the value of their assets. By paying a fixed cost and introducing new securities a firm can increase its value.

An example will make this clear. Suppose that Ω is finite and that there is a finite set of types of investors indexed by $k \in K$. Let m_k denote the vector of marginal values of consumption at date 2 measured in terms of consumption at date 1, that is,

$$m_k(\omega) = \frac{\partial U_k / \partial c_2(\omega)}{\partial U_k / \partial c_1}.$$

Then the marginal valuation of a security a by an investor of type k is (the dot product) $m_k \cdot f_a$, where f_a is the payoff function associated with security *a.* The value of the security in equilibrium must be the maximum over K of $m_k \cdot f_a$, that is, $p(a) = \max\{m_k \cdot f_a : k \in K\}$ because the investors who value it most will buy it. Then the market value of a firm with financial structure F_i must be

$$MV_i(p) = \sum_{a \in A_i} \max_{k \in K} m_k \cdot f_a,$$

where $A_i = \{a \in \mathbb{N} : f_a \in F_i\}$. Suppose that all types of investors have the same marginal valuations. Say, $m_k = m$. Then

$$MV_i(p) = \sum_{a \in A_i} m \cdot f_a = m \cdot \sum_{a \in A_i} f_a = m \cdot Z.$$

In other words, market value is independent of financial structure, and there is no benefit from issuing a complicated set of securities. Choosing a complex financial structure increases market value only if there is dis-agreement among agents about the value of securities. In effect, one is breaking the firm into pieces and selling the pieces to the *clientele* that values it most. It is this ability to increase the value of the firm that provides the incentive to innovate and allows the cost of innovation to be covered.

The Leading Example

These ideas can be illustrated in the context of the leading example intro-duced in the previous section. Suppose that the returns to the firm are the same in each state, say, $Z(\omega) = 2$ for each ω in Ω. Having returns equal in the two states maintains the symmetry of the example and greatly sim-plifies the analysis of it. There are two financial structures, denoted F_1 and F_2. F_1 is the trivial structure consisting of unlevered equity: $F_1 = \{Z\}$. The second structure consists of two securities, $F_2 = \{f_0, f_1\}$ where

$$f_0(\omega) = \begin{cases} 2 \text{ if } \omega = \omega_0 \\ 0 \text{ if } \omega = \omega_1 \end{cases}; \quad f_1(\omega) = \begin{cases} 0 \text{ if } \omega = \omega_0 \\ 2 \text{ if } \omega = \omega_1 \end{cases}.$$

So in this example there are four commodities traded at the first date: the consumption good, unlevered equity $(2, 2)$, and the two contingent securi-ties $f_0 = (2, 0)$ and $f_1 = (0, 2)$. The securities in the financial structure F_2 may seem rather special, but as we shall see, they arise quite naturally as optimal securities in certain circumstances.

The simpler structure F_1 may be treated as the status quo, and its cost C_1 normalized to 0. The second structure F_2 requires the issue of new securities so it will be more expensive: $C_2 > 0$. The market values of the two structures are given by $MV_1(p) = p(Z)$ and $MV_2(p) = p(f_0) + p(f_1)$, respectively. The firm will choose the more complex structure if the increase in market value compensates for the additional cost, that is, $p(f_0) + p(f_1) - p(Z) \geq C_2$. Otherwise it will choose the trivial structure.

As in section 4.1, there are two types of investor who are equally distributed in the population and who have the same utility function. The difference between the two types of investor is accounted for by their random future incomes; type k_0's receive $(5, 10)$ and type k_1's $(10, 5)$ in states $\{\omega_0, \omega_1\}$. The two types of investor can benefit from sharing the risks of their individual income fluctuations. In the absence of an insurance market, they can do this by holding securities. Clearly, the contingent securities issued by firms choosing the more complex financial structure F_2 are more helpful in this respect than unlevered equity.

Suppose that $C_2 \geq 4$ and that the common utility function satisfies the following conditions:

$$V'(7) = 5, \ V'(9) = 4, \ V'(10) = 2, \ V'(12) = 1.$$

Given that investors are risk neutral at date 1, $\partial U_k / \partial c_1 = 1$ and $m_k(\omega) = V'(c_2(\omega))$. This together with the fact that markets are competitive and investors and firms are price-takers allows us to find equilibrium security prices in a straightforward way since they are equal to marginal valuations.

Under these assumptions there exists an equilibrium in which no firm innovates, that is, all choose F_1. By symmetry, the investors all demand one unit of unlevered equity in this equilibrium, and their consumption at the second date will be 7 in the low state and 12 in the high state. Equilibrium prices are given by $p(Z) = 6$, and $p(f_0) = p(f_1) = 5$. To see why, note that the allocation of consumption across states is such that marginal valuations are

$$m_{k_0} = (2.5, 0.5) \text{ and } m_{k_1} = (0.5, 2.5).$$

In state ω_0 type k_0's are consuming 7, so $V'(7) = 5$ and $\partial U_{k_0} / \partial c_2 = 0.5 \times 5 = 2.5$ since the probability of ω_0 is 0.5. Similarly, in state ω_1 they are consuming 12, so $V'(12) = 1$ and $\partial U_{k_0} / \partial c_2 = 0.5 \times 1 = 0.5$. For type k_1's the analysis is symmetric. By issuing unlevered equity, a firm can achieve a market value of

$$MV_1(p) = (2.5, 0.5) \cdot (2, 2) = (0.5, 2.5) \cdot (2, 2) = 6.$$

On the other hand, by splitting its future income bundle $(2, 2)$ into two parts $(2, 0)$ and $(0, 2)$ and marketing each to the clientele that values it most, a firm can achieve a market value of

$$MV_2(p) = (2.5, 0.5) \cdot (2, 0) + (0.5, 2.5) \cdot (0, 2) = 10.$$

The increase in market value does not compensate for the increased cost, so net market value is maximized by choosing the trivial structure. Investors are also behaving optimally since their marginal valuation of $F_1 = \{Z\}$ is equal to its price.

Now suppose that $C_2 \leq 2$ but that V satisfies the same conditions as before. Then there exists an equilibrium in which all firms choose the more complex financial structure F_2. Investors of type k_i purchase two units each of the security f_i ($i = 0, 1$) and none of the other securities. This means that their consumption will be 9 in the low state and 10 in the high state. Equilibrium prices are given by $p(Z) = 6$ and $p(f_0) = p(f_1) = 4$. In this equilibrium the allocation of consumption across states is such that marginal valuations are

$$m_{k_0} = (2, 1) \text{ and } m_{k_1} = (1, 2).$$

The gain from splitting is now less: $MV_1(p) = 6$ and $MV_2(p) = 8$. But as we assumed the difference in the costs of the two financial structures is also less, it is optimal for firms to split. Once again, it is easy to check that at these prices, all agents are also behaving optimally.

When $2 < C_2 < 4$, there does not exist an equilibrium in which all of the firms make the same choice. But there does exist an equilibrium in which both financial structures are chosen. The exact proportions will be determined by the condition that firms must be indifferent between the two structures.

Existence of Equilibrium

The first task is to check that equilibrium exists. It can straightforwardly be shown that this is indeed the case.

THEOREM 2.1   Under the maintained assumptions, there exists an equilibrium.

The theorem follows by standard arguments. This is not surprising since the economy is isomorphic to an Arrow-Debreu economy in which the commodities traded are goods and securities at date 1 and the primitive preferences are assumed to be given by u_k. A full account of this and the other results is given in chapter 6.

Efficiency

When markets are incomplete there is no reason to expect that equilibrium is efficient in the usual (Pareto) sense, However, equilibrium can be shown to be *constrained* efficient. What this means is that a central planner or government could not make every agent better off if she were subject to the same transaction costs as the private sector. Instead of assumption A.7 we now have the following.

(A.7′) The planner is assumed to use only the markets for goods and securities at the first date and to be subject to the same costs of issuing securities as firms.

An attainable allocation (α, x) is said to be *constrained efficient* if and only if there does not exist another attainable allocation $(\hat{\alpha}, \hat{x})$ such that:

1. $u_k(x_k) < u_k(\hat{x}_k), \forall k \in K$;
2. $\sum_{k \in K} c_k v_k + \sum_{i \in I} C_i \alpha_i < \sum_{k \in K} \hat{c}_k v_k + \sum_{i \in I} C_i \hat{\alpha}_i$.

The first inequality has the obvious interpretation that utilities can be increased: the second implies that all entrepreneurs can be made better off by some feasible allocation of consumption at the first date. Under the maintained assumptions, this definition is equivalent to the more usual one which requires that no agent be made worse off and some be made better off. At the initial date, it would always be possible to redistribute a small amount from the better-off people to the indifferent people so that everybody's position is improved.

THEOREM 2.2 If (α, p, x) is an equilibrium then (α, x) is a constrained efficient allocation.

The theorem follows by a standard argument. If we think of the economy as one in which the primitive commodities are first-period consumption and the securities traded at the first date and the primitive preferences are given by u_k, then the economy is isomorphic to an Arrow-Debreu economy in which markets are complete. Constrained efficiency in the original economy corresponds to Pareto efficiency in the artificial Arrow-Debreu economy. The constrained efficiency of equilibrium in the original economy is thus a corollary of the First Theorem of Welfare Economics, which asserts the Pareto efficiency of equilibrium in the artificial economy.

The Extended Model

For many purposes, the model developed above is sufficient. But in order to characterize the optimal securities, it is necessary to have a model that allows firms to choose from the set of all possible financial structures rather than a finite subset. We shall briefly sketch how the model can be extended to allow for this possibility. To cope with this more general problem some new notation is needed. Let $\mathscr{F}$ denote the *compact*[4] set of securities $\{f: \Omega \to \mathbb{R} | 0 \le f \le Z\}$. To show that there exists an equilibrium when firms can choose unrestricted financial structures, the proof of theorem 2.1 can be adapted using an approximation argument. The essential idea is that the set of financial structures $\mathfrak{F}$ can be approximated using a finite set $\{F_i : i \in I\}$. Taking limits, one obtains an equilibrium of the extended model by continuity.

Optimal Securities

It is interesting to see what optimal securities might look like. In order to characterize optimal securities it is assumed that firms can choose unrestricted financial structures, that is, we consider equilibrium in the extended model. Suppose that the costs of issuing securities are primarily fixed costs, in the sense that the cost of a financial structure F_i depends only on the *number* of securities issued.

(A.15)   The cost of a financial structure depends only on the number of different securities issued: $C(F) = C(F')$ if $|F| = |F'|$, $\forall F, F' \in \mathfrak{F}$ (where $|F|$ denotes the number of securities in financial structure F).

A security is said to be *extremal* if and only if

$$f(\omega) \in \{0, Z(\omega)\}, \forall \omega \in \Omega.$$

There are two aspects to the optimality of securities. A financial structure is optimal from the point of view of the firm if it maximizes the net market value of the firm. The financial structures chosen by firms are optimal from the point of view of the investors if they span an efficient consumption allocation. The following theorem shows that extremal securities are optimal in both senses, that is, both entrepreneurs and investors are just as well off if entrepreneurs restrict themselves to choosing the extremal securities.

THEOREM 2.3   Let (α, x) be a constrained efficient allocation for an economy in which firms can choose unrestricted financial structures. Under the maintained assumptions, there exists an attainable allocation $(\hat{\alpha}, \hat{x})$ which uses only extremal securities in which the consumption of every agent is the same as in (α, x).

Suppose that a fraction of firms α_i have chosen the financial structure F_i. Suppose further that the financial structure consists of just two securities, f and $Z - f$. There exists a set of extremal securities $\{f_h\} \subset \mathcal{F}$ and numbers $\{\lambda_h\}$ such that $\lambda_h > 0$ and $\sum_h \lambda_h = 1$ and $f = \sum_h \lambda_h f_h$. For each h, define a new financial structure $F_h = \{f_h, Z_h - f_h\}$ and let a fraction $\alpha_h = \lambda_h \alpha_i$ firms choose F_h instead of F_i.

By assumption, the cost of the new financial structure is the same as the old. The net market value of a firm choosing F_h cannot increase, since that would contradict the properties of the original equilibrium. On the other hand, the aggregate value of the firms who chose F_i in the old equilibrium cannot decrease, since that would imply that investors could have obtained an equivalent portfolio more cheaply, which would contradict the definition of equilibrium. Thus, the net market value of a firm with financial structure F_h must be the same as with F_i. This shows that the new extremal financial structures are optimal in the sense of maximizing net market value.

By construction, the new securities span the old, so investors can obtain their existing consumption bundles by holding appropriate amounts of the new securities. Market clearing must hold since each unit of the old securities corresponds to a unique convex combination of the new securities. The cost of these portfolios has not changed since, by the definition of equilibrium, it cannot be less than the old value, and yet we have shown that the aggregate value has not increased. This shows that the new securities are optimal from the point of view of investors as well.

The argument above shows that we can replace the financial structure F_i by an extremal financial structure when F_i has only two securities. In the general case, where F_i has n securities, we can proceed as follows. Let $F_i = \{f_1, \ldots, f_n\}$. Using the argument above, we can replace F_i with alternative structures $F_h = \{f_h, f'_2, \ldots, f'_n\}$, where for each h, f_h is extremal but the securities $f'_2, \ldots, f'_n$ need not be. Then take the firms who are supposed to choose F_h and repeat the procedure to replace f'_2 with an extremal security. In this way, we eventually assign extremal structures to every firm in such a way that the securities issued span the original securities. The rest of the argument is essentially unchanged.   ∎

Theorem 2.3 is a spanning theorem: it shows that the efficient allocation can be achieved if firms and investors only use extremal securities. The reason is not too hard to see. Any security can be thought of as being generated by a portfolio of extremal securities. Then investors can choose to hold the portfolio of extremal securities rather than the original security. Firms are indifferent, as we have seen.

As a corollary of theorem 2.3, we see that in any equilibrium, firms are indifferent between the equilibrium structure and issuing extremal securities. One does not have to construct an alternative equilibrium to see this. It follows from a linearity property of the equilibrium price function. To see this, take a fixed but arbitrary equilibrium and let m_k denote the marginal valuation of an investor of type k. Define a valuation function v from $\mathscr{F}$ to $\mathbb{R}$ by putting

$$v(f) = \max\{m_k \cdot f \mid k \in K\}, \forall f \in \mathscr{F}.$$

Without loss of generality we can assume that $p(f) = v(f)$, since no investor will buy a security if $p(f) > v(f)$. Then the market value of a firm with market structure F is

$$v(F) \equiv \sum_f v(f) = \sum_f m_f \cdot f,$$

where m_f denotes the maximizer of $m_k \cdot f$. Now suppose that for some ω there are at least two securities f such that $f(\omega) > 0$. Then choose the value of f that maximizes $m_f(\omega)$ to receive the entire return $Z(\omega)$ and put the others equal to zero. Call the new structure F' with securities f'. Then

$$v(F') \equiv \sum_{f'} v(f') = \sum_{f'} m_{f'} \cdot f' \geq \sum_{f'} m_f \cdot f' \geq v(F),$$

as required.

The cost structure assumed here is special, although it seems to make sense when the costs of issuing securities are primarily fixed costs. If there are marketing costs, a different cost function may be more plausible, and that will affect the nature of the optimal securities. Madan and Soubra

(1991) have studied a model with marketing costs and show that interior securities, that is, securities that have a positive return in most states, can be optimal. Ross (1989) has argued that marketing costs may be an important factor in security design. These ideas are discussed further in chapter 5.

An interesting question is the *number* of securities required to support an efficient allocation. Obviously, the answer will depend on the cost function. To illustrate the possibilities, consider the case where it is prohibitively expensive to issue more than two securities. Then financial structures will consist of one or two securities at most.

THEOREM 2.4   Let (α, x) be a constrained efficient allocation and suppose that no firm chooses a financial structure with more than two securities. Under the maintained assumptions, there exists an allocation $(\hat{\alpha}, \hat{x})$ which gives every agent the same consumption as (α, x) and uses a maximum of $K(K - 1) + 1$ securities.

When a firm issues two securities, it is splitting its future income between two different investor types; if not, its value would not increase to allow it to cover the cost of splitting. For any pair of investor types there is at most one financial structure, that is, one pair of securities, needed to accomplish the net division of income that occurs in the allocation (α, x). The number of different pairs is $K(K - 1)/2$, and each one requires at most two securities. In addition, there may be a need for firms that choose the trivial financial structure. Hence the same consumption as (α, x) can be achieved with at most $K(K - 1) + 1$ securities.

This sort of argument generalizes in a natural way to cases where firms issue more securities, where there are different types of firms and so forth.

4.3   Innovation with Short Sales

The results in section 4.2 on the existence and efficiency of equilibrium are similar to those in the standard Arrow-Debreu model. The competitive nature of the model depends on the assumption of no short sales. A firm that is negligible relative to the economy as a whole can only introduce a negligible amount of a new security. In the absence of short sales, the innovation has little impact on equilibrium, and the competitive features of the standard model are preserved. When short sales are allowed, introducing a new security is like opening a new market in which a large number of traders can take positions, and this can have a large (noncompetitive) impact on the market.

An obvious question is whether the assumption that short sales are ruled out is an appropriate one. This depends on the particular circumstances that are of interest. In practice, short selling securities on stock exchanges is very costly, and only a limited amount is undertaken. To see why, consider how the process works. A short seller goes to her broker and puts in a short sale order. The broker then borrows the required securities from the margin accounts of his own firm's customers or those of other brokerage firms or from other stock lenders such as institutions. The borrowing broker must deposit 100 percent of the cash value of the securities with the lending broker as collateral. If the securities borrowed are in plentiful supply, the lending broker may rebate a portion of the interest earned on this collateral to the borrowing broker, but if they are scarce, a premium may be charged. Otherwise the lending broker keeps the entire interest earned. It is this feature of short selling that makes it so costly.

On the New York Stock Exchange the total volume of short selling is around 8 percent of total volume. Most of this arises from brokers and dealers hedging their inventory, and only about 1.5 percent is undertaken by nonmembers of the exchange (Pollack (1986)). This is perhaps not surprising given the large costs of short selling.

Thus, in some circumstances the assumption that there are no short sales or that short sales are costly is an appropriate one. For example, in the case of primes and scores discussed in chapter 2 where equity is deposited in a trust and split into two components, Jarrow and O'Hara (1989) argue that short sales constraints are binding. However, in other cases it can be argued that there are close substitutes for short selling which involve very low costs. If there are options markets, it is possible to sell a call and buy a put to obtain a position which is similar to short selling. The main differences are that with options there are no dividends to be paid, and the position is not open-ended but has a definite end date. Figlewski and Webb (1993) have argued that in practice a significant amount of the trading in options markets is a substitute for short selling. Another substitute for short selling is to sell index futures. These arguments suggest that in some cases ruling out short sales is not an appropriate assumption.

There is an alternative interpretation. When an investor sells a security short, she is essentially issuing an IOU that is identical to the original security and is backed by her personal resources. The situation in which one firm invents a new security and other firms imitate it is similar. The innovating firm is responsible for defining the security and starting the market; the imitating firms are simply issuing claims, which are identical to the new security, backed by their own future revenues.

In an empirical study of innovation, Tufano (1989) has found that the first firm to innovate bears substantially higher costs than subsequent imitators. This is similar to a situation in which one firm innovates at some cost and short sellers are able to expand the supply of that security at a lower cost.

Both these arguments suggest that the case of costless short selling is relevant. Another important reason for studying this case is theoretical: it is a standard assumption of many important theories in financial economics.

Ruling out short sales was important in the previous section because without this assumption equilibrium would not exist when firms and investors are price-takers. When issuing securities is costly, the more securities a firm has the more valuable it must be to enable these costs to be recouped. However, this is inconsistent with equilibrium if costless short sales are possible. An investor could go short in a multiple security firm and long in an identical but less valuable firm with fewer securities and make an arbitrage profit.

In this section and in chapter 7, we suggest a way of reconciling the existence of equilibrium with short sales by weakening the price-taking assumption. The usual justification for price-taking behavior is that in a large economy, agents have a negligible effect on prices; in the limit as the number of agents tends to infinity, the effect of their actions tends to zero. We start by examining this justification for price-taking behavior in a model similar to that of section 4.2 with no short sales but a finite number of firms. It is shown that the equilibrium of the finite economy converges in the limit to the competitive equilibrium with price-taking behavior. Thus, the price-taking assumption is appropriate when short sales are ruled out.

Short sales are introduced into the model in two steps. We first assume that limited short sales are possible. In this case the competitive properties of the model are maintained in the sense that as the number of firms becomes very large, no firm can affect prices. However, the equilibrium that is attained is no longer efficient. The limited short sales create an externality similar to that identified by Makowski (1983); the opportunities for improved risk sharing in the economy are no longer measured by the net supply of the securities as they were in the efficient equilibrium of section 4.2 but by the open interest in the securities.

The second step is to consider what happens when unbounded short sales are possible. It is well known from the literature on stock market economies that, in the context of a firm choosing a production plan, a change by one firm can have a large impact when there are unbounded short sales. This happens when a change in production plan alters the space spanned by investors' portfolios (see, e.g., Kreps 1979, essay II). It is not necessarily incompatible with perfect competition when there is a large number of firms. However, in the present context, the nature of the equilibrium attained is no longer competitive. Competition is necessarily imperfect if there is to be an incentive to innovate. Allowing unbounded short sales thus leads to a very different type of equilibrium to that in section 4.2.

A Finite Economy

In the versions of the basic model discussed above there is assumed to be a countably infinite number of firms. The finite version of the model is essentially the same except for the number of firms so assumption A.8 is replaced by the following:

(A.8′) There is a finite number of *firms* indexed by $n = 1, 2, \ldots, N$. Firms have random future incomes represented by a random variable Z.

Given this assumption, competitive price-taking behavior is no longer appropriate for the firms, so the definition of equilibrium has to be altered. Apart from this, the model remains the same as before. There is a finite set of financial structures $\{F_i : i \in I\}$, and the cost of issuing the associated securities is given by the cost function $C: I \to \mathbb{R}_+$. In order to focus on the strategic behavior of firms we assume there is an infinite number of investors divided into a finite set K of types. This ensures they are price-takers. We could assume a finite number of investors and allow this to increase as N increases, but this would complicate the analysis without adding any new insights. Each type k in K has preferences represented by a von Neumann–Morgenstern utility function $U_k: \mathbb{R}^2 \to \mathbb{R}$ and a future income represented by the random variable Y_k. The cross-sectional distribution of types is denoted by v. In what follows these parameters are held fixed.

Define a *finite economy of size N* as follows. There are N firms indexed $n = 1, \ldots, N$. There is a measure N of investors so that the ratio of firms to consumers is fixed at 1. The cross-sectional distribution of investor types is v. The rest of the parameters are the same as for the infinite economy. An economy of size N can be denoted by $\mathscr{E}^N = (N, \{Z\}, \{F_i\}, C, K, \{(U_k, Y_k)\}, v)$.

The Game Form

Since there is a finite number of firms, they interact strategically. Their interaction is modeled in the simplest possible way. It is assumed that equilibrium in the asset markets at date 1 is achieved in two stages.

1. At the first stage, firms simultaneously choose their financial structures taking the choices of others as given.

2. At the second stage, investors buy and sell the supply of securities determined at the first stage on a competitive auction market.

The equilibrium prices observed at the second stage depend on the choices made by firms at the first stage. When firms make their decisions at the first stage, they anticipate the prices that will result at the second stage. For this reason, they are not price-takers.

An equilibrium of this model is described in reverse. Beginning with the second stage, we describe a competitive equilibrium in the auction market, taking as given the choices made by the firms in the first stage. Then we use this equilibrium to define the game played by the firms at the first stage.

Similarly to section 4.2, let α_i denote the proportion of firms that have the financial structure i and let the vector α be a cross-sectional distribution of financial structures. The set of cross-sectional distributions for an economy of size N is then

$$\Delta^N(I) \equiv \{\alpha \in \mathbb{R}_+^I \mid \sum_{i \in I} \alpha_i = 1 \text{ and } \forall i \in I, \exists j = 0, \ldots, N, \alpha_i = j/N\}.$$

Given a cross-sectional distribution α in $\Delta^N(I)$, an *exchange equilibrium* relative to α is defined to be an ordered pair (p, x) consisting of a price system p in P and an allocation x in X for investors if (p, α, x) satisfies two of the three conditions of the competitive equilibrium defined earlier, that is, optimality for investors and market clearing:

(E.1) $\forall k \in K$, x_k maximizes $u_k(x_k)$ subject to $c_k + p \cdot d_k = 0$ and $x_k \in \mathbb{R} \times D$;

(E.2) $\forall i \in I, \forall f \in F_i, \sum_{k \in K} d_k(f) v_k = \alpha_i$.

It is next necessary to develop notation to describe the relationship between the financial structures α firms choose at the first stage and the equilibrium (p, x) that occurs at the second date. An *equilibrium selection* is a function ϕ defined from $\Delta^N(I)$ to $P \times X$ such that for every α in $\Delta^N(I)$, $\phi(\alpha)$ is an exchange equilibrium relative to α.

For any equilibrium selection, the finite game $\Gamma^N(\phi)$ the firms play at the first stage when choosing their financial structures can be defined as follows. First, let the set of players be $\{1, \ldots, N\}$. Second, the strategy set is $I \times \ldots \times I$. Finally, define the payoff functions as follows. Let α_{-n} denote the cross-sectional distribution of choices made by $N - 1$ players other than n, and let (i, α_{-n}) denote the cross-sectional distribution in which the distinguished player n chooses i and the other players' choices are represented by the distribution α_{-n}. If the choices of all N players are described by (i, α_{-n}) then the payoff to the distinguished player is denoted by $v_n(i, \alpha_{-n})$ and defined by $v_n(i, \alpha_{-n}) = MV_i(p) - C_i$, where $(p, x) = \phi(i, \alpha_{-n})$, $\forall (i, \alpha_{-n}) \in \Delta^N(I)$. Note that the payoff function is independent of n.

In what follows, we shall focus mainly on symmetric Nash equilibria, that is, Nash equilibria in which each player chooses the same mixed strategy σ in $\Delta(I)$. A *strategic equilibrium* for $\mathscr{E}^N$ is defined to be an ordered pair (σ, ϕ) consisting of an equilibrium selection ϕ and a symmetric equilibrium σ of the game $\Gamma^N(\phi)$. Using standard techniques, the following result can be demonstrated.

THEOREM 3.1 Under the maintained assumptions there exists a strategic equilibrium for $\mathscr{E}^N$.

As an illustration, consider the leading example developed in previous sections. To begin with, consider the simplest case where there is just one firm so $N = 1$ (the measure of each type of investor is 0.5 since there is one firm per investor overall). As before, suppose there are two financial structures available to it, F_1 which consists of unlevered equity $Z = (2, 2)$ and F_2 which consists of contingent securities $f_0 = (2, 0)$ and $f_1 = (0, 2)$. The investors' common utility function satisfies $V'(7) = 5$, $V'(8) = 4.6$, $V'(9) = 4$, $V'(10) = 2$, $V'(11) = 1.6$, $V'(12) = 1$.

If the firm chooses F_1 at the first stage, each type will hold one unit of unlevered equity and consume $5 + 2 = 7$ in one state and $10 + 2 = 12$ in the other. Given that the two states are equally likely, the marginal values of consumption for type k_0's are $(0.5V'(7), 0.5V'(12)) = (2.5, 0.5)$ and similarly for type k_1's they are $(0.5, 2.5)$. Since both types hold the security, the value of the firm in the second-stage equilibrium is $MV_1(p) = p(Z) = (2.5, 0.5) \cdot (2, 2) = (0.5, 2.5) \cdot (2, 2) = 6$.

On the other hand, if the firm chooses F_2 at the first stage, both types of investor will consume 9 in one state and 10 in the other, so the marginal valuations for type k_0's will be $(0.5V'(9), 0.5V'(10)) = (2, 1)$ and for type k_1's will be $(0.5V'(10), 0.5V'(9)) = (1, 2)$. Type k_0's hold the $(2, 0)$ security because they value it most, and the type k_1's hold the $(0, 2)$ security because they value it most. The total value of the firm in the second-stage exchange equilibrium is therefore $MV_2(p) = p(f_0) + p(f_1) = (2, 1) \cdot (2, 0) + (1, 2) \cdot (0, 2) = 8$.

In this example, therefore, the value of the firm will be 6 if the firm chooses F_1 and 8 if it chooses F_2. If $C_2 \geq 2$, it will choose F_1 in the strategic equilibrium; otherwise it will choose F_2.

Next, consider the case where there are two identical firms so $N = 2$. Now both firms have the choice between F_1 and F_2 at the first stage, so there are three possible second-stage exchange equilibria.

1. Both firms choose F_1.

2. Both firms choose F_2.

3. One firm chooses F_1, and the other chooses F_2.

We consider these in turn.

1. If both firms choose unlevered equity F_1, the two types of investor consume 7 in one state and 12 in the other, so similarly to before when $N = 1$, $MV_1(p) = p(Z) = (2.5, 0.5) \cdot (2, 2) = (0.5, 2.5) \cdot (2, 2) = 6$.

2. If both firms choose contingent securities F_2, it is again similar to the case where $N = 1$, so $MV_2(p) = p(f_0) + p(f_1) = (2, 1) \cdot (2, 0) + (1, 2) \cdot (0, 2) = 8$.

3. If one firm chooses F_1 and the other chooses F_2, then investors will each hold 0.5 of the $(2, 2)$ security and one unit of the extremal security that benefits them the most, so they consume $5 + 1 + 2 = 8$ in one state and $10 + 1 = 11$ in the other. The marginal values of consumption for type k_0's will be $(0.5V'(8), 0.5V'(11)) = (2.3, 0.8)$ and for type k_1's will be $(0.5V'(11), 0.5V'(8)) = (0.8, 2.3)$. Given this, the value of the firm with finan-

cial structure F_1 is $MV_1(p) = p(Z) = (2.3, 0.8) \cdot (2, 2) = (0.8, 2.3) \cdot (2, 2) = 6.2$. For the firm with financial structure F_2 the security $f_0 = (2, 0)$ will be held by type k_0's and the security $f_1 = (0, 2)$ will be held by type k_1's, so $MV_2(p) = p(f_0) + p(f_1) = (2.3, 0.8) \cdot (2, 0) + (0.8, 2.3) \cdot (0, 2) = 9.2$.

In this example there will not always be a pure strategy equilibrium. For some parameter values, there will be a mixed strategy equilibrium where firms choose F_1 with probability σ and F_2 with probability $1 - \sigma$. Given $C_1 = 0$, firms will be indifferent between these two strategies when $\sigma(6) + (1 - \sigma)(6.2) = \sigma(9.2 - C_2) + (1 - \sigma)(8 - C_2)$. The left-hand side represents the expected payoff from choosing F_1. There is a probability σ the other firm will also choose F_1 and both firms receive 6. There is a $(1 - \sigma)$ probability the other firm will choose F_2 and the firm with F_1 will receive 6.2. Similarly the right-hand side represents the expected payoff from choosing F_2. Solving for σ gives

$$\sigma = \frac{C_2 - 1.8}{1.4}.$$

Hence for $C_2 \geq 3.2$ there is a pure strategy equilibrium where both firms choose F_1, and for $C_2 \leq 1.8$ there is a pure strategy equilibrium where both firms choose F_2. For intermediate values of C_2, there is a mixed strategy equilibrium.

Other examples with $N > 2$ can be similarly constructed. As more firms are added, the range of C_2 for which a mixed strategy equilibrium exists alters as the possible levels of consumption the investors can achieve change.

Asymptotic Behavior

We next consider what happens as N tends to infinity in order to determine when price taking is an appropriate assumption. We consider two cases; in the first short sales are ruled out, but in the second they are not. Let the economy with an infinite number of firms be denoted by $\mathscr{E}^\infty = (\{Z\}, \{F_i\}, C, K, \{(U_k, Y_k)\}, v)$. Consider a sequence of strategic equilibria $\{(\sigma^N, \phi^N)\}$ such that for each N, (σ^N, ϕ^N) is an equilibrium of the finite economy of size N. There is a convergent subsequence of $\{\sigma^N\}$ which, without loss of generality, can be taken to be the original sequence. Suppose that $\sigma^N \to \sigma^\infty$. For each N, the cross-sectional distribution of financial structures is a random variable $\tilde{\alpha}^N$. But the law of large numbers implies that $\tilde{\alpha}^N$ converges in probability to σ^∞. The exchange equilibrium corresponding to $\tilde{\alpha}^N$ is also a random variable, $(\tilde{p}, \tilde{x}) = \phi(\tilde{\alpha}^N)$. This random variable does not necessarily converge without an additional assumption of continuity.

(A.16) (*Continuity Assumption*) For some (p^∞, x^∞) in $P \times X$ and any neighborhood V of (p^∞, x^∞) there exists a neighborhood V' of σ^∞ such that for some $\overline{N}$, for any α in V' and $N > \overline{N}$, $\phi^N(\alpha)$ belongs to V.

This is a strong assumption, but for technical reasons it is hard to do without. A sufficient condition for assumption A.16 is uniqueness of the exchange equilibrium for any given choice of financial structures. Although uniqueness seems to be stronger than necessary, we do not know of a weaker condition. It would be still better to have a sufficient condition that only referred to the primitives of the model.

The continuity assumption implies that $\phi^N(\tilde{\alpha}^N)$ converges to (p^∞, x^∞) in probability.

THEOREM 3.2   Consider a sequence of strategic equilibria $\{(\sigma^N, \phi^N)\}$ such that $\{\sigma^N\}$ converges to σ^∞, $\{\tilde{\alpha}^N\}$ converges in probability to α^∞, and the continuity assumption holds. Then under the maintained assumptions, $\phi^N(\tilde{\alpha}^N)$ converges to (p^∞, x^∞) in probability, and $(p^\infty, \alpha^\infty, x^\infty)$ is a competitive equilibrium for $\mathscr{E}^\infty$.

This result shows that when short sales are ruled out, the assumption of price-taking behavior is a reasonable one. It can be illustrated using the leading example. In particular, as N increases, the equilibrium converges to the competitive equilibrium described in section 4.2 where for $C_2 \geq 4$ all firms choose the financial structure F_1, for $4 > C_2 > 2$ both structures are chosen with the proportion choosing F_2 being larger the smaller is C_2, while for $C_2 \leq 2$ all choose F_2. To see how the equilibrium converges, suppose $C_2 = 3.9$. In the competitive equilibrium where there is an infinite number of firms, a large proportion choose F_1 and a small proportion choose F_2 since C_2 is close to 4. When $N = 1$ the firm will choose F_1 since $3.9 \geq 2$. Similarly when $N = 2$ both firms will choose F_1 since $3.9 \geq 3.2$. As N increases, a single firm choosing F_2 means investors' consumption in the two states moves closer to 12 and 7, so firm value moves toward 10. Eventually there will come a point where firm value exceeds 9.9, and F_2 will be chosen in equilibrium some of the time. As N tends to infinity, the value of σ in the mixed strategy equilibrium tends to the proportion of firms that chooses F_1 in the competitive equilibrium, and $1 - \sigma$ tends to the proportion that chooses F_2.

It has been assumed that firms have identical payoffs Z. In chapter 7 the case where firms have symmetric payoffs Z_n, $n = 1,\ldots,N$ is considered. What is meant by symmetric here is that the payoffs of the firms could be permuted among firms without changing the joint payoff distribution, but the payoffs are not perfect substitutes. In other words, firms may have idiosyncratic risk. It can be seen that the existence result is unchanged by this change in assumptions. The convergence result also holds because the idiosyncratic risk is diversified away as $N \to \infty$.

We next show what happens when short sales are possible.

The Short Sale Puzzle

Consider a competitive equilibrium of the economy $\mathscr{E}^\infty$. Typically we shall observe different firms adopting different financial structures. The more complex structures will be more expensive, but the greater expense is compensated for by the increase in the market value of the firm. Now suppose that short sales are allowed. In the case where all firms are assumed to have identical future returns it appears that a riskless arbitrage profit can be made. Suppose that two firms have different financial structures and as a result have different market values. Then an investor can make a riskless arbitrage profit by selling short the securities issued by the more valuable firm and going long in the securities issued by the less valuable firm. More precisely, if he sells short one unit of each of the securities issued by the more valuable firm and buys one unit of each of the securities issued by the less valuable firm, his net liablility is zero, since his liabilities and assets will just cancel out next period. But in the current period he has made a profit, since the value of what he sells exceeds the value of what he purchases. The existence of such an arbitarge opportunity is inconsistent with equilibrium, so this argument shows that we cannot have an equilibrium in which firms adopt financial structures with different costs when unlimited short sales are allowed. We are assuming here that all agents know all the prices when they make their decisions, as they do in the standard theory of competitive equilibrium.

Can we have an equilibrium in which all firms choose financial structures with the same cost? Sometimes, for example, if costs are high enough, all firms will choose the trivial structure. But typically if costs are low enough, there will be an incentive for some but not all firms to innovate. In that case, equilibrium does not exist. The fact that equilibrium does not "exist" means that in some way we have formulated the equilibrium wrongly. We shall see below exactly what is wrong with the notion of competitive equilibrium in the presence of short sales. But first, it is important to see that short sales change the properties of equilibrium even when the assumption of perfect competition is appropriate.

Externalities

Roughly speaking, perfect competition is an appropriate assumption when no agent has significant power to influence the market. In the present context, we can ensure that this condition is satisfied by assuming that the there is a finite limit on the short positions in any security issued by a single firm. This can be done in a variety of ways, some more realistic than others. Since the purpose here is just to illustrate what happens when limited short sales are allowed, the short sale constraint is introduced in the simplest way possible.

(A.14′)   Each investor is assumed to face a constraint of the form: $d(f) \geq -L\alpha_i$, $\forall f \in F_i$, $\forall i \in I$, where L is a nonnegative constant which is the same for all investors and securities.

In the sequel, we shall consider other ways of modeling equilibrium, in which decisions are made sequentially and firms may choose random strategies, before they know the prices at which they will be able to trade.

Relaxing the assumption that the constraint is the same for all investors and securities would complicate the analysis but would not affect the argument materially. The important point is that the total amount of short sales is constrained and is proportional to supply. Thus, if financial structure F_i is chosen by no firms, no short sales in the associated securities are allowed.

The definition of competitive equilibrium given earlier is simply the special case where $L = 0$. When $L \neq 0$, we shall refer to the equilibrium as a competitive equilibrium with limited short sales. The definition is the same except for the obvious alteration in the account of investors' behavior. The main difference in the properties of equilibrium is that efficiency is no longer assured. In fact, we can give conditions under which efficiency fails. Note that the definition of constrained efficiency must also be altered to allow for limited short sales.

THEOREM 3.3   Let (p, α, x) be a competitive equilibrium with limited short sales for $\mathscr{E}^\infty$. Suppose that there are two financial structures F_i and F_j satisfying the following conditions:

1. $\alpha_i = 0 < \alpha_j$ and $MV_i(p) - C_i < MV_j(p) - C_j$;
2. $d_k(f) > -L\alpha_j$, $\forall f \in F_j$, $\forall k \in K$;
3. $(1 + L)MV_i(p) - C_i > (1 + L)MV_j(p) - C_j$.

Then the equilibrium allocation is not constrained efficient.

The conditions in the theorem have straightforward interpretations. Condition 1 says that no firm chooses F_i in equilibrium (strictly, a set of measure zero) whereas some firms choose F_j (strictly, a set of positive measure). The second inequality says that F_j gives a strictly higher net market value than F_i (the weak version of the inequality is implied by definition of equilibrium). Condition 2 says that the short sale constraint is not binding for securities associated with the financial structure F_j. Condition 3 says that if the firm were to get the proceeds from the allowable short sales as well as from the original securities, then the financial structure F_i would be more profitable.

The explanation for the result is that allowing short sales introduces an *externality* into the firms' decision making. When a firm issues new securities, it increases the opportunities for risk sharing in the economy. When no short sales are allowed, the increased opportunities are measured by the increase in the value of the securities issued by the firm, that is, by the increase in market value. Thus, the social benefit from the new securities coincides with the firm's benefit, and the firm has the right incentive to issue new securities. When short sales are allowed, however, there is an additional source of risk sharing that is not taken into account by the firm. The short sales also represent a source of increased risk sharing, which is allowed by the issue of the original securities but does not benefit the firm. Thus, there is an externality which creates a divergence between the social and private benefits of innovation. This can be seen by comparing conditions 1 and 3 of the theorem. The private benefits of the two financial structures are compared in condition 1 while the social benefits are compared in condition 3. In the case envisaged in the theorem, the two comparisons yield opposite results.

The theorem can be illustrated with the leading example. Let $F_j = F_1$, $F_i = F_2$ and suppose $C_2 = 4.2$. When $L = 0$ so that short sales are not possible, all firms choose F_1 in equilibrium and have value 6. If a firm were to choose F_2, its gross value would be 10, and its net value would be $10 - 4.2 = 5.8 < 6$. In this equilibrium, conditions 1 and 2 of the theorem are satisfied but condition 3 is not. The equilibrium is efficient since the private value of F_2 is the same as the social value.

Next suppose $L = 0.1$ so that condition 3 is satisfied: $1.1 \times 10 - 4.2 = 6.8 > 1.1 \times 6 = 6.6$. The equilibrium remains unchanged; the amount received by any firm choosing F_2 is still only 10 which gives a net payoff of 5.8, and this is less than the 6 obtained with F_1. However, in terms of social optimality the situation would be improved if some firms chose F_2 instead of F_1, so the equilibrium is not efficient. To see this suppose ε of firms chose F_2 instead of F_1. What are the benefits of this switch? The benefit to investors of type k_i is $1.1 m_{k_i} \varepsilon = 5.5\varepsilon$, so the total benefit to investors is 11ε. Taking into account the cost of issuing the security means the benefit is $11\varepsilon - 4.2\varepsilon = 6.8\varepsilon$ which explains the left-hand side of the condition above.

What are the opportunity costs of the switch to F_2 from F_1? Firms are giving up the proceeds from F_1 which amount to 6ε. In addition, investors must provide the short sales of F_2. Suppose all investors short sell $L\varepsilon = 0.1\varepsilon$ of F_2. Since short selling all the securities in F_2 is equivalent to short selling F_1, the opportunity cost of this is $6 \times 0.1\varepsilon = 0.6\varepsilon$. Hence the total opportunity cost is $6\varepsilon + 0.6\varepsilon = 6.6\varepsilon$ which explains the right-hand side of the condition above.

Note that the conditions in the theorem are sufficient rather than necessary. If the short sales are provided by the people that have the lowest cost of doing this rather than everybody, a weaker condition than condition 3 holds.

Imperfect Competition

When the open interest in the securities issued by a single firm is constrained to be finite, the actions of the firm have a negligible impact on the economy, at least when the economy is very large. Things are quite different if the open interest can grow unboundedly large as the number of firms grows large. In this section we study an example in which there is no constraint on short sales. We see that the introduction of a new security by a single firm can lead to a nonnegligible effect on the economy because it opens up a new market. As a result, the firm may not be a perfect competitor even in a large economy.

The market data are taken from the leading example. Consider an economy with N firms as described in assumption A.8′. Suppose that the cross-sectional distribution of financial structures is α. An exchange equilibrium relative to α is defined in the same way as when short sales were ruled out except that the set of available portfolios must be defined differently. When no short sales are allowed, there is no essential loss of generality in assuming that investors can buy whatever securities they like at the prevailing prices. The reason is that if in equilibrium the supply of a security is zero, each investor's demand must also be zero. When short sales are allowed, the conclusion no longer follows. In order to prevent investors from trading a nonexistent security we have to add an additional constraint. Define the set of portfolios to be $D = \{d: F \to \mathbb{R}\}$ and define the set of available portfolios to be $D(\alpha) = \{d \in D \mid d(f) = 0$ if $f \in F_i \Rightarrow \alpha_i = 0,\ \forall i \in I\}$. Then the previous definition of exchange equilibrium is altered by the substitution of $D(\alpha)$ for D.

With this change in the definition there are only two possible exchange equilibria for the leading example. The reason is that with unlimited short sales, the securities associated with the structure F_2 operate like Arrow securities. If any firm chooses the financial structure F_2, markets are complete. In that case the equilibrium is independent of α. On the other hand, if no firm chooses F_2, then there is a unique equilibrium in which only unlevered equity is traded.

When one firm innovates and chooses F_2, markets are complete, and by symmetry it is clear that every investor can attain a uniform consumption allocation across states, that is, $(9.5, 9.5)$. At this allocation the marginal valuations of each type of investor will be the same. As a result, the equilibrium market value of the firm will be $(1/2)V'(9.5)\cdot 2 + (1/2)V'(9.5)\cdot 2 = 2V'(9.5) = 7$, say, independently of the market structure chosen. On the other hand, if no firm chooses F_2, the only exchange equilibrium is the one in which unlevered equity is traded, and markets remain incomplete. The equilibrium level of future consumption is 7 in the low state and 12 in the high state. As a result there is a market value of $(1/2)V'(7)\cdot 2 + (1/2)V'(12)\cdot 2 = 6 < 7$.

Several points are noteworthy about this example. The first is that whichever exchange equilibrium is observed, all firms have the same market value. This means that the firm that chooses F_2 is not better off than the firm that chooses F_1. In fact, the firm is worse off because the cost of F_2 is greater than the cost of F_1. On the other hand, all firms will be better off if at least one firm chooses F_2, as long as the cost of the structure is less than the difference in the market values, that is, $C_2 < 1$. If the cost of innovating is greater than the difference in the market values, no firm will want to innovate, but it may still be optimal from society's point of view to have the innovation. In fact, as long as the total benefit to the firms, that is, the total increase in value, is greater than the cost of one firm innovating, it is optimal to have the innovation. Since the increase in the value of all the firms is $1 \cdot N$, it will be optimal to have the innovation for some sufficiently large value of N.

The analysis of strategic equilibrium for the general case is quite easy. Let MV_I denote the market value of a firm in the (unique) exchange equilibrium corresponding to the value of $\alpha \in \Delta^N(I)$ such that $\alpha_2 = 0$ (i.e., markets are incomplete). Let MV_C denote the market value of the firm in the (unique) exchange equilibrium corresponding to any value of $\alpha \in \Delta^N(I)$ such that $\alpha_2 > 0$ (i.e., markets are complete). Let us suppose that the market value is greater when markets are complete than when they are incomplete, that is, $MV_I < MV_C$ (this need not be the case in general; see chap. 7). Let σ denote the probability that an individual firm chooses the more complex financial structure. Note that any firm would rather choose F_1, other things being equal. The incentive to choose F_2 comes from the prospect that no other firm will choose F_2, and they will all end up in the exchange equilibrium with the lower market value. The probability of this happening in a symmetric Nash equilibrium is $(1 - \sigma)^{N-1}$, and the loss if it happens is $(MV_C - MV_I)$. The firm will be indifferent between the two structures if the expected benefit of innovating is just equal to the cost, that is, $(1 - \sigma)^{N-1}(MV_C - MV_I) = C_2$. There exists a unique strategic equilibrium with mixed strategies if and only if this equation has a solution $0 < \sigma < 1$. If $MV_C - MV_I < C_2$ there is a unique strategic equilibrium in which $\sigma = 0$. Note that unless $N = 1$, there cannot be a symmetric equilibrium in which $\sigma = 1$. A firm will always prefer to be a free rider: if it is sure that someone else will bear the cost of innovation, it will choose not to innovate itself.

Let us concentrate on the mixed strategy equilibrium. It is clear from the equilibrium condition that $\sigma \to 0$ as $N \to \infty$. Furthermore, the probability that no innovation takes place is bounded away from zero: $(1 - \sigma)^{N-1} = C_2/(MV_C - MV_I) > 0$ for all N. This is necessary in order to provide an incentive for each firm to innovate. One can also see that the average number of firms that innovate is bounded:

$$\sigma N = \left(1 - \left(\frac{C_2}{MV_C - MV_I} \right)^{1/(N-1)} \right) N$$

and using L'Hôpital's rule the limiting value of σN can be shown to be $\ln\{(MV_C - MV_I)/C_2\} > 0$.

The Impact of Short Sales

In this chapter we have seen several ways in which the introduction of short selling changes the welfare analysis of financial innovation. Even if only *limited* short sales are allowed, the efficiency properties of equilibrium may be quite different. Short selling expands the supply of the security and provides additional risk sharing, but this benefit is not internalized by the innovating firm. When an innovating firm issues new securities, it only takes into account the impact on the value of the firm. It does not take into account the value of the open interest in the securities. Because of this externality, the innovation decision may be inefficient.

When *unlimited* short selling is allowed, there is an additional problem. The innovating firm may perceive that it has a large impact on equilibrium. Although the amount of the security issued by the firm itself may be negligible relative to the size of the economy, the volume of the short sales that piggyback on the original innovation may be quite large. For this reason, the firm acquires market power and becomes an imperfect competitor, which provides an additional source of inefficiency.

Imperfect competition is not simply an accident when there are unlimited short selling opportunities; it is an essential ingredient of equilibrium. In a large economy, the innovating firm will be no better off ex post, that is, after the innovation, than a firm which did not innovate. In fact, to the extent that it must bear the cost of the innovation it is worse off. The only incentive to innovate comes from the innovation's possible impact on prices. In other words, imperfect competition is necessary for innovation when the economy is large.

This is true even when there is potential competition. As we saw in the example, there may be more than one provider of the innovative securities in equilibrium, so the innovating firm is not a monopolist. In this sense, it is not true that the firm always has a large impact on equilibrium. But as we saw in the example, there must be a positive probability that no one else will innovate. Otherwise there would be no incentive for this firm to make the innovation itself. The point of the analysis is not just that an innovating firm could have a large impact on the economy. If that were all, we might be able to avoid the problem by arranging things so that several firms innovated simultaneously. Imperfect competition is essential in order to provide the necessary incentives to innovate.

As we mentioned earlier, one of the substitutes for short selling is the existence of options markets. There is empirical evidence that the introduction of an option on a firm's shares often has a significant impact on the value of the firm. This suggests that the model with unbounded short sales developed here and in chapter 7 may be of more than theoretical interest.

4.4 Market Share and Innovation by Financial Institutions

An important question in the context of financial innovation is the identity of the innovator. The possibility considered in the previous sections is that firms issue securities. Of course, they may have had the assistance of an investment bank which provides the required expertise, but in that case the bank is merely an agent of the firm whose involvement has no effect on the innovative process. The intermediary, in other words, is a veil behind which the reality of the firm's interests determines the size and nature of the innovation.

Another possibility, however, is that intermediaries such as investment banks undertake innovation on their own account. The incentives for an intermediary to innovate may differ from those of a firm. As discussed in chapter 2, Kanemasu, Litzenberger, and Rolfo (1986) investigated the stripping of Treasury securities by investment banks in the early to mid-1980s. They found this activity was initially profitable but that as more banks undertook it, profits were reduced. Tufano (1989) considered a sample of fifty-eight innovations by investment banks which did not include stripped Treasury securities. He found that banks did not charge higher fees during the initial period where they were the only issuer of a security and charged less than imitators who introduced similar securities. In the long run, the main advantage that innovating investment banks gained was a larger market share than imitators.

These empirical studies illustrate the importance of understanding the incentives intermediaries such as investment banks have to innovate. As discussed in section 4.3, the case where there is immediate imitation is similar to that where there are costless short sales. An innovating firm will bear the cost of innovation but will not receive revenues that are higher than those of a noninnovating firm. The incentive to innovate will come from general-equilibrium effects. A new security may change the value of existing holdings, and this means a firm may have an incentive to innovate. However, it is not only general-equilibrium effects that create incentives to innovate. As the results of Kanemasu, Litzenberger, and Rolfo (1986) and Tufano (1989) indicate, temporary monopoly power and increased market share provide another important incentive. In this section we develop a simple model of these incentives.

A Monopoly Investment Bank

We start with the simplest case where a monopoly investment bank introduces a security to achieve optimal risk sharing.

(A.17)   There exists a monopoly investment bank. The owners only consume at date 1, so the objective of the investment bank is to maximize date 1 profits. There are costs C of issuing a security.

The assumption that bank owners only consume at date 1 is a simplification. If they consumed at date 2 it would be necessary to consider their role as investors which would complicate the analysis without adding important insights. Apart from this and the absence of assumption A.7 the assumptions are the same as in section 4.1.

There are two types of nonintermediary agent, call them A and B. The type A's are the "investors," and type B's are the "issuers." They cannot trade directly but must use the investment bank. Since the investment bank has a monopoly, it can charge fees to both issuers and investors. There are a number of fee structures that could be implemented. If the fees are based on the size of transaction in any way, they will be distortionary. The structure that yields the investment bank the greatest amount is simply a fixed or lump-sum fee. In other words, an investor has to pay the same fee ϕ_A irrespective of the amount purchased (provided this is positive); similarly, the issuer has to pay the same fee ϕ_B irrespective of the amount issued (provided this is positive).

The monopoly investment bank has an incentive to choose a security which leads to a Pareto efficient allocation of resources. If the security could be changed so that one group could be made better off without making the other worse off, the investment bank could make this change and increase the fee it charges to the type made better off. Hence if it innovates in equilibrium it will choose the Pareto-efficient security $f(\omega_i)$ that maximizes revenues, and the fees it charges will be

$$\phi_k = EU_k^{**} - EU_k^* \quad \text{for } k = A, B,$$

where EU_k^{**} is their utility when they can use the security without paying any fees and EU_k^* is their utility when they cannot use the security. The bank's profits will be $\Pi = \phi_A + \phi_B - C$. Innovation will only occur in equilibrium when $C \leq \phi_A + \phi_B$.

The allocation of resources is Pareto optimal with a monopoly investment bank and lump-sum fees because the bank can capture all the benefits of innovation and can weigh these against the costs of innovation. In practice, of course, lump-sum fees are usually not possible, and intermediaries face the prospect of potential or actual competition. Although these reduce the incentive to innovate, they may be desirable on equity grounds in that they spread the benefits of innovation as discussed in chapter 8.

Competition through Imitation

For a given innovative security, investment banks compete over fees. The fees that they charge usually depend on the quantity of securities sold and take the form of a spread between the buying and selling price. This spread is effectively a joint fee ϕ to investors and issuers. In general, the fee can depend in a complex, nonlinear way on the amount of securities sold.[5] For simplicity, it will be assumed below that there is a constant fee per dollar of a security that is sold.

To investigate the effect of imitation, it is necessary to extend the basic model.

(A.18)   There are three dates $t = 1, 2, 3$. One-period securities are issued at dates 1 and 2.

The focus on short-term securities means that the demand for a security can be represented in simple terms as a function of the fees charged.

(A.19)   For a given security, the inverse aggregate demand curve in terms of the fees charged can be represented by $\phi = \phi(Q)$.

In order to analyze the problem of competition through imitation it is necessary to specify the costs of innovation and outline the possibilities for imitation.

(A.20)   In order to supply a new security an investment bank must pay a
development cost C. If another bank subsequently imitates the
security, its development cost is zero. The innovating bank and its
imitators must train staff to deal with the new security, and it is
this that determines capacity. For a bank to develop capacity q
costs $c(q)$.

If a bank creates a new security it is the only issuer at date 1. At date 2
other banks will imitate provided it is profitable to do so. The innovating
bank takes this into account initially when it chooses its capacity. It is
effectively a Stackelberg leader, and the imitators are Stackelberg follow-
ers. Let the innovating bank be denoted by the subscript $i = 0$ and the
other banks that enter be denoted $i = 1, \ldots, N$. Suppose the discount rate
is zero. The innovating bank's problem is then

$$\text{Max}_{q_0} \; \phi(q_0)q_0 + \phi\left(q_0 + \sum_{i=1}^{N} q_i\right)q_0 - c(q_0) - C,$$

taking q_i, $i = 1, \ldots, N$ as given.
   The representative imitator's problem is

$$\text{Max}_{q_j} \; \phi\left(q_0 + \sum_{i=1}^{N} q_i\right)q_j - c(q_j),$$

taking q_i, $i = 0, \ldots, N$, $i \neq j$ as given.
   The number of imitators is determined by the requirement that they
make nonnegative profits. It is also necessary that the innovator make a
nonnegative profit for innovation to occur.
   Since all banks are the same, it is arbitrary which bank is the innovator
and which banks are imitators. In practice it is likely that there will be
differences between banks, and the one with a comparative advantage will
be the innovator.
   The first-order condition for the innovator is

$$\phi'(q_0)q_0 + \phi(q_0) + \phi'\left(q_0 + \sum_{i=1}^{N} q_i\right)q_0 + \phi\left(q_0 + \sum_{i=1}^{N} q_i\right) - c'(q_0) = 0.$$

For the representative imitator it is

$$\phi'\left(q_0 + \sum_{i=1}^{N} q_i\right)q_j + \phi\left(q_0 + \sum_{i=1}^{N} q_i\right) - c'(q_j) = 0.$$

Provided $\phi(\cdot)$ and $c(\cdot)$ satisfy the standard conditions, so $\partial(MR - MC)/\partial q < 0$, it can be seen that $q_0 > q_i$ for $i = 1, \ldots, N$. In other words, the innovator obtains a larger market share than imitators. This occurs because the innovator is a Stackelberg leader in the capacity game and is thus able to preempt the imitators. This inequality also implies that the fee charged initially will be higher than in subsequent periods.

These results are consistent with the observation of Kanemasu, Litzenberger, and Rolfo (1986) concerning the stripping of Treasury securities. Although the larger market share prediction is consistent with Tufano's (1989) results, the results concerning the level of initial fees are not. However, the model is a simple one and abstracts from a number of important things. In particular, it is unlikely that the aggregate demand curve $\phi(q)$ is the same in every period. It is plausible that it will initially be below that in subsequent periods to reflect the learning costs and uncertainty associated with the new security. In this case market share will still be higher for the innovator, but initial fees can be at the same level or below those in subsequent periods as Tufano finds.

Tufano's result that the innovator charges a long-run price below that of imitators can be explained in a number of ways. One of the most plausible is that, in addition to the costs of developing capacity $c(q)$, there are also costs, such as marketing costs, which recur each period. As Tufano (1989, p. 214) suggests, these may be lower for innovators than imitators because "[innovation] enables a bank to enjoy economies of scale and scope by jointly producing underwriting and trading services, or to enjoy lower marketing costs by credibly signaling its intangible assets of skill or creativity."

This chapter has illustrated that even when a product can be imitated, an innovator may nevertheless have an advantage because she is the first mover. If investment banks must train staff or incur any other type of capacity cost, then they may be able to gain a larger market share as a result of being an innovator. This can result in larger profits and more than make up for the costs of innovation. The incentives to innovate will typically not be efficient unless an investment bank has a monopoly and can charge lump sum fees to issuers and investors. However, the case where there is competition has the desirable feature that the benefits of innovation are more widely spread.

Obviously, this analysis barely scratches the surface. We have treated the security as if it were an ordinary commodity with given characteristics and a given demand function. These assumptions ignore certain obvious complications.

• In practice, the demand function will be uncertain, both because the innovator cannot be sure of what the various issuers and investors want and because the issuers and investors are not sure about the nature of the new product.

• Uncertainty about what the market wants will have an impact on the design of the security, both the willingness of the innovator to try something new and the exact nature of the new security brought to market.

• Because of uncertainty about who wants what, the innovating bank will need to do market research. At this point it is important to recognize the role of the bank as a network, gathering information about missing opportunities for sharing risk.

• The bank's network is also important when it comes to marketing the security. Its ability to identify potential issuers and investors and persuade them of the advantages of the new financial product is crucial to its success.

This emphasis on uncertainty, information, and networking suggests that the market for new securities will be much more complex than the analysis in this section has allowed. Some of these ideas are discussed in chapter 5, but much research remains to be done.

4.5   Innovation in Financial Markets

In sections 4.2 and 4.3 we assumed firms issued securities, and in section 4.4 we assumed intermediaries such as investment banks issued them. Many other institutions also innovate, and the incentives and welfare properties associated with this kind of innovation can be quite different. In this section we consider what happens when an exchange issues derivative securities. The primary examples of this type of innovation are options and financial futures exchanges. As the empirical evidence discussed in chapter 2 illustrates, this type of innovation can have important general-equilibrium effects. In particular, the value of firms may be substantially changed by the innovation. As the results of Detemple and Jorion (1990) concerning the effect of introducing options demonstrate, the changes in value can be widespread and can spill over to other firms besides the firm on which the option is written. In this section we briefly consider the incentives to set up exchanges. They are considered at length in chapter 8. We start with a simple model of introducing an options exchange to focus on the issue of how such innovations are financed. The simplicity of the model means that issues concerning the design of contracts to be traded on the exchange are trivial. In the last part of the section we outline Duffie and Jackson's (1989) analysis of the design of futures contracts.

Incentives to Set up an Options Exchange

The incentives to set up an options exchange arise not from the desire to increase the market value of the firm as in sections 4.2 and 4.3 but from the fees that can be charged to traders to enter the market. The different incentives produce different results, but not necessarily better ones. Recall that when firms issue securities there may be a free rider problem if short sales are allowed. The existence of short sellers who can take a "free ride" on the first-mover's innovation will reduce the incentive to issue a new security. Even when short sales are limited there is an externality which causes the private and social benefits of innovation to diverge. The private benefit is the increase in the value of the firm, but this does not include the risk-sharing benefits resulting from the short sales. This problem does not arise in the case of an organized exchange. The exchange owner can control entry to the exchange. Only those who pay the fee can enter. She is thus in a position to extract all the surplus from potential traders. One might therefore think that the exchange owner's decision to set up an exchange is more likely to be optimal. But there are other problems, both of them arising from the general equilibrium effects of the decision to open the exchange.

The first is that the opening of an exchange may have effects on individuals who are not traders on the exchange. For example, the initiation of options trading may affect the value of the firm whose shares are being traded. These external effects are relevant to the social optimality of the exchange, but there is no evident way that the exchange owner can internalize them. Since these effects may be positive or negative, there may be too much or too little innovation. For example, if the opening of the exchange raises the value of the firm and the exchange owner cannot capture this increase, then an exchange may not be set up when it should be. On the other hand, if the opening of the exchange lowers the value of the firm and the exchange owner is not forced to compensate the shareholders, then an exchange may be set up when it should not be.

The second problem is that, even if the exchange owner can extract all the surplus from the agents in the economy, that surplus will be different after the exchange is open. From society's point of view, the exchange should be opened if the social surplus, measured as the difference between welfare before the exchange is opened and welfare after it is opened, is greater than the cost of opening the exchange. If the exchange owner can capture this ex ante surplus, he will indeed make the socially optimal decision. But what happens if the exchange owner has already sunk the costs of opening the exchange? The most that he can extract from each trader is the value of entering the exchange, that is, the difference between the trader's welfare if he enters the exchange and his welfare if he stays out. This ex post measure of welfare is generally different from the ex ante measure and will provide different, suboptimal incentives to open the exchange. If ex post surplus is greater than ex ante surplus, the exchange may be opened when it should not be; if ex post surplus is less than ex ante surplus, the exchange may not be opened when it should be. In short, we may have too little or too much innovation, just as in the case of innovation by firms when short sales are possible.

To illustrate these ideas, consider the following very simple example. There are two dates $t = 1, 2$ and a single consumption good at each date. There are two types of investors $i - 1, 2$. Each of them has risk preferences represented by the same von Neumann–Morgenstern utility function $u(c_1, c_2) = c_1 + U(c_2)$, where c_1 is consumption in the first period, c_2 is consumption in the second period, and $U' > 0$, $U'' < 0$. An agent of type i has a random future income Y_i, for $i = 1, 2$. There is a single type of firm whose future income is represented by the random variable Z. As usual, we abstract from production decisions and take the firm's income as exogenous. The firm just issues equity. The firm is assumed to be owned by an entrepreneur who wants to sell the entire firm.

We assume for simplicity that the number (or measure) of investors of each type is equal to the number (or measure) of firms.

In the absence of an options exchange, the only security investors can trade is equity in the firm. Suppose the price of equity is p. Then the maximized expected utility of an investor of type i is

$$V_i(p) = \underset{e_i}{\text{Max}}\ EU(Y_i + e_i Z) - p e_i,$$

where e_i is the investor's demand for equity. Since investors have transferable utility, we can define welfare to be the sum of maximized expected utilities and the value of the firm, $W(p) \equiv V(p) + p \equiv V_1(p) + V_2(p) + p$.

Now suppose that an options exchange is opened at date 1. A single security is traded, an option with a striking price of σ. At date 2 the option is worth $(Z - \sigma)^+ \equiv \max\{Z - \sigma, 0\}$ if the firm's future value turns out to be Z. To enter the exchange, the investor must pay a fee. Once in the exchange, she can trade as much as she wants at the equilibrium price. By charging the investor a fixed fee, the exchange owner can extract all the surplus from the investor. This makes it more likely that we will get an optimal innovation decision from the owner. At the same time, the linearity of the investor's utility in first-period consumption means that the fee will not affect the investor's demand for securities (we assume that the investor's demand is not wealth-constrained).

Example Suppose there are two states of nature at the second date. Suppose the future incomes of the firm and the two types of investor are given by the following:

$Z = (2, 1)$;

$Y_1 = (1, 1)$;

$Y_2 = (0, 1)$.

An option with a striking price of $\sigma = 1$ will yield

$$(Z - \sigma)^+ = \begin{cases} 1 \text{ if } Z = 2; \\ 0 \text{ if } Z = 1. \end{cases}$$

The ability to trade this option will give the investors access to complete markets, since by trading the option and equity they can construct an Arrow security paying one unit of the numeraire in either state. A competitive equilibrium with complete markets will be Pareto efficient and, in particular, will achieve first-best risk sharing.

The first-best allocation will give each type of investor at the second date a consumption of $3/2$ in each state. From the first-order conditions, the equilibrium price of equity will be

$$p^* = \frac{1}{2} U'\left(\frac{3}{2}\right) 2 + \frac{1}{2} U'\left(\frac{3}{2}\right) 1 = \frac{3}{2} U'\left(\frac{3}{2}\right).$$

The sum of the maximized expected utilities for the two types is

$$2U\left(\frac{3}{2}\right) - p^* = 2U\left(\frac{3}{2}\right) - \frac{3}{2}U'\left(\frac{3}{2}\right) = v^*.$$

Total welfare is

$$v^* + p^* = 2U\left(\frac{3}{2}\right).$$

Let $\hat{p}$ denote the equilibrium price of equity in the absence of an options exchange. The social surplus from opening the exchange can be denoted by S and defined by

$$S \equiv v^* + p^* - W(\hat{p}) = v^* + p^* - (V(\hat{p}) + \hat{p}).$$

The ex ante surplus for investors is denoted by S_a and defined by

$$S_a = v^* - V(\hat{p}).$$

The ex post surplus for investors is denoted by S_p and defined by

$$S_p = v^* - V(p^*).$$

The First Best Suppose the cost of opening the exchange is $c > 0$, measured in units of the consumption good at the first date. The exchange should be opened if $s > c$. If the exchange is not opened, investors of type i receive an expected utility of $V_i(\hat{p})$, and entrepreneurs receive $\hat{p}$. If the exchange is opened, then ignoring the entry fees, the investors of type i receive an expected utility of v^*, and the entrepreneurs receive p^*. Since there is transferable utility, the investors and the entrepreneurs could give up a total amount of first-period consumption equal to $v^* - V(\hat{p}) + p^* - \hat{p} = S$ and still be as well off as they were without the exchange. The maximum amount that can be transferred to the exchange owner without making the others worse off is S. Since the exchange owner's cost is c there is a Pareto improvement from opening the exchange if $S - c > 0$.

The following game will implement the first-best decision. Allow the exchange owner to make a "take it or leave it" offer to the other agents in the economy. Each entrepreneur is asked to make a payment of t_0, and each investor of type i is asked to make a net payment t_i to the exchange owner. If everyone agrees, the exchange is opened, and every investor has the right to trade freely on the exchange. Otherwise, the exchange is not set up.

If $S > c$, the exchange is opened in the unique subgame perfect equilibrium of this game. If $S < c$, there is again a unique subgame perfect equilibrium, and the exchange is not opened. If $S = c$, it is a matter of indifference whether the exchange is opened or not.

For example, if $S > c$, the unique subgame perfect equilibrium strategies involve the investors of type i paying $t_i = V_i(\hat{p}) - v^*$ and the entrepreneurs paying $t_0 = p^* - \hat{p}$. Everyone agrees to pay this charge. Note that some of these "payments" may be negative numbers, that is, they represent payments by the exchange owner as compensation for "damage" caused by the opening of the exchange.

This game is unrealistic in two respects. First, the entrepreneurs, who do not want to trade in the options market, are charged a fee by the exchange owner. (Alternatively, the entrepreneurs have veto power over the exchange and must be bribed to let it open.) Second, the charge for trading in the exchange is levied before the exchange is open and with the owner's commitment not to set up the exchange if she does not receive the full surplus. In practice, commissions and other fees are charged once an exchange is in operation, and such charges are levied only on those actually trading in the exchange. These stylized facts lead us to consider an alternative game.

Suboptimal Innovation Decisions   Now consider a different type of decision structure. First the exchange owner decides whether or not to open the exchange. If the exchange is not opened, investors trade equity only. If the exchange is opened, the owner sets entry fees t_1 and t_2 to be paid by the investors of types 1 and 2. If an investor pays the fee, she can trade on the exchange. If not, she can only trade on the equity market.

Let us restrict attention to equilibria in which investors of a given type all enter the exchange or all stay out. Since it takes two types to trade, this means that either all investors enter the exchange or all stay out. Since the exchange will not be set up unless investors are expected to enter the exchange and pay the entry fees, in equilibrium all investors will enter the exchange.

The maximum fee that can be charged an investor is the one that makes her indifferent between entering the exchange and not entering the exchange. In equilibrium, the fee for an investor of type i will be $t_i = \frac{1}{2}v^* - V_i(p^*)$. The maximum total revenue the owner can extract after the exchange has been set up is therefore equal to $v^* - v(p^*) = S_p$. The net gain to the exchange owner is $S_p - c$, and so the exchange will be set up in this case if $S_p > c$. Then the exchange will be set up even though it is suboptimal to do so if $S_p > c > S$.

Recall that there are two reasons why S_p and S differ. First, S contains a payment by or to the entrepreneurs, whereas S_p does not. The entrepreneurs may be affected by the opening of the exchange, and the exclusion of their change in utility from S_p will distort incentives. Second, the surplus measured by S_p is ex post. If the investor decides not to enter the exchange, she can trade on the equity market at the equilibrium price p^*. This determines her reservation utility and hence her ex post surplus from entering the exchange. On the other hand, if the exchange were not opened at all, she could still trade on the equity market, but at the equilibrium price $\hat{p}$. Thus, her reservation utility is different in this case, and so the maximum entry fee the owner can charge will be different.

It can also be the case that an exchange will not be set up when it is socially optimal to open one. This will happen when $S > c > S_p$.

The Effect of Options Trading on the Value of the Firm   The opening of an options exchange may raise or lower the value of the firm. Consider first the case where $\hat{p} > p^*$. Then clearly $V(\hat{p}) < V(p^*)$. The benefit the investor gets from entering the exchange will be greater ex post than it is ex ante. This will tend to increase the surplus the owner can extract and will encourage an excessive amount of innovation. On the other hand, the entrepreneurs are benefiting from the opening of the exchange because it increases the value of their firms. The fact that the owner cannot capture this benefit will tend to discourage innovation. Since these two effects go in opposite directions, it is hard to say much about the net effect. If the value of the firm is lowered by options trading, the two effects are simply reversed, and, of course, they go in opposite directions.

We can say a little more by exploiting the special structure of the model. Figure 4.1 shows the graph of the function $V(p)$. It is obvious that $V(p)$ is decreasing in p. By a standard argument, we can also show that it is convex. By the envelope theorem and the market-clearing condition, we have $V'(\hat{p}) = -1$. The convexity of $V(p)$ then implies that $V(p^*) - V(\hat{p}) \geq -1 \cdot (p^* - \hat{p})$; in other words, $V(p^*) + p^* \geq V(\hat{p}) + \hat{p}$. This condition has an interesting interpretation. It says that the sum of entrepreneurs and investors' reservation utilities must rise after the opening of the options exchange. If the exchange owner could somehow internalize the surplus of the entrepreneurs, the necessity of charging fees on an ex post basis would

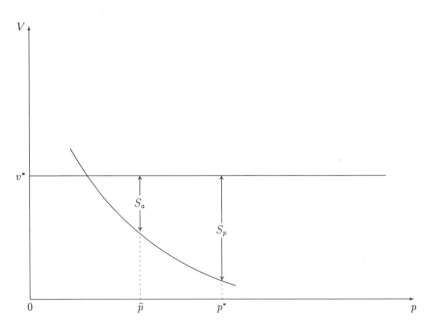

Figure 4.1
The relationship between expected utility and price

unambiguously reduce the incentive to open the exchange below the first-best level. The fact that the entrepreneurs' surplus is left out of account prevents us from drawing this simple conclusion.

The Design of Futures Contracts

In the two-person example used to illustrate the difficulties associated with opening an options exchange, the design of an optimal options contract is trivial. With two traders and complete information, first-best risk sharing is attainable through a simple contract. In other circumstances, the problem is far from trivial. Duffie and Jackson (1989) have studied the problem of designing an optimal futures contract and obtained a number of interesting results which we review briefly here.

There are K investors $k = 1, \ldots, K$, each endowed with a random endowment x_k of some numeraire good. Investors have mean-variance preferences: the utility of a random outcome x is represented by $U_k(x) = E(x) - r_k \text{var}(x)$, where $r_k > 0$ is the coefficient of risk aversion. A futures contract is a random variable f sold at a price p. To avoid unnecessary complications it is assumed that all transactions take place within a single period. Buying the contract f at a price p entitles the investor to $(f - p)$ at the end of the period.

There is a transaction cost of T per unit of the contract traded. At any value of T, the market makers are assumed to maximize the volume of transactions in order to maximize their income. Why should the market makers adopt this objective function? We can think of the futures market as a cooperative enterprise run by the market makers, whose income derives from the commissions they receive on futures contracts. The transaction cost T represents the commissions they charge for providing contracts. Since their income equals T times the volume of contracts traded, they will want to maximize volume for any given transaction cost. While this interpretation makes sense of the objective function, it makes it hard to treat T as a genuine transaction cost, that is, as something determined by the transaction technology. We shall come back to this point later.

Equilibrium with a Single Contract   Taking the contract f and the futures price p as given, the typical investor chooses a position y_k, which may be long or short, to maximize $U_k(x_k - y_k(f - p) - T|y|)$. It can be shown that the optimal position is given by the formula

$$y_k = |\alpha_k| \left(\frac{-\operatorname{cov}(f, x_k)}{\operatorname{var}(f)} + \frac{E(f) - p + |\alpha_k| T}{2r_k \operatorname{var}(f)} \right),$$

where $\alpha_k = -\operatorname{sign}(y_k)$. A collection $(y_1, \ldots, y_K, p)$ is an equilibrium, given (f, T) if y_k solves the investor's maximization problem given (p, f, T) and $\sum_k y_k = 0$.

It can be shown that there is a unique equilibrium allocation $(y_1, \ldots, y_K)$ for every choice of (f, T). But if the transaction cost T is very large relative to the risks to be hedged or if the contract f is badly designed, the open interest in the contract may be zero. In that case the price is not uniquely determined. However, if at least one of the investors has a nonzero position, the price is uniquely determined by the formula

$$p = E(f) - \frac{2}{\gamma} \operatorname{cov}(\sum_k |\alpha_k| x_k, f) + \frac{T\Gamma}{\gamma},$$

where $\alpha_k = -\operatorname{sign}(y_k)$, $\gamma = \sum_k (|\alpha_k|/r_k)$, and $\Gamma = \sum_k (\alpha_k/r_k)$.

It is easy to show from the equilibrium conditions that investors' demand is homogeneous: an equiproportional change in the contract and

transaction cost will change the investor's position by the inverse propor-
tion: for any $\lambda > 0$, $y_k(\lambda f, \lambda T) = \frac{1}{\lambda} y_k(f, T)$. Duffie and Jackson (1989) assume that transaction costs are proportional to the standard deviation of
the contract ($T = \tau SD(f)$, where $SD(f)$ is the standard deviation of the
contract), and argue that it makes sense to normalize the contracts so that
$SD(f) = 1$.

Two points should be noted here. First, it seems that transaction costs
are being treated as exogenous, rather than as a variable chosen by the
exchange. If T really represents a cost of exchanging the contract, rather
than a transfer from the investor to the market maker, it is not clear why
volume maximization is the appropriate objective. On the other hand, if T
is a fee charged by the market maker, proportionality may not be an
appropriate assumption.

The second point concerns the nature of the normalization. Even if we
accept that costs are in some sense proportional, the assumption that all
contracts with the same standard deviation have the same cost is much
stronger. It is more than a simple normalization: it implicitly restricts the
transactions cost technology in ways that may be important. A different
implicit technology may lead to quite different results.[6]

For any transaction cost T, the contract will be chosen to maximize the
volume of transactions, that is, f is chosen to

Maximize $v(f, T) = \sum_k |y_k(f, T)|$

subject to $SD(f) = 1$.

Duffie and Jackson show the contract f is volume-maximizing only if it is
perfectly correlated with the random variable $d(f)$, where

$d(f) = \gamma_L e_S - \gamma_S e_L$

$e_S = \sum_{k \in S} x_k$

$e_L = \sum_{k \in L} x_k$

$\gamma_L = \sum_{k \in L} (1/r_k)$

and

$\gamma_S = \sum_{k \in S} (1/r_k)$.

S is the set of investors who take short positions, L is the set of investors
who take long positions, e_L is the sum of endowments of the short inves-

tors, and L is the sum of endowments of the long investors. Similarly, γ_S is the sum of risk tolerances of the short investors, and γ_L is the sum of risk tolerances of the long investors. The *endowment differential* $d(f)$ is the risk-adjusted difference between the endowments on the two sides of the market.

This is a necessary condition but not sufficient. There may be several contracts that satisfy this condition, and not all of them will be volume-maximizing, as Duffie and Jackson show by example. When there are no transaction costs, a sufficient condition for a contract f to be volume-maximizing is that

1. f is perfectly correlated with the endowment differential $d(f)$ and

2. f maximizes the variance of $d(f)$.

Equilibrium with Several Contracts Typically there will be several contracts in existence when a new contract is added. The problem of designing the volume-maximizing additional contract can be analyzed in the same way. Suppose there is a set of contracts $f = (f_1, \ldots, f_n)$ in existence. For a particular contract i define the sets of long and short investors $L(i)$ and $S(i)$ in the usual way and define the endowment differential for contract i, $d(f)_i = \gamma_{L(i)} e_{S(i)} - \gamma_{S(i)} e_{L(i)}$. Suppose that the set of contracts $f = (f_1, \ldots, f_n)$ does not contain any redundant contracts, that is, no contract can be expressed as a linear combination of the remaining contracts. Let $\langle f_{-i} \rangle$ denote the linear subspace spanned by the contracts $f_{-i} = (f_1, \ldots, f_{i-1}, f_{i+1}, \ldots, f_n)$. For any random variable x, let $\pi^\perp(x|f_{-i}) = x - \pi(x|f_{-i})$, where $\pi(x|f_{-i})$ is the orthogonal projection of x onto $\langle f_{-i} \rangle$. Then it can be shown that f_i is volume-maximizing given f_{-i} only if it is perfectly correlated with $\pi^\perp(d(f)_i|f_{-i})$, the part of the endowment differential for contract i that is not spanned by the remaining contracts f_{-i}.

This characterization of the design of futures contracts assumes there is a single exchange, but the different contracts may be offered by competing exchanges. It can also be shown that the volume-maximizing contracts constitute a Nash equilibrium, under the assumptions that (1) each exchange can introduce a single contract, (2) they make their choices simultaneously, and (3) each exchange is interested in maximizing its own trading volume.

When choices are made sequentially, each exchange should take account of the effect of its choice on the choices of the exchanges that follow.

It turns out that not every contract need be volume-maximizing in a subgame perfect equilibrium.

In the static model, utility is monotonic in the size of the optimal positions. This is why it turns out that when there is a single contract, the volume-maximizing contract is Pareto optimal. With the assumption of zero transaction costs, this definition of Pareto optimality can be extended to multiple contracts. There may exist Nash equilibria in which the contracts are not Pareto optimal.

Even in the monopolistic case, where there is a single contract, the Pareto-optimality result does not carry over from a static context to a dynamic one. In a dynamic context, an investor has two ways to hedge against endowment risk. One is to take a position in a futures contract; the other is to make use of dynamic trading strategies. To some extent, these are alternatives since dynamic trading strategies allow the investor to synthesize securities that may not be provided by the market. The monopolist may have an incentive to design the contract in such a way that the investor is forced to engage in dynamic trading in order to achieve optimal risk sharing. The reason is that the more the investor has to adjust her portfolio, including her position in the futures contract, the greater the volume of trading in the futures market and the more fees the monopolist collects. Thus, a volume-maximizing monopolist may have an incentive to design a contract that does not provide an optimal hedge.

This account of contract design focuses on risk sharing in a special context. No restrictions are placed on the definition of the contract. In practice, the legal definition of an unambiguous index may be a major concern. It is assumed the contract designer has complete information. Dynamic considerations, such as the need for liquidity, cannot be dealt with adequately in this setting. Finally, as we have noted, there are questions about the underlying transaction cost technology and the market maker's objective function. These all provide important topics for future research.

4.6 Innovation by Governments

As outlined in chapter 2, governments have historically played an important role as financial innovators. In the sixteenth century, the French government pioneered the development of bonds, and in later centuries governments introduced many novel securities to improve their ability to borrow. During most of this period, governments provided the vast majority of traded securities. The shares of a number of banks and insurance companies were publicly listed, but apart from this there were relatively few other private securities. It was not until the nineteenth century that firms began to issue large quantities of securities; even as late as 1853, government obligations constituted 76 percent of the value of those listed on the London Stock Exchange.[7] If these government securities had not existed, the savings opportunities available to people would mostly have been direct investments in risky real assets. These securities enabled risk-averse people with few investment skills to avoid risk and maintain a relatively constant standard of living.

In recent years, too, governments have played an important part as financial innovators. For example, the U.S. government has played a major role in developing the market for mortgage-backed securities through its agencies the GNMA, the FNMA, and the FHLMC. The governments of a number of countries experiencing hyperinflation, including Argentina, Brazil, and Israel, have issued bonds indexed to a consumer price index or some other measure of inflation. The U.K. government has also issued substantial amounts of index-linked debt. In contrast, this type of security has not been issued by the private sector.

The many externalities and market failures that have been identified in previous sections underline why government innovation in this area may be important. Despite its apparent empirical importance, there has been very little analysis of government intervention of this type.

Chapter 9 deals with some of the issues that arise when governments issue securities. One of the classical issues in monetary theory revolves around the question of whether the government's financial policy has any real effect. The Ricardian equivalence theorem, for example, asserts that changes in the size and composition of the public debt are neutral (Barro 1974). The Ricardian theorem is true, among other things, as long as the set of debt instruments issued by the government does not change. As with the Modigliani-Miller theorem and many other irrelevance results, the argument is that investors can do or undo anything that government can do (Wallace 1981; Chamley and Polemarchakis 1984). A crucial assumption of this result is that unlimited short sales are possible; investors must be able to buy or sell an unlimited amount of all securities (Bester 1985). On the other hand, as we showed in section 4.3, if there are unlimited short sales and markets are incomplete, the government can have a large impact by introducing a small amount of a new security that expands risk-sharing opportunities. The possibility for unlimited short sales creates a discontinuity: once the market is open, a "large" open interest can develop even if the quantity of the underlying security is "small." As in section 4.2, this discontinuity disappears as soon as short sales are constrained; in that case the introduction of a new security has a limited impact. Two possibilities present themselves. The first is that unlimited short sales are assumed to be possible. In that case, the Ricardian equivalence theorem holds: changes in the stock of existing securities have no effect, but introducing new securities can have a large impact. The second possibility is that short sales are restricted and introducing small quantities of new securities has a small impact. In that case, however, the Ricardian equivalence theorem no longer holds, and changes in the quantity of existing government securities can have an impact. In both cases, the government's financial policy matters.

The important issue in the context of financial innovation is what securities governments should issue.[8] We initially consider what impact short- and long-term debt have on risk-sharing opportunities in the economy and which of these is preferred. The analysis is based on a simple overlapping generations model in which identical agents live for two periods. There is a constant returns-to-scale, risky investment technology. Individuals are born with a nonrandom endowment. Part of the endowment is consumed in their youth, and part is invested in the risky asset to provide consumption in their old age. In the absence of government securities or taxes, all the risk is borne by the old. The lack of risk sharing is due to the incompleteness of markets. This incompleteness raises the possibility that government debt can lead to a Pareto improvement in welfare.

For example, can the government make everybody better off in a stationary equilibrium by issuing one-period bonds? If there were no bonds, agents would find themselves in a stationary autarkic equilibrium. The expected utility of consumers at time t is denoted by

$$EU = U_1(e - y) + E[U_2(yR^{t+1})|R^t], \tag{4.8}$$

where $U_1(\cdot)$ and $U_2(\cdot)$ are utilities in youth and old age, respectively, with $U' > 0$ and $U'' < 0$, e is the nonrandom endowment, y is the investment in the risky asset, and R^t is the random gross rate of return on investment at time t.[9]

Suppose that the government issues a fixed quantity b of bonds per person who is born each period. These are sold at price v_1 and redeemed at price 1. In order to ensure the budget balances, a lump sum tax (or transfer) of h is levied on the young. The budget constraint of the government in every period is therefore

$$v_1 b + h = b, \tag{4.9}$$

and the expected utility of consumers is given by

$$EU = U_1(e - y - v_1 b - h) + EU_2[(yR^{t+1} + b)|R^t]. \tag{4.10}$$

Substituting expression 4.9 and 4.10 gives

$$EU = U_1(e - y - b) + EU_2[(yR^{t+1} + b)|R^t]. \tag{4.11}$$

It can be seen immediately from this formula that the debt policy described is equivalent to a tax-transfer scheme where the government taxes each young person by an amount b and distributes b to each old person every period.

The condition for a small issue of one-period bonds (or an equivalent tax-transfer scheme) to be Pareto improving is found by differentiating expression 4.11 with respect to b and evaluating at $b = 0$:

$$-U_1'(e - y) + E[U_2'(yR^{t+1})|R^t] > 0. \tag{4.12}$$

The price of the bond issue, v_1, is determined by investors' first-order condition:

$$-v_1 U_1'(e - y) + E[U_2'(yR^{t+1})|R^t] = 0. \tag{4.13}$$

Substituting expression 4.13 into 4.12, it can be seen that the issuance of debt is Pareto improving if and only if

$$v_1 > 1. \tag{4.14}$$

In other words, the net rate of return on one-period bonds $(1/v_1) - 1$ must be negative to make everybody better off.

To see whether this condition might be satisfied, suppose there is no discounting and

$$U_1 = U_2 = \ln C \tag{4.15}$$

where C is consumption. The return on the risky asset R is independent and identically distributed through time. The distribution is log normal with mean and variance

$$E[\ln(R)] = \mu - \frac{1}{2}\sigma^2; \; V[\ln(R)] = \sigma^2. \tag{4.16}$$

These assumptions imply that $E[R] - \exp(\mu)$ so that for $\mu > 0$ the net rate of return on the risky asset will be positive. The condition 4.14 becomes

$$v_1 = \exp(-\mu + \sigma^2) > 1$$

or equivalently

$$\mu - \sigma^2 < 0. \tag{4.17}$$

This condition will be satisfied, and the net rate of return on the risky asset will be positive provided μ is positive and σ^2 is large enough.

The introduction of one-period bonds improves risk sharing by allowing agents to hedge the risky investment technology. They are better off because the bond allows their consumption in states where the payoff of the risky asset is low to be increased; this is more important the greater the variance of the risky asset. The introduction of two-period bonds can allow further improvements in risk sharing, perhaps surprisingly, because the resale price of the longer dated securities is risky. Suppose R is positively serially correlated. In this case a high realization of R will mean expected future returns on the risky asset are high. The intermediate-date bond price will then be low because the bonds are relatively unattractive. This negative correlation means that two-period bonds provide a hedge against the fluctuations in the return of the risky asset.

To see this more formally, suppose that each period the government issues an amount b of two-period bonds at price v_2 and does not issue any one-period bonds. At the end of each period these bonds are repurchased at the one-period bond price v_1, so the only bonds in existence in any period are two-period bonds. In this case the government's budget constraint (2) becomes

$$v_2 b + h = v_1 b, \tag{4.18}$$

and the expected utility of the investors becomes

$$EU = U_1(e - y - v_2 b - h) + EU_2[(yR^{t+1} + v_1 b)|R^t]. \tag{4.19}$$

Substituting expression 4.18 into 4.19 and, for a particular generation, denoting the one-period bond price when they are young by v_1^t and when they are old by v_1^{t+1} gives

$$EU = U_1(e - y - v_1^t b) + EU_2[(yR^{t+1} + v_1^{t+1}b)|R^t]. \tag{4.20}$$

Just as before it can be seen that issuing bonds is equivalent to a tax-transfer scheme. Now, however, the scheme is state contingent because v_1^t will depend on R^t. To see this note that when considering small bond issues, v_1^t is determined as in condition 4.13 by the first order condition

$$-v_1^t U_1'(e - y) + E[U_2'(yR^{t+1})|R^t] = 0. \tag{4.21}$$

Positive serial correlation implies that when R^t is high the next period's return R^{t+1} will also be high on average. Given $U'' < 0$, the expected marginal utility of consumption $E[U_2'(yR^{t+1})|R^t]$ will therefore be low and v_1^t will be low. Thus R^t and v_1^t are negatively correlated which provides the possibility for improved risk sharing; falls in the return R^t are offset by an increase in v_1^t.

Differentiating expression 4.20 at $b = 0$ gives the condition for utility to be improved by the introduction of two-period bonds:

$$-v_1^t U_1'(e - y) + E[v_1^{t+1} U_2'(yR^{t+1})|R^t] > 0. \tag{4.22}$$

The first-order condition which determines v_2 when $b = 0$ is

$$-v_2^t U_1'(e - y) + E[v_1^{t+1} U_2'(yR^{t+1})|R^t] = 0. \tag{4.23}$$

Combining expressions 4.22 and 4.23, it can be seen the condition for a Pareto improvement is no longer $v_1 > 1$ but is now that in every state

$$v_2^t > v_1^t. \tag{4.24}$$

This condition can again be illustrated using the example with logarithmic utility and lognormal returns specified in expressions 4.15 and 4.16. The condition 4.22 for the introduction of two-period bonds to be Pareto improving becomes

$$-v_1^t + E\left[\frac{v_1^{t+1}}{R^{t+1}}\middle| R^t\right] > 0 \tag{4.25}$$

where $v_1^t = E[R^{t+1}|R^t]$. Under the previous assumption that R^t is independently and identically distributed, v_1^t is a constant, so two-period bonds are nonrandom and essentially equivalent to one-period bonds. It can be seen that in this case expression 4.25 becomes $v_1 > 1$ as with one-period bonds.

Next suppose that R^t is positively serially correlated. In order to keep the calculations tractable suppose that $\ln(R)$ follows a random walk with a drift of $-\frac{1}{2}\sigma^2$, and a normally distributed innovation with mean zero and variance σ^2. This implies that $E[R^{t+1}|R^t] = R^t$.

The condition for one-period bonds to be Pareto improving can be shown to be

$$\mu - \sigma^2 < 0 \quad \text{where } \mu \equiv \ln(R^t) \tag{4.26}$$

while the condition for two-period bonds is

$$\mu - 2\sigma^2 < 0 \quad \text{where } \mu \equiv \ln(R^t). \tag{4.27}$$

Hence two-period bonds can lead to a Pareto improvement in circumstances where one-period bonds cannot. The positive serial correlation of R^t leads to a negative correlation between R^t and v_1^t which means two-period bonds are a better hedge against the risk associated with R^t.

Strictly speaking, the assumption that $\ln(R)$ follows a random walk means that expressions 4.26 and 4.27 cannot be satisfied for all possible values of R^t. There is a positive probability that R^t will become very large because the changes each period are unbounded and over time there will be a large number of changes. This means that expressions 4.26 and 4.27 cannot be satisfied in every state. However, the assumption allows the conditions to be stated in a simple form and gives the basic idea; it can be thought of as the limiting case of bounded support and high serial correlation.

In the simple model above, the introduction of one-period and two-period bonds was equivalent to a tax-transfer scheme. A natural question is what is the relationship between government financial schemes and tax-transfer schemes in more complex models? It is shown in chapter 9 that the two are not equivalent. While any financial policy can be implemented by a tax-transfer scheme, the reverse is not true. To see this, consider an autarkic equilibrium. Assuming the government has all the information it requires, any feasible allocation can be implemented with a tax-transfer scheme. If the government uses a financial policy instead, there is the constraint that the financial market must be in equilibrium. This means that the set of allocations that can be achieved is a subset of what can be achieved with tax-transfer schemes.

These results concerning the relationship between tax-transfer schemes and financial policies rely on full information being costlessly available.

In practice, the information necessary to implement the two policies is different. If this factor is taken into account, introducing securities may dominate. For example, in the simple illustrations above the tax-transfer scheme required information on who was old and who was young. As developed in expressions 4.9 and 4.10, this was also true for the financial policy as a lump sum tax was levied on the young to cover any shortfall in revenue. However, this is not necessary. Suppose instead a lump sum tax of ℓ was imposed on everybody to cover any shortfall in revenue. Now the government budget constraint is

$$v_1 b + 2\ell = b, \tag{4.28}$$

and the expected utility of consumers is

$$EU = U_1(e - y - v_1 b - \ell) + EU_2[(yR^{t+1} + b - \ell)|R^t]. \tag{4.29}$$

Substituting expression 4.28 into 4.29 gives

$$EU = U_1(e - y - (b - \ell)) + EU_2[(yR^{t+1} + b - \ell)|R^t]. \tag{4.30}$$

The bonds are again equivalent to a tax-transfer scheme which takes $b - \ell$ from the young and gives it to the old each period. It is then possible to proceed just as before and derive conditions for Pareto-improving changes. Now no information about age is required if bonds are used, whereas information on who is old and who is young is required for the tax-transfer scheme. Hence the informational requirements of financial policy can be substantially less than for a tax-transfer scheme.

The financial policy the government pursues in the models above is simply to provide a risk-free security. Another natural question is: Why can't the private sector do this? There are a number of reasons why governments should play an important role in providing securities. One of the recurring themes of the previous sections is that the incentives private agents have to innovate are rarely socially optimal. A government interested in improving welfare rather than profit maximization may therefore be able to step in when the private sector is unwilling to.

A government may also have an advantage compared to the private sector in providing securities. The ability to tax is an important aspect of this; the government can issue securities which are default-free. In contrast, private issuers have the possibility of going bankrupt. One important advantage the government has is that the penalties for not paying taxes are usually much larger than the penalties for default. Another is their low transaction costs for issuing default-free securities. If the private sector were to issue securities with the same characteristics as those issued by the government, it would be necessary to write a large number of highly contingent contracts with many individuals and firms. The government, on the other hand, does not need to write these contracts since the contingent liabilities are implied by the tax code without an explicit contract. In addition, most of the costs of acquiring information for the tax system are fixed. Using it to provide revenue for securities costs little on the margin given that revenue is needed for other government expenditures.

Some companies are similar in a number of ways to the government. For example, corporations such as AT&T and IBM have large income streams and can potentially issue some debt that has a low risk of default. However, even these firms are subject to significant change through time. They may be reorganized as AT&T was, their financial position may deteriorate so that the risk of bankruptcy becomes significant as in the case of General Motors, or they may change the nature of their business substantially as USX has done. One of the characteristics of stable governments is that they do not change their organization very much over time. This means that they may have a distinct advantage over corporations for issuing long-dated securities.

Another important advantage that the government has is that it does not suffer from a coordination problem as private agents do. For example, it may be desirable to issue index-linked bonds to allow some segments of the population to insure against changes in the cost of living. Although all firms may be better off from issuing index-linked securities, it may be that any individual firm that does it is put at a disadvantage. If inflation rapidly increases, then a firm with index-linked debt may be forced out of its product market by firms that have not undertaken this type of commitment. The government does not suffer from this type of problem.

Taxation also provides another important distinction between the government and private issuers. Many aspects of taxation are security specific. For example, interest on firms' debt is tax-deductible, but dividends on equity are not. In order to obtain the tax advantages of debts, firms must issue securities that the courts will recognize as debt. This may severely restrict the types of security private agents can issue. The government on the other hand is not restricted in this way; if necessary, it can change the tax code to provide an exemption.

The welfare effects of government financial innovation are potentially large. For example, in many countries the existence of government bonds allows a significant increase in welfare because of the lack of alternative ways to share risk and smooth consumption over time; the elimination of these government securities would substantially reduce the level of welfare. Many risks remain which cannot be shared using existing securities. Currently, most governments do not devote much attention to the forms of financial innovation they should pursue. This is unfortunate as the potential gains may be very large. In chapter 2 it was pointed out that the introduction of options markets may have resulted in a 69 percent increase in the value of the stocks on the major U.S. exchanges. In contrast, the cost of setting up the options exchanges was very small. This suggests the net benefits from innovation can potentially be large. In the case of options the private sector had incentives to introduce the securities. There may be many other types of security which the government could introduce at a relatively small cost which would have a large impact on welfare where appropriate private incentives do not exist. Mortgage-backed securities provide an example where the government has sponsored markets which have been successful and raised the welfare levels of borrowers and lenders. Financial innovation is an area of public policy which should be given more attention than at present.

4.7   Information and Innovation

An important limitation of the analysis above is that investors are assumed to have full information about the securities they are buying. In practice, it appears that one of the important features of introducing a genuinely novel security is that investors are uncertain about what it is that they are actually buying. This kind of uncertainty is different from the uncertainty that an investor faces when she buys a familiar security. All securities are to some extent risky, normally because of the randomness of the underlying asset's returns. Even if a corporate bond promises a fixed stream of payments of principal and interest, there is a positive probability that the payments will not be made. This kind of uncertainty is the same for all investors: all have the same interest in determining what the actual returns will be. In the case of a genuinely new security, other issues arise. An investor may simply not know what is being offered or whether it will contribute in any way to improving her ability to hedge or increase the returns to her portfolio. We refer to this kind of uncertainty as *product uncertainty*, because it is like the uncertainty faced by a consumer buying a new product for the first time.

This kind of uncertainty may be an important obstacle to financial innovation. Like any other form of uncertainty, it will cause investors to demand a premium if they are to hold the new security, thus reducing the price the issuer can get. If the price is too low, the issuer may not find it worthwhile issuing the security in the first place. It turns out this type of uncertainty can lead to inefficiencies which are quite different from those we have dealt with so far. One example is provided by the gains from *standardization*. If a novel security must earn an uncertainty premium, there is an incentive to issue standard securities which do not bear this premium. The private returns from standardization may lead to coordination failure, that is, the market may fail to innovate, or it may coordinate on the "wrong" security. The existence of private gains from standardization is suggested by the fact that when firms raise external capital by issuing securities, they almost always use one of a small number of financial instruments: debt, equity, convertible debt, preferred shares, warrants, etc. Chapter 10 develops this analysis in more depth.

It may be helpful to give a couple of examples to illustrate the empirical relevance of these ideas. The first example is the introduction of *original issue discount (OID) or zero-coupon bonds*. As discussed in chapter 2, these bonds had been issued on a limited scale by state governments starting in the 1960s, but it was not until the early 1980s that they were widely used. At that time the tax code allowed interest to be amortized on a straight-line basis that took no account of compounding. When interest rates rose substantially, this provision created an extremely profitable opportunity for tax arbitrage.[10] The tax code was altered by the Tax Equity and Fiscal Responsibility Act of 1982 (TEFRA), and firms stopped issuing the OID bonds. However, even after the removal of the tax-arbitrage opportunity, there was a demand for the bonds, and investment banks supplied the market by stripping the interest from conventional bonds.[11] Evidently the experience gained by the market had created a demand for a previously unfamiliar asset. The "technology" of OID bonds was known prior to 1980, but it took the unusually large tax-arbitrage incentive to spur their introduction. However, once introduced, the experience gained by the market eliminated the uncertainty premium, and demand remained.

The second example suggests that even a "standard" (old) security may have an uncertainty premium attached to it. Hirshleifer (1988) has analyzed a model of futures markets in which investors have to pay a fixed setup cost to operate in the market. He interprets this fixed cost as representing the unfamiliarity of some investors with commodity futures. In equilibrium, the fixed cost causes residual risk to be priced.[12] The pricing of residual risk is related to the hedging positions of commodity producers. In a recent paper Bessembinder (1992) has verified empirically that there is a significant relationship between residual risk and hedging positions and commodity risk premia. This evidence supports the hypothesis of market segmentation, which can be explained by the information costs of trading unfamiliar securities.

In order to reduce the product uncertainty associated with new financial products, investors may be led to acquire costly information. In what follows, we shall be interested in cases where this information has two special features. The first is that the information acquired by the investors is *nontransferable*. It is either hard to communicate to other investors or is irrelevant to them. This property is important, because this kind of information cannot be obtained by observing prices or other investors' behavior. Every investor must gather information for herself. The second feature is that the information is *generic*: it concerns types of securities rather than the particular security issued by a single entrepreneur. This ensures that there are private gains from standardization. These two characteristics are crucial in generating the possibility of coordination failure discussed below. Here are a few examples of information that is generic and nontransferable.

Suppose a new claim has a return which is contingent on some macroeconomic variable, such as an exchange rate or an interest rate. If the investor does not know how these macroeconomic variables are correlated with her own income, say, she will be unable to evaluate the riskiness of the claim correctly.

Suppose that a new security has a return that is contingent on accounting data about the firm. An investor who is unfamiliar with accounting systems will have difficulty evaluating the riskiness of this asset.

Another example is a security involving unfamiliar legal provisions. These may be difficult for an investor to evaluate, either because they have not been tested in the courts or because the investor, having no experience of how these provisions work in practice, is unable to work out their implications in circumstances that she can foresee.

An investor's uncertainty about financial structures is formally represented as uncertainty about preferences. This may seem odd, but in fact it is quite a natural way of representing uncertainty about new securities. What matters for any investor's choice is her preference over portfolios. If the investor does not know what is a good choice, we can either say she does not know the properties of the securities or she does not know her own preferences. The advantage of the latter is that it ensures the uncertainty concerns a piece of information that is nontransferable and generic.

Each investor receives a personal preference shock which affects the value of claims to her. If the investor does not know her own type, this creates an additional source of uncertainty about the value of a new claim. Suppose there is a finite set K of types of investors. Each investor of type k in K receives a preference shock Y_k. The preferences of investors of type k are represented by a von Neumann–Morgenstern utility function $U(\cdot, Y_k)$. Uncertainty about k implies uncertainty about the induced preferences over portfolios.

Initially investors are completely ignorant of their types. To discover more about their preferences, they can purchase information in the form of an information structure H, where H is a partition of the set of types K. When she acquires an information structure, an investor learns in which cell of the partition her true type lies.

The Model

Some changes are required in the basic model that has been used so far. It is now necessary to allow idiosyncratic risk in the asset returns. The return to asset n is represented by the random variable Z_n for $n = 1, 2, \ldots, \infty$. In general, these asset returns Z_n are determined by a combination of macroeconomic or economy-wide and idiosyncratic shocks. There is a symmetry condition on the joint probability distribution of asset returns: although the assets are not necessarily perfect substitutes, they would make similar contributions to a well-diversified portfolio.

As before there is a finite set of financial structures. Associated with each financial structure F_i is a random vector X_i, representing the contingencies in the financial structure. A claim is a function of the return to the underlying asset and the contingencies associated with the financial structure. Then if entrepreneur n issues a claim $f \in F_i$, the payoff to the claim is $f(Z_n, X_i)$.

The countable number of investors is divided into a finite set K of investor types. Initially, investors are ignorant of their type, that is, they are ex ante identical. They have a common prior distribution over types denoted by v. Types are assumed to be independently distributed, so the law of large numbers ensures that the cross-sectional distribution of types is almost surely equal to v. Investors' preferences are represented by a concave and strictly increasing von Neumann–Morgenstern utility function. Each investor receives an income of $Y_0 > 0$ units of the consumption good at date 1. At the second date, an investor of type k receives a random income Y_k.

Investors acquire information about their types by purchasing an information structure. There is a finite set of information structures $\mathscr{H} = \{H_j : j \in J\}$. Each information structure H_j is a partition of the set of types K. The cost of purchasing H_j is denoted by C_j. Without loss of generality, we can assume that each investor purchases at most one information structure. By a suitable relabeling, each combination of structures can be treated as an information structure in its own right. With this convention, there will exist a null structure that gives no information and a maximal structure that is finer than every other structure.

An equilibrium of the model is a fairly straightforward adaptation of the equilibrium concept introduced in section 4.2. We define equilibrium informally in the context of an extended example presented in the next section.

An Example

To illustrate the general framework, consider the following example. The random variables $\{Z_n\}$ are i.i.d., taking the values 0 and 1 with equal probability. There are two financial structures. One is the trivial financial structure $F_0 = \{f\}$ consisting of unlevered equity. The second is slightly more complex. It consists of two claims $F_1 = \{f_A, f_B\}$. There is a contingency X taking the values A and B with probability $1/2$. The claims are defined by putting

$$f_A(Z_n, X) = \begin{cases} Z_n & \text{if } X = B \\ 0 & \text{otherwise} \end{cases},$$

and $f_B(Z_n, X) = Z_n - f_A(Z_n, X)$. The two claims split the return to the underlying asset according to the value of X, giving the entire return to one

claim or the other. To simplify the story it is assumed that the costs
associated with both structures are zero.

There are two types of investors, indexed by $k = A, B$. Investors' incomes are correlated with the contingency X:

$$Y_A = \begin{cases} 1 & \text{if } X = A \\ 0 & \text{otherwise} \end{cases},$$

and $Y_B = 1 - Y_A$. The utility function is assumed to be quadratic over the
relevant range:

$$U(c_1, c_2) = c_1 + ac_2 - \frac{b}{2}(c_2)^2, \text{ (with } a > 2b > 0).$$

There are two information structures. The trivial information structure
$H_0 = \{\{A, B\}\}$ gives no information. The other, $H_1 = \{\{A\}, \{B\}\}$ reveals
an investor's true type. The costs of choosing H_0 and H_1 are zero and
$C > 0$, respectively. Each investor has a prior probability of 1/2 of
belonging to either type.

Coordination Failure

Using this example, we can demonstrate the possibility of coordination
failure. We can interpret the example as an illustration of the idea that
there may be too much "standardization" or that the market may choose
the wrong standard. The intuitive argument is simple. Consider an equilibrium in which all firms are issuing standard securities. Suppose that a
single firm wants to issue a "nonstandard" security. Without further information, investors will not be willing to pay a price that will induce the
deviant firm to issue the security. The question then is whether it is worthwhile for the investors to become informed. It may not be. If an investor
makes a large investment in the new security, she is taking on a large
amount of the idiosyncratic risk associated with that particular firm. On
the other hand, if she buys a small amount of the new security, her surplus
from the transaction will not compensate her for the cost of becoming
informed. Thus, she may not wish to become informed. As a result, the
price of the security remains low, and the firm, anticipating this, decides
not to issue the nonstandard security. Thus, only standard securities are
issued in equilibrium.

Another story can be told, however. Suppose that a large number of
firms decided to issue the nonstandard securities. Then it may be worth-

while for the investors to become informed. They could avoid the idiosyncratic risk attached to individual firms by diversifying and at the same time recoup the cost of becoming informed by purchasing a large number of the new securities. Then the price of the nonstandard securities will be higher, and the firms will find it worthwhile to issue them. We have found a second equilibrium in which all firms issue the nonstandard securities, that is, the nonstandard securities become the standard ones.

An Efficient Equilibrium

There is a large number of agents, and no short sales are allowed, so it is appropriate to assume that they are all price-takers. Given the prices for all claims, the decision of the firms is simply to choose the financial structure that maximizes the net market value of the firm. The investors have a slightly more complex decision problem. First, an investor has to choose an information structure. Next, having chosen the information structure, she must decide on a portfolio of claims to hold, conditional on the information set that she observes. (The investor should be thought of as choosing a portfolio for each information set that can result from her choice of information structure.) These choices maximize the investor's expected utility subject to her budget constraint. The budget constraint requires the investor to balance her budget across all the information sets following from a given information structure. It allows the investor to insure against the outcome of the information process. With this definition of equilibrium, we can use the standard definition of constrained efficiency. Demand and supply for each type of claim are required to balance in equilibrium.

Attention is restricted to symmetric equilibria in the usual way. The behavior of firms and investors is represented by the respective cross-sectional distributions of their choices. Claims of the same type, that is, having the same payoff function and coming from the same financial structure, are priced in the same way. Moreover, these claims are traded on the same market, even though they are not perfect substitutes because of their idiosyncratic risk.

In what follows, an entrepreneur is said to *innovate* if she chooses the more complex financial structure F_1. Similarly, an investor is said to become *informed* if she chooses the information structure H_1. We begin by describing a "good" equilibrium in which all firms innovate and all investors become informed.

We assume that Y_0 is sufficiently large so that consumption is always positive at the first date. Other constraints on parameters will be added as the analysis proceeds.

Suppose that all investors become informed and all entrepreneurs (except one) innovate. Investors of type A buy only claims of type A and investors of type B buy only claims of type B. Since there is an equal proportion of investors of each type, markets clear if each investor buys two units of the preferred claim. For example, an investor of type A holds a (diversified) portfolio of two units of claim A which pays 1 when $X = B$ and 0 when $X = A$. The investor's income Y_A is 1 when $X = A$ and 0 when $X = B$, that is, it is perfectly negatively correlated with the portfolio return. Holding this portfolio, each investor will achieve a constant level of consumption, equal to one unit, in each state.

Let p_A and p_B denote the prices of the claims A and B, respectively. Put $p_A = p_B = \frac{1}{4}u'(1)$, where $u'(c) \equiv a - bc$. Then it is easy to check that, at these prices, it is optimal for each investor to demand two units of the preferred claim if she becomes informed.

Letting $p = \frac{1}{2}u'(1)$ denote the price of a unit of unlevered equity, it is obvious that an entrepreneur is indifferent between the two financial structures. Then it is (weakly) optimal for entrepreneurs to innovate.

To show that we have an equilibrium, it only remains to prove that no investor would be better off choosing the trivial information structure. Suppose that an investor remained uninformed and purchased d units of equity. A (diversified) unit of equity pays 1/2 almost surely, so the investor's expected utility is $Y_0 - pd + \frac{1}{2}u(\frac{1}{2}d) + \frac{1}{2}u(1 + \frac{1}{2}d)$. The first-order condition for a maximum is $\frac{1}{4}(u'(\frac{1}{2}d) + u'(1 + \frac{1}{2}d)) = p = \frac{1}{2}u'(1)$. Using the linearity of marginal utility one can solve this equation to find that $d = 1$. (At this point one should check the first-order conditions to make sure that the investor does not want to hold any of claims A and B.) Since $d = 1$, the uninformed investor pays the same amount for her portfolio as the informed investor does for hers. Thus, the difference in expected utility is accounted for by the cost of information and the difference in second-period consumption. The investor will strictly prefer to be informed if and only if

$$\frac{1}{2}u\left(\frac{1}{2}\right) + \frac{1}{2}u\left(\frac{3}{2}\right) < u(1) - C. \tag{4.31}$$

This inequality will be assumed to hold.

This equilibrium is constrained efficient in the usual sense, that is, a planner using the same transactions technology could not improve on the allocation for everyone. This result is not trivial, even in the context of an example. A general argument is given in chapter 10.

It turns out that there is always an equilibrium of this type in the general model. This result can be stated as follows:

THEOREM 7.1   For any economy $\mathscr{E}$ satisfying the maintained assumptions, there exists a constrained efficient equilibrium.

If information were free, then every equilibrium would be constrained efficient. This shows that information costs are the source of any inefficiency.

THEOREM 7.2   Suppose that $\mathscr{E}$ is an economy satisfying the maintained assumptions. If $C_j = 0$ for every j in J, then any equilibrium of $\mathscr{E}$ is constrained efficient.

The proofs of theorems 7.1 and 7.2 are given in chapter 10.

An Inefficient Equilibrium

Suppose that no investor becomes informed and no entrepreneur (except one) innovates. The price system is assumed to be the same as in the full innovation equilibrium, that is, $p_A = p_B = p/2 = u'(1)/4$. At these prices, entrepreneurs are obviously indifferent between the two financial structures. Also, by the argument given above, an uninformed investor will choose to hold one unit of unlevered equity and none of the other claims. This implies that markets clear. To show that this is an equilibrium, then, it is necessary and sufficient to show that an investor does not want to become informed.

Suppose that the investor who becomes informed discovers she is of type A (the other case is exactly symmetrical). She chooses a portfolio (d, d_A, d_B), where d is the amount of unlevered equity and d_A and d_B are the amounts of claims A and B, respectively. Recalling that the securities A and B are issued by a single entrepreneur, the expected utility associated with this portfolio is

$$Y_0 - pd - p_A d_A - p_B d_B + \frac{1}{4}\left(u\left(\frac{1}{2}d\right) + u\left(\frac{1}{2}d + d_A\right) + u\left(1 + \frac{1}{2}d\right) \right.$$
$$\left. + u\left(1 + \frac{1}{2}d + d_B\right)\right).$$

The necessary and sufficient conditions for an optimum are

$$\frac{1}{4}\left(u'\left(\frac{1}{2}d\right) + u'\left(\frac{1}{2}d + d_A\right) + u'\left(1 + \frac{1}{2}d\right) + u'\left(1 + \frac{1}{2}d + d_B\right)\right)\frac{1}{2} \leq p,$$

$$\frac{1}{4}u'\left(\frac{1}{2}d + d_A\right) \leq p_A,$$

$$\frac{1}{4}u'\left(\frac{1}{2}d + 1 + d_B\right) \leq p_B,$$

together with the usual complementary slackness conditions. Using the linearity of marginal utility, these conditions can be solved to yield the solution $d = d_A = 2/3$ and $d_B = 0$. Expected utility is easily calculated to be

$$Y_0 - p - C + \frac{1}{4}\left(u\left(\frac{1}{3}\right) + u(1) + 2u\left(\frac{4}{3}\right)\right).$$

Note that the informed investor's portfolio costs exactly as much as the uninformed investor's portfolio. Thus, an investor will strictly prefer to be uninformed if and only if

$$\frac{1}{4}\left(u\left(\frac{1}{3}\right) + u(1) + 2u\left(\frac{4}{3}\right)\right) - C < \frac{1}{2}\left(u\left(\frac{1}{2}\right) + u\left(\frac{3}{2}\right)\right). \tag{4.32}$$

Thus there exists an equilibrium with no innovation ($\alpha_1 = 0$) if condition 4.32 is satisfied.

Since u is strictly concave,

$$u(1) > \frac{1}{2}\left(u\left(\frac{1}{2}\right) + u\left(\frac{3}{2}\right)\right)$$

and

$$u(1) > \frac{1}{4}\left(u\left(\frac{1}{3}\right) + u(1) + 2u\left(\frac{4}{3}\right)\right).$$

Then it is clear by inspection that there exists a value of C that simultaneously satisfies inequalities 4.31 and 4.32. This completes the demonstration that the economy has two equilibria. By construction, the full innovation equilibrium dominates the no-innovation equilibrium. In fact, these equilibria are Pareto-ranked ex post, that is, after agents know their types.

THEOREM 7.3   There exists an economy, satisfying the maintained assumptions, that has two, Pareto-ranked equilibria.

The coordination problems associated with gathering new information about securities is just one of many that are associated with asymmetric information. Some of the issues that asymmetric information raises are discussed at greater length in the next chapter.

Notes

1. This argument assumes that the costs of bankruptcy are proportional so that the greater the shortfall the greater the cost. Fixed costs of bankruptcy would cause a discontinuity, which would create technical complications.

2. Although the direct utility function is strictly concave, the indirect utility function will not be, in general, because the securities are not linearly independent. In the example above, $f_0 = f_1 + f_2$, so a portfolio $d = (1, 0, 0)$ consisting of only the first security will yield the same future utility as a portfolio $d' = (0, 1, 1)$ including only the second and third. Any convex combination of d and d' will be indifferent to the investor.

3. Because there is a countable number of firms, the cross-sectional distribution is not well defined for an arbitrary allocation of financial structures to firms unless we adopt some conventions. First of all, we assume a fixed ordering of firms $j = 1, 2, \ldots, \infty$. Second, fix an allocation of financial structures to firms, say, $\{i_j\}_{j=1}^{\infty}$, where i_j is the choice of firm j. Then for any subset $j = 1, \ldots, N$ and any financial structure F_i we can define α_i^N to be the proportion of firms choosing financial structure i:

$$\alpha_i^N = \#\{j \le N | i_j = i\}/N.$$

Finally, we say that α_i is the proportion of firms choosing financial structure F_i if and only if $\alpha_i = \lim_{n \to \infty} \alpha_i^N$. In what follows we only need to know the cross-sectional distribution, so the loss of information in not specifying the allocation $\{i_j\}$ is immaterial.

4. As long as Ω is finite, $\mathscr{F}$ is a product of compact intervals and hence compact in the product topology. If Ω is a compact metric space, and $\mathscr{F}$ consists of measurable functions, then $\mathscr{F}$ will be a compact set if endowed with the weak topology.

5. The problem of choosing a fee is similar to the problem of choosing optimal commodity taxation, and the issue of who bears the fee is related to the issue of tax incidence. See Atkinson and Stiglitz (1980) for an analysis of optimal commodity taxation and tax incidence.

6. In order to satisfactorily deal with the problem of setting transaction fees it is necessary to look at an integer programming problem since investors are restricted to trading whole units of contracts on the exchange. If the exchange bears any transaction costs to trading larger numbers of contracts, the exchange will not want face values to be too low. On the other hand, small face values will be more convenient to investors. We are grateful to Matt Jackson for pointing this out.

7. Michie (1987), p. 54.

8. The discussion in the remainder of this section draws heavily on Blanchard (1990).

9. Superscripts denoting timing are not included where the context makes this clear.

10. The interest on an OID bond is represented by the discount, that is, the difference between the face value of the bond and its issue price. For tax purposes, this amount was

amortized over the life of the bond using a straight-line formula. Since the formula ignored compounding, it allowed interest to be deducted from income faster than it was implicitly being paid, thus yielding an enormous profit to the issuer. See Finnerty (1988) for details and further references.

11. Banks would buy bonds and then sell the income stream derived from the coupons separately from the principal amount that would be paid at maturity.

12. Investors are usually assumed to eliminate the purely idiosyncratic or "residual" risk associated with any security through diversification. Consequently, the price of the security does not reflect the presence of such risk. With setup costs, investors require an additional incentive to trade the securities, and this takes the form of a reward for bearing residual risk.

5 Other Approaches and Future Research

As the historical account in Chapter 2 indicates, financial innovation has many aspects. We have focused on risk sharing. Even within this narrow focus, many issues have not been addressed. For example, the models we have developed have mostly assumed a short time horizon. When extended to more than one or two periods, the analysis may change significantly. A more important limitation of our treatment, however, is that risk sharing is only one motivation for financial innovation. Other important factors include reduction of transaction costs, corporate control, and information. In this chapter we briefly consider some alternative theories of financial innovation. A number of them are pursued at greater length in chapter 11, which contains a survey of recent contributions to the theory of security design.

5.1 Other Risk-Sharing Issues

We have considered financial innovation as a means of improving risk sharing. We have made progress in terms of developing a basic framework, but many questions have not been addressed. We start with a discussion of some of the remaining issues.

Dynamics

Most of the models we have considered have one or two time periods. Many interesting questions involving dynamics require a richer environment. Hart and Moore (1989) analyze a situation in which an entrepreneur wishes to raise funds to undertake a project when contracting possibilities are incomplete. Both the entrepreneur and the outside investor can observe the project payoffs at each date. Third parties, such as the courts, cannot observe them, so payoffs cannot be contracted on. The focus of Hart and Moore's analysis is the problem of providing an incentive for the entrepreneur to repay the borrowed funds. Among other things, it is shown that debt is an optimal contract and that incentives to repay are provided by the ability of the creditor to seize the entrepreneur's assets. The relationship between incentives to pay, risk sharing, and security design in other situations is an important topic for future research.

One of the important distinguishing features of actual securities is whether their payoffs are contractually fixed or are at the discretion of the board of directors. Understanding why one arrangement or the other is chosen should help to provide an understanding of security design and the way in which risk is shared in practice. At one extreme is common stock. Dividends are not guaranteed in advance but instead are left to the discretion of the board of directors. At the other extreme is debt, where interest payments are fixed. If the interest is not paid, the firm is in default, and the bondholders can force the firm into bankruptcy. Although not fully guaranteed, the payments are guaranteed to the fullest extent possible. An intermediate case is preferred stock, where the payment is fixed but is made at the discretion of the board of directors. The main restriction which ensures that payments are actually made is the requirement that no dividends can be paid on common stock until the cumulative backlog on preferred stock has been paid. Preferred stockholders cannot force bankruptcy if a dividend is omitted, nor can they replace the board of directors.

The underlying reasons for these differences between equity, debt, and preferred stock cannot readily be understood in a static framework. In a two-period model, the firm is liquidated at the last date, and the resulting cash is distributed. It is easy to identify the profits of the firm, and there is no role for discretion by a board of directors elected by shareholders; there are no interesting trade-offs. In multiperiod models there may be more scope for understanding this, why dividends are left to the directors' discretion, because of the effect current actions have on the beliefs of investors. In addition, account must be taken not just of the immediate clientele, but also of the future clienteles whose characteristics are as yet unknown. Allowing discretion by a representative group of shareholders may provide the flexibility to adapt the securities to these future clienteles.

Another important issue that cannot be addressed in a static framework is the role of dynamic trading strategies in completing markets. Harrison and Kreps (1978) and Duffie and Huang (1985) have shown that in frictionless continuous time models, trading a few securities can be equivalent to having a complete set of Arrow-Debreu state-contingent securities. If there are transaction costs of trading, then markets will usually not be dynamically complete. The principles of security design in this type of situation and its relationship to security design in terms of the models developed in chapter 4 is an important issue for future research. The combination of continuous-time techniques with other imperfections such as liquidation costs is another important area of research. Anderson and Sundaresan (1993) have combined the techniques of continuous-time finance with bargaining theory to develop techniques for valuing and designing debt contracts. This approach looks very promising in terms of providing practical techniques of security design.

Intermediaries and Risk Sharing

In the United States and United Kingdom many companies' securities are listed on the stock market. In contrast, in France and Germany (and until recently Japan) relatively few companies are listed; instead most securities are held by banks. These different institutional structures imply that risk may be spread across the population in different ways. In the stock-market–based systems of the United States and United Kingdom, information about future economic prospects is rapidly incorporated into stock prices. As a result, holders of securities bear the risk directly; a fall in values means that those planning to consume in the short run bear considerable consumption risk. In contrast, in bank-based systems the effects of new information on the value of securities are not public. The depositors in banks, who are the indirect holders of the securities, do not suffer any immediate loss or gain when there is a change in value; those planning to consume in the short run bear very little risk. Instead the interest rate paid on bank deposits is adjusted to deal with the change in prospects, and the risk is spread over many groups. The distribution of risks with the two structures is therefore very different. One important research problem is to identify the advantages and disadvantages of these two systems in terms of the sharing of risk.

A second task is to identify conditions under which agents have the correct incentives to provide the socially optimal system. For example, it may be that a bank-based system of sharing risk, of the type that exists in France and Germany, is unable to survive in a competitive environment where every type of financial innovation is allowed. If adverse shocks are met by cuts in the interest rate paid on deposits, as opposed to changes in the capitalized value of securities, the average return paid out after a drop in value may be lower than the yield of the underlying portfolio. This creates an arbitrage opportunity. Mutual funds consisting of securities similar to those held by the banks can be set up. If depositors are free to withdraw their money and invest directly in the funds, bank-based risk sharing of the type described will not be feasible. Thus a competitive financial system with unlimited financial innovation may not allow ex ante optimal risk sharing, and restrictions on financial innovation may be desirable. This issue is particularly important in light of the current proposals to integrate the European Community's financial markets. Depositors in French and German banks may have an incentive to withdraw their deposits after a fall in security values and invest in British financial markets.

Another example where countries' risk-sharing systems differ is the mortgage market. In the United States, mortgages are provided by a wide range of intermediaries, and many different types of contracts, including fixed rate and variable rate mortgages, are available. By contrast, in the United Kingdom, mortgages are primarily provided by building societies and banks, and only variable rate contracts are available. Again, an important issue is which type of system allows optimal risk sharing and whether financial innovation needs to be regulated in order for the optimal system to be provided.

Hedging Personal Risks

Most of the discussion in the previous sections has been concerned with firm or production risks, but much of the risk that individuals bear is personal. Some of these risks, such as the chance of becoming unemployed, are related to firm risk, while others such as health risk are not. Insurance companies provide opportunities for sharing some of these risks, for example, by selling health insurance. However, other types of insurance, such as insurance against unemployment risk, are provided by governments or are not provided at all. In many cases the market failure that has led to government provision or to nonprovision is clear. For example, there are moral hazards that make the private provision of unemployment insurance infeasible and make the government the only viable provider. However, there are examples of risks where this is not the case.

Most individual's s primary asset is their human capital. This is subject to significant fluctuations in value as industries grow and decline. With the end of the cold war the defense industry is in decline. Those people who have nontransferable skills have suffered a large uninsured capital loss. In this case there appear to be very few moral hazards that rule out the existence of insurance markets. One way of providing insurance would be to have futures or options contracts based on output in a particular industry. This security would allow people to hedge their human capital risk. As yet such securities do not, of course, exist. They could perhaps be synthesized by, for example, shorting a diversified portfolio of stocks in an industry. The transaction costs of doing this are large, however. Another example of a personal asset that is difficult to hedge is housing. Shiller (1992) has suggested a design for a futures market that would allow such risks to be shared, but as yet no such markets exist. Financial innovation that allows hedging of personal risks as opposed to corporate risks may become important in the future.

Risk sharing is only one of many reasons for financial innovation. In the remaining sections we consider some of the other motivations for innovation that appear to be important.

5.2   Transaction Costs

The traditional theory of financial intermediation argues that intermediaries arise to minimize transaction costs (see, e.g., Gurley and Shaw 1960). Merton (1989) and Ross (1989) have made a similar argument for financial innovation. In this view the prime purpose of many of the innovations that have been observed such as options and futures markets is to reduce transaction costs rather than to improve risk-sharing possibilities. For example, options and futures markets greatly reduce the transaction costs of hedging. In most such cases, however, the motivation for trade is risk sharing; reducing transaction costs simply facilitates risk sharing. In this section we briefly review the transaction cost approach to financial innovation.

Trading Costs

Hakansson (1979) has pointed out that standard options-pricing theory contains a paradox. In order to price the options, it is assumed that markets are effectively complete through dynamic trading strategies and that the options are redundant assets. But in this case there is no reason for the options to exist since there are full risk-sharing opportunities without them.

Merton (1989) has suggested a solution to this dilemma. He argues that individuals may face high transaction costs, but that intermediaries and derivative markets will arise to take advantage of these market imperfections. Large intermediaries will have low transaction costs because of their size. For them markets will be effectively complete because they can synthesize securities using dynamic trading strategies. They can issue these securities at low cost and provide individuals with their desired consumption patterns. This would be very expensive if individuals were to do it themselves, and intermediaries can make a profit from the cost differential. Similarly, derivative securities markets may arise to allow individuals, who do not have direct access to equivalent dynamic trading strategies, to trade cheaply. The use of options-pricing theory and more generally contingent claims analysis is valid because of the presence of the institutional traders with low transaction costs. In this view financial innovation gives wider access to risk-sharing possibilities and reduces transaction costs.

Marketing Costs

Ross (1989) has emphasized the interaction of marketing costs with agency problems between investors and intermediaries as a cause of financial innovation. He distinguishes between "high-grade" and "low-grade" investments and between transparent, translucent, and opaque financial intermediaries. High-grade investments are those like publicly traded equity and bonds whose characteristics are well known; low-grade investments are those like loans to firms and individuals where the characteristics are unique. Transparent intermediaries are those like mutual funds that primarily make high-grade investments. Translucent intermediaries are those like pension funds that invest primarily in high-grade securities but have a few low-grade investments. Opaque intermediaries are those like S&L's and insurance companies that have a large proportion of low-grade investments and a small proportion of high-grade investments.

In transparent intermediaries, agency problems are relatively trivial. At the other end of the spectrum, agency problems can be severe in opaque intermediaries. In order to ensure they are able to meet their commitments, some form of government regulation or private monitoring, both of which put a lower bound on the proportion of low-grade assets, is desirable. As a result of this constraint, opaque intermediaries may need to sell off low-grade assets from time to time.

Since low-grade assets cannot be easily assessed, they must be carefully marketed. This is primarily the job of investment banks. They have networks of investors with whom they deal regularly and who can potentially absorb the low-grade investments. Part of the cost of marketing to these networks is fixed, and there are learning effects. Both of these factors imply the average cost of marketing securities will decline as scale increases, so it is efficient to bundle them into large packages. This leads to innovation, as the investment bank will develop a new security to package the low-grade securities.

The importance of marketing costs has also been recognized by a number of other authors. Madan and Soubra (1991) combine Ross's approach with that of section 4.2 by focusing on the transaction costs of marketing securities. They assume that widening the appeal of a security reduces the marketing costs. In this framework it is shown that standard securities such as debt, equity, and warrants can be optimal. They also suggest techniques which can be applied to security design in practice.

Pesendorfer (1991) has also considered financial innovation in a model that is related to Ross (1989). He assumes there are standard securities that can be traded with zero costs. Intermediaries purchase these and repackage them to create intermediated securities. These need to be marketed, and marketing is costly. As we assumed in section 4.2, there are short sale constraints for intermediated securities; without these, short selling would be equivalent to issuing securities and avoiding marketing costs.

Three main results are obtained. It is shown that innovation can improve agents' welfare even if markets are as complete as before. This is because innovation can allow the costs of marketing to be reduced. The second result is that the level of innovation is not necessarily constrained efficient. This is because no intermediary has access to all standard security markets, so there is no mechanism to coordinate innovations. As a result it is possible to get stuck at equilibri· where there is too little innovation. If two intermediaries were to innovate simultaneously in these equilibria, everybody could be better off because of complementarities provided by the innovation. Since there is no mechanism to coordinate them and individually it is not worthwhile for either of them to do it, they do not innovate. The final result concerns the role of innovation in eliminating indeterminacy. Balasko and Cass (1989) and Geanakoplos and Mas-Colell (1989), among others, have shown that if securities pay off in nominal units of account and markets are incomplete, then there is an indeterminacy in real equilibrium allocations. The reason is that payoffs to securities are specified in nominal terms, so changing the numeraire changes the real value of the securities and the space spanned by their payoffs. When markets are complete this cannot happen, since changing the numeraire does not change the span of the set of securities. Pesendorfer (1991) shows that as marketing costs tend to zero, the markets become complete, and any real indeterminacy is eliminated.

Marketing costs are clearly an important aspect of new securities and products. The work that has been done to date captures various aspects of these costs. However, many important aspects remain unaddressed. For example, investment banks maintain costly networks to market securities. What is the impact of these on the process of financial innovation? Are there network externalities as in the industrial organization literature discussed in chapter 3 or not?

5.3 Corporate Control

When markets are complete, it is well known that investors agree unanimously on the optimal policy of a firm. However, when markets are incomplete or investors have divergent views, this may no longer be the case, and the issue of control becomes important. In the United States the control of a solvent corporation is usually determined by majority voting with each share of common stock being allocated one vote. Owners of debt securities do not have control rights unless the firm goes bankrupt. In Europe control rights are often allocated differently, with some classes of shares having multiple votes and others having one or none. One of the most important issues in financial innovation is to develop an understanding of the different mechanisms for determining corporate control.

Allocation of Control

There is a large literature on the allocation of control rights. One branch considers the allocation of control among different securityholders. Aghion and Bolton (1992) consider an entrepreneur who has insufficient resources to finance a project she wishes to undertake and must therefore borrow from outside investors. These outside investors are only interested in the monetary profits they receive, whereas the entrepreneur is concerned about the effort required to produce the profits as well as the money she receives. The important feature of Aghion and Bolton's model is that contracting possibilities are incomplete so that the conflict of interests between the entrepreneur and the outside investors cannot be solved by a contract specifying entrepreneurial effort and reward. Instead, an efficient allocation of resources is achieved by allocating control using debt and the institution of bankruptcy. This ensures that when earnings, and hence future prospects, are good, the entrepreneur decides whether or not the profits from expansion are worth the effort she must supply. However, when earnings and future prospects are bad, the outside investors make the liquidation decision and frustrate the entrepreneur's attempt to expand.

Zender (1991) also develops a model based on the allocation of control rights where the use of debt and equity is optimal. The project to be undertaken requires two investors to provide the financing; individually, neither has sufficient resources. In order for there to be the correct incentives to make the proper decisions efficiently, only one of the investors can be assigned control. One of the investors is therefore given equity and is made the residual claimant, while the other receives debt and does not obtain control unless the decisions are improperly made and the firm goes bankrupt.

Allocation of Voting Rights

The second branch of the literature has considered the question of control in terms of the way in which voting rights should be allocated. The issue that has been of particular concern is to identify the circumstances where the use of one vote per share and majority voting are optimal.

Grossman and Hart's (1988) starting point is the fact that when securities are widely held there is a free rider problem; individual shareholders do not have an incentive to expend sufficient resources to monitor management. The situation where voting rights matter most is when outside "rivals" monitor the "incumbent management" and make a takeover bid. Grossman and Hart consider the corporate charter an entrepreneur should adopt to maximize the initial value of the firm. The important determinant of the allocation of voting rights in their model is the distribution of the private benefits of control between the rival and incumbent management. If there is an asymmetry, so that one group has much larger benefits than the other, then one share one vote is optimal because it maximizes the amount that has to be paid to acquire control; concentrating votes makes it cheaper to acquire control because fewer shares have to be bought. If there are symmetric private benefits of control, then concentrating votes is optimal since it makes rivals and incumbents compete and pay for the private benefits of control. Grossman and Hart argue that the asymmetric case is relevant because the extent to which incumbent managers can extract private benefits is limited by the law, and they suggest that this is why one share one vote is so prevalent.

Harris and Raviv (1988) consider a model that is closely related to Grossman and Hart's. However, they distinguish between privately optimal arrangements, where the corporate charter is chosen to maximize the initial value of the firm, as in Grossman and Hart, and the socially optimal arrangement, which takes into account the private benefits accruing to rival and incumbent management teams. Also, they assume each voter can be pivotal. It is shown that one share one vote majority rule is socially optimal because it ensures that the team that generates the greatest total amount gains control; any deviation gives an advantage to the incumbent or rival that may allow her to gain control, even though she would generate a lower total amount. In contrast to Grossman and Hart, they focus on the case where both rivals and incumbents have private benefits of control. They therefore argue that issuing two sets of securities, one with all the voting rights and one with all the dividends, is privately optimal because it makes them compete for the right to extract the private benefits. This suggests an important empirical issue, namely, the extent to which private benefits differ between incumbents and rivals.

Blair, Golbe, and Gerard (1989) consider a model similar to that of Harris and Raviv (1988) except that they assume the rival and incumbent bid simultaneously, whereas Harris and Raviv assume they bid sequentially. This difference in assumptions leads to an important difference in results. In contrast to Harris and Raviv (1988), they find that in the absence of taxes, one share one vote majority rule and extreme securities that unbundle voting and cash flows are equivalent, and both lead to social optimality. The main concern of Blair, Golbe, and Gerard is to consider the effect of capital gains taxes on the allocation of voting rights and cash flows. If there are capital gains taxes, then welfare is improved if extreme securities are used. This is because a lock-in effect means capital gains taxes may prevent a superior rival from winning if there is one share one vote majority rule; tax liabilities may be higher when the rival wins than when the incumbent wins. Allowing separate trading of votes alleviates this effect.

Harris and Raviv (1989) consider the allocation of voting rights and cash flows when the firm is not restricted to issuing equity using a model similar to that of Grossman and Hart (1988). They focus on private optimality and assume there are asymmetric private benefits of control. The task of the entrepreneur who owns the firm initially is to design securities that prevent an incumbent management with private benefits from maintaining control when a superior rival appears. This means that the cost of resisting takeovers must be maximized. As in the papers focusing only on equity, one share one vote among voting securities is an important component of optimal design since it means that control cannot be acquired cheaply by the party with private benefits. In addition, nonvoting risky securities should not be sold to outside investors; if a nonvoting security is sold to outside investors it should be risk-free debt. The reason is that these two measures maximize the cost of obtaining control and so tend to favor the superior rival.

The results in the literature on voting rights and control appear to depend on whether there are symmetric or asymmetric private benefits of control. More important, they do not appear to explain satisfactorily differences in corporate control mechanisms in Europe, Japan, and the United States. The development of models that can explain international differences in methods of allocating control would be an important contribution to this area.

The allocation of voting rights in order to maximize the cost of resisting takeovers is not the only explanation of one share one vote. Bagwell and Judd (1989) instead consider the optimality of majority rule where control is concerned with payout and investment decisions. Initially, all investors are identical, corporate charters are designed, and securities are issued to finance firms' investments. Investors discover whether they prefer early or late consumption and how risk averse they are. Then firms decide on how much to pay out and whether to invest in risky or safe projects. In an ideal world, investors can acquire the shares of firms that adopt their preferred policies. In this case majority rule is optimal since, within firms, shareholders are homogeneous. The problem is that if investors face high costs of reallocating their portfolios, such as capital gains taxes that produce lock-in effects, the reallocation of investors will not be optimal. In this case firms' shareholders are not homogeneous, and majority rule is no longer optimal. Instead, when the costs of reallocation are high, corporate charters should specify a utilitarian form of objective function where the weights assigned to each type correspond to their representation in the population.

Maug (1992) considers the important issue of the role of outside boards of directors. In his model, investment in firm-specific human capital by managers is necessary for the firm to be productive, and the level of skill that managers attain cannot be contracted on. The use of debt and liquidation when bankruptcy occurs has the drawback that managers' incentives to invest in firm-specific human capital are reduced because bankruptcy may occur in states where it is suboptimal. Maug shows that by introducing an outside board of directors it is possible to reduce this inefficiency.

Bagwell and Judd's and Maug's models illustrate that the allocation of voting rights and control may be important even when there is no prospect of takeover. They focus on two particular situations of this type, but there are many others. For example, when there are differences in beliefs about the effects of various policies the firm might adopt, the allocation of control by appropriate design of securities and corporate charters is important. The existing literature on corporate control illustrates the range of issues but has not yet provided robust answers to many of the questions addressed.

5.4   Information

Section 4.7 analyzed a coordination failure that arose because of the costs of learning about a new security. Information costs affect the design of securities in many ways. We consider some of these here.

Adverse Selection and Noncontingent Contracts

Standard contract theory suggests that optimal contracts should be contingent on all relevant information which in most cases implies they will be extremely complex (see Hart and Holmstrom 1987). However, an important feature of many existing financial contracts is that they are not contingent on information which appears to be relevant. For example, standard debt contracts are not contingent on the firm's earnings. This appears to be inconsistent with optimal risk sharing, which requires that borrowers and lenders have equal marginal rates of substitution between states. Although there are forms of debt contract, such as income bonds, where payments are contingent on the earnings of the firm, they are rarely used. A number of papers have developed theories based on adverse selection in which noncontingent securities like standard debt are optimal.

Nachman and Noe (1990) consider a model where a firm issues a security to investors in order to undertake an investment which generates an uncertain output. The probability distribution of outputs depends on whether the firm is good or bad. The firm knows its type, but investors do not. A good firm's output stochastically dominates that of a bad firm. It is assumed that the security is monotonic in the sense that the payment to investors is nondecreasing in the firm's earnings. A good firm would like to signal its type by reducing the payment it makes when output is high and increasing it when output is low. Firms pool at a debt contract which is stable in a sense related to the Cho and Kreps (1987) Intuitive Criterion. A good firm cannot separate itself by increasing payments in low-output states, since this would violate feasibility, or by reducing payments in the high-output states, since this would violate monotonicity. The equilibrium contract is thus noncontingent, in the sense that the payment is equal to the lesser of a constant or total earnings.

In a related paper De and Kale (1993) assume that a firm can use some combination of two types of contract, fixed-periodic-obligation debt (FD) and no-periodic-obligation debt (ND). Standard debt is an example of an FD security, and income bonds are an example of an ND security. The firm issues securities that are priced by the market. Investors infer that firms that offer ND contracts are more likely to be bad firms since they have a higher chance of benefiting from the low payments if earnings are low. The unique equilibrium that is stable in the sense of universal divinity (Banks and Sobel 1988) involves only FD being used by firms. As in Nachman and Noe's model, the restriction of contract forms to combinations of FD and ND prevents firms trying to signal their type.

Allen and Gale (1992) develop a model where adverse selection interacts with measurement distortion and leads to noncontingent securities being used. In practice, securities cannot be made contingent on "states of nature." Some type of measurement system, an accounting system, for example, is necessary to generate the variables such as earnings on which payoffs are contingent. These measurement systems can be distorted at some cost by firms if they have sufficient incentive to do so. It is argued that one case of interest is where the cost of distorting the measurement system is positively correlated with firm type, so good firms have a high cost of distortion and bad firms have a low cost. In this case, bad firms are more likely to offer securities such as income bonds, where payments are contingent on earnings, since the net benefits of distorting are greater for bad firms. The equilibrium in which firms offer a noncontingent contract is then universally divine; investors deduce that any firm offering a contingent contract is likely to be bad since they gain the most from the contingency.

Acquisition of Information

One of the determinants of a security's value is the amount of information that investors gather. This raises the possibility that securities will be designed to affect the extent to which information is acquired in order to maximize value. Boot and Thakor (1993) have considered a noisy rational expectations model of this type. A firm, which can have a high or low value, sells its securities to investors. The firm knows its own value, but investors do not unless they pay to become informed. There is a group of liquidity traders whose demand for securities is exogenously determined and random; this ensures that asset prices are noisy and do not fully reveal firm type. The investors who do not choose to become informed are the residual holders of the security. All traders are risk neutral. The informed traders cannot borrow or sell short; if they find out the firm has high value they invest all their wealth in it, and if it has low value they invest nothing in it. The price is determined by the residual holders who will only hold it if price is equal to the expected value of the stock conditional on the sum of the liquidity and informed traders' demands. In equilibrium, the profits of the informed are just sufficient to cover the cost of buying the information.

Good firms want there to be as many informed investors as possible because this creates a high demand for their securities and increases the amount the firms receive. By splitting its cash flow into a safe and a risky portion, that is, into debt and equity, a good firm provides better incentives for investors to become informed. The reason is that the fluctuations in price of the risky component are increased, and this raises the profits an informed investor earns. As a result more investors become informed, and the value of the firm is raised. Bad firms always find it worthwhile to mimic the good firms so they can receive the average value of the two. Thus in equilibrium all firms find it worthwhile to split.

One extension of the model is where the information informed investors receive does not perfectly signal firm type and there are many firms. In this case it is worthwhile to bundle the securities and then to split this portfolio into a safe and risky component. This allows the idiosyncratic risk associated with the signals to be eliminated and for the firms to receive more because people are better informed. This result is consistent with the fact that financial intermediaries such as collateralized mortgage obligations pool securities and then issue multiple claims against them.

Demange and Laroque (1992) also consider the relationship between private information and the design of securities in a noisy rational expectations model. Entrepreneurs who have a large stake in a single company will want to diversify their holdings. However, if they have privileged information, other investors will be reluctant to trade with them; in extreme cases, they will not be able to diversify at all. Demange and Laroque show that entrepreneurs can overcome this problem, to some extent, by designing the securities they sell so they are uncorrelated with their information. The optimal security design trades off insurance opportunities with speculative gains. The issue of whether having privileged information is beneficial to entrepreneurs is also addressed. When there are only a few highly risk-averse outside investors who condition their beliefs on prices, it is shown that the entrepreneur may be better off with privileged information; otherwise she will be worse off because of her inability to diversify.

The influence of information acquisition on securities prices is an important one. This suggests that models such as those of Boot and Thakor (1992) and Demange and Laroque (1992), in which this is the main determinant of security design, are likely to contribute significantly to our understanding of the motivating factors for financial innovation.

5.5 Conclusion

Traditional theories have taken the market structure and the financial securities traded in them as given. The theory of financial innovation attempts to endogenize market structure and explain the nature of the securities traded. The historical review in chapter 2 demonstrates that financial innovation has occurred for several thousand years and has accelerated considerably in recent decades. The dramatic changes in financial markets in the 1970s and 1980s suggest that theories need to account for financial innovation; it is not possible to ignore this even as a first approximation, as traditional theories have done. We have sketched some basic models that allow innovation to be incorporated at a fundamental level of analysis. These models are developed in the following chapters in more depth. As this section has illustrated, there exist many other approaches to modeling financial innovation. As yet, our understanding of financial innovation is at an early stage, and much work remains to be done.

References to Chapters 1–5

Abken, P. A. (1991). "Beyond Plain Vanilla: A Taxonomy of Swaps," Federal Reserve Bank of Atlanta, *Economic Review* (March/April) 12–29.

Aghion, P., and P. Bolton (1992). "An Incomplete Contracts Approach to Financial Contracting," *Review of Economic Studies* 59:473–494.

Alderson, M. J., K. C. Brown, and S. L. Lummer (1987). "Dutch Auction Rate Preferred Stock," *Financial Management* 16:68–73.

Allen, F., and D. Gale (1992). "Measurement Distortion and Missing Contingencies in Optimal Contracts," *Economic Theory* 2:1–26.

Anderson, R. W., and C. J. Harris (1986). "A Model of Innovation with Application to New Financial Products," *Oxford Economic Papers* 38:203–218.

Anderson, R. W., and S. Sundaresan (1993). "Design and Valuation of Debt Contracts," mimeo, Columbia University.

Arrow, K. (1962). "Economic Welfare and the Allocation of Resources for Inventions," in *The Rate and Direction of Inventive Activity*, edited by R. Nelson, Princeton: Princeton University Press.

Atkinson, A. B., and J. E. Stiglitz (1980). *Lectures on Public Economics*, New York: McGraw-Hill.

Bagwell, L., and K. L. Judd (1989). "Transaction Costs and Corporate Control," Working Paper 67, Kellogg Graduate School of Management, Northwestern University.

Balasko, Y., and D. Cass (1989). "The Structure of Financial Equilibrium with Exogenous Yields: I. Unrestricted Participation," *Econometrica* 57:135–162.

Banks, J., and J. Sobel (1988). "Equilibrium Selection in Signaling Games," *Econometrica* 55:647–662.

Barnea, A., R. Haugen, and L. Senbet (1985). *Agency Problems and Financial Contracting*, Englewood Cliffs, NJ: Prentice-Hall.

Barro, R. (1974). "Are Bonds Net Wealth?" *Journal of Political Economy* 87:1095–1118.

Baskin, J. B. (1988). "The Development of Corporate Financial Markets in Britain and the United States, 1600–1914: Overcoming Asymmetric Information," *Business History Review* 62:199–237.

Besen, S. M., and L. L. Johnson (1986). "Compatibility Standards, Competition and Innovation in the Broadcasting Industry," Report R-3453-NSF, Rand Corporation.

Besen, S. M., and G. Saloner (1987). "Compatibility Standards and the Market for Telecommunications Services," Working Paper E-87-15, Hoover Institution, Stanford.

Bessembinder, H. (1992). "Systematic Risk, Hedging Pressure, and Risk Premiums in Futures Markets," *Review of Financial Studies* 5:637–667.

Bester, H. (1985). "Screening vs. Rationing in Credit Markets with Imperfect Information," *American Economic Review* 57:850–855.

Bhattacharya, S., J. Glazer, and D. E. M. Sappington (1990). "Sharing Productive Knowledge in Internally Financed R&D Contests," *Journal of Industrial Economics* 39:187–208.

Black, D. G. (1986). "Success and Failure of Futures Contracts: Theory and Evidence," *Monograph Series in Finance and Economics*, No. 1986-1, Salomon Brothers Center for the Study of Financial Institutions, New York University.

Blair, D. H., D. L. Golbe, and J. M. Gerard (1989). "Unbundling the Voting Rights and Profit Claims of Common Shares," *Journal of Political Economy* 97:420–433.

Blanchard, O. J. (1990). "Comments on The Efficient Design of Public Debt by Douglas Gale," in *Public Debt Management: Theory and History*, edited by R. Dornbusch and M. Draghi, Cambridge: Cambridge University Press, 47-51.

Boot, A., and A. Thakor (1993). "Security Design," *Journal of Finance*, 48:1349-1378.

Chamley, C., and H. Polemarchakis (1984). "Asset Markets, General Equilibrium and the Neutrality of Money," *Review of Economic Studies* 51:129-138.

Chatfield, M. (1977). *A History of Accounting Thought*, revised edition, New York: Krieger.

Cho, I.-K., and D. Kreps (1987). "Signaling Games and Stable Equilibria," *Quarterly Journal of Economics* 102:179-222.

Conrad, J. (1989). "The Price of Option Introduction," *Journal of Finance* 44:487-498.

Cuny, C. J. (1993). "The Role of Liquidity in Futures Market Innovations," *Review of Financial Studies*, 6:57-78.

Dasgupta, P., and J. Stiglitz (1980). "Uncertainty, Industrial Structure, and the Speed of R&D," *Bell Journal of Economics* 11:1-28.

De, S., and J. Kale (1993). "Contingent Payments and Debt Contracts," *Financial Management*, 22:106-122.

DeAngelo, H., and E. M. Rice (1983). "Antitakeover Charter Amendments and Stockholder Wealth," *Journal of Financial Economics* 11:329-360.

Demange, G., and G. Laroque (1992). "Private Information and the Control of Securities," Document 92-22, DELTA.

Detemple, J., and P. Jorion (1988). "Option Listing and Stock Returns," First Boston Working Paper 89-13, Columbia University.

Detemple, J., and P. Jorion (1990). "Option Listing and Stock Returns: An Empirical Analysis," *Journal of Banking and Finance* 14:781-801.

Detemple, J., and L. Selden (1991). "A General Equilibrium Analysis of Option and Stock Market Interactions," *International Economic Review* 32:279-303.

Dewing, A. S. (1934). *A Study of Corporation Securities*, New York: Ronald Press.

Dewing, A. S. (1955). *The Financial Policy of Corporations*, 5th edition, New York: Ronald Press.

Duffie, D. (1989). *Futures Markets*, Englewood Cliffs, NJ: Prentice-Hall.

Duffie, D., and C. Huang (1985). "Implementing Arrow-Debreu Equilibria by Continuous Trading of Few Long-Lived Securities," *Econometrica* 53:1337-1356.

Duffie, D., and M. O. Jackson (1989). "Optimal Innovation of Futures Contracts," *Review of Financial Studies* 2:275-296.

Farrell, J., and G. Saloner (1985). "Standardization, Compatibility and Innovation," *Rand Journal of Economics* 16:70-83.

Felgram, S. (1987). "Interest Swaps: Risk and Prices," *New England Economics Review*, Federal Reserve Bank of Boston, December.

Figlewski, S., and G. Webb (1993). "Options, Short Sales, and Market Incompleteness," *Journal of Finance* 48:761-777.

Finnerty, J. D. (1988). "Financial Engineering in Corporate Finance: An Overview," *Financial Management* 17:14-33.

Finnerty, J. D. (1993). "An Overview of Corporate Securities Innovation," *Journal of Applied Corporate Finance* 4:23-39.

Fisher, L., I. E. Brick, and F. K. W. Ng (1983). "Tax Incentives and Financial Innovation: The Case of Zero-Coupon and Other Deep-Discount Corporate Bonds," *Financial Review* 18:292–305.

Fraser, D. R., and M. J. Alderson (1993). "Financial Innovations and Excesses Revisited: The Case of Auction Rate Preferred Stock," *Financial Management*, 22:61–75.

Fudenberg, D., R. Gilbert, J. Stiglitz and J. Tirole (1983). "Preemption, Leapfrogging, and Competition in Patent Races," *European Economic Review* 22:3–31.

Geanakoplos, J. and A. Mas-Colell (1989). "Real Indeterminacy with Financial Assets," *Journal of Economic Theory* 47:22–38.

Gehrig, T. (1992). "Natural Oligopoly in Intermediated Markets," mimeo, Institut für Volkswirtschaft, University of Basel.

Gilbert, R., and D. Newbery (1982). "Preemptive Patenting and the Persistence of Monopoly," *American Economic Review* 74:238–242.

Green, R. C. (1984). "Investment Incentives, Debt and Warrants," *Journal of Financial Economics* 13:115–136.

Grossman, S. J., and O. D. Hart (1988). "One Share/One Vote and the Market for Corporate Control," *Journal of Financial Economics* 20:175–202.

Grossman, S. J., and J. E. Stiglitz (1980). "On the impossibility of informationally Efficient Markets," *American Economic Review* 70:393–408.

Gurley, J., and E. Shaw (1960). *Money in a Theory of Finance*, Washington: Brookings.

Guthmann, H. G., and H. Dougall (1962). *Corporate Financial Policy*, 4th edition, Englewood Cliffs, NJ: Prentice-Hall.

Hakansson, N. H. (1979). "The Fantastic World of Finance: Progress and the Free Lunch," *Journal of Financial and Quantitative Analysis* 14:717–734.

Harris, C. J., and J. Vickers (1985). "Perfect Equilibrium in a Model of a Race," *Review of Economic Studies* 54:1–22.

Harris, M., and A. Raviv (1988). "Corporate Governance: Voting Rights and Majority Rule," *Journal of Financial Economics* 20:55–86.

Harris, M., and A. Raviv (1989). "The Design of Securities," *Journal of Financial Economics* 24:255–287.

Harrison, M., and D. Kreps (1978). "Speculative Investor Behavior in a Stock Market with Heterogeneous Expectations," *Quarterly Journal of Economics* 89:519–542.

Hart, O. D. (1979). "On Shareholder Unanimity in Large Stock Market Economies," *Econometrica* 47:1057–1084.

Hart, O. D., and B. Holmstrom (1987). "Theory of Contracts," in *Advances in Economic Theory*, edited by Truman Bewley, Econometric Society Monographs, Fifth World Congress, New York: Cambridge University Press.

Hart, O. D., and J. Moore (1989). "Default and Renegotiation: A Dynamic Model of Debt," Working Paper 89-069, Harvard Business School.

Hayes, S. L., and P. M. Hubbard (1990). *Investment Banking*, Boston: Harvard Business School Press.

Hirshleifer, D. (1988). "Residual Risk, Trading Costs and Commodity Futures Risk Premia," *Review of Financial Studies* 1:173–193.

Hirshleifer, J. (1971). "The Private and Social Value of Information and the Reward to Inventive Activity," *American Economic Review* 61:561–574.

Hull, J. (1991). *Introduction to Futures and Options Markets*, Englewood Cliffs, NJ: Prentice-Hall.

International Swap Dealers Association Market Survey (1992).

Jarrell. G. A., and A. B. Poulsen (1987). "Shark Repellents and Stock Prices: The Effects of Antitakeover Amendments since 1980," *Journal of Financial Economics* 19:127–168.

Jarrow, R, A., and M. O'Hara (1989). "Primes and Scores: An Essay on Market Imperfections," *Journal of Finance* 44:1263–1287.

Jensen, M. C., and W. H. Meckling (1976). "Theory of the Firm: Managerial Behavior, Agency Costs and Ownership Structure," *Journal of Financial Economics* 3:305–360.

Kamien, M. I., and N. L. Schwartz (1978). "Potential Rivalry, Monopoly Profits and the Pace of Inventive Activity," *Review of Economic Studies* 45:547–557.

Kanemasu, H., R. H. Litzenberger, and J. Rolfo (1986). "Financial Innovation in an Incomplete Market: An Empirical Study of Stripped Government Securities," Rodney L. White Center Working Paper 26-86, University of Pennsylvania.

Katz, M. (1986). "An Analysis of Cooperative Research and Development," *Rand Journal of Economics* 17:527–543.

Katz, M., and C. Shapiro (1985). "Network Externalities, Competition and Compatibility," *American Economic Review* 75:424–440.

Katz, M., and C. Shapiro (1986a). "Technology Adoption in the Presence of Network Externalities," *Journal of Political Economy* 94:822–841.

Katz, M., and C. Shapiro (1986b). "Product Compatibility Choice in a Market with Technological Progress," *Oxford Economic Papers* 38:146–165.

Kellenbenz, H. (1957). Introduction to *Confusion de Confusiones*, translated by H. Kellenbenz, No. 13 (1987), The Kress Library Series of Publications, The Kress Library of Business and Economics, Harvard University, Cambridge, MA.

Kim, W. S., and C. M. Young (1991). "The Effect of Traded Option Introduction on Shareholder Wealth," *Journal of Financial Research* 14:141–151.

Klemkosky, R. C., and T. S. Maness (1980). "The Impact of Options on the Underlying Securities," *Journal of Portfolio Management* 7:12–18.

Klette, T., and D. de Meza (1986). "Is the Market Biased against R&D?" *Rand Journal of Economics* 17:133–139.

Kreps, D. (1979) . "Three Essays on Capital Markets," IMSSS Technical Report No. 298, Stanford University.

Linn, S. C., and J. J. McConnell (1983). "An Empirical Investigation of the Impact of 'Antitakeover' Amendments on Common Stock Prices," *Journal of Financial Economics* 11:361–399.

Litan, R. E. (1991). "The Revolution in U.S. Finance: Past, Present, and Future," The Frank M. Engle Lecture 1991, The American College, Bryn Mawr, PA.

Madan, D., and B. Soubra (1991). "Design and Marketing of Financial Products," *Review of Financial Studies* 4:361–384.

Makowski, L. (1983). "Competitive Stock Markets," *Review of Economic Studies* 50:305–330.

Malatesta, P. H., and R. A. Walkling (1988). "Poison Pill Securities: Stockholder Wealth, Profitabililty, and Ownership Structure," *Journal of Financial Economics* 20:347 –376.

Marshall, J. F., and K. R. Kapner (1990). *Understanding Swap Finance*, Cincinnati: South-Western.

Masuoka, T. (1991). "Asset and Liability Management in the Developing Countries: Modern Financial Techniques," mimeo, World Bank.

Maug, E. (1992). "Capital Structure and Organizational Form: Alternative Governance Structures to Force Liquidation," mimeo, London School of Economics.

Merton, R. C. (1989). "On the Application of the Continuous-Time Theory of Finance to Financial Intermediation and Insurance," *Geneva Papers on Risk and Insurance* 14:225–261.

Merton, R. C. (1990). "The Financial System and Economic Performance," *Journal of Financial Services Research* 4:263–300.

Michie, R. (1987). *The London and New York Stock Exchanges 1850–1914*, London: Allen and Unwin.

Miller, M. H. (1986). "Financial Innovation: The Last Twenty Years and the Next," *Journal of Financial and Quantitative Analysis* 21:459–471.

Morgan, E. V., and W. A. Thomas (1969). *The London Stock Exchange: Its History and Functions*, 2nd edition, New York: St. Martin's Press.

Nachman, D., and T. Noe (1990). "Design of Securities under Asymmetric Information," mimeo, Georgia State University.

Neal, L. (1990). *The Rise of Financial Capitalism: International Capital Markets in the Age of Reason*, Cambridge: Cambridge University Press.

Pesendorfer, W. (1991). "Financial Innovation in a General Equilibrium Model," mimeo, UCLA.

Petruzzi, C., M. Del Valle, and S. Judlowe (1988). "Patent and Copyright Protection for Innovations in Finance," *Financial Management* 17:66–71.

Pollack, I. M. (1986). "Short-Sale Regulation of NASDAQ Securities," NASDAQ Pamphlet.

Price, J. A. M., and S. K. Henderson (1984). *Currency and Interest Rate Swaps*, London: Butterworths.

Reinganum, J. (1984). "Practical Implications of Game Theoretic Models of R&D," *American Economic Review* 74:61–66.

Ross, S. (1989). "Institutional Markets, Financial Marketing and Financial Innovation," *Journal of Finance* 44:541–556.

Ryngaert, M. (1988). "The Effect of Poison Pills on Shareholder Wealth," *Journal of Financial Economics* 20:377–417.

Scherer, F. M. (1967). "Resource and Development Resource Allocation under Rivalry," *Quarterly Journal of Economics* 81:359–394.

Schwarz, E. W., J. M. Hill and T. Schneeweis (1986). *Financial Futures*, Homewood, ILL: Irwin.

Shiller, R. J. (1992). "Broadening the Scope of Our International Asset Markets: Index Numbers and the Standardization of Assets," mimeo, Department of Economics, Yale University.

Silber, W. L. (1981). "Innovation, Competition, and New Contract Design in Futures Markets," *Journal of Futures Markets* 1:123–155.

Spratlin, J. S., and P. Vianna (1986). *An Investor's Guide to CMOs*, New York: Salomon Brothers.

Tirole, J. (1988). *The Theory of Industrial Organization*, Cambridge, MA: MIT Press.

Titman, S. (1990). "Interest Rate Swaps and Corporate Financing Choices," Working Paper 16–90, Anderson Graduate School of Management, UCLA.

Trennepohl, G., and W. Dukes (1979). "CBOE Options and Stock Volatility," *Review of Business and Economic Research* 14:49–60.

Tufano, P. (1989). "Financial Innovation and First-Mover Advantages," *Journal of Financial Economics* 25:213–240.

Tufano, P. (1991). "Business Failure as a Stimulus to Innovation: An Institutional and Historical Perspective," Working Paper 91-039, Harvard Business School.

Van Horne, J. C. (1985). "Of Financial Innovation and Excesses," *Journal of Finance* 40:621–631.

Vega, J. P. de la. (1688). *Confusion de Confusiones*, translated by H. Kellenbenz, No. 13 (1987), The Kress Library Series of Publications, The Kress Library of Business and Economics, Harvard University, Cambridge, MA.

Vila, J.-L. (1987). "Speculation and the Public Interest," CARESS Working Paper 87-25, University of Pennsylvania.

Wallace, N. (1981). "A Modigliani-Miller Theorem for Open Market Operations," *American Economic Review* 71:267–274.

Walmsley, J. (1988). *The New Financial Instruments: An Investor's Guide*, New York: John Wiley and Sons.

Walmsley, J. (1991). *Global Investing*, London: Macmillan.

Walter, I., and R. C. Smith (1990). "European Investment Banking: Structure, Transactions Flow and Regulation," in *European Banking in the 1990s*, edited by Jean Dermine. Oxford, U.K.: Blackwell.

Watt, W. H., P. K. Yadav, and P. Draper (1992). "The Impact of Option Listing on Underlying Stock Returns: The UK Evidence," *The Journal of Business Finance and Accounting* 19:485–503.

Whiteside, M., P. W. Dukes, and P. M. Dunne (1983). "Short Term Impact of Option Trading on Underlying Securities," *Journal of Financial Research* 6:313–321.

Winger, B. J., C. R. Chen, J. D. Martin, J. W. Petty, and S. C. Hayden (1986). "Adjustable Rate Preferred Stock," *Financial Management* 15:48–57.

Working, H. (1953). "Futures Trading and Hedging," *American Economic Review* 43:314–343.

Yawitz, J. B., and K. J. Maloney (1983). "Evaluating the Decision to Issue Original Issue Discount Bonds," *Financial Management* 12:36–46.

Zender, J. F. (1991). "Optimal Financial Instruments," *Journal of Finance* 46:1645–1664.

II MODELS OF FINANCIAL INNOVATION AND RISK SHARING

6 Optimal Security Design

It is widely acknowledged that there has been a significant increase in the amount of financial innovation in recent years (see, for example, Miller 1986). A vast number of new securities with novel features have been introduced. These include not only corporate securities, such as zero coupon bonds and floating rate bonds, but also other types of securities, such as financial futures, options on indexes, and money market funds, to name but a few. An important question concerns how such securities should be optimally designed; in other words, how should the payoffs to a security be allocated across states of nature in order to maximize the amount the issuer receives? Unfortunately, with a few exceptions (see, for example, Duffie and Jackson 1986 and Silber 1981 on the design of futures contracts and Williams 1986 on corporate securities as optimal contracts when there is asymmetric information), traditional theories have little to say on this issue. In this chapter our aim is to develop a benchmark model of security design by investigating the simple case where only firms issue financial claims.

The literature on firms' capital structure decisions assumes that a firm can issue only debt and equity. It does not consider the more basic question of whether debt and equity are the best securities the firm can issue. The result of Modigliani and Miller (1958) and of subsequent authors (such as Stiglitz 1969 and 1974, Baron 1974 and 1976, and Hellwig 1981) that capital structure is irrelevant when markets are complete (assuming no taxes or frictions) suggests that the form of securities issued in this case is also unimportant. Although the result that capital structure is important when markets are incomplete indicates that the form of securities may also matter, it throws little light on their optimal design.

In order to develop a theory of optimal security design, it is clearly necessary to develop a framework in which markets are incomplete. Traditional general equilibrium theories with incomplete markets, such as Diamond (1967), Radner (1972), and Hart (1975), have taken those markets which are open and those which are closed as exogenous. The usual justification for considering incomplete markets is the existence of transaction costs of some sort. However, the relationship between these transaction costs and the securities that are the optimal ones for agents to issue is not considered.

This chapter originally appeared in *The Review of Financial Studies* 1988, vol 1, no. 3, 229–263, © 1989 The Review of Financial Studies 0893-9454/89. Reprinted with permission.

The purpose of this chapter is to incorporate explicitly the transaction costs of issuing securities in order to determine their optimal design. We suppose that firms bear fixed costs of issuing securities and allocate pay-offs to securities across states. Thus, the securities that are traded are chosen optimally and the incomplete-market structure is endogenous. The model is intended to be a simple one that can act as a benchmark. It is an abstraction that gives insight rather than a realistic description of what we observe.

Two important issues must be addressed when constructing this type of model. The first is precisely who can issue securities and what the costs of doing this are. We assume that firms can issue one security for some fixed cost and a second security for some additional amount. The payoffs to these securities are generated by the assets of the firm. Individual investors are unable to issue securities. In particular, we assume that individuals cannot short-sell firms' securities. If individuals could do this without cost, then there could not exist an equilibrium in which firms issue costly securities. The reason is that the short sellers are effectively able to expand the supply of a firm's security more cheaply than firms can. However, in order for a firm to be willing to issue securities, it must be able to recoup the cost of doing so. If firms face competition from short sellers who face no costs, this will be impossible. The short selling of one firm's securities by another is also excluded, as this leads to nonexistence in the same way.

The justification for these assumptions is that short selling is fundamentally different from issuing securities backed by real assets. The existence of tangible and visible assets reduces the moral-hazard problems associated with the exchange of promises of future payment. In reality, it appears that short selling is very costly and is only rarely done. For most of the analysis, it is assumed that the costs are such that there is no short selling; however, at one point this assumption is relaxed to illustrate what happens when limited short selling is possible at a low cost.

The second issue concerns the knowledge that agents have about the prices of those securities which in principle could be issued by firms but which in equilibrium are not. We assume that both the firms and the consumers are aware of these prices. The trading process that we have in mind is analogous to the Lloyd's of London insurance market, where a price can be obtained for a policy insuring any risk whether or not such policies are actively traded. Our approach is therefore different from that taken by Hart (1979), who assumes that there is an asymmetry between firms and producers: Firms know the prices that would be obtained for securities that are not issued; consumers do not.

We obtain five main results:

1. The constrained efficiency (and existence) of equilibrium is demonstrated.

2. In our model, the number of securities that are issued in equilibrium can exceed the number of states and yet markets are incomplete in the sense that first-best risk sharing is not achieved. When technologies are convex in an appropriate sense, we show that an upper bound on the number of securities issued in equilibrium is $|J| \cdot |I|^2$, where $|J|$ is the number of different types of firms and $|I|$ is the number of different types of consumers.

3. As a point of reference, we consider examples where firms are constrained to use debt and equity but these securities are costly to issue. We show that Modigliani and Miller's (1958) irrelevance result does not hold: the value of firms has to depend on their financial structure to give them an incentive to issue the costly securities. In equilibrium both debt and equity are issued, provided the costs are sufficiently low.

4. If firms are not restricted to issuing debt and equity, but can allocate earnings between two securities in any way they choose, then the optimal securities need not be debt and equity. In fact, under fairly general conditions debt and equity *cannot* be optimal securities. When the firm issues two securities, each one is targeted at a particular clientele. Typically, in any state all the firm's output is allocated to the group that values it most.

5. The role of the no-short-sale assumption is shown to be critical. As argued above, if costless short sales are allowed, then equilibrium fails to exist. Financial structure must affect firm value in order to provide an incentive for firms to issue securities. Without frictions of some kind or another, there will be arbitrage opportunities that preclude the existence of equilibrium. We illustrate what happens when limited short selling is possible at low cost. In this case equilibrium may or may not exist, depending on the cost of issuing securities.

Following the well-known paper by Miller (1977), a large literature on tax clienteles has arisen (recent examples are Dybvig and Ross 1986, Dammon and Green 1987, and Ross 1987). There are a number of parallels between this literature and our chapter. In the tax clientele literature, individuals with different marginal tax rates value assets differently at the margin. In order to maximize their market value, firms market their securities to particular tax clienteles. In equilibrium, securities are held by the clientele that values them most. Because of the different marginal valuations of different clienteles, tax arbitrage possibilities may arise and equilibrium may not exist unless arbitrage possibilities are limited by constraining short sales, assuming progressive taxation or some other means.

In any model with no short sales and incomplete markets, different investors will typically value assets differently at the margin. In such a setting, firms can increase their market value by issuing securities that take advantage of the different marginal valuations of these different "clienteles." In contrast to the tax clientele perspective, securities are endogenous in our model. Firms design securities to suit particular groups, whereas in the tax clientele literature the form of the securities issued by firms is determined by the tax code. Another distinction is that our clienteles result from differences in preferences and endowments (together with incomplete markets) rather than from tax structure. However, we also need a short-sale constraint to ensure that equilibrium exists, because the different marginal valuations of different investors would present arbitrage opportunities if unbounded short sales were allowed. In addition, in both cases asset supplies determine marginal valuations and hence the form of equilibrium.

Grossman and Stiglitz (1980) discuss a model in which the incentives to trade arise primarily from differences in beliefs. In contrast, in our model the incentives to trade arise from differences in endowments and risk preferences. Nevertheless, in both instances there is an analogous problem concerning the existence of equilibrium. In their model, if endowments are nonstochastic then prices fully reveal traders' information. However, this means that it is not worthwhile acquiring costly information. But if nobody acquires information, it will be worthwhile to do so. Hence, no equilibrium exists. In our model, the gross amount received by firms that issue multiple securities must be strictly greater than the gross amount received by a single-security firm, so that the costs of issuing securities can be recouped. However, if short sales are costless, this creates an arbitrage opportunity. But if no firm issues multiple securities, it will be worthwhile doing so. Hence, no equilibrium exists unless there are costs of short selling.

The chapter proceeds as follows. Section 6.1 gives an informal description of the model; a formally precise definition is contained in the technical appendix. Section 6.2 contains an analysis of the general model; the more complex formal proofs are again in the appendix. The next two sections develop illustrative examples. Some readers may prefer to read these before section 6.2. For purposes of comparison, section 6.3 shows what happens when there are costs of issuing securities but firms are constrained to issue debt and equity, and section 6.4 considers the case where firms are free to allocate their earnings in a particular state to two securities in any way they desire. Section 6.5 considers the role of short-sale constraints. Finally, section 6.6 contains concluding remarks.

6.1   The Model

The formal definition of the model is given in the appendix. An intuitive description of its main features is given here.

There are two dates ($t = 0, 1$), and there is a finite set of states of nature ($s \in S$) that occur with probability π_s. All agents have the same informational structure: There is no information at the first date, and the true state is revealed at the second. At each date there is a single consumption good. There is a finite set of types of producers ($j \in J$) and a finite set of types of consumers ($i \in I$). There is a continuum of agents of each type. For simplicity's sake, it is assumed below (except where otherwise stated and in the appendix) that the measure of each type of producer and each type of consumer is 1.

6.1.1   Producers

A type of producer is defined by a security set and a cost function. When a firm chooses an element from its security set, it is choosing both its production plan and its financial structure. A producer of type $j \in J$ has a set of production plans Y_j to choose from. A particular production plan is represented by $y_j = (y_j(s))_{s \in S}$, where $y_j(s)$ denotes the output of the good in state s at date 1 for every $s \in S$.

It is assumed that any production plan can have at most two types of claims issued against it. The analysis can readily be extended to allow for more than two claims, but this makes the exposition more cumbersome and so is not pursued here. The two claims are indexed by $k = 1, 2$. A financial structure is a specification of the claims against the production plan. In the case where the claims are debt and equity, the financial structure corresponds to the mix between debt and equity that the firm uses. Just as there is a continuum of mixes of debt and equity that a firm can adopt, there is a continuum of financial structures that a firm can choose. For each distinct production plan, the corresponding set of possible financial structures can also be thought of as distinct. Hence, without loss of generality, it is possible to describe a firm's joint choice of production plan and financial structure by its choice of financial structure alone. The financial structures available to the firm are indexed by $e \in E_j$. The index set E_j is referred to as the set of available financial structures. For any financial structure $e \in E_j$ and $k = 1, 2$, let $r^k(e)$ denote the vector of dividends corresponding to the kth claim in the financial structure e. Thus, the properties of different financial structures and different claims are completely described by the dividend functions r^1 and r^2.

The dividend functions are assumed to satisfy certain natural conditions. Dividends are always nonnegative: $r^1(e) \geq 0$ and $r^2(e) \geq 0$ for all structures $e \in E_j$. In other words, we restrict attention to securities satisfying limited liability. If securities could have negative payoffs, this would be similar to individuals short-selling securities. The reasons for assuming that short sales are costly are discussed in the introduction and in section 6.5; similar comments are applicable here. Inactivity is possible; that is, if the producer decides not to operate, then $r^1(e) = r^2(e) = 0$. Dividends are assumed to exhaust the production plan; that is, $r^1(e) + r^2(e) \equiv y_j$. Also, it is possible to issue equity only: $r^1(e) = y_j$ and $r^2(e) = 0$.

The cost function of producers of type $j \in J$ is denoted by C_j. For any financial structure $e \in E_j$, $C_j(e)$ is the cost of operating a firm with a financial structure e. The cost of operating the firm includes the cost of inputs to the production process (i.e., investment) as well as the costs of issuing securities. If a producer decides not to operate a firm and thus issues no securities, no cost is incurred. The null structure corresponding to this action is denoted by $e = 0$, and thus $C_j(0) = 0$.

Producers derive no utility from future consumption. Every producer maximizes his (current) profit, taking as given the market value of firms with different financial structures. Let $v^k(e)$ denote the market value of the kth claim on a firm with financial structure e for $k = 1, 2$, and $e \in E_j$. Then the market value (MV) of a firm with financial structure e is $v^1(e) + v^2(e) \equiv \mathrm{MV}(e)$, say. A producer of type j chooses e to solve

$$\max_{e \in E_j} \mathrm{MV}(e) - C_j(e).$$

Since the producers' problem is nonconvex, there may not be a unique maximum. Let v_j denote the distribution of financial structures chosen by producers of type j; that is, for any measurable set $H \subset E_j$, $v_j(H)$ is the measure of producers of type j who choose financial structures $e \in H$.

For simplicity, we have assumed that producers (i.e., the original owners of the firms) consume only at $t = 0$. The objective function of the firm would be the same if the firm had several original owners who consumed at both $t = 0$ and $t = 1$. When a firm is small, its decisions do not affect the set of securities available to the economy as a whole; either the securities issued by the firm are already spanned by other firms' securities or they must be priced so that in equilibrium consumers hold negligible amounts. In either case the only effect of the choice of a change in financial structure is on the wealth of the firm's owners. So value maximization is consistent with utility maximization and will be unanimously approved by the firm's owners. This was shown by Hart (1979) in a different context.

6.1.2 Consumers

Let Ω denote the set of nonnegative consumption bundles. For any consumption bundle $x \in \Omega$, it is useful to write $x = (x^0, x^1)$, where x^0 denotes consumption at date 0 and where $x^1 = (x^1(s))_{s \in S}$ is the vector of consumption levels in different states at date 1. That is, $x^1(s)$ is the consumption level in state s at date 1 for every $s \in S$.

A consumer type $i \in I$ is characterized by a utility function and an endowment of goods. The utility function of type i consumers is denoted by $U_i(x)$. Preferences are assumed to be well-behaved: U_i is strictly increasing and strictly quasi-concave. The consumer's endowment is denoted by $w_i \in \Omega$.

A portfolio is represented by an ordered pair $\alpha = (\alpha^1, \alpha^2)$ of measures on the set $E \equiv \bigcup_{j \in J} E_j$. For any measurable set $H \subset E$, $\alpha^k(H)$ is the number of units of the kth claim on firms with financial structures $e \in H$ held in the portfolio. Since short sales are not allowed, portfolios are nonnegative: $\alpha^k(H) \geq 0$ for any measurable set $H \subset E$ and any $k = 1, 2$.

Recall that $v^k(e)$ is the price in terms of consumption at date 0 of the kth claim on a firm with financial structure e for any $k = 1, 2$ and $e \in E_j$. For any security price function $v = (v^1, v^2)$, the value of a portfolio $\alpha \in A$ is denoted by $\alpha * v$, where

$$\alpha * v \equiv \sum_{k=1}^{2} \int_E v^k \, d\alpha^k.$$

Similarly, the income at date 1 from a portfolio $\alpha \in A$ is denoted by $\alpha * r$, where

$$\alpha * r \equiv \sum_{k=1}^{2} \int_{E} r^k \, d\alpha^k.$$

In this notation the budget constraints of a consumer of type i can be written as follows:

$$x^0 = w_i^0 - \alpha * v$$

$$x^1 = w_i^1 + \alpha * r.$$

(The budget constraints are written as equations because U_i is assumed to be strictly increasing.) For any security price function v and any choice of portfolio $\alpha \in A$, the budget constraints define a unique consumption bundle $x = \xi_i(\alpha, v)$. So the consumer's problem is to choose a portfolio α to maximize utility, subject to the requirement that the consumption bundle $\xi_i(\alpha, v)$ implied by α and v is feasible. Formally,

$$\max_{\alpha \in A} U_i[\xi_i(\alpha, v)] \text{ s.t. } \xi_i(\alpha, v) \geq 0.$$

6.1.3   Equilibrium

We define our equilibrium concept in two stages. First we outline a Walrasian type of equilibrium concept, and then we add an extra condition. Our notion of equilibrium is similar to that suggested by Hart (1979), but with one important difference, which is pointed out below.

In Walrasian equilibrium all agents maximize (expected) utility, taking prices for both issued and unissued securities as given, and all markets clear at the prevailing prices. Formally, a Walrasian equilibrium must specify a price function $v = (v^1, v^2)$, a portfolio $\alpha_i = (\alpha_i^1, \alpha_i^2)$ for each type of consumer $i \in I$, and a distribution v_j of financial structures for each type of producer $j \in J$. The equilibrium conditions are:

(E1)   For every type $i \in I$, α_i maximizes the consumers' utility, subject to their budget constraints and to the nonnegativity constraints, given the price function v.

(E2)   For every type $j \in J$, all the mass v_j is concentrated on financial structures that maximize profits.

(E3)   Markets must clear: $\sum_{i \in I} \alpha_i = \sum_{j \in J} v_j$.

In equilibrium each firm takes the securities issued by other firms as given, and in a large economy a single firm's securities form a negligible part of any investor's portfolio. Thus, the firm expects its securities to be priced according to investors' marginal valuation of a unit of the security. These marginal valuations will be independent of the firm's actions because any individual holds a negligible amount of its securities. This is the sense in which our concept of equilibrium involves price taking by firms. The *rational conjecture condition* says that the price that firms expect to receive if they issue a security is the maximum amount that any individual would be prepared to pay for a very small quantity of it. For any consumer type $i \in I$ with an equilibrium consumption bundle $x_i \in \Omega$, let $p_i(x_i)$ denote the vector of marginal rates of substitution defined by

$$p_i(x_i) = \frac{\dfrac{\partial U_i(x_i)}{\partial x^1}}{\dfrac{\partial U_i(x_i)}{\partial x^0}}.$$

If we write $p_i(x_i) = (p_{is}(x_i))$, then $p_{is}(x_i)$ is the amount of date 0 consumption that a consumer of type i is willing to give up in exchange for an extra unit of consumption in state s at date 1 for any $s \in S$. Suppose that a security offers a vector of dividends $r^k(e)$ at date 1. Suppose also that every consumer has positive consumption at date 0. For some very small quantity ε of this security, a consumer of type i ought to be willing to pay $\varepsilon p_i(x_i) \cdot r^k(e)$ units of consumption at date 0. In other words, the price that he should pay is $p_i(x_i) \cdot r^k(e)$. The equilibrium price $v^k(e)$ should be the maximum such willingness to pay; that is,

$$v^k(e) = \max_{i \in I} p_i(x_i) \cdot r^k(e)$$

for every claim $k = 1, 2$ and financial structure $e \in E_j$. (If not all consumers have positive consumption at date 0, the maximum should be taken over the set of types that do.)

An *equilibrium* is defined to be a Walrasian equilibrium that satisfies the rational conjecture condition. This condition does not affect the equilibrium allocation in any substantive way. It is automatically satisfied in Walrasian equilibrium for every security that is actually issued. Because of the restrictions on short sales, this is not the case for securities that are not issued. However, if it is not satisfied for unissued securities in some

Walrasian equilibrium, then one can satisfy it simply by reducing the value of $v^k(e)$ appropriately without making any other change in the Walrasian equilibrium.

Hart (1979) distinguishes between markets that are open and markets that are closed. If a particular security is not issued by any firm, he assumes that market to be closed. Also, consumers are not allowed to trade in that security and they do not observe a market-clearing price for that security. On the other hand, producers know the price that would clear the market if a small quantity of a nonissued security were to be introduced.

An equilibrium as we have defined it differs from Hart's in one important respect. As far as producers are concerned, the two concepts are the same; it really makes no difference whether producers see prices quoted for every possible security or have rational conjectures about what prices would be if a new security were issued. For consumers, on the other hand, it makes a difference whether they can trade every security at the quoted price, even if they choose not to trade some of them in equilibrium. In other words, there is a difference between a closed market and a market that is open but inactive because no trade takes place at the prevailing price. The importance of this difference is discussed in section 6.2.

6.2 General Properties of Equilibrium

The first property we note is that the equilibria of our model are all constrained-efficient. An equilibrium is said to be constrained-efficient if a planner who is subject to the same transaction costs as individual agents cannot make everyone better off. In this context the condition "subject to the same transaction costs" is interpreted to mean that the planner can reallocate securities and consumption only at the first date. (The formal definition of *constrained efficiency* that we use is given in the appendix.)

Under this interpretation the constrained efficiency of equilibrium is not surprising. Using the budget constraints to solve for second-period consumption, we can express the utility of any agent in terms of first-period consumption and of the portfolio of securities he holds at the end of the period. Then the economy is seen to be isomorphic to an Arrow-Debreu economy in which only first-period consumption and securities are traded. Pareto efficiency in this Arrow-Debreu economy is equivalent to constrained efficiency in the original. So our result can be seen as a special case or application of the first fundamental theorem of welfare economics. Thus, we have the following result:

THEOREM 2.1   Every equilibrium is constrained-efficient.

Proof. See the appendix.   ∎

This result is not surprising when seen in the right perspective. Nevertheless, it stands in sharp contrast to the claims of Hart (1980) and Makowski (1980); both authors argue in the context of a product-differentiation model formally similar to ours that "equilibrium" need not be efficient. The reason for this difference of opinion can be traced to their definition of equilibrium. It is important to understand the difference between their concept and ours because there are substantive modeling issues involved. Both Hart (1980) and Makowski (1980) use a concept of equilibrium introduced in Hart (1979). As outlined in section 6.1, Hart's concept is as follows. Prices are quoted for securities that are actually issued in equilibrium. If a security is not issued, there is no market for it; no price is quoted, and consumers simply assume that it cannot be bought. On the other hand, firms must make conjectures about the price at which a security could be sold if it were to be introduced; otherwise, they could not make an optimal decision about which security to offer. These conjectures are assumed to be rational; that is, the conjectured price equals that maximum price at which the economy would absorb a small amount of the security. The rest of the definition is standard. Let us call Hart's concept a *conjectural equilibrium* to distinguish it from our *Walrasian equilibrium*.

This sketch of conjectural equilibrium allows us to see the essential cause of market failure in the Hart-Makowski model and why it is absent in ours. There is a complementarity between products in their models that may lead to a pecuniary externality. This externality can easily be explained by an example. Suppose that nuts and bolts can be produced only by different firms. Nuts and bolts have value only if consumed together. If nuts are not produced, the marginal value of a bolt is zero, so bolts will not be produced either. The same argument shows that nuts will not be produced if bolts are not produced. Thus, both types of firms are maximizing profits at zero output given the behavior of the other and their own (rational) conjectures. Yet this conjectural equilibrium is not efficient, since a coordinated increase in the output of both products could make everyone better off.

The same kind of phenomenon clearly could occur in our model if we analyzed it by using the conjectural equilibrium concept. Think of an economy with two types of firms, each of which has positive output in one state only (thus, each type of firm can issue essentially one kind of security), and suppose that consumers have indifference curves for consumption in these two states that do not intersect the axes (for example, a Cobb-Douglas utility function). These consumers will not value consumption in one of these states unless they have positive consumption in the other. Thus, we may have a conjectural equilibrium in which neither type of firm produces output and issues securities. This is an equilibrium for firms because they rightly conjecture that their securities would be worthless if issued in isolation. Consumers are in equilibrium, on the other hand, because the markets for both securities are assumed to be closed if the supply of the securities is zero. The reason why this cannot happen in our model is that prices are quoted for every security whether it is actually issued or not. If the prices of both securities were zero, firms would be maximizing profit at zero output, but consumers would not be maximizing utility if they thought they could buy at the prevailing price and they still demanded none. So markets will not clear at a zero output level. In the Hart-Makowski version of the model, on the other hand, the securities markets are closed to consumers. They do not need to worry about clearing these markets.

At some level it probably seems natural to assume that a market does not exist if the corresponding good or security is not being produced. This kind of reasoning is encouraged by a tendency to equate markets with a gathering of people for the purchase and sale of commodities. But when we speak of a market existing in a Walrasian model, this is not what we have in mind. The existence of a market in this context is just another kind of equilibrium condition. A market "exists" if and only if a market-clearing price prevails; that is, buyers and sellers can agree on a common price at which they all think they can trade any amount that is small relative to the economy as a whole. It is not immediately obvious why the existence of a market in this sense should depend on a nonzero amount of the corresponding commodity being traded. For example, at Lloyd's of London it is possible to obtain a price for insuring any risk even though no policy of that type is actively traded. Similarly, investment banks will quote prices for tailor-made securities.

There may be reasons why a market does not exist in this sense, but these reasons are not apparent in the Hart-Makowski model. There are no transaction costs; as soon as a firm decides to produce a positive amount of some commodity, a market, that is to say, a market-clearing price, springs costlessly into existence. Nor is it clear that there are other obstacles to the free flow of information implied by a market-clearing price. After all, producers correctly conjecture the prices at which they can sell a nonexistent product even without the aid of a market. So it is not clear why, in equilibrium, there should not be a market-clearing price for every commodity. To say that some of these conditions will not be satisfied because the corresponding markets do not "exist" is tautologous. The existence of a market *means* that an equilibrium condition is satisfied, nothing more.

The next result concerns the existence of equilibrium.

THEOREM 2.2   Under the maintained assumptions the equilibrium set is nonempty.

Proof.   See the appendix.   ∎

This theorem does not require comment except to note the role of the no-short-sales assumption in guaranteeing the existence of equilibrium. This assumption is needed in order to prevent the equalization of marginal rates of substitution everywhere. As we noted in the introduction, some divergence of marginal valuations between different consumer types is necessary in order to give firms an incentive to create costly securities.

The next question to be addressed is the number of securities needed in equilibrium. Without essential loss of generality, it can be assumed that there is only one type of firm: $|J| = 1$. It will be clear that the argument generalizes easily. Initially, suppose that the number of securities is finite. Let Y be a convex, compact set of output vectors and let

$$E = \{(\rho_1, \rho_2) \in \mathbf{R}_+^S \times \mathbf{R}_+^S | \rho_1 + \rho_2 = y \in Y\}.$$

Let $\bar{E}$ denote the set of nontrivial splits; that is, $\bar{E} = \{e \in E | r^k(e) \neq 0, k = 1, 2\}$. Assume also that costs are *convex* in the following sense: $(\lambda_1 + \lambda_2)C(e_3) \leq \lambda_1 C(e_1) + \lambda_2 C(e_3)$ for any $\lambda_1, \lambda_2 \geq 0$ and $e_1, e_2, e_3 \in \bar{E}$ such that $(\lambda_1 + \lambda_2)r(e_3) = \lambda_1 r(e_1) + \lambda_2 r(e_2)$.

This definition of convexity is quite general in that it allows costs to vary with financial structure as well as with the number of securities. For example, financial structures with a large proportion of debt may be more costly to issue than financial structures with a small amount of debt. Thus, the issuing costs for an expensive two-security financial structure could be several times greater than the issuing costs for a relatively cheap two-security financial structure. However, a case of particular interest, which is considered below in some detail, is that in which the costs of issuing securities depend only on the number issued and are independent of the qualitative properties of the securities.

Without loss of generality, consider a pair of consumer types i_1 and i_2 who jointly own firms with financial structures e_1 and e_2 in $\bar{E}$. We can assume, again without loss of generality, that consumer types i_k own all of the kth security. Let λ_1 denote the measure of firms with structure e_1 owned by these consumers, and let λ_2 denote the measure of firms with structure e_2 owned by these consumers. By convexity of Y there exists a financial structure $e_3 \in \bar{E}$ such that

$$(\lambda_1 + \lambda_2) r^i(e_3) = \lambda_1 r^i(e_1) + \lambda_2 r^i(e_2)$$

for $i = 1, 2$. Thus, we can replace the firms that have financial structures e_1 and e_2 with an equal measure of firms that have financial structure e_3 and leave consumers equally well off. The convexity assumption on C ensures that firms are equally well off choosing the financial structure e_3:

$$\sum_{k=1}^{2} v^k(e_3) - C(e_3) \geq \sum_{k=1}^{2} p_k(x_k) \cdot r^k(e_3) - C(e_3)$$

$$\geq (\lambda_1 + \lambda_2)^{-1} \sum_{b=1}^{2} \lambda_b \left\{ \sum_{k=1}^{2} p_k(x_k) \cdot r^k(e_b) - C(e_b) \right\}$$

$$\geq (\lambda_1 + \lambda_2)^{-1} \sum_{b=1}^{2} \lambda_b \left\{ \sum_{k=1}^{2} v^k(e_b) - C(e_b) \right\}.$$

Since $\sum_k v^k(e_1) - C(e_1) = \sum_k v^k(e_2) - C(e_2)$, the preceding calculation shows that e_3 is optimal. In this way we have shown that for every pair (i_1, i_2) of consumer types, there need be only one (nontrivial) financial structure.

We may also need firms with trivial financial structures (i.e., firms that issue only one security). But making the appropriate convexity assumptions, there will need to be only one security (i.e., one trivial financial structure) per consumer type. Then the total number of securities in equilibrium (or in any constrained-efficient allocation) need not exceed $|I| \cdot |I - 1| + |I| = |I|^2$. The extension to $|J|$ types of firms is immediate.

THEOREM 2.3   With convex technologies the number of securities needed in equilibrium is less than or equal to $|J| \cdot |I|^2$.

Note that in "proving" theorem 2.3 we have assumed that the number of securities is finite to start with. Since any finite measure can be approximated arbitrarily closely by a measure with finite support, the argument can be extended to the general case simply by "taking limits."

It is interesting to compare theorem 2.3 with results obtained in standard stock market economies (Hart 1977). When each firm issues only a single security (equity), the number of securities needed is $|J| \cdot |I|$. For each type of firm $j \in J$, each consumer type gets its own tailor-made company (production plan), and this is clearly the best that one can do. We allow firms to vary production plans and financial structures, whereas Hart allows them only to vary production plans. The $|J| \cdot |I|$ securities in Hart's model correspond to the $|J| \cdot |I|$ firms with trivial (one-security) financial structures in our model. In addition, however, there are potentially $|J| \cdot |I| \cdot |I - 1|$ cases where a pair of investors effectively choose a production plan and split it optimally between them. Theorem 2.3 gives only an upper bound; the actual number of securities might be less if, for example, the number of states was very small.

Finally, we consider the form that optimal securities take. Until now we have combined production costs with the costs of issuing securities and have described them both by the cost function $\{C_j\}$. In the last part of this section we assume that production costs are convex and that the costs of issuing securities are fixed. More precisely, we assume that a firm issuing one security incurs a cost c_1 and that a firm issuing two securities incurs a cost $c_1 + c_2$. These costs are independent of the qualitative properties of the securities issued. When these conditions are satisfied, we say that the costs of issuing securities are *fixed* costs. Under these conditions there is no loss of generality in assuming that securities take a special form. A security is *extreme* if, in any state of nature, it promises either the entire product of the firm or nothing. These are the only securities that need to be considered when issuing costs are fixed.

THEOREM 2.4   Suppose that issuing costs are fixed costs. Then for any equilibrium there exists another equilibrium in which the consumption of every agent and the production of every firm are the same and in which only extreme securities are issued.

Proof. Consider a fixed, but arbitrary, firm with output vector y. Let X be the set of extreme points of the set $R \equiv \{0 \leq r \leq y\}$. Then $x \in X$ implies $x(s) \in \{0, y(s)\}$ for any state $s \in S$. Any nontrivial financial structure consistent with the output vector y can be identified with a vector $r \in R$: if $e \in \bar{E}$ and $r^1(e) + r^2(e) = y$, then put $r_1(e) = r$ and $r^2(e) = y - r$. For any $r \in R$ there exists a set $\{x_k\} \subset X$ and a set of numbers $\{\alpha_k\}$ such that $\alpha_k > 0$, $\sum_k \alpha_k = 1$, and $r = \sum_k \alpha_k x_k$. Suppose that a measure $m > 0$ of firms choose a production plan y and issue securities with payoffs r and $y - r$, respectively. For each k let a measure $\alpha_k m$ choose a production plan y and issue securities with payoffs x_k and $y - x_k$, respectively.

By assumption, the cost to the firm has not changed. The value of the firm is also unchanged. From the definition of equilibrium the value of a firm issuing $(x_k, y - x_k)$ cannot be greater than the value of one issuing $(r, y - r)$. However, the aggregate value of the firms cannot be less; otherwise, consumers would never have purchased the original securities. Thus, firms are maximizing profits with the new financial structures.

Since the new securities span the old, consumers can obtain their existing consumption bundles by holding appropriate amounts of the new securities. Market clearing must hold since each unit of old securities corresponds to a unique convex combination of extreme securities. Finally, the cost to consumers has not changed since, by the definition of equilibrium, the cost of each consumer's portfolio cannot decrease and yet the aggregate value must be the same.   ∎

We have proved the theorem for the case where firms issue two securities. It can be seen that the result also applies where firms are permitted to issue more than two securities.

In section 6.4 we give examples which illustrate that the optimal securities involve splitting the firm's income stream so that in every state all payoffs are allocated to the security held by the group that values it most. Before doing this, we provide a point of reference by considering the case where firms can issue only standard securities.

6.3   Examples with Debt and Equity

This section develops illustrations of the case where firms are restricted to issuing debt and equity. This situation can arise if the legal system is such that debt and equity are the only types of securities that can be used. The defining characteristic of debt is that the *par payment* (i.e., the promised payment) is the same in all states. In states where the output of the firm is below the par payment, the debt holders receive the entire output. If the firm's output is above the par payment in all states, the debt is *safe*; otherwise, it is *risky*.

In all the examples it is assumed that there is one type of producer and that the measure of firms is 1. The set of output vectors that each firm can produce is $Y = \{0, \bar{y}\}$. If a firm does not operate so that its output vector is 0, its costs are also 0. If a firm operates and produces the output vector $\bar{y}$, its costs are c_1 if it issues one security and $c_1 + c_2$ if it issues two securities; in other words, the marginal cost of issuing the second security is c_2. Example 1a is a specific illustration where c_1 is assumed to be zero and c_2 is strictly positive. Example 1b is a more general version of 1a where c_1 and c_2 are both positive.

There are two types of consumers, and the measure of each group is 1. Consumers have a von Neumann–Morgenstern utility function $\hat{U}_i$. In this case, for any consumption bundle $x \in \Omega$, $U_i(x)$, is the expected utility of x, where

$$U_i(x) = \sum_{s \in S} \pi_s \hat{U}_i(x^0, x^1(s)).$$

Example 1a   As mentioned above, in this illustration $c_1 = 0$ and $c_2 > 0$. There are two states ($s = 1, 2$) that are equally likely, so $\pi_s = 0.5$. It is assumed that the output vector $\bar{y}$ that each firm can produce when it operates is

$$\bar{y}(1) = 1 \qquad \bar{y}(2) = 2.$$

The two types of consumers ($i = a, n$) have von Neumann–Morgenstern utility functions

$$\hat{U}_a = x^0 + V(x^1) \qquad \text{with } V' > 0, V'' < 0$$

$$\hat{U}_n = x^0 + x^1.$$

Hence, group a is risk-averse in date 1 consumption and group n is risk-neutral. When a specific functional form is used for V, it is assumed that

$$V(x^1) = 2 \ln(1 + x^1).$$

It is helpful to define the marginal utility of consumption of type i in state s as

$$\mu_{is}(x^1) = \frac{p_{is}(x_i)}{\pi_s}$$

so that

$$\mu_{ns} = 1.$$

Since $c_1 = 0$, all firms operate and issue at least one security. First, consider the case where c_2 is sufficiently large that firms issue only one security, which must be equity:

$$r^1(s) = \bar{y}(s) \qquad \text{for all } s.$$

It follows from the definition of equilibrium that the price that firms expect to receive if they issue a security is the maximum amount that any individual would be prepared to pay for a very small quantity of it. Hence, the value of the one-security firms' equity is

$$v^1 = \max_{i=1,2} \sum \pi_s \mu_{is} \bar{y}(s) = \sum \pi_s \mu_s \bar{y}(s)$$

where the term μ_s is used to denote the marginal utility of consumption that is relevant for determining market values. Now $\mu_s = \mu_{as} > 1$ for all s if endowments are such that only the risk-averse group holds the security, and $\mu_s = \mu_{ns} = 1$ for all s if they are such that the risk-neutral group holds the security. Consider the case where both groups hold the security, so that $\mu_s = \mu_{ns} = 1$ for all s and $v^1 = 1.5$. The situation in which the supply of the security is sufficiently small that only the risk-averse group holds it can be similarly analyzed.

It can straightforwardly be shown that the risk-averse group s demand for the firms' equity is

$$\alpha^1* = 0.629$$

(where α^1* is used here and below to denote the demand of the risk-averse group when $v^1 = 1.5$). The risk-neutral group holds the remaining 0.371 of the security. The total value of a firm is $v^1 = 1.5$. The marginal utilities of consumption for the risk-averse group are

$$\mu_{a1} = 1.228 \qquad \mu_{a2} = 0.886.$$

Next, suppose that a firm issues debt so that the payoffs to its securities are as shown in table 6.1. Given that all other firms are issuing

Table 6.1
Payoffs to debt and equity securities in example 1

Claim	Payoff		Price
	State 1	State 2	
r^1	1	1	1.057
r^2	0	1	0.500

Note: Suppose that a firm issues debt (claim r^1) and equity (claim r^2) when all other firms issue just one security. The risk-averse group values the debt most because it allows this group to smooth its consumption. The risk-averse group bids the debt's price above its expected payoff of 1 to $(0.5)(1)(1.228 + 0.886) = 1.057$, where 0.5 is the probability of the two states, 1 is the debt's payoff in both states, and 1.228 and 0.886 are the group's marginal utilities of consumption in the two states. At this price the risk-neutral group would like to short-sell the debt but is constrained by the short-sale restriction. Similarly, the firm's equity is valued most by the risk-neutral group, which bids its price to $(0.5)(1) = 0.5$, and the short-sale constraint binds on the risk-averse group.

equity which is priced with $\mu_s = \mu_{ns} = 1$ for all s, it follows that the risk-averse group will value this firm's debt the most because $\sum \pi_s \mu_{as} = 1.057 > \sum \pi_s \mu_{ns} = 1.000$. Since the risk-averse group holds all of this debt, its price is determined by the group's marginal utilities of consumption μ_{as} and is thus 1.057. This firm's equity is valued the most by the risk-neutral group since $\mu_{n2} = 1.000 > \mu_{a2} = 0.886$. Because the risk-neutral group holds all of this equity, its price is 0.5. Thus, the total value of such a firm is $1.557 - c_2$.

It can be seen that the capital structure shown in table 6.1 is in fact the optimal one for a firm issuing debt and equity in this situation. The cost of issuing a second security is independent of its payoffs. Since the debt is held by the risk-averse group, its value would increase by only $\pi_2 \mu_{a2} = 0.443$ for each unit of output that the par payment on the debt is increased above 1. This is less than the $\pi_2 \mu_{n2} = 0.5$ that the risk-neutral group would be prepared to pay if the payoff were allocated to the equity it holds. Thus, such a change would lower the value of the firm. Similarly, a reduction in the par payment on the debt will also reduce the value of the firm since the risk-averse group values these marginal payoffs more than the risk-neutral group does. A similar argument holds in all two-state examples: it is always optimal for a firm to issue the maximum amount of risk-free debt possible. It can easily be seen that this is a special feature of the two-state case; with three or more states, firms can find it optimal to issue either risky or risk-free debt, depending on the parameter values.

Thus, for $c_2 > 0.057$ only equity will be issued by firms, and for $c_2 <$ 0.057 some proportion of the firms will issue both debt and equity; therefore, three types of securities will exist in total: the one-security firms' equity and the two-security firms' debt and equity. The risk-neutral group of consumers holds the equity of both the one- and two-security firms. The risk-averse group holds the equity of the one-security firms and the debt of the two-security firms. The prices of both types of equity claims are equal to their expected return, and the price of the debt is such that firms are indifferent between issuing one or two securities. The debt is priced above its expected return in order to compensate firms for the cost that they bear in issuing it; for example, if $c_2 = 0.05$, then the price of the debt is 1.05, the price of the equity of a two-security firm is 0.5, and the price of the equity of a one-security firm is 1.5. The proportion of firms issuing two securities is 0.111, and the proportion issuing one is 0.889. The risk-averse group holds 0.556 of the one-security firms' equity. As $c_2 \to 0$, more firms issue debt. When $c_2 = 0$, the debt's price is equal to its expected return and the risk-averse group holds just debt, while the risk-neutral group holds the rest of the securities. There is *full risk sharing* in the sense that all firms allocate their output between their security holders efficiently (i.e., either marginal utilities of consumption at $t = 1$ are equated or all output goes to the group with the highest marginal utility; in the case here, marginal utilities are equated).

Example 1b   Consider next what happens when c_1 and c_2 are both positive. (To allow the above results to be placed in context, here we shall analyze a generalization of example 1a.) Now the only restrictions on the utility function are that $V'(1) = 1$ and $V'(0)$ is finite (i.e., $V(x^1) = 2\ln(1 + x^1)$ is a special case of this); otherwise, the details are the same as in example 1a.

Figure 6.1 illustrates the relationship between the issuing costs and the number of securities issued. Example 1a corresponds to the c_2 axis where $c_1 = 0$. For $c_2 > 0.5[1 - V'(2\alpha^{1*})]$ ($=0.057$ in example 1a), there are only one-security firms, and so the total number of securities issued is 1. For $c_2 < 0.5[1 - V'(2\alpha^{1*})]$, some firms issue debt and equity and the remainder only equity, so that three securities are issued in total. The line labeled "Debt-and-equity boundary" represents the remainder of the boundary between the regions where one and three securities are issued. (The line labeled "Optimal securities boundary" is discussed in section 6.4.)

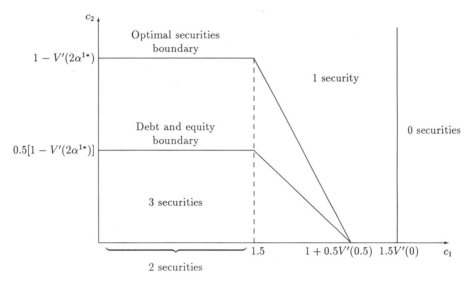

Figure 6.1
The relationship between the issuing costs and the total number of securities issued in examples 1 and 2

These examples have two equally likely states and one firm type with output (1, 2) in the two states. The symbol c_1 represents the cost of a firm issuing one security, and c_2 represents the cost of a firm issuing a second security. The marginal utility of consumption of risk-averse and risk-neutral investors is $V'(\cdot)$ and 1, respectively. The number of securities in the figure refers to the total number of securities issued by all firms (e.g., three if some firms issue two contingent claims and others issue only equity). The debt-and-equity boundary is the locus of costs in example 1b at which the solution switches from all firms issuing equity to some firms issuing equity and others issuing both debt and equity. The optimal securities boundary is the locus of costs in example 2b at which the solution switches from all firms issuing equity to some firms issuing equity and others issuing two optimally designed securities.

It is not worthwhile for any firms to operate and issue a security unless $c_1 < 1.5V'(0)$. For values of c_1 above this level, no investment is undertaken and no securities are issued. As c_1 falls below $1.5\ V'(0)$, more firms operate and issue one security. Initially, these are held entirely by the risk-averse group since $V'(0) > 1$, and so $\mu_{as} > \mu_{ns} = 1$ for all s. Eventually there comes a value $c_1 = 1 + 0.5V'(0.5)$ where group a's demand is 0.5, so that $\mu_{a2} = 1$. For $c_1 \leq 1 + 0.5V'(0.5)$, $\mu_{a2} \leq \mu_{n2} = 1$. For sufficiently small c_2, it becomes worthwhile for some firms to issue debt and equity since the risk-neutral group will be prepared to pay $\mu_{n2} = 1$ ($\geq \mu_{a2}$) per unit of expected income in state 2 and will hold the two-security firm's equity. The debt and one-security firms' equity are held by the risk-averse group. As c_2 rises, the boundary also rises, because $\mu_{n2} - \mu_{a2}$ must be sufficiently large to allow two-security firms to recoup their additional costs. Along the boundary, v^2 falls and α^2 increases. It is this that causes $\mu_{n2} - \mu_{a2}$ to rise.

When $c_1 = 1.5$ it is profitable for one-security firms to operate and be held by the risk-neutral group. At this point there is *full investment* in the sense that all firms operate and issue at least one security. Since the risk-neutral group holds at least some of the one-security firms' equity, it is priced at 1.5. There is no further scope for a fall in the price of the one-security firms' equity, and so the boundary is horizontal as c_1 falls from 1.5 to 0.

The only region where two types of securities are issued in total is along the c_1 axis where $c_2 = 0$ between 0 and 1.5. Here all firms operate, and since the marginal cost of issuing a second security is zero, they issue enough debt for the risk-averse group to smooth completely its consumption across states. Thus, in this region there is full investment and full risk sharing.

Another feature of this example is worth noting. Even though there are only two states, there can nevertheless be three securities in existence without there being complete markets in the sense that full risk sharing is possible. The reason for this is that there are no short sales. Thus, when there are costs of issuing securities and when there are constraints on short sales, the question of whether or not the number of securities is greater or less than the number of states is of less significance than when these factors are ignored.

The standard Modigliani-Miller theory, adapted to include corporate taxes and bankruptcy costs, suggests that firms choose their capital structure to trade off the tax advantage of debt against the cost of going bankrupt. Jensen and Meckling (1976), among others, have argued that a weakness of the theory is that it predicts that before the existence of the corporate income tax, debt would not be used at all since bankruptcy was costly. Of course, debt was widely used before the introduction of the tax. They argue that this demonstrates the importance of other factors, such as asymmetric information, in determining firms' capital structures. The examples above illustrate that, together with having no short sales, the costs of issuing securities are also a form of friction which are consistent with the existence of interior optimal debt ratios even when there is no tax advantage to debt. (The no-short-sale constraint may represent a cost, possibly arising from asymmetric information.)

Myers (1984) has stressed that conventional theories of capital structure are inconsistent with the observation that similar firms in the same industry often have significantly different debt/equity ratios. It can be seen that the illustrative examples above have this feature. In equilibrium, firms of the same type are indifferent between having an optimally levered capital structure and being unlevered because of nonconvexities. In more complex examples with more types of consumers and firms, it is possible for there to be many equally profitable optimal levels of leverage for firms of the same type. Allen (1987) also suggests a theory that is consistent with similar firms having different debt ratios. However, in Allen's model the asymmetric nature of the equilibrium results from the strategic interaction of firms in an imperfectly competitive product market. In contrast, here the asymmetric nature of equilibrium arises because it provides better risk-sharing opportunities for investors.

6.4 Examples with Optimal Securities

In this section it is assumed that firms are not restricted to issuing debt and equity. Instead, when they issue two securities they are free to allocate the firm's output in a particular state between the two securities in any way they wish. It is shown that the optimal securities are not debt and equity; nevertheless, they do have a particularly simple form.

Before discussing specific examples, we make some general observations about the optimality of debt and equity when the issuing costs are positive. *If consumers have smooth preferences, then it is never optimal to issue debt and equity.* The argument is as follows. If issuing two securities is costly, the firm will issue two securities only if this increases the firm's gross value. A necessary condition for this is the existence of two types of consumers, each of which values one of the optimal securities more highly than the other type does. For example, a firm of type j chooses a financial structure $e \in E_j$ and sells security $r^1(e)$ to type 1 consumers and security $r^2(e)$ to type 2 consumers. Then

$$v^1(e) = p_1(x_1) \cdot r^1(e) > p_2(x_2) \cdot r^1(e)$$

$$v^2(e) = p_2(x_2) \cdot r^2(e) > p_1(x_1) \cdot r^2(e).$$

If either of these inequalities were violated, it would be more profitable for the firm to issue a single security to one of these types. A necessary condition for these inequalities to hold is that for each type there is a state in which the firm has positive output and that this type has a higher marginal valuation than the other type. Then each security must be allocated the entire output in one state at least, so the securities cannot correspond to (risky) debt and equity.

The importance of the smoothness of consumers' preferences is that it ensures that for any $e \in E_j$ and $i \in I$, $v^k(e) \geq p_i(x_i) \cdot r^k(e)$. This condition must hold in any Walrasian equilibrium, even if we do not impose the rational conjecture condition (cf. section 6.1). Thus, if there exists a structure $\hat{e} \in E_j$ such that

$$p_1(x_1) \cdot r^1(\hat{e}) + p_2(x_2) \cdot r^2(\hat{e}) > p_1(x_1) \cdot r^1(e) + p_2(x_2) \cdot r^2(e)$$

it immediately follows that $v^1(\hat{e}) + v^2(\hat{e}) > v^1(e) + v^2(e)$, contradicting the optimality of $e \in E_j$. This is the formal justification for the last step in the above argument showing that debt and equity are not optimal. The argument breaks down, however, if preferences are not smooth. Take an example like example 1a in section 6.3, but replace the utility function of type a with

$$\hat{U}_a = x^0 + 2 \min\{x^1, 1\}.$$

If the costs of issuing securities are positive but sufficiently small, it will be optimal for firms to issue securities having returns $(1, 1)$ and $(0, 1)$, respectively (i.e., debt and equity).

Example 2a   Consider first an example with the same structure and parameter values as Example 1a. As before, when c_2 is large so that all firms issue only equity, group a's demand is 0.629, $\mu_{a1} = 1.228$, and $\mu_{a2} = 0.886$. If a firm were to issue debt as its second security, it would obtain $(0.5)(1.228) + (0.5)(0.886) = 1.057$ for it and $(0.5)(1) = 0.5$ for its equity. However, this is not the best it can do. It can clearly increase its receipts by reducing the payment on its r^1 security in state 2 and increasing the payment on the other security. The r^1 security is held by the risk-averse group, which values each unit of expected revenue in state 2 at only 0.886, whereas the r^2 security is held by the risk-neutral group, which values each unit at 1.000. Similarly, the firm should not reduce the payment on the r^1 security in state 1 since it is held by the risk-averse group, which values each unit at 1.228, whereas the risk-neutral group values each unit at only 1.000. This means that the optimal pair of securities for a firm to issue has the payoffs and prices shown in table 6.2.

Table 6.2
Payoffs to optimal securities in example 2

Claim	Payoff		Price
	State 1	State 2	
r^1	1	0	0.614
r^2	0	2	1.000

Note: The optimal securities involve giving all the firm's payoffs to the security that is held by the group with the highest marginal utility of consumption (MUC) in that state. In state 1 the risk-averse group has an MUC of 1.228, whereas the risk-neutral group has an MUC of 1. Thus, claim r^1, which is held by the risk-averse group, has a payoff of 1; and r^2, which is held by the risk-neutral group, has a payoff of 0. In state 2 the MUCs are 0.886 and 1, respectively, so all the output is allocated to the r^2 claim and none to the r^1 claim. The gross value of the firm rises from 1.057, when the debt and equity are issued, to 1.614.

The optimal securities thus have a particularly simple form. All the output in a particular state should be allocated to the security held by the group that values it most. This feature of optimal securities is quite general. It is due to the fact that firms' objective functions are linear, which arises from the competitive nature of the model. It does not depend on the existence only of two states and of two groups, one risk-neutral and one risk-averse.

The total value of a firm that issues two securities when all other firms issue one security is $1.614 - v_2$. Hence, firms will start issuing debt and equity at the critical cost $c_2^* = 0.114$. This contrasts with the case where firms issue debt and equity where the critical level $c_2^* = 0.057$ is much lower. Thus, optimal securities can permit a strictly better allocation of risk for a given (positive) issue cost than can debt and equity.

The claims issued by two-security firms in this example are, in effect, pure contingent claims. This feature arises from the fact that the number of states of nature is the same as the maximum number of securities that a firm can issue. If the number of states exceeds the number of securities, some optimal claims will have positive payoffs in more than one state. To illustrate this, let us consider an example similar to that above but with three equally probable states of nature in which firms' outputs are $\bar{y} = (1, 2, 3)$. In the case where c_2 is large, so that only one-security firms exist, the marginal utilities of consumption of the risk-averse group in the three states are $\mu_a = (1.374, 1.046, 0.845)$, respectively. A two-security firm would maximize its value by issuing a claim that paid $(1, 2, 0)$ for the risk-averse group and a claim with payoffs $(0, 0, 3)$ for the risk-neutral group. It is also possible to construct examples where all the payoffs in state 2 go to the risk-neutral group; for example, if $\bar{y} = (1, 2.5, 3)$, then $\mu_a = (1.408, 0.975, 0.885)$. The only case in which it is optimal for both securities to have a positive payoff in state 2 is when both groups have the same marginal utility of consumption in that state; for example, if $\bar{y} = (1, 2.3, 3)$, then $\mu_a = (1.394, 1.000, 0.868)$.

Example 2b Figure 6.1 illustrates what happens when c_1 and c_2 are both positive. The line labeled "Optimal securities boundary" is now the boundary between the region with three securities and the region with one security. The explanation of the form of the boundary is similar to that given in example 1b. The difference is that with optimal securities it is possible to allocate output more efficiently to those who value it most; with debt the problem is that firms cannot give less in state 2 than in state 1. As a result, the optimal securities boundary is shifted out relative to the debt-and-equity boundary. The two boundaries coincide only when they intersect with the c_1 axis at $1 + 0.5V'(0.5)$. In that case both boundaries are determined by the condition that the amount of a one-security firm's equity held by the risk-averse group is such that $\mu_{a1} = \mu_{n1} = 1$. This is unaffected by the form of the second security. It is only when $c_2 > 0$ and it is necessary that $\mu_{a1} = \mu_{n1} + c_2 > 1$ that the form of the second security makes a difference.

Example 3 The only region in figure 6.1 in which two securities in total are issued is when $c_2 = 0$ and c_1 is between 0 and 1.5. However, it is possible to construct examples where the total number of securities is 2 even when c_1 and c_2 are strictly positive. To illustrate this, let us consider another case with two groups of consumers and one type of producer. Both groups have the same (risk-averse) utility function but differ in their endowment in the two (equally likely) states at $t = 1$. Group 1 receives 1 unit of output in state 1 and 0 units in state 2. For group 2, the reverse is true. When a firm operates, its output vector $\bar{y}$ is

$$\bar{y}(1) = \bar{y}(2) = 1.$$

Hence, the example is symmetric and it is this, as opposed to the risk neutrality assumed before, which simplifies it. The measure of consumers of each type and of producers is 1. The utility functions of consumers are the same as those for group a in examples 1b and 2b.

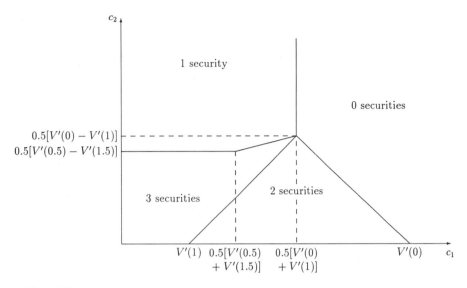

Figure 6.2a
The relationship between the issuing costs and the total number of securities issued in example 3

The example has two equally likely states and one firm type with output (1, 1) in the two states. There are two groups of consumers who differ by the state in which they receive their endowment (the utility function is common). As in figure 6.1, c_1 represents the cost of a firm issuing one security, and c_2 represents the cost of a firm issuing a second security. The number of securities in the figure refers to the total number of securities issued by all firms (e.g., three if some firms issue two contingent claims and others issue only equity).

Figure 6.2a illustrates the relationship between the issuing costs and the total number of securities issued. When just one security is issued, then it must be equity with a payoff of 1 in both states. Thus, it will not be worth issuing just one security unless $c_1 \leq 0.5[V'(1) + V'(0)]$. Again, the best that a two-security firm can do involves splitting itself in such a way that all the output in a particular state is allocated to the group of security holders that values it most. Thus, the optimal securities have the payoffs shown in table 6.3. The prices shown are the gross values, given that the two groups consume only their endowments It will be worth issuing at least two securities whenever $c_1 + c_2 \leq V'(0)$. It follows that no securities at all will be issued to the right of the boundary with the kink at $(0.5[V'(1) + V'(0)], 0.5[V'(0) - V'(1)])$.

For c_2 below the kink and to the left of this boundary, firms will find it worthwhile to issue two securities, as shown in figure 6.2a. In this region

Table 6.3
Payoffs to optimal securities in example 3

Claim	Payoff		Price
	State 1	State 2	
r^1	1	0	0.5 $V'(0)$
r^2	0	1	0.5 $V'(0)$

Note: Again, the best that a two-security firm can do involves splitting itself in such a way that all the output in a particular state is allocated to the group that values it most. Claim r^1 is held by the group that is endowed with output only in state 2. When investors consume only their endowments, they bid claim r^1's price to $(0.5)(1)V'(0) = 0.5\ V'(0)$, where 0.5 and 1 are the state 1 probability and payoff, respectively, and $V'(0)$ is the group's marginal utility of consumption in state 1. Similarly, claim r^2 is held by the group that is endowed with output only in state 1.

there is full risk sharing but not full investment: all the firms that operate allocate their output between their security holders efficiently, but not all firms that could operate do so. As c_1 falls, more firms operate. When $c_2 = 0$, the point where all firms invest is reached when $c_1 = V'(1)$. To the left of this, all firms still issue only two securities and there is both full risk sharing and full investment. For small values of c_2, those firms which issue two securities must do at least as well as those which issue one. For sufficiently small values of c_1, firms are indifferent between issuing one and two securities. But for large values it is not worthwhile issuing just one: firms can do strictly better by issuing two. The points at which all firms issue two securities but are indifferent between this and issuing only one gives the boundary between the regions where two and three securities are issued in total.

All firms find it optimal to issue only one security above and to the left of the kink at $(0.5[V'(1) + V'(0)], 0.5[V'(0) - V'(1)])$. The boundary between this and the region where three securities are issued in total occurs at the points where all firms issue one security but are indifferent between this and issuing two. Thus, when $c_1 = 0$ and all firms issue at least one security that is held equally by the two groups, it occurs at the point where $c_2 = 0.5[V'(0.5) - V'(1.5)]$. In the case shown in figure 6.2a, $V''' > 0$ and the point is below $0.5[V'(0) - V'(1)]$; otherwise, it would be above. When c_1 is sufficiently small, all firms operate and the boundary is horizontal. However, when $c_1 > 0.5[V'(0.5) + V'(1.5)]$ the boundary slopes up as c_1 increases and the amount of equity held in the one-security region falls.

Figure 6.2b shows how the efficiency of investment and risk sharing is affected by the issuing costs. As can be seen, (1) provided that the marginal

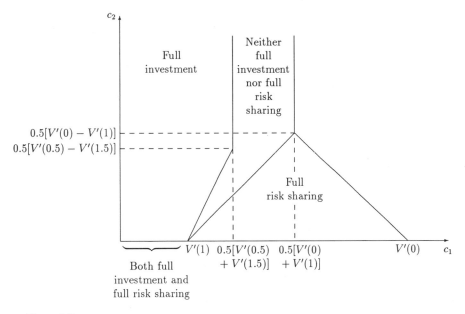

Figure 6.2b
The relationship between issuing costs, risk sharing, and investment in example 3
See the legend for figure 6.2a. In the region labeled "Full risk sharing," firms allocate their output to investors efficiently, and in the region labeled "Full investment," all firms operate.

cost of issuing the first security is sufficiently low, there is full investment efficiency, and (2) provided that the marginal cost of issuing the second security is sufficiently low, there is full risk-sharing efficiency. When both are high, there is a compromise between the two. The only case where there is full investment and full risk sharing, so that the allocation is fully efficient, is when $c_2 = 0$ and c_1 is sufficiently small.

In summary, this section has developed simple examples to illustrate the optimal design of securities. It has been shown that debt and equity are not optimal securities even in cases where one group is risk-neutral and one is risk-averse. Instead, it is optimal to split the firm in a particularly simple way. The firm should be marketed to the pair of groups of security holders that leads to the highest valuation of the firm. The output in each state should be allocated to the group that values it most highly, with the other getting zero in that state. Only in states where both groups value consumption equally is it optimal to have both security holders receiving positive payoffs. However, theorem 2.4 in section 6.2 shows that even in this situation there always exists an equivalent equilibrium where securities are extreme in the sense that all output is allocated to one or the other of the groups of security holders. Theorem 2.4 also demonstrates that the result that optimal securities should be extreme holds in much more complex environments than the simple two-group, two-state example illustrated here.

Of course, in reality firms do issue debt and equity. However, as pointed out in the introduction, the model is meant to be an abstraction that gives insight: the result demonstrates that the basic principle of security design is that the firm should be split in such a way that in any state all the payoffs are allocated to the group that values them most. We have not taken into account all the relevant institutional details. By extending the model to allow for richer institutional and tax environments, more directly descriptive results should be obtainable. For example, we have not incorporated the tax deductibility of interest or possibilities for intermediation. What we might actually expect to obtain in a model incorporating these factors is firms issuing debt to get its tax advantages and intermediaries repackaging it to get any risk-sharing advantages.

The Role of Short-Sale Constraints

With issuing costs, financial structure must matter in order to provide an incentive to firms to issue securities. This potentially creates arbitrage possibilities that must be ruled out by some sort of friction if the existence of equilibrium is to be assured. In every case above it is assumed that short sales are so costly that they are not undertaken. In practice, the costs of undertaking short selling (including both the direct costs and those resulting from the way in which short sales are taxed) are large and the actual amount that is done, by nonmembers of exchanges is small (see, for example, Pollack 1986). The purpose of this section is to consider the case where there are costs but these are not sufficient to rule out all short sales.

Suppose that there are just fixed costs of short selling; there will still be a nonexistence problem, as described in the introduction. It is again possible to construct a perfectly hedged portfolio and earn a profit equal to c_2 for each firm that is short-sold. By taking a sufficiently large position, it will always be possible to make a profit that is larger than the fixed costs. Hence, some marginal cost of short selling is necessary if an equilibrium is to exist with short sales. A constant marginal cost is not sufficient since this either rules out short sales completely if it is greater than c_2 per firm or fails to prevent the nonexistence problem if it is less than this. Hence, the case of interest is where there is a nonlinear cost of short selling.

There are two obvious possibilities: The costs depend either on the number of shares short-sold or on the value of the shares short-sold. Given the arbitrariness of assuming any number of shares in a firm, it is perhaps easier to adopt the latter approach here. In particular it is assumed that the costs of short selling, σ, are an increasing convex function of the total value of securities, Z, that is short-sold. For purposes of illustration. it is convenient to assume that

$$\sigma = Z^2.$$

In the equilibrium of example 2a, the short-sale constraints bind on both the risk-neutral and the risk-averse groups. The risk-neutral group would of course like to short-sell the r^1 security with payoffs $(1, 0)$ since its price is greater than its expected return. However, the risk-averse group would also like to short-sell the r^2 security with payoffs $(0, 2)$. This is because by combining this with a long position in the one-security firm's equity, they can effectively create the r^1 security at a price equal to its expected return. Thus, what happens when there are nonlinear cost and when only limited short selling is possible is that the n's expand the supply of the r^1 security and the a's expand the supply of the r^2 security.

Consider what happens at the critical value $c_2^* = 0.114$, where introducing a two-security firm at prices $v^1 = 1.000$ and $v^2 = 0.614$ becomes worthwhile. As soon as some firm issues r^1 and r^2, the two groups will short-sell them, thereby expanding the supplies of both. The price of r^1 in particular must then fall in order to equate demand and supply. But at a lower price it is not worthwhile for any firm to issue two securities. Hence, similar to the case with unlimited short sales, no equilibrium exists. In order for an equilibrium to exist, c_2 must be sufficiently small that at the price where demand equals supply for r^1 it is nevertheless worthwhile for a firm to issue two securities. For all values of c_2 below the critical level $c_2^{**} = 0.076$, where this becomes feasible, an equilibrium exists. At this point the n's short-sell an amount 0.115 of r^1 and the a's short-sell an amount 0.038 of r^2. However, between c_2^* and c_2^{**} no equilibrium exists.

The possibility of short selling effectively introduces another way for securities to be issued. Since in the example considered in this section the costs of short selling are quadratic, it is always worthwhile for individuals to issue a limited amount of securities. For small amounts, they have a cost advantage over firms in expanding the supply of the security. At least for low values of c_2, this expanded low-cost supply of the security leads to a better allocation of risk than would occur without short selling. The problem is that for intermediate values of c_2, the competition between firms and individuals can lead to the nonexistence of equilibrium.

6.6   Concluding Remarks

This chapter develops a framework for considering the question of optimal security design. Since this is of interest only when markets are incomplete, a model is used in which the absence of full risk-sharing possibilities is due to the existence of transaction costs for issuing securities. In constructing any model of this type, two questions must be addressed. The first concerns the form of friction that must be introduced so that equilibrium can exist. The second involves the way in which the markets for unissued securities are represented. The approaches taken above of introducing costs of short sales and of assuming that both the firms and the consumers know the prices of unissued securities are not the only alternatives for resolving these questions. Their main advantage is that they provide a simple and tractable benchmark.

Within this framework many issues remain to be addressed. Among other things, an important question that we hope to pursue in future research concerns the optimal design of securities in multiperiod models. In addition to implications for capital structure, such analyses should also have implications for dividend policy. The role of the assumptions concerning short sales and unissued securities also points to the importance of research aimed at providing a more detailed understanding of the microstructure of markets.

We have avoided some difficult questions concerning the existence of equilibrium by assuming no short sales. In the context of the tax clientele literature, Schaefer (1982) argues that short-sale constraints will be necessary for the existence of equilibrium if there exist differentially taxed assets that have perfectly correlated pretax and after-tax payoffs. However, Dammon and Green (1987) have shown that if firms' payoffs have unique risk, then equilibrium can exist without short-sale constraints. In ongoing research we are considering extensions of the approach used in this chapter—extensions in which short sales are not limited by the assumption that they are too costly and in which firms' payoffs have unique risk.

Appendix

Formal Definition of the Model

There are two dates ($t = 0, 1$) and a finite set of states of nature ($s \in S$). All agents have the same informational structure: There is no information at the first date, and the true state is revealed at the second. At each date there is a single consumption good. Since commodities are distinguished by the date and state in which they are delivered, the commodity space is $\mathbf{R}^{|S|+1}$. There is a finite set of types of consumers ($i \in I$) and a finite set of types of producers ($j \in J$) To justify the assumption of perfect competition, we assume that there is a continuum of agents of each type. For each $i \in I$, let $m_i > 0$ denote the measure of consumers of type i; for each $j \in J$, let $n_j > 0$ denote the measure of producers of type j.

Producers A type of producer is defined by a security set and a cost function. The security set of type $j \in J$ is denoted by E_j, which is simply an index set. Any production plan can have at most two types of claims issued against it; for any $e \in E_j$, these two claims are indexed by $k = 1, 2$. The properties of the different securities are described by two dividend functions (r^1, r^2) defined on the global security set $E = \bigcup_{j \in J} E_j$; thus, $r^k(e)$ denotes the vector of dividends corresponding to the kth claim in financial structure e. The dividend functions define the production plan, or output vector, associated with each financial structure: $y_j(e) \equiv r^1(e) + r^2(e)$ for any $e \in E_j$. Let $Y_j = \{y_j(e) | e \in E_j\}$ denote the set of feasible output vectors for firms of type $j \in J$. Securities are assumed to satisfy the following conditions:

A1a. E_j is a compact metric space for every $j \in J$.

A1b. For all $j \in J$ there exists $e \in E_j$ such that $r^1(e) = r^2(e) = 0$.

A1c. For all $j \in J$ and any $y \in Y_j$ there exists $e \in E_j$ such that $r^1(e) = y$ and $r^2(e) = 0$.

A2. $r^k: E \to \mathbf{R}_+^{|S|}$ is a continuous function.

Since E is an index set, assumptions A1a and A2 are technical conveniences. Assumption A1b represents the possibility of issuing no securities (i.e., the producer decides not to produce any output). Assumption A1c says that it is possible to issue a single security (equity).

The cost function of producers of type $j \in J$ is denoted by C_j: $E_j \to \mathbf{R}_+$. $C_j(e)$ is the cost, in units of output at date 0, of operating a firm with financial structure $e \in E_j$. Without essential loss of generality, we may assume that these costs include the cost of inputs to the production process (i.e., investment). It is natural to assume that

A3a. $C_j(e) = 0$ if $e \in E_j$ and $r^1(e) = r^2(e) = 0$.

A3b. C_j: $E_j \to \mathbf{R}_+$ is lower-semicontinuous.

Every producer is assumed to maximize his profit, taking as given the market value of the different kinds of firms he can operate. Let MV(e) denote the value of a firm with structure $e \in E$, measured in units of consumption goods at date 0. Then a producer of type $j \in J$ chooses $e \in E_j$ to maximize MV(e) $-$ $C_j(e)$. The producer takes prices (and hence MV) as given; he does not need to concern himself with the actions of other agents. Not all producers of the same type will choose the same financial structure, because the objective function is not quasi-concave. The equilibrium choices of the jth type are represented by a measure v_j defined on E_j. A measure like v_j is called a distribution; for any measurable set $H \subset E_j$, $v_j(H)$ is the measure of producers of type j who choose securities of type $e \in H$. A distribution v_j is admissible iff $v_j(E_j) = n_j$ (i.e., if all producers of type j are accounted for). N_j denotes the set of admissible distributions of producers of type $j \in J$. Then for each $j \in J$ we can define the optimal security correspondence ψ_j by putting

$$\psi_j(\text{MV}) = \arg\max_{v \in N_j} \int_{E_j} (\text{MV} - C_j)\, dv$$

for any market-value function MV. Under price-taking behavior, individual profit maximization is equivalent to aggregate profit maximization.

Consumers Every consumer is characterized by a consumption set, a portfolio set, a utility function, and an endowment. All consumers have the same consumption set $\Omega = \mathbf{R}_+^{|S|+1}$ with generic element $x \in \Omega$. It is convenient to partition the consumption set $\Omega = \Omega^0 \times \Omega^1$ and to partition consumption bundles $x = (x^0, x^1) \in \Omega^0 \times \Omega^1$. ($x^0 \in \mathbf{R}_+$ denotes consumption at date 0, and $x^1 \in \mathbf{R}_+^{|S|}$ denotes consumption at date 1.) The utility function of consumers of type $i \in I$ is denoted by U_i: $\Omega \to \mathbf{R}$; the endowment is denoted by $w_i \in \Omega$.

A portfolio is a nonnegative, vector-valued measure $\alpha = (\alpha^1, \alpha^2)$ defined on E. For any measurable set $H \subset E$ and any $k = 1, 2$, $\alpha^k(H)$ is the number of units of the kth claim on a firm with structure $e \in E$ held in the portfolio. No short sales are allowed, so α has values in $\mathbf{R}_+^2$. All consumers have the same set of admissible portfolios denoted by A.

A consumer of type $i \in I$ is characterized by the array (Ω, A, U_i, w_i). We assume that each type satisfies the following properties:

A4a. $U_i: \Omega \to \mathbf{R}$ is strictly quasi-concave and strictly increasing for every $i \in I$.

A4b. U_j is C^1 on the interior of Ω and continuous at the boundary for every $i \in I$.

Assumption A4 allows us to define a function $p_i:$ int $\Omega \to \mathbf{R}^{|S|}$ for each $i \in I$ by putting

$$p_i(x) = \frac{\partial U_i/\partial x^1}{\partial U_i/\partial x^0}$$

for every $x \in$ int Ω. Since U_j is strictly increasing, $p_i(x) \gg 0$ for every $x \in$ int Ω.

A security price function is a function $v \equiv (v^1, v^2)$ defined on E to $\mathbf{R}_+^2$. For any $e \in E$ and $k = 1, 2$, $v^k(e)$ is the price, measured in units of consumption of date 0, of the kth claim in the financial structure e. We restrict attention to continuous price functions. For any admissible portfolio $a \in A$, the value of the portfolio is defined by $\alpha * v$, where

$$\alpha * v = \sum_{k=1}^{2} \int_E v^k \, d\alpha^k.$$

Similarly, the total income at date 1 from a portfolio $a \in A$ is denoted by $\alpha * r$, where $r = (r^1, r^2)$ and

$$\alpha * r = \sum_{k=1}^{2} \int_E r^k \, d\alpha^k.$$

In this notation we can write the budget constraints for a consumer of type $I \in I$ as follows:

$$x^0 = w_i^0 - \alpha * v$$

$$x^1 = w_i^1 + \alpha * r.$$

(The budget constraints are equations because U_i is strictly increasing.) Using these equations, we can write the consumption bundle x as a function of α and v. So we write $x = \xi_i(\alpha, v)$ for every $i \in I$. Then we define the budget set for type $i \in I$ to be

$$\beta_i(v) = \{\alpha \in A \mid \xi_i(\alpha, v) \in \Omega\}$$

for every price function v. The optimal portfolio correspondence is defined by putting

$$\phi_i(v) = \underset{\alpha \in \beta_i(v)}{\arg\max} \ U_i(\xi_i(\alpha, v))$$

for any price function v.

Equilibrium   We define our concept of equilibrium in two stages. First we outline a Walrasian type of concept; then we add an extra condition suggested by Hart (1979). In Walrasian equilibrium all agents maximize utility, taking prices as given, and all markets clear at the prevailing prices. An equilibrium must specify a portfolio α_i for each type of consumer $i \in I$, a distribution v_j for each type of producer $j \in J$, and a continuous price function $v: E \to \mathbf{R}_+^2$. We define a Walrasian equilibrium to be an array $\langle (\alpha_i)_{i \in I}, (v_j)_{j \in J}, v \rangle$ satisfying the following properties:

$$\alpha_i \in \phi_i(v) \qquad \text{for every } i \in I \tag{E1}$$

$$v_j \in \psi_j(v^1 + v^2) \qquad \text{for every } j \in J \tag{E2}$$

$$\sum_{i \in I} \alpha_i = \sum_{j \in J} v_j. \tag{E3}$$

Properties (E1) and (E2) require utility maximization on the part of consumers and producers, respectively; (E3) requires market clearing.

In a large economy the securities issued by any producer are negligible relative to the size of the economy as a whole. Without loss of generality, we can assume that if a new security is issued, it will be widely held and each consumer will hold a negligible amount of it. In that case a security is valued according to the marginal rates of substitution of those who hold it. The *rational conjecture condition* can be written as follows:

$$v^k(e) = \max\{p_i(\xi_i(\alpha_i, v)) \cdot r^k(e)\} \qquad \text{for every } e \in E \text{ and } k = 1, 2. \tag{E4}$$

The maximum in condition (E4) is taken over $\{i \in I \mid \xi_i^0(\alpha_j, v) > 0\}$. An equilibrium is defined to be a Walrasian equilibrium that satisfies (E4).

Condition (E4) does not affect the equilibrium allocation in any substantive way. (E4) is automatically satisfied in Walrasian equilibrium for every security that is actually issued. If (E4) is not satisfied in some Walrasian equilibrium, one can satisfy it simply by reducing the value of $v^k(e)$ appropriately without making any other change in the Walrasian equilibrium.

Efficiency   The appropriate concept of efficiency is constrained efficiency. We ask whether a central planner can make everyone better off by using only the markets and technologies available to private individuals. (Under our assumptions there is no difference between making everyone better off and making some people better off and no one worse off.) The allocation at date 1 is determined by trades in securities at date 0. Therefore, an equilibrium is constrained-efficient iff it is impossible to make everyone better off by means of transfers of goods and securities at date 0. Formally, an equilibrium $\langle (\alpha_i)_{i \in I}, (v_j)_{j \in J}, v \rangle$ is constrained-efficient iff there does not exist an obtainable allocation $\langle (\hat{\alpha}_i)_{i \in I}, (\hat{v}_j)_{j \in J} \rangle$ and transfers $(\tau_h)_{h \in I \cup J}$ satisfying these conditions:

(a) $\hat{\alpha}_i \in A$, $\hat{v}_j \in N_j$, and $\tau_h \in \mathbf{R}$ for every $i \in I$, $j \in J$, and $h \in I \cup J$.

(b) $\sum_{i \in I} m_i \hat{\alpha}_i = \sum_{j \in J} \hat{v}_j$ and $\sum_{i \in I} m_i \tau_i + \sum_{j \in J} n_j \tau_j = 0$.

(c) $\int_{E_j} (v^1 + v^2 - C_j) \, dv_j < \int_{E_j} (v^1 + v^2 - C_j) \, d\hat{v}_j + \tau_j$ for every $j \in J$.

(d) $U_i[\xi_i(\alpha_i, v)] < U_i[\xi_i(\hat{\alpha}_i, v) + (\tau_i, 0)]$ for every $i \in I$.

(The fact that we use the equilibrium price function v in the definition of constrained efficiency is immaterial. It simply allows us to use the notation introduced earlier.)

Proof of Theorems 2.1 and 2.2

THEOREM 2.1   Every equilibrium is constrained-efficient.

Proof.   Suppose not. Then in the previous notation

$$\xi_i^0(\hat{\alpha}_i, v) + \hat{\alpha}_i * v + \tau_i > w_i^0 \qquad (i \in I)$$

and

$$\int_{E_j} [v^1 + v^2 - C_j + \tau_j] \, d\hat{v}_j > \int_{E_j} [v^1 + v^2 - C_j] \, dv_j \qquad (j \in J). \qquad (1)$$

Adding up, we get

$$\sum_{i \in I} m_i \{ \xi_i^0(\hat{\alpha}_i, v) + \hat{\alpha}_i * v + \tau_i \} > \sum_{i \in I} m_i w_i^0. \tag{2}$$

The attainability condition for the new allocation has the form

$$\sum_{i \in I} m_i \xi_i^0(\hat{\alpha}_i, v) + \sum_{j \in J} \hat{v}_j * v = \sum_{i \in I} m_i w_i^0.$$

Then substituting from condition (b) above yields

$$\sum_{i \in I} m_i \{ \xi_i^0(\hat{\alpha}_i, v) + \hat{\alpha}_i * v \} = \sum_{i \in I} m_i w_i^0$$

so equation 2 and condition (b) imply that $\sum_{j \in J} \int_{E_j} \tau_j d\hat{v}_j < 0$. From the equilibrium conditions we know that

$$\int_{E_j} (v^1 + v^2 - C_j) d\hat{v}_j \le \int_{E_j} (v^1 + v^2 - C_j) dv_j$$

so for some $j \in J$, equation 1 is violated.   ∎

THEOREM 2.2   Under the maintained assumptions the equilibrium set is nonempty.

Proof.   For each $q = 1, 2, \ldots,$ let E_j^q be a finite subset of E_j satisfying the same properties as E_j and such that $E_j^q \to E_j$ as $q \to \infty$, where convergence of E_j^q is with respect to the Hausdorff metric. We prove existence for the economy with E_j replaced by E_j^q for all $j \in J$, and then the theorem follows by taking limits.

Let $E^q = \bigcup_{j \in J} E_j^q$ and let A^q denote the set of nonnegative measures on E^q to $\mathbf{R}^2$ with the property that

$$\alpha^k(\{e\}) \le \frac{n_j + 1}{\min\{m_i\}}$$

for any $e \in E_j$; $k = 1, 2$; $j \in J$; and $\alpha \in a^q$. Thus, any portfolio α observed in equilibrium must certainly belong to A^q. For each $i \in I$, let $\beta_i^q(v) = \beta_i(v) \cap A^q$ and define $\phi_i^q(v)$ by

$$\phi_i^q(v) = \arg\max_{\alpha \in \beta_i^q(v)} U_i[\xi_i(\alpha, v)]$$

for any $e \in E^q$, $k = 1, 2$, and any consumption bundle x_i.

Let

$$V^q = \{v: E^q \to \mathbf{R}^2 | v^1(e) + v^2(e) \le K\}$$

where K is very large. Then

$$\phi_i^q: V^q \to A^q$$

is upper hemicontinuous (u.h.c.), nonempty, and convex-valued. Similarly, define ψ_j^q by putting N_j^q equal to the set of nonnegative real-valued measures on E_j^q such that $v_j(E_j^q) = n_j$ for all $v_j \in N_j^q$, and then

$$\psi_j^q(v) = \arg\max_{v \in N_j^q} \sum_{k=1}^{2} \int E_j^q (MV - C_j)\, dv^k$$

for any $v \in V^q$. Then the usual arguments show that

$$\psi_j^q: V^q \to M(E_j^q)$$

is u.h.c., nonempty, and convex-valued. Define a correspondence

$$\zeta^q: V^q \to \mathbf{R}^{E_q} \times \mathbf{R}^{E_q}$$

by

$$\zeta^q(v) = \sum_{i \in I} m_i \phi_i^q(v) - \sum_{j \in J} \hat{\psi}_j^q(v)$$

for every $v \in V^q$, where $\hat{\psi}_j^q(v) = \{(v, v) | v \in \psi_j^q(v)\}$. Then ζ^q inherits the properties of (ψ_j^q) and (ϕ_i^q). Choose K in the definition of V^q so that in any attainable allocation, $p_i(x_i) \cdot r^k(e) < K$.

By a standard fixed-point argument there exists $(z^q, v^q) \in \mathbf{R}_+^{E_q} \times \mathbf{R}_+^{E_q} \times V^q$ such that $z^q \in \zeta^q(v^q)$ and $v^q * z^q \ge V^q * z^q$. If $z^{qk}(e) > 0$, then $v^{qk}(e) = K$, but in that case $\alpha^k(e) = 0$ for any $\alpha \in \phi_i^q(v^q)$ and any $i \in I$, a contradiction. Conversely, $z^{qk}(e) < 0$ implies that $v^{qk}(e) = 0$, in which case $\alpha^k(e) = (n_j + 1)/\min\{m_i\}$ for some j, where $e \in E_j$ and $\alpha \in \phi_i^q(v^q)$. (Unless $r^k(e) = 0$; in that case, put $z^{qk}(e) = 0$ without loss of generality.) Again we have a contradiction. So $z^q = 0$.

It is straightforward to check that conditions (a) to (c) of the definition of equilibrium are satisfied (i.e., none of the artificial constraints is binding). To ensure condition (d), simply replace $v^q(e)$ by

$$\min\{v^q(e), \max p_i(\xi_i(\alpha_i, v^q))\}$$

where $\alpha_i \in \phi_i^q(v^q)$ and the maximum is taken over $\{i \in I | \xi_i^0(\alpha_i, v^q) > 0\}$. (Note that strict quasi-concavity of U_i implies that $\xi_i(\alpha_i, v^q)$ is unique.) It is easy to check that this does not disturb the other equilibrium conditions for any $v: E^q \to \mathbf{R}_+^2$.

For each E^q we have an equilibrium $\{(\alpha_i^q), (v_j^q), v^q\}$ for the corresponding economy. The measures (α_i^q) and (v_j^q) can be extended to all of E in an obvious way; so can v^q, and condition (d) tells us that this extension is continuous. Since (α_i^q) and (v_i^q) are bounded, there exist weakly convergent subsequences, which we can take to be the original sequence. Along this sequence $\xi_i(\alpha_i^q, v^q)$ is unique for each i and q, so we can choose a further subsequence along which $\xi_i(\alpha^q, v^q)$ converges. (Obviously $\{\xi_i(\alpha^q, v^q)\}$ is bounded.) Along this sequence v^q converges to a continuous function $v: E \to \mathbf{R}_+^2$. We claim that the limit point $\{(\alpha_i), (v_j), v\}$ is the required equilibrium. By continuity, conditions (c) and (d) are satisfied. Suppose, contrary to what we want to prove, that condition (a) is not satisfied. Then there exists, for some $i \in I$, an $\hat{\alpha}_i \in \beta_i(v)$ that is preferred to α_i. This is impossible unless $\hat{\alpha}_i * v > 0$, so without loss of generality we can assume that $w_i^0 - \hat{\alpha}_i * v > 0$ by continuity. Since $\alpha * r \geq 0$ for any $\alpha \in A^q$, for q sufficiently large we can find $\hat{\alpha}^q \in \beta_i^q(v^q)$ arbitrarily close to $\hat{\alpha}_i$ in the weak sense. (This requires the facts that E is compact and $v^q \to v$ uniformly on E.) But for q large enough and $\hat{\alpha}^q$ close enough to $\hat{\alpha}_i$, $\hat{\alpha}^q$ must be preferred to α_i^q, a contradiction. This proves condition (a), and the proof of condition (b) is similar.   ∎

Note

An earlier version of this paper was presented at the 1988 Western Finance Association meeting at Napa. Financial support from the NSF (Grant Nos. SES-8420171/SES-8813719 and SES-8520224/SES-8720589 for the two authors, respectively) is gratefully acknowledged. We thank seminar participants at the London School of Economics, the City University of New York, and the ESRC Economic Theory Study Group meeting at the University of Warwick, and also Fischer Black, Michael Brennan, Ed Green, Joe Haubrich, Kose John, Shuman Lee, a referee, and particularly Chester Spatt for many helpful comments and suggestions.

References

Allen, F., 1987, "Capital Structure and Imperfect Competition in Product Markets," Working Paper 11-87, Rodney L. White Center, Wharton School, University of Pennsylvania.

Baron, D. P., 1974, "Default Risk, Home-Made Leverage and the Modigliani-Miller Theorem," *American Economic Review*, 62, 176–182.

Baron, D. P., 1976, "Default Risk and the Modigliani-Miller Theorem: A Synthesis," *American Economic Review* 64, 204–212.

Dammon, R. M., and R. C. Green, 1987, "Tax Arbitrage and the Existence of Equilibrium Prices for Financial Assets," *Journal of Finance*, 42, 1143–1166.

Diamond, P A., 1967, "The Role of a Stock Market in a General Equilibrium Model with Technological Uncertainty," *American Economic Review*, 57, 759–766.

Duffie, D., and M. O. Jackson, 1986, "Optimal Innovation of Futures Contracts," Research Paper 917, Stanford Graduate School of Business.

Dybvig, P. H., and S. A. Ross, 1986, "Tax Clienteles and Asset Pricing," *Journal of Finance*, 41, 751–762.

Grossman, S. J., and J. E. Stiglitz, 1980, "On the Impossibility of Informationally Efficient Markets," *American Economic Review*, 70, 393–408.

Hart, O. D., 1975, "On the Optimality of Equilibrium when Market Structure is Incomplete," *Journal of Economic Theory*, 11, 418–443.

Hart, O. D., 1977, "Take-Over Bids and Stock Market Equilibrium," *Journal of Economic Theory*, 16, 53–83.

Hart, O. D., 1979, "On Shareholder Unanimity in Large Stock Market Economies," *Econometrica*, 47, 1057–1084.

Hart, O. D., 1980, "Perfect Competition and Optimal Product Differentiation," *Journal of Economic Theory*, 22, 279–312.

Hellwig, M. F., 1981, "Bankruptcy, Limited Liability and the Modigliani-Miller Theorem," *American Economic Review*, 71, 155–170.

Jensen, M. C., and W. H. Meckling, 1976, "Theory of the Firm: Managerial Behavior, Agency Costs and Ownership Structure," *Journal of Financial Economics*, 3, 305–360.

Makowski, L., 1980, "Perfect Competition, the Profit Criterion and the Organization of Economic Activity," *Journal of Economic Theory*, 22, 222–242.

Miller, M. H., 1977, "Debt and Taxes," *Journal of Finance*, 32, 261–275.

Miller, M. H., 1986, "Financial Innovation: The Last Twenty Years and the Next," *Journal of Financial and Quantitative Analysis*, 21, 459–471.

Modigliani, F., and M. H. Miller, 1958, "The Cost of Capital, Corporation Finance, and the Theory of Finance," *American Economic Review*, 48, 162–197.

Myers, S. C., 1984, "The Capital Structure Puzzle," *Journal of Finance*, 39, 575–592.

Pollack, I. M., 1986, *Short-Sale Regulation of NASDAQ Securities*, NASDAQ pamphlet.

Radner, R., 1972, "Existence of Equilibrium Plans, Prices and Price Expectations in a Sequence of Markets," *Econotnetrica*, 40, 289–303.

Ross, S. A., 1987, "Arbitrage and Martingales with Taxation," *Journal of Political Economy*, 95, 371–393.

Schaefer, S. A., 1982, "Taxes and Security Market Equilibrium," in W. F. Sharpe and C. M. Cootner (eds.), *Financial Economics Essays in Honor of Paul Cootner*, Prentice-Hall, Englewood Cliffs, N.J., pp. 159–178.

Silber, W. L., 1981, "Innovation, Competition and New Contract Design in Futures Markets," *Journal of Futures, Markets*, 1, 123–155.

Stiglitz, J. E., 1969, "A Re-Examination of the Modigliani-Miller Theorem," *American Economic Review*, 59, 784–793.

Stiglitz, J. E., 1974, "On the Irrelevance of Corporate Financial Policy," *American Economic Review*, 64, 851–866.

Williams, J. T., 1986, "Bonds, Stocks and Options as Optimal Contracts between Corporate Claimants," mimeo, Graduate School of Business Administration, New York University.

7 Arbitrage, Short Sales, and Financial Innovation

7.1 Introduction

The Arrow-Debreu-McKenzie model of general equilibrium assumes that markets are complete so that all contingent commodities can be traded. The theory has now been extended to deal with the more realistic case of incomplete markets, where some commodities cannot be traded.[1] However, even this literature typically assumes a given market structure.[2] The assumption of a given market structure is quite restrictive, as one can see from recent developments in financial markets. The unprecedented rate of financial innovation makes it clear that market structure is neither constant nor exogenous.

In this chapter we consider some of the implications of endogenizing market structure by allowing firms to issue new securities. We begin by defining an equilibrium in an economy with a finite number of firms and a continuum of investors. Then we study the behavior of the equilibrium as the number of firms becomes unboundedly large. When the number of firms is finite, one expects the economy to be imperfectly competitive; but as the number of firms becomes large, one expects price-taking competition to obtain.[3] Under certain conditions, that may be the case here, but only if short sales are strictly limited. If investors are allowed to undertake unlimited short sales, then we can show that:

(I)   Firms do not necessarily become price-takers in the limit.

(II) Financial innovation is not necessarily efficient.

(III) Even when the cost of issuing new securities is negligible, markets may not be complete.

These results are disturbing because the assumption of unlimited short sales plays a crucial role in financial theory. A number of important classical results rely on spanning arguments that require agents to take short positions. Some examples are the use of Arrow securities (Arrow 1964), the Modigliani-Miller theorem (Modigliani-Miller 1958; Hellwig 1981), the arbitrage pricing theory of Ross (1976), and the options pricing theory of Black-Scholes (1973). But when financial innovation is allowed, it appears that short sales are incompatible with efficiency and price-taking

This article originally appeared in *Econometrica*, vol. 59, no. 4 (July 1991) 1041–1068. Reprinted with permission.

behavior. So the attractive properties of the classical theory appear to be threatened by the possibility of financial innovation.

Although our formal analysis is concerned with the impact of short sales on innovation, it has a wider relevance. In an empirical study of financial innovation by investment banks, Tufano (1988) has found that the first firm to innovate bears substantially higher costs than subsequent imitators. Moreover, the first-mover does not charge a higher price for his product during the brief period of monopoly before imitative products appear. His data show that there is a problem for innovators in recouping their costs. (He suggests the incentive to innovate comes from increased market share.) In our model, all firms move simultaneously and bear the same costs. However, the short-sellers play a role analogous to the imitators in Tufano's study. This suggests that similar techniques might be used to study the effects of imitation, with similar results.[4]

In section 7.2 we describe the basic model. There is a finite number of firms with a random future income. Each firm is owned by an entrepreneur who wants to maximize his current consumption. He does this by selling claims against his future income to investors. When no short sales are allowed, the incentive to issue new securities is straightforward. Because it is costly to issue claims, markets will be incomplete. Then different types of investors will typically put different values on the same security. In order to maximize the market value of the firm, an entrepreneur will issue a variety of claims against the future returns of the firm. In effect, he is "splitting" the firm and marketing each piece to the clientele that values it most.

When unlimited short sales are allowed, things are more complicated. For example, it is well known from the literature on stock market economies that a firm's choice of production plan can have a large impact on the economy when unlimited short sales are allowed. By introducing a new production plan, the firm can change the dimension of the space spanned by investors' portfolios (see, for example, Kreps 1979, essay II). Similarly, in the present context, the introduction of a new security by a single firm can have a large impact on the economy if it increases the span of the securities in the economy. But if each security is issued by a large number of firms, it is not clear that perfect competition is incompatible with short sales. One of the central points of this paper is that competition is necessarily " imperfect" if there is to be any incentive to innovate.

In section 7.3, we study an example that illustrates this idea. In the example, firms are assumed to have identical returns. Then arbitrage ensures that in equilibrium all firms have the same market value. This means that ex post, after the entrepreneurs have made their decisions, there is no incentive to innovate. An entrepreneur who has issued innovative securities is worse off than one who does not, since he has incurred a cost of innovation and yet realizes the same market value. Nonetheless, there may be an incentive to innovate ex ante, before the entrepreneurs make their decisions. By introducing innovative securities, an entrepreneur may influence the prices that prevail ex post and hence change the market values of all firms, his own along with others'. Furthermore, this effect may persist even when the number of entrepreneurs and assets becomes unboundedly large.

The crucial assumption of the example studied in section 7.3 is that the future returns of firms are perfectly correlated. In section 7.4 we argue that similar conclusions should hold in the general case, when returns exhibit idiosyncratic risk. Without the assumption of perfect correlation, arbitrage is risky, the market values of firms may not be equalized, and there may be an ex post incentive to innovate. But if a large number of entrepreneurs choose the same financial structure (issue the same types of securities), the idiosyncratic risk can be diversified away. Then the market value of firms with the same financial structure must be equalized and the ex post incentive to innovate disappears for those firms. There are two ways that the incentive to innovate can be preserved. First, if only a small number of entrepreneurs issues a particular security, each of the entrepreneurs may perceive that he has a large impact on the equilibrium price. Second, because the returns to individual firms exhibit idiosyncratic risk, arbitrage may be unprofitable when the number of innovating firms is small and so there may remain an ex post incentive to innovate. In either case, the incentive to innovate is preserved only if there is imperfect competition and this conclusion should hold even in the limit, when the number of firms becomes unboundedly large.

Section 7.5 contains some further examples of the limiting behavior of equilibrium as the economy becomes unboundedly large. Those examples show that non-price-taking behavior and inefficiency persist in the limit when short sales are unconstrained and there is idiosyncratic risk.

In section 7.6 we study the case where short sales are strictly limited. Under certain conditions, we can obtain a competitive limit theorem, that is, agents behave as price-takers asymptotically. However, because short sales create a "pecuniary externality," equilibrium need not be efficient. The existence of this externality was first recognized by Makowski (1983), in the context of a stock market economy.[5] When there are no short sales, the increase in the value of the firm coincides with the social gain from the innovation. When there are limited short sales, there is an additional source of social benefit that is not taken into account by the firm's owner. The short sales allow greater risk sharing; but the value of this risk sharing is not captured by the increase in the firm's value. Roughly speaking, it is the change in the value of the open interest rather than the change in the value of the firm that measures the social benefit of an innovation. Because of the divergence between social and private benefit, innovation may be inefficient, even if entrepreneurs are price-takers.

The results obtained here are in stark contrast to those obtained in an earlier paper (Allen and Gale 1988; hereafter AG). In that paper, we studied a model of financial innovation which differed from the model discussed here in two respects. First, in AG we assumed either that short sales were not allowed or that they were effectively limited by costs. Second, we assumed a continuum of firms, comprising a finite number of types. In contrast to the results obtained here, the model studied in AG exhibited the following properties:

(I′)   By definition, firms behaved as price-takers.

(II′)   Financial innovation was efficient.[6]

(III′)   When the costs of creating new securities were negligible, markets were complete.

Also, as we pointed out in AG, if unlimited short sales were allowed, equilibrium typically did not exist. Incentives for innovation exist in a price-taking equilibrium only if the value of the firm is perceived to depend on its financial structure. But, as we have seen, the dependence of market value on financial structure gives rise to an arbitrage opportunity which is inconsistent with equilibrium. Evidently, the concept of equilibrium used in AG is inappropriate when short sales are allowed.

7.2   A Model of Financial Equilibrium

Time is divided into two periods or *dates* indexed by $\tau = 1, 2$. At each date there is a single consumption good, which can be thought of as "income" or "money." Asset returns and prices are measured in terms of this numeraire good.

Economic agents are assumed to be of two kinds, *entrepreneurs* and *investors*. Entrepreneurs are assumed to be risk neutral and are only interested in consumption at the first date.[7] Each entrepreneur owns an asset which produces a random return at the second date. In order to maximize consumption at the first date, the entrepreneurs will want to sell their assets to the investors. They do this by issuing claims against the returns of the assets; this provides the motivation for financial innovation. Unlike entrepreneurs, investors are risk averse and are interested in consumption at both dates. In equilibrium, they purchase the claims issued by the entrepreneurs and consume the returns at the second date.

Equilibrium at the first date is achieved in two stages. In the first stage, entrepreneurs decide what kinds of claims to issue against the assets they own. At the second stage, these claims are traded on a competitive auction market. At date 2 the asset returns are realized and the claims issued at date 1 are paid off.

We begin by describing an economy with a finite number N of entrepreneurs and a continuum of investors. Later, we shall be interested in the asymptotic behavior of the economy as N becomes unboundedly large.

Asset Returns

There is a countable set of assets indexed by $n = 1, 2, \ldots, \infty$ Each asset n is represented by a random variable Z_n which gives the asset's return at date 2 in terms of the consumption good. Let G_N denote the joint probability distribution of the random variables $\{Z_n\}_{n \in N}$.[8] That is, for any $z = (z_1, \ldots, z_n) \in \mathbb{R}^N$, $G_N(z) = \text{Prob}\{Z_n \leq z_n : n \in N\}$. The asset returns are assumed to satisfy the following conditions.

ASSUMPTION 1   (a) Z_n is nonnegative with probability 1 and has finite expected value; (b) G_N is symmetric, i.e., for any permutation $\pi: N \to N$ and any $z \in \mathbb{R}^N$,

$$G_N(z_1, \ldots, z_N) = G_N(z_{\pi(1)}, \ldots, z_{\pi(N)}).$$

Symmetry does not imply that assets are perfect substitutes, although it is consistent with perfect substitutability. Typically, we will want to assume that assets exhibit some idiosyncratic risk, in which case they will *not* be perfect substitutes. On the other hand, symmetry does imply that assets make similar contributions to a well diversified portfolio.[9]

Financial Structures

When markets are incomplete, it may be possible to increase the value of an asset by "splitting" it, that is, by issuing more than one type of claim against it. A claim is a measurable function $f: \mathbb{R}_+ \to \mathbb{R}_+$. If the underlying asset shows a return of z units, the claim entitles the bearer to $f(z)$ units of the numeraire good at date 2. The collection of claims issued by an entrepreneur is called a *financial structure*. There is a finite number of financial structures indexed by $i = 1, \ldots, I$. The set of claims associated with the ith structure is denoted by F_i. F_i is assumed to be finite. The claims associated with the financial structure are assumed to exhaust the returns to the asset. Thus, for any i in I,

$$\sum_{f \in F_i} f(z) = z, \quad \forall z \in \mathbb{R}_+. \tag{2.1}$$

Issuing claims is assumed to be costly. The cost of the ith financial structure is $C_i \geq 0$ units of the numeraire good at date 1.

To illustrate these ideas, suppose the asset owned by the entrepreneur is a "firm" and that the entrepreneur wants to issue debt and equity. The random variable Z_n represents the future income of the "firm." The financial structure chosen by the entrepreneur will consist of two claims, $F_0 = \{f_0, f_1\}$, where f_0 corresponds to debt and f_1 corresponds to equity. Suppose that R is the face value of the debt. Then $f_0(z) = \min\{R, z\}$ and $f_1(z) = \max\{z - R, 0\}$, for any $z \geq 0$.

Investors

There is a continuum of investors divided into a finite set K of investor types. An investor of type k has a von Neumann–Morgenstern utility function $U_k: \mathbb{R} \times \mathbb{R} \to \mathbb{R}.$[10] If c_τ denotes consumption at date τ, the associated utility is $U_k(c_1, c_2)$. Preferences are assumed to satisfy the following standard conditions.

ASSUMPTION 2 U_k is concave, strictly increasing, and bounded above, for all $k \in K$.

We also impose the following nonstandard condition.

ASSUMPTION 3   Let $\{(c_n, W_n)\}$ be a fixed but arbitrary sequence where, for each n, c_n is a real number and W_n is a random variable. Suppose that for any $\varepsilon > 0$ and $M > 0$, $\mathrm{Prob}\{W_n \leq -M\} \geq \varepsilon$ for infinitely many values of n. Then $\liminf E[U_k(c_n, W_n)] = -\infty$.

What assumption 3 says is that expected utility becomes very negative if there is a small amount of mass very far down the tail of the distribution of second period consumption.[11] Investors are assumed to have a zero endowment of the consumption good at each date.[12]

The cross-sectional distribution of investors' types is denoted by $\alpha = (\alpha_1, \ldots, \alpha_k)$, where $\alpha_k > 0$ for every k in K and $\sum_{k \in K} \alpha_k = 1$. α_k denotes the proportion of investors who are of type k. In an economy of size N, the total measure of investors is assumed to be N so the measure of investors of type k is $\alpha_k N$.

Equilibrium is defined in two stages. First, we define equilibrium for the auction market, given the claims to be traded. Then we describe how claims are issued at the first stage, in anticipation of the auction market equilibrium at the second stage. This two-stage concept of equilibrium is fairly standard, having been used in similar contexts by Hart (1979) and Jones (1987), for example. It is the natural way to model the interaction among a finite number of oligopolistic sellers and a continuum of competitive buyers.

Exchange Equilibrium

Equilibrium in the auction market is assumed to be *symmetric*. The symmetry of equilibrium restricts equilibrium in three ways. First, investors of the same type exhibit the same equilibrium behavior. Second, if two entrepreneurs choose the same financial structure, their claims are priced in the same way. Third, if two entrepreneurs choose the same financial structure, investors demand the same amount of the corresponding claims from each entrepreneur. This last restriction is consistent with optimality in view of the symmetry of asset returns.[14] The assumption of symmetry considerably simplifies the asymptotic analysis in the sequel. Symmetry is not needed for existence but for reasons of space we have decided to restrict attention to symmetric equilibria from the outset.

The cross-sectional distribution of financial structures is denoted by $\beta \in \Delta_N(I)$, where $\Delta_N(I)$ denotes the set of vectors $\beta = (\beta_1, \ldots, \beta_I)$ satisfying

$$\sum_{i \in I} \beta_i = 1 \quad \text{and,} \quad \forall i \in I, \quad \beta_i = n/N \quad \text{for some integer } n \geq 0. \tag{2.2}$$

β_i is the proportion of entrepreneurs choosing financial structure i and $\beta_i N$ is the number choosing financial structure i. It is assumed that the equilibrium in the auction market depends only on the cross-sectional distri-

bution of financial structures; this is an additional symmetry property
imposed on the equilibrium.

The claims traded in the auction market are indexed by $A = \{(f, i): f \in F_i\}$. Also, let A_i denote the set of claims associated with F_i.[14]
Let $A(\beta)$ denote the set of *available* claims, where $A(\beta)$ is defined by

$$A(\beta) = \{(f, i) \in A \mid \beta_i > 0\}. \tag{2.3}$$

A *portfolio* is a function $d: A \to \mathbb{R}_+$, where $d(a)$ is the investor's position in
claims of type a. Note that $d(a)$ is the investor's total position in claims of
type a: if three entrepreneurs issue this type of claim, the investor buys
$d(a)/3$ units from each of them.[16] The set of portfolios is denoted by D and
the set of available portfolios by $D(\beta)$, where

$$D(\beta) = \{d \in D \mid d(a) = 0 \text{ if } a \notin A(\beta)\}. \tag{2.4}$$

In the sequel, it is sometimes assumed that investors can undertake limited
short sales. Let L denote the number of units of each claim issued by
entrepreneurs that can be sold short by investors. For most purposes, we
are interested in the cases $L = 0$ and $L = \infty$. Each investor is assumed to
receive a fraction $1/N$ of the total ration, or L/N units per entrepreneur.
Then if $\beta_i N$ entrepreneurs choose financial structure F_i, the maximum size
of an investor's short position in some claim f in F_i is $(L/N)\beta_i N = L\beta_i$. The
short sale constraint can thus be written $d(a) \geq -L\beta_i$ for each a in A_i. In
what follows, we let $D(\beta, L)$ denote the set of available portfolios that
satisfy the short sale constraint.[16]

For any cross-sectional distribution of financial structures $\beta \in \Delta_N(I)$ and
any portfolio $d \in D\beta)$, let $W_N(d, \beta)$ denote the total return to the portfolio
at date 2. $W_N(d, \beta)$ is defined as follows. Let $(i_1, \ldots, i_N)$ denote any assignment of financial structures that has the cross-sectional distribution β. Let
$N_i = \{n \in N \mid i_n = i\}$ denote the set of entrepreneurs with the ith financial
structure. Then

$$W_n(d, \beta) = \sum_{i \in I} \sum_{f \in F_i} \sum_{n \in N_i} \frac{d(f, i)f(Z_n)}{\beta_i N}. \tag{2.5}$$

The right-hand side of (2.5) is independent of the particular assignment
$(i_1, \ldots, i_N)$ by virtue of assumption 1, so $W_n(\cdot)$ is well defined. Using (2.5),
define an indirect utility function $u_k^N: \mathbb{R} \times D(\beta) \times \Delta_N(I) \to \mathbb{R}$ by putting

$$u_k^N(c, d, \beta) = E[U_k(c, W_N(d, \beta))],$$

$$\forall k \in K, \forall (c, d, \beta) \in \mathbb{R} \times D(\beta) \times \Delta_N(I). \tag{2.6}$$

$u_k^N(c, d, \beta)$ is the expected utility derived by an investor of type k from first-period consumption c and the portfolio d when the cross-sectional distribution of financial structures is β.

A *price system* is a function $p: A \to \mathbb{R}_+$. An *allocation* is an array $x = (x_k) = ((c_k, d_k)) \in (\mathbb{R} \times D)^K$. Let P denote the set of price systems and X the set of allocations. An allocation is *attainable* relative to β if $(c_k, d_k) \in \mathbb{R} \times D(\beta)$, for every k, and

$$\sum_{k \in K} d_k(f, i)\alpha_k = \beta_i, \qquad \forall (f, i) \in A. \tag{2.7}$$

Now we can define a *symmetric exchange equilibrium* (SEE) relative to β to be a price system p and an attainable allocation x relative to β, such that

$$\forall k \in K, \qquad x_k \text{ maximizes } u_k^N(c, d, \beta)$$

$$\text{subject to } c + p \cdot d = 0 \text{ and } d \in D(\beta, L). \tag{2.8}$$

THEOREM 2.1   If assumptions 1 through 3 are satisfied, there exists a SEE relative to β for every $\beta \in \Delta_N(I)$.

Standard arguments suffice to prove the existence of equilibrium when $L < \infty$. To show existence in the case $L = \infty$, we consider a sequence of economies in which L grows without bound. If certain unnecessary "wash trades" are eliminated, assumption 3 implies that for L sufficiently large the short sale constraint is not binding. Essentially, there is enough risk aversion so that short positions do not grow unboundedly large. Then we have the desired equilibrium. Since the arguments are standard apart from this one part, the proof is omitted. (See Allen and Gale 1989 for details.)

Financial Equilibrium of the Full Model

Now we analyze the choice of financial structures at the first stage. An *equilibrium selection* is a function $\phi: \Delta_N(I) \to P \times X$ associating a SEE relative to β with every cross-sectional distribution β in $\Delta_N(I)$. For any equilibrium selection ϕ, define a finite symmetric game $\Gamma(\phi)$ as follows. Let N be the set of *players* and let $\Delta(I)$ be the set of *mixed strategies*. For any $n \in N$ and $\beta_{-n} \in \Delta_{N-1}(I)$, let (i, β_{-n}) denote the cross-sectional distribution of financial structures when player n chooses i and the choices of the rest are given by the cross-sectional distribution β_{-n}. The second-stage equilibrium resulting from the choice of (i, β_{-n}) is $(p, x) = \phi(i, \beta_{-n})$ and the payoff to player n is given by

$$v(i, \beta_{-n}) = \sum_{a \in A_i} p(a) - C_i. \tag{2.9}$$

Suppose that player n chooses a mixed strategy $\sigma \in \Delta(I)$ and the other players choose $\sigma^* \in \Delta(I)$. The payoff to player n will be given by

$$v(\sigma, \sigma^*; \phi) = \sum_{i \in I} \sum_{B_{-n} \in \Delta_{N-1}(I)} \mathrm{Prob}(\beta_{-n} | \sigma^*) \sigma_i v(i, \beta_{-n}). \tag{2.10}$$

The *payoff function* v is evidently symmetric, i.e., independent of n, by virtue of the symmetry of exchange equilibrium. Define the game $\Gamma(\phi)$ by putting $\Gamma(\phi) = (N, \Delta(I), v)$. A *symmetric Nash equilibrium* (SNE) is defined to be a mixed strategy $\sigma^* \in \Delta(I)$ satisfying

$$\sigma^* \in \arg\max\{v(\sigma, \sigma^*; \phi): \sigma \in \Delta(I)\}. \tag{2.11}$$

By a variant of the standard argument, we can show the existence of a mixed strategy satisfying (2.11).

We define a *symmetric financial equilibrium* (SFE) to be a mixed strategy σ and an equilibrium selection ϕ such that σ is a SNE of $\Gamma(\phi)$.

THEOREM 2.2   If assumptions 1 through 3 are satisfied, there exists a SFE.

Proof   Immediate from theorem 2.1 and the preceding discussion.   ∎

The crucial properties of the model that ensure existence are (i) the finiteness of the entrepreneurs' strategy sets and (ii) the use of mixed strategies. The question of the existence of equilibrium has arisen in similar settings (Hart 1979, Jones 1987). However, these authors focused on pure strategy equilibria, without providing an existence theorem.

7.3   The Incentive to Innovate

In this section we study an extended example to illustrate the impact of short sales on the incentive to innovate. We assume there are two states of nature $\Omega = \{\omega_1, \omega_2\}$ and that all asset returns are perfectly correlated. Then asset returns can be represented by an ordered pair (z_1, z_2), that is,

$$Z_j(\omega_i) = z_i \qquad \text{for} \qquad i = 1, 2 \text{ and } j = 1, \ldots, N. \tag{3.1}$$

Entrepreneurs have a choice of two financial structures, F_1 and F_2. The first consists of equity alone. The second allows the entrepreneur to issue two securities, one giving a claim to the entire return to the asset in state ω_1 and the other giving a claim to the return in state ω_2. Formally,

$$F_i = \begin{cases} \{f_0\} = \{(z_1, z_2)\} & \text{if } i = 1, \\ \{(f_1, f_2)\} = \{(z_1, 0), (0, z_2)\} & \text{if } i = 2, \end{cases} \tag{3.2}$$

where again we identify a claim with an ordered pair indicating the payoff in each state. Issuing one claim is assumed to be costless (we can think of this as the status quo). Issuing two claims has a positive cost γ. Formally, the cost function is defined by

$$C_i = \begin{cases} 0 & \text{if } i = 1, \\ \gamma & \text{if } i = 2. \end{cases} \tag{3.3}$$

There are two types of investors $k = 1, 2$. Their preferences are described by the von Neumann–Morgenstern utility functions U_k, where

$$U_k(c_1, c_2) = c_1 + V_k(c_2), \quad \text{for } k = 1, 2. \tag{3.4}$$

Note the assumption of "transferable utility." We assume that there are equal measures of investors of each type.

Suppose that unlimited short sales are allowed, that is, $L = \infty$. Then there is a unique SEE for each cross-sectional distribution of financial structures. In fact, there are only two possible SEE whatever the cross-sectional distribution of financial structures. To see this, consider two cases. First, suppose that all entrepreneurs choose the financial structure F_1. In that case, investors can only trade equity: the definition of equilibrium does not allow them to trade short or long in the securities f_1 and f_2, which have not been issued. As a result, markets are incomplete: there are two states but only one security. Since investors' preferences satisfy "transferable utility," the SEE is unique and the market value of the firm will be given by the price of equity $p(f_0)$.

Next, suppose that at least one entrepreneur chooses the more complex financial structure $F_2 = \{f_1, f_2\}$. The claims offered in this structure are indistinguishable from Arrow securities. Investors can span the entire space of contingent commodities by trading in these securities and markets are effectively complete. As in the first case, transferable utility implies that there is a unique SEE relative to this choice of financial structures. The completeness of markets has two important implications for the nature of the SEE. The first is that the SEE is independent of the number of entrepreneurs who choose F_2. As long as F_2 is chosen by at least one entrepreneur, investors can split the other assets themselves by taking appropriate positions in the claims f_1 and f_2. The second implication is that the market value of all firms must be the same. That is,

$$p(f_0) = p(f_1) + p(f_2) \tag{3.5}$$

in equilibrium. Otherwise, investors could achieve a riskless arbitrage profit. Thus, the entrepreneur who chooses to split his asset is no better off ex post than those entrepreneurs who choose not to split. In fact, he is worse off to the extent that he has born the cost $\gamma > 0$ of issuing the new securities.

Example 1   To illustrate the two SEE, we have calculated a numerical example. Suppose that the asset returns are $(z_1, z_2) = (0.5, 2.5)$ and the investors preferences are given by

$$U_1(c_1, c_2) = 5 + c_1 - \exp(-ac_2), \quad \text{where } a = 10, \tag{3.6a}$$

$$U_2(c_1, c_2) = 5 + c_1 + \ln(c_2). \tag{3.6b}$$

If no one innovates, the equilibrium values are given in table 7.1. We refer to this equilibrium as the *incomplete markets* SEE.

Because investors' preferences satisfy transferable utility, it is easy to calculate the marginal value of a security to an investor. Let $\mu_k(\omega)$ denote the marginal utility of consumption at the second date to an investor of type k in state ω and let $f(\omega)$ denote the return to one unit of claim f in state ω. Then the marginal value of claim f to a type k investor in equilibrium must be

$$\mu_k(\omega_1)f(\omega_1) + \mu_k(\omega_2)f(\omega_2).$$

If the claim is actually issued in equilibrium, then the price must be equal to the marginal value for all types k.

Using the data in table 7.1, we see that the marginal valuation of claim f_0 is the same for both types and is equal to the equilibrium price $p(f_0) = 0.58583$. On the other hand, the two types of investors value the unissued

Table 7.1
Equilibrium with incomplete markets

Investor type	Equilibrium demand for equity	Consumption		Marginal utility of consumption		
		State ω_1	State ω_2	State ω_1	State ω_2	Utility
1	0.29303	0.14652	0.73258	2.31042	0.00658	4.71248
2	1.70697	0.85348	4.26742	1.17167	0.23433	4.64629

Market value $= 0.58583$

securities f_1 and f_2 differently. For example, a type 1 investor would place a value of 0.57761 on the claim $(0.5, 0)$ which is greater than the value placed on it by a type 2 investor. A type 2 investor would place a value of 0.29291 on the claim $(0, 2.5)$, which is higher than the value placed on it by the type 1 investor. In other words, different clienteles value the claims differently. These differences in marginal valuation stem from the incompleteness of markets and the resulting differences in marginal rates of substitution across states.

If one or more entrepreneurs chooses to innovate, the equilibrium values are given in table 7.2. We refer to this as the *complete markets SEE*. In this case, marginal rates of substitution across states are equalized between the two types of investor. As a result, the marginal value of all claims is equalized between types of investor and the market value of assets is independent of financial structure.

As we have seen, the SEE can be extremely sensitive to the choice of financial structure by a single entrepreneur. If every entrepreneur chooses F_1, markets are incomplete; but if a single entrepreneur chooses F_2, markets are complete. This property of the model is exactly analogous to the property of stock market economies noted by Kreps (1979), who showed that the change of a single firm's production plan could have a large impact on the economy when short sales are allowed. However, this observation is not a statement about equilibrium. It does not imply that entrepreneurs will have a large impact, at the margin, *in equilibrium*. We will now show that in our model entrepreneurs must have a large impact, at the margin, in equilibrium, in order to have an incentive to innovate.

Whenever one of the entrepreneurs chooses to innovate by selecting the financial structure F_2, the market value of the asset ex post is independent of the financial structure. We describe this state of affairs by saying that

Table 7.2
Equilibrium with complete markets

Investor type	Consumption		Marginal utility of consumption		Utility
	State ω_1	State ω_2	State ω_1	State ω_2	
1	0.20706	0.38323	1.26113	0.21660	4.75405
2	0.79294	4.61677	1.26113	0.21660	4.64884

Market value = 0.58603

there is no *ex post incentive to innovate*. Why would an entrepreneur ever innovate in these circumstances? The answer is that there may be an *ex ante incentive to innovate* even if there is no incentive ex post. The ex ante incentive comes from the ability of the entrepreneur to use his choice of financial structure to influence the prices in the SEE. In other words, it comes from imperfect competition. In example 1, the market value of the "firm" is higher in the complete markets SEE than in the incomplete markets SEE. Even after taking account of the cost of innovating, an entrepreneur may be better off in the SEE with complete markets than in the SEE with incomplete markets. By innovating, the entrepreneur ensures that he will end up in the preferred equilibrium.

Suppose, for example, that there are two entrepreneurs ($N = 2$). Let MV_I denote the market value of the asset when markets are incomplete and let MV_C denote the market value of the asset when markets are complete. If no one innovates, the market value is MV_I; if one or more innovates, the market value is MV_C. By innovating, a single entrepreneur can raise market value by $MV_C - MV_I$. Of course, each entrepreneur would prefer the other to bear the costs of issuing the second claim, since they achieve the same market value ex post. In a mixed strategy equilibrium, the incentive to innovate comes from the possibility that the other entrepreneur will not innovate. If σ is the probability that an entrepreneur innovates, then an entrepreneur will be indifferent between innovating and not innovating if and only if $\sigma MV_C + (1 - \sigma)MV_I = MV_C - \gamma$. Thus, in a mixed strategy SFE σ must satisfy

$$\sigma = \frac{MV_C - MV_I - \gamma}{MV_C - MV_I}. \tag{3.7}$$

In example 1, $MV_C - MV_I = 0.00020$ so neither entrepreneur will issue two claims unless $\gamma \leq 0.00020$. If, say, $\gamma = 0.00005$, then $\sigma = 0.25$. As γ becomes smaller, the probability with which each entrepreneur innovates becomes larger. In the limit as γ approaches 0, they each innovate with probability 1.

Now suppose that the number of entrepreneurs is an arbitrary integer N. All entrepreneurs randomize, choosing F_2 with probability σ. In equilibrium, entrepreneurs must be indifferent between the two financial structures, that is,

$$[1 - (1 - \sigma)^{N-1}]MV_C + (1 - \sigma)^{N-1}MV_I = MV_C - \gamma. \tag{3.8}$$

Solving for the equilibrium value of σ we find that

$$\sigma = 1 - (\gamma/(MV_C - MV_I))^{1/(N-1)}. \tag{3.9}$$

Clearly, σ approaches 0 as N approaches ∞. Moreover, using L'Hôpital's rule, it can be shown that $\sigma N \to \ln\{(MV_C - MV_I)/\gamma\}$. The average number of innovators is finite even when the potential number is infinite. For example, when $\gamma = 0.00005$ the average number who innovate is 1.38629 in the limit. Note also that the probability that no one innovates is bounded away from zero. In fact, from (3.8) we see that $(1 - \sigma)^N$ converges to $\gamma/(MV_C - MV_I)$.

Several aspects of this example are noteworthy.

(i) First, arbitrage among the different claims issued guarantees that in equilibrium all assets have the same market value, independently of financial structure.

(ii) Even when N is very large, entrepreneurs do not become price-takers. By changing his choice of financial structure, for example, choosing F_2 with probability 1, an entrepreneur can have a significant effect on the probability distribution of prices in the SEE.

(iii) Hence, even though there is no ex post incentive to innovate, there is an ex ante incentive to innovate. An entrepreneur can alter prices by innovating, so as to increase the market value of all assets.

(iv) Markets do not become complete in the limit. The probability of no innovation is bounded away from zero.

7.4 Arbitrage Pricing in the General Case

An essential property of the example studied in section 7.3 is the fact that asset returns are perfectly correlated. Arbitrage between assets with different financial structures is riskless so the market value of an asset must be independent of the financial structure. Otherwise investors could make an arbitrage profit. When market value is independent of financial structure, there is no ex post incentive for innovation. The entrepreneur who innovates is worse off to the extent that he bears the cost of the more costly financial structure. To have an ex ante incentive to innovate, we need imperfect competition, that is, the choice of an individual entrepreneur must change the SEE prices.

When asset returns exhibit idiosyncratic risk, the argument is not so simple. Since all arbitrage is risky, it is not clear that arbitrage will equalize market values and eliminate the ex post incentive to innovate. However, under certain conditions the earlier conclusion will obtain, that is, imperfect competition must persist in order to provide an incentive to innovate. The argument goes as follows. Suppose that some entrepreneurs innovate, choosing a costly financial structure F_i, say, while the rest choose the status quo structure, F_h. If the number of entrepreneurs choosing F_i is large, then diversification among the claims issued by the innovating entrepreneurs can eliminate the idiosyncratic risk element. As a result, arbitrage implies that the market values of these assets must be the same as the market values of the assets with the structure F_h. That is, there is no ex post incentive to innovate. The implication then is that in order to have an (ex post or ex ante) incentive to innovate we need imperfect competition. The incentive can arise in two ways: the number of innovators may be small, so that there is an ex post incentive, or an individual entrepreneur's decision to innovate may affect prices, so that there is an ex ante incentive, or both incentives may operate.

We begin by introducing an assumption to ensure that, when the number of claims of a given type is large, it is possible to diversify away all idiosyncratic risk.

ASSUMPTION 4   There exists a random variable Z_∞ such that, for any sequence of sets $\{J_N\}$ such that $J_N \subset \{1,\ldots,N\}$ and $|J_N| \to \infty$ and for any $f \in \bigcup F_i$, $\sum_{j \in J_N} |J_N|^{-1} f(Z_j)$ converges to $E[f(Z_j)|Z_\infty]$ in probability.

Assumption 4 is satisfied if $\{Z_n\}$ is a family of i.i.d. random variables, for example. A more interesting case is given by

$$Z_n = Z_\infty + \varepsilon_n, \tag{4.1}$$

where $\{\varepsilon_n\}$ are i.i.d. and Z_∞ is an arbitrary random variable.

Consider a sequence of economies increasing in size. For each economy of size N, let β^N be a cross-sectional distribution of financial structures and let (p^N, x^N) be a SEE relative to β^n. Let $I^* \subset I$ denote the set of structures $i \in I$ such that $\beta_i^N N \to \infty$ as $N \to \infty$. For every N define the market value of an asset with financial structure $i \in I$ by the equation

$$MV_i^N = \sum_{f \in F_i} p^N(f, i). \tag{4.2}$$

We are interested in the behavior of the market values as the size of the economy becomes very large.

THEOREM 4.1   Suppose that assumptions 1 through 4 are satisfied and suppose that $\{(p^N, x^N)\}$ is a convergent sequence. Then there exists a constant $\bar{m}$ such that $MV_i^N \to \bar{m}$ for every $i \in I^*$, where I^* is the set of structures such that $\beta_i^N N \to \infty$ as $N \to \infty$.

Proof   See the appendix.   ∎

The theorem says that all assets with financial structures in I^* have the same market value in the limit. The intuition behind this result is straightforward. If it were not true there would exist, in the limit, two infinite sets of similar assets, one of which had uniformly higher market values than the other. Since these two sets of assets are infinite, assumption 4 implies that diversification eliminates idiosyncratic risk. By shorting the overvalued set and buying the undervalued set it is possible to construct an arbitrage portfolio which, in the limit. is riskless and yields a positive profit. The existence of such a portfolio is inconsistent with equilibrium.

Remark 1   It is tempting to interpret this result in the spirit of the Modigliani-Miller Theorem (MMT). The MMT states that under certain conditions corporate financial structure is irrelevant. More specifically, it implies that a firm's market value will be independent of its financial structure, where financial structure is identified with the debt-equity ratio.[17] On the surface, this sounds like theorem 4.1 but there are important differences. In the first place, the MMT is a statement about the effect of the firm's choices. It says that whatever debt-equity ratio the firm chooses, the market value of the firm will be the same. Theorem 4.1, on the other hand, is a statement about the financial structures chosen in equilibrium. It says that *in equilibrium* the market value of most assets will be the same. It does not assert the irrelevance of financial structure. In particular, it does not say that the market value would be unaffected if the entrepreneur were to choose a different financial structure, one which is not observed in equilibrium.

A second and more subtle difference is that theorem 4.1 leaves out of account any subset of assets that is finite and hence negligible in the limit. By "negligible in the limit" we mean that the fraction of assets in this subset converges to zero as N approaches infinity. A set which is negligible in this sense may not be negligible in terms of its importance for risk-sharing in the economy. In particular, because of the possibility of short sales, the open interest in the claims on a negligible set of assets may be nonnegligible in the limit.[18] In the next section, we see that this is precisely what happens.

7.5   Further Examples of Symmetric Financial Equilibrium

In this section, we again use examples to investigate the asymptotic properties of equilibrium when there are unlimited short sales. In example 2 asset returns exhibit purely idiosyncratic risk. In the limit, as N becomes large, there is no "innovation." "Innovation" is not needed because there is no aggregate uncertainty. This is an example where, even with unlimited short sales, there is price-taking in the limit.

Example 3 extends the preceding example by introducing systematic, economy-wide risk. The conclusions here are similar to those obtained in example 1, thus showing that at least some of the conclusions of section 7.3 are robust to the introduction of idiosyncratic risk.

In examples 1, 2, and 3 there is no ex post incentive to innovate since market values of assets are equalized independently of financial structure. Example 4 shows that there can be an ex post incentive to innovate.

Example 1 showed that there might be too little incentive to innovate. Example 5 shows that, on the contrary, there may be too much. That is, entrepreneurs may innovate when it is socially undesirable for them to do so.

Example 2   As before we assume that there are only two possible levels of asset returns, 0.5 and 2.5. But now asset returns are assumed to be i.i.d., taking each value with equal probability. The other assumptions are the same as in example 1.

With N assets there are now 2^N states of nature. Even if every entrepreneur chooses to innovate and issue two claims, markets will be incomplete. The reason is simply that claims are functions of the returns to the underlying asset. Nevertheless, this example is straightforward to analyze. Since each asset has only two possible returns, it is always possible to construct a portfolio with a constant payoff across states if at least one entrepreneur issues two nontrivial claims.[19] This portfolio is effectively debt. Since any claim can be artificially created out of debt and equity, the MMT holds. As a result, all assets have the same market value, regardless of their financial structure. (This is only true when asset returns have two values, of course.)

From the preceding discussion, we see that there are only two possible SEE. One of them results if all entrepreneurs choose the financial structure F_1; the other results if one or more choose the financial structure F_2 and the remainder choose F_1. Let the market values of an asset in these SEE be denoted by MV_I and MV_D respectively. The analysis of the SFE is similar to the example in section 7.4. Suppose to begin with that $N = 2$. Entrepreneurs will randomize over financial structures, choosing F_2 with probability σ. In equilibrium, $\sigma = (MV_D - MV_I - \gamma)/(MV_D - MV_I)$. It can be shown that $MV_I = 0.56987$ and $MV_D = 0.57406$ so that $MV_D - MV_I = 0.00419$. Entrepreneurs will issue two claims only if $\gamma \leq 0.00419$. For example, if $\gamma = 0.00209$, then $\sigma = 0.5$.

Now consider an arbitrary economy of size N. As N becomes large, investors are able to diversify away most of the idiosyncratic risk simply by holding equity. The return from holding a representative portfolio is 1.5 per asset. The value of the asset is 0.56149 independently of financial structure. In the limit all risk is eliminated and there is no need for financial innovation. It is not worthwhile for an entrepreneur to issue two claims since it does not alter the second-stage equilibrium in any way.

This is an example in which entrepreneurs do become price-takers in the limit. The reason is, of course, that the claims in the second financial structure F_2 are eventually redundant. This example also shows that the amount of innovation may decline as the size of the market increases.

Example 3   The next example differs from the preceding one in two respects. First, there are assumed to be two "macrostates," Good and Bad, each of which occurs with probability 0.5. In the good state, an asset's return is 0.5 with probability 0.25 and 2.5 with probability 0.75. In the bad state, these probabilities are reversed: the return is 0.5 with probability 0.75 and 2.5 with probability 0.25. Second, there are assumed to be N entrepreneurs and $2N$ investors.

The case where there are two entrepreneurs can be analyzed in the same way as the preceding-example. The main difference is that as N increases, the idiosyncratic risk associated with each asset is diversified away but there remains the risk attributable to the macrostate. A representative portfolio yields a return of 2 in the good state and 1 in the bad state. In this case, even as N becomes very large, there is an incentive to innovate and some entrepreneurs will issue two claims.

It is again relatively simple to calculate equilibrium in the limit. By the earlier argument, if anyone innovates, a portfolio equivalent to risk-free debt can be constructed and the MMT holds. There are only two possible SEE at the second stage. One of them occurs if no one innovates; the other occurs if at least one entrepreneur innovates, in which case the equilibrium is the same as if debt and equity were traded.

It follows that, in the limit, if anyone innovates it will be possible to construct portfolios equivalent to contingent commodities on the macro-states. It can be shown that $MV_C = 1.21340$ and $MV_I = 1.20845$ so $MV_C - MV_I = 0.00495$ in the limit. As in the perfectly correlated case (example 1), σN converges to $\ln\{(MV_C - MV_I)/\gamma\}$. For example, if $\gamma = 0.00124$, then the average number of entrepreneurs who innovate in the limit is 1.38428. Again, the probability that no one innovates is bounded away from zero.

This example shows that the characteristics of example 1 are not attributable to the assumption of perfectly correlated asset returns. Also, unlike example 2, which had purely idiosyncratic risk, there is an incentive to innovate in the limit, when all idiosyncratic risk has been diversified away.

Example 4   All of the examples so far have had the very special property that in the second-stage SEE all assets have the same market value independently of financial structure. Ex post, there is no incentive to innovate. The incentive to innovate has come exclusively from the ex ante expectation that the innovation will change the equilibrium. In this section, we consider an example where, ex post, the entrepreneur who innovates achieves a higher market value than the entrepreneur who does not.

There are three levels of returns: 1, 2 and 3. All three are equally likely. As in the first examples, the number of investors and entrepreneurs is the same. There is no cost if the entrepreneur wants to issue equity only. Thus, $F_1 = \{(1, 2, 3)\}$ and $C_1 = 0$. The other financial structures have the form

$$F_i = \{(a, b, c), (1, 2, 3) - (a, b, c)\} \tag{5.1}$$

where $a = 0, 1$, $b = 0, 1, 2$, and $c = 0, 1, 2, 3$. Investors have the usual preferences. It can be shown that when there are two entrepreneurs ($N = 2$) there exists a SFE in which all entrepreneurs randomize between F_1 and the financial structure $F_i = \{(0, 1, 1), (1, 1, 2)\}$. Let σ denote the probability that they choose the structure with two claims. If both entrepreneurs innovate, the market value of their assets is 0.55305 in the SEE. If neither innovates the market value is 0.55298. When one innovates and the other does not, the innovator's market value is 0.55340 and the non-innovators' market value is 0.55283.

It is weakly optimal to innovate if and only if

$$0.55305\sigma + 0.55340(1 - \sigma) - \gamma \geq 0.55283\sigma + 0.55298(1 - \sigma) \tag{5.2}$$

or, rearranging, $\sigma \leq (0.00042 - \gamma)/0.00020$. It can be seen that for $\gamma \leq 0.00022$ there exists a pure strategy equilibrium in which both entrepreneurs innovate. In the previous examples, the only symmetric pure strategy equilibria were those in which no one innovated. When there is no ex post incentive to innovate, innovation will occur in a pure strategy equilibrium only if it is asymmetric. Specifically, at most one entrepreneur will innovate. For values of γ above 0.00022, mixed strategies are used in equilibrium.

Example 5 We have seen that innovation may not occur when it is socially desirable. More surprisingly, it may occur when it is socially undesirable.

Consider example 1 but change the ratio of entrepreneurs to investors to be 0.25 : 1. In this case, completion of the market reduces the investors' utilities by 0.00262 for type $k = 1$ and 0.02128 for type $k = 2$. The market value of assets increases by 0.05617 so that the overall increase in the sum of utilities (ignoring the cost of the innovation) is 0.03227. It can be seen that for $0.03227 < \gamma < 0.05617$ entrepreneurs will have an incentive to innovate—and *will* innovate with positive probability in a SFE—but welfare will be reduced.

The possibility of making unlimited short sales does increase the opportunities for risk sharing. However, as a result of the inefficient incentives for innovation, everybody may be worse off. In example 6 (below), we take the data from example 1 and consider what would happen if no short sales were allowed. It turns out that there is some innovation if $0.00020 < \gamma < 0.28468$ and short sales are not allowed, but none if they are. Everyone is better off when no short sales are allowed, even if there are no transfers at the first date. In other words, the constrained SFE Pareto dominates the unconstrained SFE.

7.6   Efficiency of Competitive Equilibrium

In this section we examine the asymptotic properties of equilibrium under the assumption that investors can only make limited short sales ($L < \infty$)

In Allen and Gale (1989) we showed that, under certain conditions, the SFE of a sequence of finite economies converge to a competitive (price-taking) equilibrium in the limit. In what follows we simply assume, without stating formal conditions, that a SFE converges in the limit to a competitive, price-taking equilibrium as the size of the economy becomes unboundedly large.[20]

We define a large economy as follows. There is a large number of entrepreneurs and investors. (Formally, we want a countably infinite number of entrepreneurs and a continuum of investors. In what follows, equilibrium is defined in terms of distributions of types and structures, so the set of agents is not mentioned explicitly.) As usual, each entrepreneur n is characterized by an asset with a random return Z_n. There is a finite number of financial structures $\{F_i\}$ with cost function $\{C_i\}$. The asset returns are assumed to satisfy (A.1) and (A.4). If $\beta_i > 0$ the number of entrepreneurs choosing F_i is infinite. Then it must be possible to diversify away all idiosyncratic risk from the claims $a \in A_i$. If $\beta_i = 0$, then investors will not be able to purchase any of the claims $a \in A_i$ in equilibrium. In either case, we can *define* the return to a (well-diversified) unit of claim a to be

$$R_a(Z_\infty) \equiv E[f(Z_n)|Z_\infty], \qquad \forall a = (f, i) \in A.$$

There is a finite number of investor types $k \in K$, each characterized by the von Neumann–Morgenstern utility function U_k. The proportion (measure) of investors of type k is α_k. (A.2) and (A.3) are satisfied for each k. Define an indirect utility function by putting

$$W(d) = \sum_{a \in A} d(a) R_a(Z_\infty) \qquad \forall d \in D \qquad \text{and}$$

$$u_k(c, d) = E[U_k(c, W(d))] \qquad \forall k \in K, \forall (c, d) \in \mathbb{R} \times D.$$

Let $D(\beta, L)$ denote the set of portfolios available to investors, where

$$D(\beta, L) = \{d \in D \,|\, d(a) \geq -\beta_i L, \forall a \in A_i, \forall i \in I\}$$

and β is the cross-sectional distribution of financial structures. For any $p \in P$, let $MV_i(p)$ denote the market value of an asset with financial structure F_i, that is, $MV_i(p) \equiv \sum_{a \in A_i} p(a)$. Then a *competitive equilibrium* for a large economy is an array (σ, p, x) in $\Delta(I) \times P \times X$ such that σ is profit-maximizing at the prevailing prices, that is,

$$\sigma_i > 0 \text{ implies that } i \text{ maximizes } MV_i(p) - C_i, \tag{6.1}$$

and (p, x) is a SEE relative to σ, that is, x is an attainable allocation relative to $\beta = \sigma$ and

$$\forall k \in K, \qquad x_k = (c_k, d_k) \text{ maximizes } u_k(c, d)$$

$$\text{subject to } c + p \cdot d = 0 \text{ and } d \in D(\beta, L). \tag{6.2}$$

Note that the definition of $D(\beta, L)$ used here differs from the one used in section 7.2. In section 7.2 investors were forbidden to trade short or long in any security that was not issued by some firm. In other words, if a particular security was not issued by an entrepreneur, the market for that security remained *closed*. Here we allow investors to trade in any security subject only to the short sale constraint. This means that all markets are *open*, whether or not the corresponding security has been issued by any entrepreneur. Of course, if $\beta_i = 0$ then the market-clearing condition and the short sale constraint together imply that there is no trade in the claims belonging to A_i. However, the fact that markets in these claims are open means that there is a market-clearing price for each claim $a \in A_i$. This notion of equilibrium, which is used in AG, is therefore stronger than the one used in section 7.2.[21]

The question we want to answer is whether an equilibrium of this kind is efficient in some sense. Since markets are incomplete there is no reason to expect that the equilibrium is Pareto efficient. Neither is this concept of efficiency necessarily appropriate. Instead, we use a notion of constrained efficiency.[22] An equilibrium (σ, p, x) is said to be *constrained efficient* if there does not exist an allocation (σ', x') such that x' is attainable for σ', every investor is better off, and (σ', x') uses less resources at the first date:

$$\sum_{k \in K} c'_k \alpha_k + \sum_{i \in I} C_i \sigma'_i < \sum_{k \in K} c_k \alpha_k + \sum_{i \in I} C_i \sigma_i.$$

This last condition ensures that entrepreneurs can be made better off.

If no short sales are allowed, the economy is isomorphic to an Arrow-Debreu economy in which the only traded commodities are current consumption and claims. Not surprisingly, the equilibrium inherits the efficiency properties of the Arrow-Debreu model.

THEOREM 6.1   If $L = 0$ any equilibrium of a large economy is constrained efficient.

The proof, which is omitted, uses standard "revealed preference" arguments. (See Allen and Gale 1989 for details.)

The more surprising result is that, even in this competitive equilibrium, there can be inefficiencies if short sales are allowed.

THEOREM 6.2   Let (σ, p, x) be a fixed but arbitrary equilibrium of a large economy. Suppose that u_k is continuously differentiable for every k in K and suppose that for some financial structures F_i and F_j, the following conditions are satisfied:

(i) $\sigma_i = 0 < \sigma_j$ and $MV_i(p) - C_i < MV_j(p) - C_j$;

(ii) $d_k(a) > -L\beta_j$ for all $a \in A_j$;

(iii) $(1 + L)MV_i(p) - C_i > (1 + L)MV_j(p) - C_j$.

Then the equilibrium allocation is not constrained efficient.

Proof   See the appendix.

The first condition in the theorem says that structure j is chosen in equilibrium and is strictly more profitable than i. The second says that the short-sale constraint is not binding for the claims associated with F_j. This means that, at the margin, one unit of a claim $a \in A_j$ is worth exactly $p(a)$ units of first-period consumption to any investor. In this sense, we can say that the value of one unit of an asset with financial structure F_j is $MV_j(p)$.

The meaning of condition (iii) can be understood as follows. Suppose that a small measure $\varepsilon > 0$ of entrepreneurs switch from F_j to F_i. Investors' holdings in claims $a \in A_j$ must be reduced by ε (we do not need to worry about the short sale constraint, since it is not binding) and the value of this reduction to them in terms of first-period consumption is $MV_j(p)\varepsilon$. On the other hand, we can increase holdings of claims $a \in A_i$ by $\varepsilon(1 + L)$, including short sales, and the value of this in terms of first-period consumption is $MV_i(p)(1 + L)\varepsilon$ since each claim can be given to someone whose marginal valuation is equal to the price. To provide the necessary short sales, have every investor go short εL units in each claim $a \in A_i$. The value of this is $MV_j(p)\varepsilon L$, not $MV_i(p)\varepsilon L$, since investors are in effect shorting the whole asset. Then the net effect on investors' welfare, measured in first-period consumption, is $MV_i(p)(1 + L)\varepsilon - MV_j(p)(1 + L)\varepsilon$. The cost of producing the claims has increased by $(C_i - C_j)\varepsilon$. It is possible to make everyone better off by redistributing first-period consumption if the increase in investors' welfare is greater than the increase in cost, that is,

$$MV_i(p)(1 + L)\varepsilon - MV_j(p)(1 + L)\varepsilon > (C_i - C_j)\varepsilon.$$

But this is exactly what condition (iii) claims.

Example 6 We can illustrate the theorem using the data from example 1. (But now we assume there is a large number of entrepreneurs and investors.) Suppose first of all that $L = 0$, that is, no short sales are allowed. If γ is sufficiently large, there is a unique equilibrium in which no entrepreneur chooses to innovate, that is, $\sigma_1 = 1$ and $\sigma_2 = 0$. The equilibrium values are given in table 7.1. (The equilibrium values are the same as in the incomplete markets SEE of example 1 because in that SEE investors do not want to make short sales.)

The equilibrium price of the single claim issued is 0.58583. If an entrepreneur splits his "firm" by issuing two claims, the claim (0.5, 0) will be purchased only by investors of type 1. Its value to them is 0.57761. Similarly, the claim (0, 2.5) will be purchased only by investors of type 2 at a price of 0.29291. Thus, the market value of the split "firm" will be 0.87052. So it is optimal for the entrepreneur to choose the simpler structure F_1 if and only if $\gamma \geq 0.87052 - 0.58583 = 0.28469$. In this case the marginal social benefit from financial innovation (splitting) is measured by the increase in the value of the "firm" so entrepreneurs make the efficient decision.

Now suppose that limited short sales are possible without cost. The equilibrium is unchanged as long as $\gamma \geq 0.28469$. However, the social benefit of innovation is now greater than the private benefit to entrepreneurs. In fact the marginal social benefit to splitting is at least $(1 + L)0.87051 - (1 + L)0.58583$. If this is greater than γ then efficiency requires that some "firms" split. Note that in the proof of the theorem we assume that short sales are evenly distributed across investors. If we had instead allocated these short sales to the investors who valued them most (valued the claim least), then the social benefit of the innovation would have been greater. In the example, the marginal social benefit would be $(1 + 2L)0.87053$.

Remark 2 Example 6 allows us to illustrate the nonexistence problem pointed out in AG. Suppose that there is a continuum of entrepreneurs and a continuum of investors. Taking the data from example 1, we can calculate the market-clearing prices for a Walrasian equilibrium. As before, there are only two cases that need to be considered. Either no one innovates and markets are incomplete (table 7.1) or a positive measure of entrepreneurs innovates and markets are complete (table 7.2). The difference here is that entrepreneurs are price-takers: they do not take account of the effect of their actions on the second-stage equilibrium.[23]

Consider first the case where all entrepreneurs choose F_1 and markets are incomplete. As we saw in the discussion of example 6, in a price-taking equilibrium, the market value of a "split" asset will be $0.57761 + 0.29291 = 0.87052$. So it would be optimal for an entrepreneur to choose the financial structure F_2 as long as the perceived increase in market value were greater than the cost, that is, as long as $\gamma < 0.87052 - 0.58583 = 0.28469$.

On the other hand, if a positive measure of entrepreneurs chooses the financial structure F_2, markets are complete and all investors have the same marginal rates of substitution. The market value of an asset is independent of its financial structure. In that case, there is no incentive for an entrepreneur to choose the more expensive financial structure.

Thus, as long as $\gamma < 0.28469$, there cannot exist a price-taking, competitive equilibrium. Assuming that a positive measure of entrepreneurs chooses F_2, we have shown they would be better off choosing F_1. Assuming that they all choose F_1, we have shown they would be better off choosing F_2. The problem is that entrepreneurs are not taking account of the effect of their choices on the equilibrium prices.[24] This assumption may not be justified even when there is a continuum of agents.

7.7 Concluding Remarks

This chapter has considered a model where the set of traded securities is endogenous and short sales are possible. It has been shown that if firms move first, issuing securities that are subsequently traded on a competitive market, equilibrium exists but may not be efficient. The analysis here has focused on securities issued by firms. Of course, this is not the only kind of financial innovation that occurs. In Allen and Gale (1990) we consider the incentives for third parties to set up exchanges on which derivative securities (options) are traded. In this institutional framework, the innovator can control entry to the exchange and thus capture more of the rents from innovation. However, inefficiency may arise for other reasons. Much remains to be done in the direction of modeling the market microstructure in a detailed way. This is an interesting area for future research.

Appendix

PROOF OF THEOREM 4.1   The proof is by contradiction. Let (p^∞, x^∞) denote the limit of the sequence (p^N, x^N) and let $x^\infty = ((c_k^\infty, d_k^\infty))$. Suppose, contrary to what is to be proved, that there exist structures i_0 and i_1 in I^* such that $MV_{i_0}^N \to m_0$ and $MV_{i_1}^N \to m_1$ as $N \to \infty$, where $m_1 > m_0$. Define a sequence of portfolios $\{\delta^N\}$ for some fixed but arbitrary investor-type k as follows. Put

$$
\delta^N(a) = \begin{cases} d_k^N(a) & \text{if } a \in A \backslash (A_{i_0} \cup A_{i_1}), \\ d_k^N(a) - 1 & \text{if } a \in A_{i_1}, \\ d_k^N(a) + 1 & \text{if } a \in A_{i_0}. \end{cases}
$$

By assumption 4, there exists a subsequence, which can be taken to be the original sequence, along which $W_N(d_k^N, \beta_k^N)$ converges in probability to W_∞, say. Then by assumption 4 and the definition of $W_N(d, \beta)$,

$$
W_N(\delta^N, \beta^N) = W_N(d_k^N, \beta^N) + (\beta_{i_0}^N N)^{-1} \sum_{n \in S_0^N} Z_n - (\beta_{i_1}^N N)^{-1} \sum_{n \in S_1^N} Z_n
$$
$$
\to W_\infty + E[Z_n | Z_\infty] - E[Z_n | Z_\infty]
$$
$$
= W_\infty
$$

where, for each N, S_0^N and S_1^N are disjoint subsets of $\{1, \ldots, N\}$ with the property that $|S_j^N| = \beta_{i_j}^N N$ for $j = 0, 1$ From the budget constraint, however, (γ^N, δ^N) is an affordable choice for the investor of type k, where γ^N is defined by

$$
\gamma^N = -p^N \cdot \delta^N = c_k^N - MV_{i_0}^N + MV_{i_1}^N \geq c_k^N + (m_1 - m_0) - \varepsilon
$$

for N sufficiently large. Therefore,

$$
u_k^N(\gamma^N, \delta^N, \beta^N) \geq u_k^N(c_k^N + (m_1 - m_0) - \varepsilon, \delta^N, \beta^N)
$$
$$
= E[U_k(c_k^N + (m_1 - m_0) - \varepsilon, W_N(\delta^N, \beta^N))]
$$
$$
\to E[U_k(c_k^\infty + (m_1 - m_0) - \varepsilon, W_\infty)].
$$

Since $\varepsilon > 0$ is arbitrary and $u_k^N(c_k^N, d_k^N, \beta^N) \to E[U_k(c_k^\infty, W_\infty)]$, we must have $u_k^N(\gamma^N, \delta^N, \beta^N) > u_k^N(c_k^N, d_k^N, \beta^N)$ for N sufficiently large, contradicting the definition of equilibrium.   ∎

PROOF OF THEOREM 6.2   Let (σ, p, x) be a fixed but arbitrary equilibrium. Assume that for every investor of type k, the indirect utility function $u_k(c, d)$ is continuously differentiable. In equilibrium. the following Kuhn-Tucker conditions must be satisfied:

$$\frac{\partial u_k(c_k, d_k)}{\partial c_k} = \lambda_k \quad \text{and}$$

$$\frac{\partial u_k(c_k, d_k)}{\partial d_k} \le \lambda_k p,$$

with equality where $d_k(a) > -L\beta_i$, for any a in A_i. Without loss of generality, we can assume that for every claim a in A, there exists some type who is prepared to buy the claim at the margin, that is, $\partial u_k(c_k, d_k)/\partial d_k = \lambda_k p$. (If not, simply reduce prices until the condition is satisfied.)

Suppose there are two financial structures i and j satisfying the conditions (i) to (iii) of the theorem. Now consider a change in the equilibrium allocation that, by construction, satisfies the constraints in the definition of constrained efficiency. First, define σ' by putting:

$$\sigma'_h = \begin{cases} \sigma_h & \text{for } h \neq i, j, \\ \delta_i + \varepsilon & \text{for } h = i, \\ \sigma_j - \varepsilon & \text{for } h = j. \end{cases}$$

A small measure $\varepsilon > 0$ of entrepreneurs has switched from structure i to structure j. Define a new allocation of portfolios $d' = (d'_k)$ by putting:

$$d'_k(a) = \begin{cases} d_k(a) & \text{for } a \notin A_i \cup A_j, \\ d_k(a) - \varepsilon L + \theta_k(a)\varepsilon & \text{for } a \in A_i, \\ d_k(a) - \theta_k(a)\varepsilon & \text{for } a \in A_j. \end{cases}$$

The investors' holdings are unchanged except for claims associated with the structures i and j. All agents are assumed to sell short εL units of the claims associated with F_i and to buy back a nonnegative quantity $\theta_k(a)\varepsilon$ of each claim a in A_i. Furthermore, we assume that $\theta_k(a) = 0$ unless type k is willing to hold the claim at the margin. It is clear from the construction and from our initial hypotheses that the short-sale constraint will be satisfied for every claim. To ensure that the resulting allocation is feasible, we assume that $\sum_{k \in K} \theta_k(a)\alpha_k = 1 + L$, for every $a \in A_i$, and $\sum_{k \in K} \theta_k(a)\alpha_k = -1$, for every $a \in A_j$.

By inspection, it can be seen that the portfolio allocation d' satisfies the conditions in the definition of constrained efficiency. Now define a consumption allocation $c' = (c'_k)$ by putting $c'_k = c_k + \gamma_k \varepsilon$, for each k in K. That is, each investor of type k receives a transfer of $\gamma_k \varepsilon$ units of the consumption good at the first date. From the differentiability assumption, an investor of type k will be better off for $\varepsilon > 0$ sufficiently small if

$$\frac{\partial u_k(c_k, d_k)}{\partial c_k}\gamma_k + \sum_{a \in A_i} \frac{\partial u_k(c_k, d_k)}{\partial d_k(a)}(\theta_k(a) - L) + \sum_{a \in A_j} \frac{\partial u_k(c_k, d_k)}{\partial d_k(a)}\theta_k(a) > 0. \quad (A.1)$$

From the symmetry assumption and the definition of the indirect utility function, note that:

$$\sum_{a \in A_i} \frac{\partial u_k(c_k, d_k)}{\partial d_k(a)} = \sum_{a \in A_j} \frac{\partial u_k(c_k, d_k)}{\partial d_k(a)} \leq \sum_{a \in A_j} \lambda_k p(a).$$

Substituting from this inequality and from the first-order conditions into (A.1), we see that (A.1) will be satisfied if

$$\lambda_k \gamma_k + \sum_{a \in A_i} \lambda_k p(a)\theta_k(a) + \sum_{a \in A_j} \lambda_k p_k(a)\theta_k(a) - \sum_{a \in A_j} \lambda_k p(a)L > 0. \quad (A.2)$$

Dividing (A.2) by λ_k/α_k and summing over k yields

$$\sum_{k \in K} \gamma_k \alpha_k + \sum_{k \in K} \sum_{a \in A_i} p(a)\alpha_k \theta_k(a) + \sum_{k \in K} \sum_{a \in A_j} p_k(a)\alpha_k \theta_k(a) - \sum_{a \in A_j} p(a)L > 0$$

or

$$\sum_{k \in K} \gamma_k \alpha_k + MV_i(p)(1 + L) - MV_j(p)(1 + L) > 0.$$

Now in order to show that the equilibrium is not constrained efficient, it is sufficient to show that

$$\sum_{k \in K} \alpha_k \gamma_k + C_i - C_j < 0. \quad (A.3)$$

for some choice of γ_k consistent with (A.2). From inspection of these inequalities, it is clear that we can choose $\{\gamma_k\}$ to satisfy both (A.2) and (A.3) if and only if

$$MV_i(p)(1 + L) - MV_j(p)(1 + L) > C_i - C_j.$$

Since this is precisely what our initial hypothesis (iii) claims, we have proved the theorem. ∎

Notes

Earlier versions of this paper were presented at a conference at Northwestern University, joint seminars at Carnegie-Mellon University and the University of Pittsburgh, and at Harvard University and Massachusetts Institute of Technology, and seminars at the University of Texas at Austin, Johns Hopkins University, SITE, Stanford University, and the University of Maryland. We thank all the participants for their comments and suggestions, especially Larry Jones. We are indebted to Joe Ostroy for pointing out the existence of relevant work by other writers. We have also received helpful comments from Andreu Mas-Colell and three anonymous referees. Financial support from the NSF in the form of Grants SES-8813719, SES-8920048, SES-8720589, and SES-8920586 is gratefully acknowledged.

1. The seminal contributions were made by Diamond (1967), Radner (1972), and Hart (1975). Cass (1988) surveys later developments by himself, Balasko, Duffie, Geanakoplos, Magill, Mas-Colell, Polemarchakis, Shafer, and others. (See references.)

2. Exceptions are the recent work by Allen and Gale (1988) and Duffie and Jackson (1989).

3. There are finite market games in which agents behave like price-takers in equilibrium, for example, Bertrand pricing games. However, in the present model. a large number of firms is a necessary condition for competitive behavior.

4. Another empirical question is how important are short sales quantitatively? It appears that on the NYSE, short sale volume is only 8% of the volume of regular trading and most of that is technical trading (Pollack 1986). However, the enormous volume of trading in derivative securities may to some extent be a substitute for short sales. In an empirical analysis, Figlewski and Webb (1990) argue that options trading is a substitute for short sales. To the extent that our analysis applies to this case, it may be quantitatively very important. See Allen and Gale (1990) for a discussion of the impact of derivative security markets.

5. We are grateful to Joe Ostroy for pointing out the connection between our work and Makowski's.

6. More precisely, we showed that the equilibrium was constrained efficient. An allocation was defined to be constrained efficient if a planner who was subject to the same cost of issuing securities could not make everyone better off by making transfers of goods and securities at the first date.

7. More precisely, we assume that entrepreneurs are not around at date 2 and so cannot engage in short sales.

8. We adopt the usual abuse of notation and let N stand for the set $\{1, \ldots, N\}$.

9. In this sense there is a single *type* of asset. The results of this chapter could easily be extended to a finite number of types. Assumption I simplifies the analysis without significantly reducing the insight we obtain from it.

10. Note that consumption is not assumed to be bounded below. When short sales are allowed, the assumption that consumption be nonnegative with probability one is excessively strong. On the other hand, we want to avoid the difficulties of modelling bankruptcy. We allow negative consumption and attach high disutility to low values of consumption as a proxy for costly bankruptcy. (See assumption 3.)

11. Assumption 3 is implied by assumption 2 if, in addition, the utility function is additively separable. This property is not shared by some nonadditively separable utility functions, however. A counterexample is given by $U_k(c_1, c_2) = -\exp\{-c_1 - c_2\}$.

12. This is simply a normalization in view of the fact that consumption is not bounded below.

13. Suppose that two entrepreneurs n_0 and n_1 choose the ith financial structure. Let i_n denote the financial structure chosen by entrepreneur n, let $p(f, n)$ denote the price, and let $d(f, n)$ denote the amount of claim $f \in F_i$ (where $i = i_n$) purchased from entrepreneur n. Suppose that $d(f, n_1) \neq d(f, n_1)$ for some $f \in F_i$. Then define a new portfolio $d'(f, n)$ by putting

$$d'(f, n) = \begin{cases} d(f, n) & \forall f \in F_{i_n}, \forall n \in N \setminus \{n_0, n_1\}, \\ d(f, n_1) & \forall f \in F_{i_n}, n = n_0, \\ d(f, n_0) & \forall f \in F_{i_n}, n = n_1. \end{cases}$$

In defining d' we have simply transposed the quantities of claims purchased from the two entrepreneurs. From assumption 2 it follows that the probability distribution of the returns to the portfolio d is the same as the probability distribution of the returns from the portfolio d'. Certainly the cost is the same since $p(f, n_0) = p(f, n_1)$ for all $f \in F_i$ in a symmetric equilibrium. We can define a third portfolio by putting $d'' = (d + d')/2$. Then d'' has the same cost as the other two portfolios and must be weakly preferred by assumption 1.

14. The argument in footnote 13 shows that it is enough to distinguish claims by their payoff function and by the financial structure to which they belong.

15. As usual, a negative value of $d(a)$ represents a short position. In that case, the investor shorts $d(a)/3$ units of the claim issued by each entrepreneur.

16. The crucial point here is that the constraint limits the *total* amount of short selling. The constraint can be motivated as follows. Under current practice on the NYSE, an investor wanting to take a short position must borrow shares from another investor. Thus the total size of the short positions must be limited by the amount of the underlying stock available. If only stock held on margin can be borrowed, the total short position will be less than the amount of stock. If borrowed stock can be re-lent, the total short positions may exceed the amount of the underlying stock.

The constraint in the model does not fit this story exactly. It assumes that each investor receives a fixed quota independently of his desire to take a short position. This is only one rationing mechanism among many and not necessarily the most plausible. For example, it does not allow the total amount of short selling to be re-allocated among investors wanting to take short positions. But it has the advantage of being simple and allows us to make our point. Alternative rationing schemes which endogenize the ration of individual investors can be handled using the methods of Drèze (1975) but only at the cost of greatly complicating the model and without any significant gain in insight.

17. The argument is that as the firm increases (decreases) the amount of its debt outstanding, an investor can exactly offset the effect on his own portfolio by increasing (decreasing) the amount of debt he holds. An investor should therefore be indifferent to the firm's debt-equity ratio and so the market value of the firm should not be affected by it either.

18. This possibility would seem to be important in the context of the Arbitrage Pricing Theory of Ross (1976). His pricing formula holds for all but a negligible set of assets. More precisely, for any $\varepsilon > 0$, the expected returns are ε-close to the predicted value for all but a finite number of assets. However, a set of assets which has negligible cardinality need not be negligible in any other sense. In particular, it may provide important risk sharing opportunities.

19. Let D denote a constant random variable. A claim is called nontrivial if it is not zero or the identity map. Then for any nontrivial claim f and any asset Z_n, there exist numbers r_1 and r_2 such that $D = r_1(Z_n - f(Z_n)) + r_2 f(Z_n)$. A portfolio consisting of r_2 units of f and r_1 units of the residual claim is effectively debt. Once debt is available, any claim can be created out of debt and equity. Let f be any claim. Then there exist numbers r_1 and r_2 such that $f = r_1 D + r_2 Z_n$, that is, a portfolio consisting of r_1 units of debt and r_2 units of equity is equivalent to f.

20. Strictly speaking, we proved this for the case $L = 0$ but the proof is identical for $0 < L < \infty$. There are two important assumptions needed for this result. One is a continuity assumption that says, roughly speaking, that the SEE depend continuously on the cross-sectional distributions of financial structures. The second is an assumption about asset returns. It ensures that idiosyncratic risk can be eliminated through diversification. This assumption was introduced as assumption 4 in section 7.4. In a large economy, the law of large numbers ensures that the cross-sectional distribution of financial structures is nonstochastic and equal to the mixed strategy σ. As a result, the SEE resulting from the entrepreneurs' choices is nonstochastic and independent of the choice of any individual entrepreneur (here we need the continuity assumption). Entrepreneurs can take the prices in the auction market as given when they make their choices. so we are dealing essentially with a competitive price-taking equilibrium.

21. It is not obvious that this stronger notion of competitive equilibrium will be the limit of a sequence of SFE as the number of assets becomes unboundedly large. Nonetheless, we have shown in Allen and Gale (1989) that, if a certain continuity condition is satisfied and $L < \infty$, then the limit of a sequence of SFE as $N \to \infty$ is indeed a competitive equilibrium in this stronger sense. The same would not be true if $L = \infty$.

22. The efficiency notion we use is essentially the same as that proposed by Grossman (1977) and Grossman and Hart (1979). A stronger concept is proposed by Geanakoplos and Polemarchakis (1986).

23. Hart (1975) provides another example of nonexistence of equilibrium when unbounded short sales are allowed. Hart's problem differs from ours both in its source and in its severity. In Hart's model, the subspace of the commodity space that can be spanned by assets depends on prices in a discontinuous way. However, the discontinuity is nongeneric (see Duffie and Shafer 1985 and 1986). The problem discussed here is generic and seems to arise from a misspecification of equilibrium.

24. Imperfect competition is thus seen to be an important ingredient in establishing the existence of equilibrium by providing entrepreneurs with incentives they could not have in a perfectly competitive equilibrium. A similar use is made of imperfect competition by Jackson (1988). Grossman and Stiglitz (1980) argued that rational expectations equilibrium might not exist. If prices revealed all the relevant information no one would have an incentive to become informed. in which case prices could not be informative. Jackson shows that if only a few agents become informed, they will have market power, which may provide them with an incentive to become informed even if prices reveal all their information. The argument made by Grossman and Stiglitz (1980) depends on an inappropriate use of the price-taking assumption.

References

Allen, F., and D. Gale (1988): "Optimal Security Design," *Review of Financial Studies*, 1, 229–263.

———— (1989): "Arbitrage, Short Sales and Financial Innovation," Rodney White Center for Financial Research (Working Paper #10-89), University of Pennsylvania.

———— (1990): "Incomplete Markets and Incentives to Set up an Options Exchange," *Geneva Papers on Risk and Insurance Theory*, 15, 17–46.

Arrow, K. (1964): "The Role of Securities in the Optimal Allocation of Risk-Bearing," *Review of Economic Studies*, 31, 91–96.

Black, F., and M. Scholes (1973): "The Pricing of Options and Corporate Liabilities," *Journal of Political Economy*, 81, 637–659.

Cass, D. (1988): "Perfect Equilibrium with Incomplete Financial Markets: An Elementary Exposition," CARESS Working Paper 88-15, University of Pennsylvania (mimeo).

Diamond, P. (1967): "The Role of a Stock Market in a General Equilibrium Model with Technological Uncertainty," *American Economic Review*, 57, 759–766.

Drèze, J. (1975): "Existence of an Equilibrium under Price Rigidity and Quantity Rationing," *International Economic Review*, 16, 301–320.

Duffie, D. (1987): "Stochastic Equilibria with Incomplete Financial Markets," *Journal of Economic Theory*, 41, 405–416.

Duffie, D., and M. Jackson (1989): Optimal Innovation of Futures Contracts, *Review of Financial Studies*, 2, 275–296.

Duffie, D., and W. Shafer (1985): Equilibrium with Incomplete Markets: I A Model of Generic Existence," *Journal of Mathematical Economics*, 14, 285–300.

——— (1986): "Equilibrium with Incomplete Markets: II Generic Existence in Stochastic Economies," *Journal of Mathematical Economics*, 15, 199–216.

Figlewski, S., and G. Webb (1990): "Options, Short Sales and Market Incompleteness," Stern School of Business, New York University (mimeo).

Geanakoplos, J., and A. Mas Colell (1989): "Real Indeterminacy with Financial Assets," *Journal of Economic Theory*, 47, 22–38.

Geanakoplos, J., and H. Polemarchakis (1986): "Existence, Regularity and Constrained Suboptimality of Competitive Allocations when the Asset Market is Incomplete" *Uncertainty, Information and Communication: Essays in Honor of Kenneth J. Arrow, Volume III*, ed. by W. Heller, R. Starr, and D. Starrett. Cambridge: Cambridge University Press.

Grossman, S. (1977): "A Characterization of Equilibrium in Incomplete Markets," *Journal of Economic Theory*, 15, 1–15.

Grossman, S., and O. Hart (1979): "A Theory of Competitive Equilibrium in Stock Market Economies," *Econometrica*, 47, 293–330.

Grossman, S., and J. Stiglitz (1980): "On the Impossibility of Informationally Efficient Markets," *American Economic Review*, 70, 393–408.

Hart, O. (1975): "On the Optimality of Equilibrium when Market Structure is Incomplete," *Journal of Economic Theory*, 11, 418–443.

——— (1979): "On Shareholder Unanimity in Large Stock Market Economies," *Econometrica*, 47, 1057–1084.

Hellwig, M. (1981): "Bankruptcy, Limited Liability and the Modigliani-Miller Theorem," *American Economic Review*, 71, 155–170.

Jackson, M. (1988): "Equilibrium, Price Formation and the Value of Information in Economies with Privately Informed Agents," Northwestern University (mimeo).

Jones, L. (1987): "The Efficiency of Monopolistically Competitive Equilibria in Large Economies: Commodity Differentiation with Gross Substitutes," *Journal of Economic Theory*, 41, 356–391.

Kreps, D. (1979): "Three Essays on Capital Markets," IMSSS Technical Report #298, Stanford University (mimeo).

Makowski, L. (1983): "Competitive Stock Markets," *Review of Economic Studies*, 50, 305–330.

Modigliani, F. and M. Miller (1958): 'The Cost of Capital, Corporation Finance and the Theory of Finance." *American Economic Review*, 48, 162–197.

Pollack, 1. (1986): *Short-Sale Regulation of NASDAQ Securities*, NASDAQ Pamphlet.

Radner, R. (1972): "Existence of Equilibrium Plans, Prices and Price Expectations in a Sequence of Markets," *Econometrica*, 40, 289–303.

Ross, S. (1976): "The Arbitrage Theory of Capital Asset Pricing," *Journal of Economic Theory*, 13, 341–360.

Tufano, P. (1988): "Financial Innovations and First-Mover Advantages: An Empirical Analysis." Harvard Business School (mimeo).

8 Incomplete Markets and Incentives to Set Up an Options Exchange

8.1 Introduction

In many economic analyses, whether markets are complete or incomplete is critical to the results. However, traditional models with incomplete markets take the market structure as exogenous. The number of securities that are traded is limited but the origin of these limitations is not explicitly considered. It is usually argued that securities are costly but these costs are not modeled. In Allen and Gale (1988a, 1988b) we consider models where the costs of issuing securities are incorporated into the analysis and the market structure of the economy is endogenous. An important limitation of these two papers is that only firms issue securities. There are no markets for derivative securities such as options or intermediaries such as banks. The purpose of the present chapter is to consider a situation where an options exchange is set up endogenously.

We consider a simple stylized model with one type of firm and two types of investors. There is a profit-maximizing exchange owner who has a monopoly right to set up an exchange for options written on the equity of the firms. The costs of setting up the exchange are fixed and independent of the volume of options traded. These costs are recouped by charging lump sum fees. There are two dates: at each of these there is a single consumption good. At the first date the exchange owner decides whether to set up the exchange. Then the firms' equity and (if the options exchange is set up) the derivative security are traded. At the second date the state of the world becomes known and this determines the payoffs on the securities.

Five main results are obtained.

1. We begin by studying the benchmark case in which the exchange owner can charge investors and firms (possibly negative) lump sum fees. He can make every agent's agreement to pay these fees a necessary condition for setting up the exchange. Under these two assumptions the equilibrium market structure is efficient in the sense used in Allen and Gale (1988a): a central planner who is subject to the same transactions costs as individual agents could not make everyone better off by re-allocating securities and consumption at the first date.

2. Subsequently we consider a version of the model which reflects institutional practice more closely. The exchange is first set up and investors

This chapter originally appeared in *Geneva Papers on Risk and Insurance Theory* special issue entitled "The Allocation of Risk with Incomplete Asset Markets" edited by Herakles Polemarchakis, vol. 15, no. 1 (March, 1990) 17–46. Reprinted by permission.

are then charged fees for the privilege of trading derivative securities. In this case it is shown that the market structure of the economy is not always efficient. In some circumstances an options exchange is not set up in equilibrium, yet a central planner could make everybody better off by setting up an exchange and using lump sum taxes to reallocate first-period consumption and securities appropriately. Perhaps more surprisingly, there exist situations where an options exchange is set up in equilibrium even though everybody could be better off if an exchange were not set up.

3. When an exchange is established. the exchange owner does not always have the correct incentives to choose the socially efficient set of options to be traded. There exist situations where it is profitable for the exchange owner to choose a set of options that does not complete the market even though, at the same cost, he could make markets complete.

4. The value of firms is affected by the existence of an options exchange. Firm values can be increased or decreased by the existence of an exchange. Thus the incentives of a third party to issue securities differ significantly from those of firms.

5. Firms' decisions concerning their capital structure and the exchange owner's decision of whether or not to set up an options exchange are interrelated. This interrelationship can lead to an inefficiency. For example, it may be relatively expensive for firms to improve investors' risk sharing opportunities by issuing debt and levered equity but relatively cheap for an options exchange to improve investors' risk sharing opportunities by issuing a derivative security. Nevertheless, in equilibrium, firms may issue debt and levered equity and as a result the exchange owner may not find it profitable to set up an exchange even though a Pareto superior allocation is feasible if an exchange is set up.

Why do these results arise? In the benchmark model, the exchange owner makes a proposal to all of the firms and investors in the economy. He announces the derivative security that will be traded and the fees that will be charged to each agent. These fees can be negative in which case they are transfers needed to gain the approval of the recipients. Agents can accept or reject this proposal. If all agents accept, the exchange is opened; if any agent refuses, the exchange remains closed. Each agent knows that if he refuses to pay the charge, the exchange will not be set up. Therefore, his decision will be based on a comparison of his utility in two different equilibria, one with an open exchange and one without. Agents will agree to the exchange owner's proposal only if they would be at least as well off in the equilibrium with an open exchange as they would be in the equilibrium with a closed exchange. When the exchange owner can demand lump sum fees from all agents and make every agent's agreement a precondition of opening the exchange, he can capture all of the surplus. In that case his decisions are the same as those of a central planner who is subject to the same transaction costs. That is why the first-best market structure is obtained in equilibrium.

In the benchmark model we have made a number of special assumptions in order to ensure an efficient equilibrium market structure is obtained. Some of these assumptions are not satisfied in practice. The second version of the model that we look at is designed to reflect these institutional realities. In this version the exchange owner first decides whether to set up the options exchange. Then, once the exchange has been set up, he announces the fees that must be paid by any agent who wants to trade on the exchange. This version of the model differs from the benchmark in two crucial ways. First, the exchange owner cannot charge fees to the firms, since they do not want to trade on the exchange. Second, refusal of an investor to pay the charge will result only in his exclusion from the exchange, not in the exchange being closed (as in the benchmark case). Therefore his decision will be based on a comparison of his utility levels with and without access to the options exchange but within the same equilibrium.

Both of these differences affect the rents that the exchange owner can collect. If he cannot charge fees to the firms he may not be able to capture all of the surplus from opening the exchange. On the other hand, if the opening of the exchange reduces firms' values, he is not required to compensate them. In either case, he may not have the correct incentives to choose an efficient market structure. The treatment of investors is more subtle. In the benchmark model, the charge an investor is willing to pay depends on a comparison of two equilibria, one with an options exchange and one without. Therefore the maximum charge that can be extracted from an investor reflects the true value to him of opening the exchange. In the other model, the maximum charge that can be extracted from an investor reflects the value of access to the exchange in an equilibrium in which the exchange already exists. This may be greater or less than the value of opening the exchange. For all these reasons the market structure obtained in equilibrium may not be efficient.

The third result, concerning the choice of the type of option traded, arises for a similar reason. Entry charges depend on a comparison within the equilibrium. The exchange owner can find it advantageous to choose a contract which only improves risk sharing opportunities to a limited extent because this leads to security prices which allow him to charge high entry fees.

The fourth result, that firms' value can be increased or decreased by the introduction or options, is due to the fact that investors' demand for firms' equity depends on the availability of alternative securities. For example, if no options are available risk averse investors may need to hold large amounts of equity to ensure that they have enough consumption when the payoffs are low. However, if they have access to puts on a firm's equity they may hold less of it than they would do in the absence of the put. As a result the price of the firm's equity can be lower if the put is available than if it is not and the firms' owners may be made worse off by the introduction of an options exchange.

The fifth result, concerning the relationship between firms' capital structure decisions and the existence of an exchange. arises because the amount the exchange can charge for entry depends on investors' opportunities outside the exchange. If some firms issue debt and levered equity this means the alternative if investors stay outside the exchange is more attractive than if all firms just issue equity. As a result, the maximum feasible entry charge may be lower and this may make the exchange unprofitable. This can happen even in situations where setting up an options exchange to improve investors' risk sharing possibilities is relatively cheap compared to some firms issuing debt and levered equity. Thus the equilibrium allocation where some firms issue two securities and no exchange is set up may be inefficient; a Pareto superior allocation may be feasible if firms just issue one security and an exchange is set up.

Ross (1976), Green and Jarrow (1987) and Green and Spear (1987) have shown that by increasing the number of securities that are traded it is possible to complete markets and hence improve risk sharing in the economy. Their analyses do not take account of the costs of setting up the markets or the incentives of exchange owners. Although opportunities for risk sharing may be improved, it is not clear that the exchange owners have the correct incentives to complete markets and that the benefits outweigh the costs. This is the issue that our analysis focuses on.

These models deal with the limiting case in which markets are approximately complete. When markets are far from complete the introduction of an extra market may not enhance efficiency. Hart (1975) and Newbery and Stiglitz (1984) show that increasing the number of markets can make everybody worse off. The reason is that risk sharing opportunities can be altered by the introduction of a new market. In contrast, in our model the reason that everybody can be worse off with an options market than without one is rather different. It is because there are transaction costs associated with setting up markets. The way in which exchange owners recoup these costs may not provide the correct incentives.

Geanakoplos and Polemarchakis (1987) have studied the efficiency of competitive equilibrium in economies where securities have payoffs denominated in terms of an abstract unit of account. Although the set of securities is given (and incomplete) the real characteristics of the securities can change when the prices of goods (measured in terms of the abstract unit of account) are changed. In this sense securities are endogenous. In a typical equilibrium it would be possible to make everyone better off by manipulating the prices and hence the securities. But price-taking agents do not perceive this possibility. In our analysis, achieving the first best requires a comparison of equilibria, as in the benchmark model. Similarly to Geanakoplos and Polemarchakis (1987) there is an inefficiency when agents take the equilibrium as given, as in the institutional model.

The chapter proceeds as follows. Section 8.2 outlines the benchmark model. Section 8.3 shows that in this case the equilibrium market structure of the economy is socially efficient. Section 8.4 considers a model which is closer to institutional practice and demonstrates that the equilibrium market structure of the economy is not necessarily optimal. Section 8.5 looks at the issue of multiple equilibria. Section 8.6 considers the interactions between firms' capital structure decisions and the existence of an options exchange. Finally, section 8.7 contains concluding remarks.

8.2   A Benchmark Model

To illustrate these ideas we use an elementary model of asset market equilibrium. The basic ideas are taken from two earlier papers (Allen and Gale 1988a and 1988b).

There are two dates, indexed by $t = 1, 2$ and a finite set of states of nature, indexed by $s \in S$. Every economic agent has the same information structure: there is no information at the first date and the true state is revealed at the second. At each date there is a single consumption good that can be thought of as "income" or "money."

There is a continuum of identical firms. The set of firms has unit measure except where otherwise stated. A firm's profits at $t = 2$ are represented by a random variable $Z_0: S \to \mathbb{R}_+$. For each $s \in S$, $Z_0(s)$ represents the profits of the firm in state s. To begin with we shall assume that firms are passive: they do not have any decisions to make. Each firm is owned and controlled by a single entrepreneur. The entrepreneur values consumption only at the first date. Consequently, he wants to sell his equity in the firm in order to maximize his consumption at the first date. Since the value of the firm is determined by the market, the firm/entrepreneur is merely a passive consumer.

There are two types of investors, indexed by $i = a, b$. Each type of investor is a continuum and, for simplicity, we assume that each continuum has unit measure. Investors are risk averse and value consumption at each date. An investor's consumption set is denoted by X, where X is the set of functions from $SU\{1\}$ to $\mathbb{R}$. For any $\xi \in X$, $\xi(1)$ denotes consumption at date 1 and $\xi(s)$ denotes consumption at date 2 in state $s \in S$. The preferences of an investor of type i are represented by a utility function $U_i: X \to \mathbb{R}$ for each type $i = a, b$. If an investor chooses a consumption bundle $\xi \in X$ then his utility is given by $U_i(\xi)$. Each investor has an initial endowment $0 \in X$.

In addition to firms and investors there is an agent, called the exchange owner, who has the right to set up an options exchange for the trading of derivative securities. There is a fixed cost of setting up the exchange which is equal to y units of first-period consumption. We assume that only a single security can be traded on the exchange. The derivative security is represented by a function $Z_1: S \to \mathbb{R}$. One unit of the security entitles the owner $Z_1(s)$ units of the consumption good at the second date in state s, for every $s \in S$. The economy's endowment of the derivative security is equal to zero. The exchange owner chooses whether to open the exchange and, if the exchange is opened, what security should be traded. Since he only values consumption at the first date, he makes these decisions with a view to maximizing his first-period consumption.

Equilibrium at date 1 is determined in two stages. At stage 0, it is decided whether the options exchange should open and, if so, what kind of derivative security should be traded and what fees should be levied on the firms and investors. At stage 1, investors trade securities on the available markets. The definition of equilibrium begins with stage 1.

Equilibrium at Stage 1

The owner's decision to open the options exchange is indicated by the dummy variable α. The exchange is closed if $\alpha = 0$ and it is open if $\alpha = 1$. The vector of securities that can be traded at stage 1 is denoted by $Z = (Z_0, Z_1)$, where Z_0, is the underlying stock and Z_1 is the derivative security. Finally, let $e = (e_a, e_b, e_f)$ denote the vector of fees (positive or negative) imposed by the owner of the exchange at stage 1. For each $i = a, b, e_i$, is the fee imposed on an investor of type i and e_f is the fee levied on a firm.

Suppose that at stage 0 it has been decided to open the exchange ($\alpha = 1$). In that case investors can trade in both securities at stage 1. Let $v = (v_0, v_1)$ denote the vector of security prices, where v_0(resp. v_1) is the price of the underlying stock (resp. derivative security) measured in terms of consumption at date 1. An investor takes the security prices v as given and chooses a consumption level c and a portfolio $d = (d_0, d_1)$ where d_0 (resp. d_1) is his demand for the equity of the firm (resp. the derivative security). Short sales of equity are not allowed: $d_0 \geq 0$. (This assumption allows the concepts developed in Allen and Gale 1988a to be used in section 8.6 where firms issue both debt and equity. It is discussed further there.) An investor's endowment is normalized to zero at each date. Then the budget constraint of an investor of type $i = a, b$ can be written:

$$c + v \cdot d + e_i = 0, \qquad \text{for } i = a, b. \tag{1}$$

Now suppose that the exchange is not open at stage 1 ($\alpha = 0$). In that case there is no derivative security and there are no fees imposed on the investors and firms. Nonetheless it is convenient to use the same notation for this case as well. An investor is assumed to choose a pair (c, d) subject to the constraints:

$$c + v \cdot d \leq 0 \quad \text{and} \quad d_1 = 0. \tag{2}$$

The first of these constraints is the budget constraint; the second reflects the fact that he cannot trade the derivative security.

In this notation, $B_i^\alpha(v, e)$ will denote the budget set of an investor $i = a, b$ when the prevailing security prices are v, for any choice of (α, Z, e). Define $B_i^\alpha(v, e)$ by putting

$$B_i^\alpha(v, e) = \begin{cases} \{(c_i, d_i) \in \mathbb{R}^3 | c + v \cdot d + e_i \leq 0\} & \text{if } \alpha = 1; \\ \{(c_i, d_i) \in \mathbb{R}^3 | c + v \cdot d \leq 0 \text{ and } d_1 = 0\} & \text{if } \alpha = 0. \end{cases} \tag{3}$$

This allows us to give a concise definition of equilibrium.

DEFINITION Let (α, Z, e) be given. Equilibrium in stage 1, relative to (α, Z, e), is defined by an array $\{v, (c_i, d_i)\}$, consisting of a price vector v and a choice (c_i, d_i) for each type of investor $i = a, b$, that satisfies the following conditions:

(i) $(c_i, d_i) \in \arg\max_{B_i^\alpha(v, e)} U_i(c_i, d_i \cdot Z)$ for $i = a, b$;

(ii) $\sum_i d_i = (1, 0)$.

Condition (i) simply says that each investor is maximizing his utility subject to the appropriate budget constraint and to the available markets. Condition (ii) is the market-clearing condition. If the security markets clear then Walras's law ensures the goods market clears as well. Note that equilibrium in stage 1 does not refer explicitly to firms or to the exchange owner. Firms are passive participants in the equilibrium. They simply consume the value of their equity v_0. The exchange owner has made all his decisions at stage 0.

Let $\Phi^\alpha(Z, e)$ denote the set of stage 1 equilibria relative to (α, Z, e). Let $u_i^\alpha(v, e, Z)$ denote the maximum utility attainable when security prices are given by v and the stage 0 choices are given by (α, Z, e). That is

$$u_i^\alpha(v, Z, e) = \sup_{B_i^\alpha(v, e)} U_i(c_i, d_i \cdot Z) \text{ for } i = a, b. \tag{4}$$

Also, define the utility of firms to be $u_f^\alpha(v, Z, e) = v_0$ if $\alpha = 0$ and $v_0 - e_f$ if $\alpha = 1$.

Equilibrium at Stage 0

The exchange owner chooses the derivative security Z_0 that is to be traded on the exchange, the fees e that are to be charged for entry to the exchange and finally decides whether to open the exchange ($\alpha = 1$) or to leave it closed ($\alpha = 0$). Firms and investors are assumed to have a veto on the opening of the exchange. The veto works as follows. The exchange owner announces the derivative security Z_1 he would like to have traded and the fee structure he would like to charge. All agents accept or reject. If one (or more) agent rejects, the exchange cannot be opened ($\alpha = 0$). On the other hand, if they all accept then the exchange owner is given the choice of whether to open the exchange. Notice that the exchange owner is allowed to impose fees on all agents, including the firms, who will not actually use the exchange. Even firms may have an interest in seeing the exchange open, however, because of its effect on the value of their equity. The fees charged can be negative, in which case they constitute a transfer to the agent. These transfers may be necessary in order to obtain the agreement of all the agents to the exchange opening. This mechanism for choosing the market structure is patently artificial. The reason for studying it is simply that it produces an efficient choice of market structure. In subsequent sections we shall look at a model that conforms more closely to the practices of actual institutions.

Suppose that the exchange owner has announced his choice of Z_1 and e. Whether the firms and investors will accept this proposal depends on the equilibrium they anticipate in the second stage following a decision to open the exchange ($\alpha = 1$) or let it remain closed ($\alpha = 0$). In effect, these agents are comparing two equilibria and deciding which they prefer. Suppose the two equilibria are denoted by $\{v^\alpha, (c_i^\alpha, d_i^\alpha)\}$ for $\alpha = 0, 1$. It will be individually rational for an agent of type $i = a, b, f$ to accept the exchange owner's proposal if and only if:

$$u_i^0(v^0, e, Z) \leq u_i^1(v^1, e, Z). \tag{5}$$

This constraint must be satisfied if the exchange owner wants to open the exchange. On the other hand, he is not compelled to open the exchange even if all the agents accept his proposal, so there is no loss of generality in assuming that his proposal is always individually rational for all agents. We can also assume, again without loss of generality, that agents accept the proposal whenever the individual rationality constraint is satisfied. If not, the exchange owner could always win unanimous approval by decreasing slightly every agent's fee. In a perfect equilibrium agents would always accept when the individual rationality constraint was just satisfied. This leads us to the following definition.

DEFINITION A pre-equilibrium is defined by an array $\{(v^\alpha, (c_i^\alpha, d_i^\alpha)), \alpha, e, Z\}$ consisting of a second stage equilibrium $(v^\alpha, (c_i^\alpha, d_i^\alpha))$ for each $\alpha = 0, 1$, a decision a whether to open the exchange, a fee structure e and a choice of securities Z, that satisfies the following conditions:

(i) $u_i^0(v^0, e, Z) \leq u_i^1(v^1, e, Z)$ for $i = a, b, f$;

(ii) $(v^\alpha, (c_i^\alpha, d_i^\alpha)) \in \Phi^\alpha(e, Z)$ for $\alpha = 0, 1$;

(iii) Z_0 is given.

A pre-equilibrium is called a full equilibrium if there does not consist another pre-equilibrium that yields higher profits $\alpha(\sum_{i=a,b,f} e_i - \gamma)$ to the exchange owner.

Notice that in the definition of full equilibrium we are not only assuming that the exchange owner maximizes profits with respect to his choice of (α, e, Z). We also implicitly allow him to choose the equilibrium that will follow at the second stage. In section 8.5 we consider what would happen if some other selection procedure were followed.

8.3   Constrained Efficiency

In this section we consider the efficiency of the equilibrium market structure in the benchmark model. The efficiency concept we use is similar to the one used in Allen and Gale (1988a). An equilibrium is said to be constrained efficient if a central planner who is subject to the same transaction costs as individual agents, cannot make some agents better off without making some agents worse off. In this context, the condition "subject to the same transaction costs" is interpreted to the mean that the planner can only change the market structure and reallocate securities and consumption at the first date. We show that, in this sense, the equilibrium market structure in the benchmark model is efficient.

ASSUMPTION U_j is continuous, strictly increasing and quasi-concave for $i = a, b$.

Under this assumption, whenever it is possible to make some agents better off without making any agents worse off, it is possible to make all agents strictly better off. Since firms and the exchange are only interested in first-period consumption, utility is effectively "transferable" between them. An allocation is Pareto-dominated, then, if and only if there exists an alternative allocation that makes investors at least as well off and leaves more consumption for the firms and the exchange owner. This suggests the following definition.

DEFINITION   An equilibrium allocation $\{(c_i, d_i), \alpha, Z\}$ is constrained efficient if there does not exist another allocation $\{(c_i', d_i') a', Z'\}$ such that:

(i) $U_i(c_i, d_i \cdot Z) \leq U_i(c_i', d_i' \cdot Z')$ for $i = a, b$;

(ii) $\sum_i c_i + \alpha\gamma > \sum_i c_i' + \alpha'\gamma$;

(iii) $\sum_i d_i' = (1, 0)$ and, if $\alpha' = 0$, $d_{i1}' = 0$ for $i = a, b$.

To prove that the equilibrium choice of market structure is constrained efficient, we assume that there exists a better allocation and obtain a contradiction. We need to consider two different cases. Suppose first that there exists a Pareto-preferred allocation that involves opening the exchange. It can be shown that this implies the existence of a Pareto-preferred allocation that can be supported as an equilibrium. That is, there exists a pre-equilibrium that yields higher profits for the exchange owner than the given equilibrium, contradicting the definition of equilibrium.

In the second case, we suppose the equilibrium can be Pareto-improved on by an allocation in which the exchange is closed. When the exchange is closed, the model is isomorphic to an Arrow-Debreu model in which the commodities are consumption and equity. The usual argument suffices to prove constrained efficiency holding the market structure constant. Using this property, we can show that in the original equilibrium there must exist some investor or firm who would be better off in the second stage equilibrium if the exchange were closed. But that agent should have vetoed the exchange, contradicting the definition of equilibrium.

Proposition 1   If $\{(v^\alpha, (c_i^\alpha, d_i^\alpha)), \alpha, e, Z\}$ is a full equilibrium of the benchmark model then the associated allocation $\{(c_i, d_i), \alpha, Z\}$ is constrained efficient.

Proof   Suppose, contrary to what we want to prove, that the allocation is not constrained efficient. Let $\{(c_i', d_i'), \alpha', Z'\}$ be the alternative, Pareto-preferred allocation.

First consider the case where $\alpha' = 1$. Under the maintained assumption there is no loss of generality in taking $\{(c_i', d_i')\}$ to minimize $\sum_i c_i'$ subject to the individual rationality constraint $U_i(c_i^0, d_i^0 \cdot Z) \leq U_i(c_i', d_i' \cdot Z')$ for $i = a, b$. By the usual supporting hyperplane argument, we can show that the allocation $\{(c_i', d_i')\}$ can be supported as an equilibrium at the second stage. More precisely, under the maintained assumption, there exists a price vector v' and fee structure e' such that $(c_i', d_i') \in \arg\max U_i(c, d \cdot Z')$, where the maximum is taken over the budget set $B_i^1(v', e')$. Define $e_f' = v_0^0 - v_0'$. It is straightforward to check that $\{(v^0, (c_i^0, d_i^0)), (v', (c_i', d_i')), (\alpha', e', Z')\}$ is a pre-equilibrium. By hypothesis, this pre-equilibrium yields higher profits for the exchange owner than the full equilibrium, a contradiction.

Second, consider the case where $\alpha = 0$. We begin by noting that the second stage equilibrium $\{v^0, (c_i^0, d_i^0)\}$ is constrained efficient when the market structure is taken as given. To show this, suppose to the contrary that there is a Pareto-preferred allocation $\{(c_i', d_i'), \alpha', Z'\}$ with $\alpha' = 0$. Since $\alpha' = 0$ we can assume without loss of generality that $Z' = Z$. From the definition of stage 1 equilibrium, $c_i + v \cdot d_i \leq c_i' + v \cdot d_i'$ for $i = a, b$. Since $\sum_i d_i = (1, 0)$, this implies that $\sum_i c_i + \alpha\gamma \leq \sum_i c_i' + \alpha'\gamma$, as required. Now suppose that the equilibrium allocation $\{(c_i, d_i), \alpha, Z\}$ is Pareto-dominated by the alternative allocation $\{(c_i', d_i'), \alpha', Z'\}$. Without loss of generality we can assume that the alternative allocation $\{(c_i', d_i'), \alpha', Z'\}$ makes firms and both types of investor strictly better off. Since $\{v^0, (c_i^0, d_i^0)\}$ is constrained efficient, at least one type of investor or firm must be at least as well off at $\{v^0, (c_i^0, d_i^0)\}$ as he is in the alternative allocation $\{(c_i', d_i'), \alpha', Z'\}$. But this means that the individual rationality constraint cannot be satisfied, contradicting the definition of equilibrium.   ∎

8.4 An Institutional Model

A number of features of the benchmark model differ from actual practice. First, the investors who are going to trade in the exchange do not in practice agree to make payments before the exchange is set up. Second, firms and investors do not in practice have a veto over the opening of the exchange. In fact, the firms whose value forms the basis for the derivative security do not receive or make payments to the owner of the exchange. Finally, we do not observe lump sum payments for the right to trade on the exchange. The fees charged to investors depend in a more or less complex way on the volume of the security traded. The second version of the model we consider is intended to correspond more closely to actual institutional practice. In particular, we assume that the exchange is set up before investors are asked to pay for the right to trade on the exchange. If any investor refuses to pay, he is denied access to the exchange and can only trade shares in the firms. We also assume that there is no payment between the exchange owner and the firms ($e_f = 0$). For simplicity, we retain the assumption that the investors pay lump sum fees. We shall refer to this set of assumptions as the institutional model, to distinguish it from the benchmark model described in the previous section.

If the exchange owner decides not to open the exchange ($\alpha = 0$) then the definition of second stage equilibrium is the same as in the benchmark model. If the owner does open the exchange ($\alpha = 1$) then investors face a more complex problem than before. They must first decide whether to pay the entry fee and then choose an optimal consumption level and portfolio from the appropriate budget set. The description of equilibrium can he considerably simplified, however, if we recognize that in equilibrium all investors will enter the exchange. Since we only consider symmetric equilibria, either all investors of type i will pay the entry fee or none will. However, there can he no trade on the exchange unless both types of investors enter. Thus, in equilibrium, either all investors enter the exchange or none do. The exchange owner will never open the exchange unless he can recoup his costs, so the only equilibria we need to consider are those in which all investors decide to enter the exchange.

With this simplification, an equilibrium at the second stage can be described by the same definition given in section 8.2. The only change is that it must now be rational for investors to accept the proposed fees after the exchange has been set up. This requirement can he captured by changing thc individual rationality conditions in the definition of equilibrium at stage 0. Suppose that $\{v, (c_i, d_i)\}$ is a stage I equilibrium relative to (α, e, Z), where $\alpha = 1$. It is individually rational for an investor of type $i = a, b$ to pay the fee e_i and enter the exchange if and only if the following inequality is satisfied:

$$u_i^0(v, e, Z) \leq u_i^1(v, e, Z). \tag{6}$$

Contrast this individual rationality constraint with the earlier one. In the benchmark model the investor can veto the options exchange. If he refuses to pay the fee he finds himself in a different equilibrium, facing different prices as well as different markets. In the present model, the exchange is open whether he decides to pay the fee or not. If he refuses to pay the fee, he finds himself excluded from the market for the derivative security; but he is in the same equilibrium, facing the same prices.

DEFINITION   A pre-equilibrium of the institutional model is defined by an array $\{(v^\alpha, (c_i^\alpha, d_i^\alpha)), \alpha, e, Z\}$ consisting of a second stage equilibrium $(v^\alpha, (c_i^\alpha, d_i^\alpha))$ for each $\alpha = 0, 1$, a decision α whether to open the exchange, a fee structure $e = (e_a, e_b)$ and a choice of securities Z, that satisfies the following conditions.

(i) $u_i^0(v^1, e, Z) \leq u_i^1(v^1, e, Z)$ for $i = a, b$;

(ii) $(v^\alpha, (c_i^\alpha, d_i^\alpha)) \in \Phi^\alpha(e, Z)$ for $\alpha = 0, 1$;

(iii) Z_0 is given.

A pre-equilibrium is called a full equilibrium if there does not exist another pre-equilibrium that yields higher profits $\alpha(\sum_{i=a,b} e_i - \gamma)$.

Now we can see clearly the difference between the two definitions of equilibrium. In the benchmark model, the individual rationality constraint applies to all firms and investors. Furthermore, it requires that *setting up the exchange* be individually rational. In deciding whether to accept the exchange owner's proposal, an agent in the benchmark model is comparing his utility levels in two different equilibria, one with an open exchange and one without. He will agree to pay the exchange owner's charge (accept his transfer) only if his utility will be at least as great in the equilibrium with an options exchange as in the equilibrium without it. The maximum charge that can be extracted from him thus reflects the true economic value, to him, of opening the exchange. In this sense, the rents the exchange owner can extract reflect the true economic value of the exchange, so it is perhaps not surprising that he is led to choose an efficient market structure.

In the institutional model, by contrast, the individual rationality constraint applies only to investors. Firms need not be compensated if the opening of the exchange damages them by reducing their value; nor can they be asked for payments if it benefits them by increasing their value. Furthermore, the investors' individual rationality constraints have changed. In the benchmark model, individual rationality for an investor depended on an *inter-equilibrium* comparison. In the institutional model it depends on an *intra-equilibrium* comparison. If an investor refuses to pay the exchange owner's charges, the alternative is to remain outside the options exchange trading only in the ordinary equity market. He will pay the charge only if his utility with access to the exchange is at least as great as his utility without access to the exchange, in the *same equilibrium*. The maximum charge that can be extracted from the investor thus reflects the value of access to the exchange, *within a fixed equilibrium*.

Once the exchange has been opened, the bargaining power of the exchange owner to extract rents is different from what it was before the exchange opened. It may be greater; it may be less. There is no reason to think that the exchange owner's incentives in the institutional model will lead to an efficient choice of market structure.

We demonstrate next, by means of example, that this is the case: in the institutional model the equilibrium market structure is not necessarily efficient. We start by considering two-state examples; in this case all options are equivalent in the sense that they complete the market so the decision of which type of contract to offer is unimportant. Later we consider three-state examples to show how the type of option contract offered matters.

Our second result is the following.

Proposition 2 In the institutional model, the equilibrium market structure is not necessarily constrained efficient: (i) there are parameter values such that an equilibrium exists in which an exchange is not set up but Pareto superior allocations could be reached if an exchange were set up; and (ii) there are also parameter values such that an equilibrium exists in which an exchange is set up but Pareto superior allocations could be reached if an exchange were not set up.

Proof The proposition is demonstrated by means of examples. Example 1(i) shows the first part of the proposition and example 1(ii) the second part.

Example 1(i)   There are two equally-probable states of nature. There is one type of producer with outputs $(1, 2)$ in the two states respectively. The measure of firms is 2.

The cost of setting up an options exchange is 0.002. This is independent of the security structure offered by the exchange.

There are two groups of consumers $(i = a, b)$. The measure of both groups of consumer is 1 and their initial endowment is 5. They have von Neumann–Morgenstern utility functions of the form:

$$W_i(x^1, x^2) = x^1 - \exp(-\rho_i x^2) \tag{7}$$

where $\rho_a = 1$ and $\rho_b = 2$. Note that the utility function is linear in first-period consumption. This is an assumption we use in all the examples. It has strong implications for the nature of equilibrium. In particular, since agents have transferable utilities we can identify potential Pareto improvements by looking at the sum of agents' utilities.

First consider the stage 1 equilibrium when no options are available. In this case the only security that is traded is the firms' equity with payoffs (1, 2). It can readily be shown that the equilibrium values of variables of interest are as in table 8.1(i)a.

Since there are only two states, any option (except a call with a striking price of 0) leads to complete markets. For the sake of illustration suppose the exchange offers a put with a striking price of 2 which has payoffs (1, 0). In this case the equilibrium values of the variables of interest are given in table 8.1(i)b.

Table 8.1(i)c summarizes the differences between table 8.1(i)a and table 8.1(i)b. It can be seen that both groups of consumers are better off with complete markets than with incomplete markets: $\Delta W_a = 0.00256$; $\Delta W_b = 0.00256$. However, the value of the firm has fallen so that producers are worse off: $\Delta Firm\ Value = -0.00170$. Hence in terms of first period consumption the gross social gain is the sum of these three terms which is 0.0034. Since the cost of setting up an exchange is only 0.002, the net social gain is 0.0014. A social planner with the ability to reallocate first-period consumption and securities would be better off to set up the exchange.

What incentives does the exchange owner have? The amount that he can charge depends on the utility levels of the two groups if they were denied access to the options exchange. In other words, the amount that can be charged in terms of first period consumption is equal to the difference between the utility level with complete markets and the utility level that can be obtained with access to the equity market alone at the complete markets price of 0.25360. Table 8.1(i)d gives the details of this comparison.

It can be seen that since $0.00168 < 0.002$ the options exchange would not be set up in this case even though it is socially efficient for an exchange to be set up. This demonstrates part (i) of proposition 1.

Example 1(ii) The details of this example are identical to those of example 1(i) with two exceptions. The first is that the measure of firms is 0.4 instead of 2 and the second is that the cost of setting up the options exchange is 0.004 instead of 0.002.

The solutions to this example are given in tables 8.1(ii)a–8.1(ii)d. In this case even though it is undesirable to set up an exchange, nevertheless the exchange owner has an incentive to do so. This demonstrates part (ii) of the proposition.   ∎

The reason proposition 2 holds is that the amount the exchange owner can charge depends on traders' reservation utilities if they do not partici-

Table 8.1(i)a
Equilibrium in example 1(i) with incomplete markets

Group	Equilibrium demand for equity	Consumption State 1	Consumption State 2	Marginal utility of consumption State 1	Marginal utility of consumption State 2	Utility
a	1.15918	1.15918	2.31836	0.31374	0.09843	4.49796
b	0.84082	0.84082	1.68164	0.37214	0.06924	4.67498

The value of a firm = 0.25531

Table 8.1(i)b
Equilibrium in example 1(i) with complete markets

Group	Equilibrium demand for equity	Consumption State 1	Consumption State 2	Marginal utility of consumption State 1	Marginal utility of consumption State 2	Utility
a	1.21781	1.10228	2.43562	0.33211	0.08754	4.50052
b	0.78219	0.89772	1.56438	0.33211	0.08754	4.67754

The value of a firm = 0.25360

Table 8.1(i)c
A comparison between complete and incomplete markets in example 1(i)

Change in group a's utility	0.00256
Change in group b's utility	0.00256
Change in firm value	−0.00170
Total change	0.00340
Surplus from options exchange	0.00140

Table 8.1(i)d
Charges for access to the options exchange in example 1(i)

Group	Demand for equity at $v_0 = 0.25360$	Consumption State 1	Consumption State 2	Utility	Charge for entry to the options exchange
a	1.16400	1.16400	2.32800	4.49995	0.00057
b	0.84347	0.84347	1.68694	4.67643	0.00111

The total charge for entry to the options exchange = 0.00168
The total profit from setting up the exchange = −0.00032

Table 8.1(ii)a
Equilibrium in example 1(ii) with incomplete markets

Group	Equilibrium demand for equity	Consumption		Marginal utility of consumption		Utility
		State 1	State 2	State 1	State 2	
a	0.12110	0.12110	0.24219	0.88595	0.78491	4.01588
b	0.27890	0.27890	0.55781	1.14493	0.65543	4.20745

The value of a firm $= 1.22788$

Table 8.1(ii)b
Equilibrium in example 1(ii) with complete markets

Group	Equilibrium demand for equity	Consumption		Marginal utility of consumption		Utility
		State 1	State 2	State 1	State 2	
a	0.15114	0.03562	0.30228	0.96501	0.73913	4.01903
b	0.24989	0.36438	0.49772	0.96501	0.73913	4.21421

The value of a firm $= 1.22163$

Table 8.1(ii)c
A comparison between complete and incomplete markets in example 1(ii)

Change in group a's utility	0.00315
Change in group b's utility	0.00676
Change in firm value	-0.00624
Total change	0.00367
Surplus from options exchange	-0.00030

Table 8.1(ii)d
Charges for access to the options exchange in example 1(ii)

Group	Demand for equity at $v_0 = 1.22163$ without access	Consumption		Utility	Charge for entry to the options exchange
		State 1	State 2		
a	0.12421	0.12421	0.24841	4.01665	0.00238
b	0.28057	0.28057	0.56114	4.20920	0.00501

The total charge for entry to the options exchange $= 0.00740$
The total profit from setting up the exchange $= 0.00340$

pate in the market. In other words, it depends on an intra-equilibrium comparison rather than an inter-equilibrium comparison. The constraint $e_f = 0$ is not crucial for these results to hold; they would also hold if firms could be charged.

One point to notice is that it does not depend on the owner of the exchange being able to discriminate in terms of the fees charged to buyers and sellers. Even if the owner is restricted to charging them the same amount it can be seen that his decision in both of these particular examples is the same as when he can discriminate.

Part (ii) of the proposition is perhaps the more interesting result. It shows that moving to complete markets can lead to an allocation that is Pareto dominated by an allocation that could be reached with incomplete markets. It also shows that leaving the creation of derivative markets to profit-seeking behavior can lead to there being too many markets. Although the result has been derived in terms of a model where an exchange owner has a monopoly right to offer derivative securities, a similar result seems likely to hold in a number of other institutional settings. For example, suppose there is an incumbent exchange and that potential entrants can set up rival exchanges if the incumbent's profits are too high. This will limit the entry fee that the incumbent exchange charges but otherwise the model will be similar. Consider example 1(ii) but with a cost of setting up the exchange of 0.00739 so that establishing an exchange is just profitable for the incumbent. The profits in this case will be such that the potential entrants do not enter. Competition does not solve the problem.

Another interesting variant of the model is the case where the exchange is a non-profit organization. This is closer to the institutional structure that we actually observe. The problem here is to specify an objective function for the exchange. One possibility is that the exchange can use any surplus that is generated to increase the utilities of its members. For example, the offices provided to members or the salaries paid to employees could be higher than is strictly necessary. In this case the exchange will behave in much the same way as the profit-seeking exchange modelled here. Thus the fact that we observe non-profit exchanges where a large volume of securities is traded does not necessarily mean that such institutions are welfare improving; in fact the reverse can be true.

So far it has been demonstrated that the incentives to set up an exchange are not necessarily the correct ones. However, conditional on the exchange being set up the equilibrium market structure is efficient in the examples considered. We turn next to the question of whether, given the correct decision to set up, the exchange owner has the correct incentives to offer the socially desirable set of contracts.

Proposition 3   It can be more profitable for the options exchange to offer a security which fails to complete the market even though a security is available (at the same cost) which does this.

Proof   The proposition is again demonstrated by means of an example.

Example 2   There are three states of nature, $s = 1, 2, 3$, with probabilities $(0.5, 0.25, 0.25)$ respectively. The firms have outputs $(0.08, 1.8, 2)$ in the three states respectively. The measure of firms is 1.

The cost of setting up an options exchange which offers one or two options is 0.001. In other words the marginal cost of offering a second option is zero.

There are two groups of investors $(i = a, b)$. Investors of type a have exponential utility functions as in (7) with $\rho_a = 20$. For positive second-period consumption, investors of type b have logarithmic utility functions of the form.

$$W_b = x^1 + \ln(x^2).\tag{8}$$

For zero and negative second-period consumption their utility is $-\infty$. The measure of both groups of investors is 1 and their initial endowment is 5.

First consider the stage 1 equilibrium when no options are available. In this case the only security that is traded is the firms' equity with payoffs $(0.08, 1.8, 2)$. It can be shown that the equilibrium values of the variables of interest are as in table 8.2a. Now suppose that markets are complete. The equilibrium consumption allocations are given in table 8.2b. A derivative security which will support this equilibrium allocation has payoffs $(0.01393, 0.17409, 0.17974)$. Table 8.2c contains a comparison of the case where there are complete markets with the case where markets are incomplete. It can be seen that the surplus from setting up an exchange is more than enough to cover the cost of doing so. Hence an exchange which issues a security that completes the market is welfare enhancing.

Note that this is the first example in which the derivative security is not an option. The markets could also be made complete by issuing two options. An example is a put with a striking price of 0.18 which will give

Table 8.2a
Equilibrium in example 2 with incomplete markets

Group	Equilibrium demand for equity	Consumption state			Marginal utility of consumption			Utility
		1	2	3	1	2	3	
a	0.09998	0.00800	0.17997	0.19996	17.0434	0.54682	0.36657	4.45141
b	0.90002	0.07200	1.62003	1.80004	13.8886	0.61727	0.55554	2.95203

The value of a firm = 1.11109

Table 8.2b
Equilibrium in example 2 with complete markets

Group	Consumption state			Marginal utility of consumption			Utility
	1	2	3	1	2	3	
a	0.01393	0.17409	0.17974	15.1361	0.61504	0.54937	4.45015
b	0.06607	1.62591	1.82026	15.1361	0.61504	0.54937	2.91272

The value of a firm = 1.15690

Table 8.2c
A comparison between complete and incomplete markets in example 2

Change in group a's utility	−0.00126
Change in group b's utility	−0.03931
Change in firm value	0.04581
Total change	0.00524
Surplus from options exchange	0.00424

Table 8.2d
Charges for access to the exchange in example 2 with complete markets

Group	Demand for equity at $v_0 = 1.15690$ without access	Consumption state			Utility	Charge for entry to the options exchange
		1	2	3		
a	0.09745	0.00780	0.17541	0.19490	4.44689	0.00326
b	0.86438	0.06914	1.55588	1.72876	2.91163	0.00110

The total charge for entry to the options exchange = 0.00436
The total profit from setting up the exchange = 0.00336

Table 8.2e
Equilibrium in example 2 with a put option with payoffs (1, 0, 0)

Group	Equilibrium demand for equity	Consumption state			Marginal utility of consumption			Utility
		1	2	3	1	2	3	
a	0.09335	0.01393	0.16802	0.18669	15.1361	0.69438	0.47801	4.45469
b	0.90665	0.06607	1.63198	1.81331	15.1361	0.61275	0.55148	2.95803

The value of a firm = 1.10692

Table 8.2f
A comparison between complete markets and partially incomplete markets with a put option with payoffs (1, 0, 0) in example 2

Change in group a's utility	−0.00454
Change in group b's utility	−0.04530
Change in firm value	0.04998
Total change	0.00013

Table 8.2g
A comparison between partially incomplete markets with a put option with payoffs (1, 0, 0) and incomplete markets in example 2

Change in group a's utility	0.00328
Change in group b's utility	0.00600
Change in firm value	−0.00417
Total change	0.00511
Surplus from options exchange	0.00411

Table 8.2h
Charges for access to the options exchange in example 2 with put option (1, 0, 0)

Group	Demand for equity at $v_0 = 1.10692$ without access	Consumption state			Utility	Charge for entry to the options exchange
		1	2	3		
a	0.10022	0.00802	0.18040	0.20044	4.45183	0.00286
b	0.90341	0.07227	1.62614	1.80682	2.95579	0.00224

The total charge for entry to the options exchange = 0.00510
The total profit from setting up the exchange = 0.00410

payoffs of $(0.1, 0, 0)$ and a call with a striking price of 1.8 which will give payoffs of $(0, 0, 0.2)$. This case can be analyzed by extending the model in the obvious way by allowing for two derivative securities rather than one. The results are similar.

Consider next how much the exchange owner can raise by offering a security which completes the market. Table 8.2d contains the relevant values. It can be seen that it is indeed profitable to do this. However, offering a security which completes the market is not the only possible strategy for the exchange. For example, it could offer a security that leaves markets incomplete. Suppose it just offers a put option with striking price 1.08 so that the option has payoffs $(1, 0, 0)$. The stage 1 equilibrium values of interest are shown in table 8.2e. Table 8.2f compares this with the complete markets equilibrium. It can be seen that the social surplus from the derivative security that completes markets is greater than the social surplus from the derivative security that does not complete markets. Table 8.2g compares the equilibrium with the derivative security that does not complete markets with the equilibrium with no derivative securities. The latter equilibrium is worse.

Which is the most profitable strategy for the exchange owner? Table 8.2h shows the amount that can be charged by the exchange if it offers a put with payoffs $(1, 0, 0)$. A comparison with table 8.2d shows it is more profitable to do this than to offer the security that completes the market. This demonstrates proposition 3. ∎

Hence, the owner may have the wrong incentives to offer the efficient security. He can be better off distorting the security offered even when there is zero marginal cost to completing the market.

It can he seen from example 1 that introducing an options exchange that completes the market reduces the value of the firm. In other words producers are made worse off by having an option written on the equity of their firm. In example 2 the reverse is true. The original owners of the firm are made better off by the introduction of an options exchange that completes the market. This gives the following proposition.

Proposition 4   The value of the firm can be increased or decreased by the introduction of an options exchange.

We have assumed above that the owners of firms are a different group from investors and are only concerned with first period consumption. An alternative assumption is that the people that own the firms are also concerned about second period consumption and so are investors as well as owners. In the benchmark model this change would mean that the exchange owner would not need to make separate charges to firms. Instead the fee charged each investor would vary with the amount of shares owned and the change in firm value would be internalised by investors. Apart from this the analysis would be unchanged since utility is transferable. In the institutional version of the model investors take prices as given so their behavior is not altered. The results in propositions 2–4 are again unchanged because utility is transferable.

8.5   Equilibrium Selections and Multiple Equilibria

In section 8.4 we imposed a restriction that must now be reconsidered. We assumed that the exchange owner could select the equilibrium that would be observed at the second stage. Of course, if the second-stage-equilibrium is unique, this restriction is immaterial. However, when there is more than one equilibrium at stage 1, the selection procedure affects the nature of the analysis in rather subtle ways. In this section we discuss briefly an alternative way of modelling equilibrium, one which does not give the exchange owner the power to choose the second-stage-equilibrium.

We continue to assume, as we did in section 8.4, that investors of a given type behave symmetrically. This means, in particular, that when $\alpha = 1$ either all investors of type i enter the exchange or they all stay out. In section 8.4 we argued that, since no trade could occur unless both types entered, either all investors enter at the second stage or all stay out. Similarly, we argued that attention could be restricted to equilibria in which investors enter the exchange, since these are the only equilibria in which the owner would find it profitable to open an exchange. These arguments appeal to the properties of a full equilibrium. In the language of game theory, we are assuming that we can restrict attention to the equilibrium path. Once we drop the assumption that the exchange owner can choose the second-stage-equilibrium we have to take account of second-stage-equilibria that cannot be reached along the equilibrium path. Off the equilibrium path, it may well happen that the opening of the exchange is followed by a second-stage-equilibrium in which investors do not enter the exchange. Furthermore, this possibility may he relevant for the analysis of the full equilibrium, even though it cannot occur along the equilibrium path.

Let λ_i be a dummy variable taking the value 0 if no investors of type $i = a, b$ enter the exchange and 1 if they all enter. Suppose that the exchange is opened ($\alpha = 1$) but that no investors enter the exchange ($\lambda_i = 0$ for $i = a, b$). Since there is no activity on the exchange, the price of the derivative security cannot be determined by supply and demand. Nonetheless, we can define an equilibrium. It is a situation in which, at the prevailing prices, no investor is willing to pay the entry fee. In other respects, a first-stage-equilibrium in which $\alpha = 1$ and $\lambda_i = 0$ for $i = a, b$ is identical to an equilibrium in which $\alpha = 0$.

DEFINITION   Let (α, e, Z) be given. Suppose that $\alpha = 0$. An equilibrium at stage 2 is an array $\{v, (c_i, d_i)\}$, consisting of price vector v and a choice (c_i, d_i) for each type of investor $i = a, b$, that satisfies the following conditions:

(i) $(c_i, d_i) \in \underset{B_i^0(v, e)}{\arg\max} \, U_i(c_i, d_i \cdot Z)$ for $i = a, b$;

(ii) $\sum_i d_i = (1, 0)$.

If $\alpha = 1$, on the other hand, equilibrium at stage 2 is defined by an array $\{v, (c_i, d_i), (\lambda_i)\}$, consisting of a price vector v, a choice (c_i, d_i) for each type $i = a, b$ and a number $\lambda_i = 0, 1$ for each type $i = a, b$, that satisfies the following conditions:

(i) $(c_i, d_i) \in \underset{B_i^{\lambda i}(v, e)}{\arg\max} \, U_i(c_i, d_i \cdot Z)$ for $i = a, b$;

(ii) $\sum_i d_i = (1, 0)$;

(iii) $\lambda_i \in \arg\max \lambda_i u_i^1(v, e, Z) + (1 - \lambda_i) u_i^0(v, e, Z)$ for $i = a, b$.

Note that in condition (i) the budget set from which the investor chooses depends on the value of λ_i. For example, if $\lambda_i = 1$ then the appropriate budget set is $B_i^1(v, e)$. Condition (iii) ensures that the investors' decision to enter the exchange is optimal at the prevailing prices.

An equilibrium selection is a function $\phi^{\alpha}(e, Z)$ that associates an equilibrium at stage 1, relative to (α, e, Z), with every choice of (α, e, Z) at stage 0. In the definition of equilibrium given in section 8.4, it is implicitly assumed that the exchange owner can choose the equilibrium selection as well as the value of (α, e, Z). Now we assume that the equilibrium selection is taken as given. The earlier definition gives the exchange owner a strong "first-mover advantage," allowing him to manipulate the second-stage-equilibrium: the new definition takes away this advantage. It is much more in the spirit of the non-cooperative, Nash equilibrium. Of course, the old equilibrium will be a special case of the new definition for some choice of $\phi^\alpha(e, Z)$.

DEFINITION   Let $\phi^\alpha(e, Z)$ be a given equilibrium selection. A pre-equilibrium is defined by an array $\{(v^0, (c_i^0, d_i^0)), (v^1, (c_i^1, d_i^1), (\lambda_i^1)), \alpha, e, Z\}$, consisting of the second-stage equilibria $(v^0, (c_i^0, d_i^0))$ and $(v^1, (c_i^1, d_i^1), (\lambda_i^1))$ corresponding to $\alpha = 0, 1$, the decision α whether to open the exchange, the fee structure $a = (e_a, e_b)$ and the choice of securities Z, that satisfies the following conditions:

(i) $(v^0, (c_i^0, d_i^0)) = \phi^0(e, Z)$ and $(v^1, (c_i^1, d_i^1), (\lambda_i^1)) = \phi^1(e, Z)$;

(ii) Z_0 is given.

A pre-equilibrium is called a full equilibrium if there does not exist another pre-equilibrium, relative to the given equilibrium selection ϕ, that yields higher profits $\alpha(\sum_{i=a,b} \lambda_i e_i - \gamma)$.

The individual rationality condition has disappeared from the definition; condition (iii) of the definition of second-stage-equilibrium has made it redundant. Condition (i) says that the second-stage-equilibrium is determined by the owner's choice of (α, e, Z) and by the selection ϕ, which the owner must take as given. Note also the change in the definition of profits: the owner collects fees only from the investors who enter the exchange.

The main impact of taking the equilibrium selection as a given is that it increases the number of possible equilibria. It is not surprising that the second-stage-equilibria may not be unique. What is less obvious is that the existence of more than one second-stage-equilibrium may lead to a continuum of full equilibria. An analysis of this indeterminacy of equilibrium is out of place here; but we can easily indicate the essential problem. Suppose that in the first stage the exchange owner decides to open the exchange. Let $(\hat{\alpha}, \hat{e}, \hat{Z})$ denote the equilibrium choices of the owner at the first stage and suppose that for any (α, e, Z) sufficiently close to $(\hat{\alpha}, \hat{e}, \hat{Z})$ there exist two second-stage-equilibria, one in which all investors enter the exchange and one in which none of them do. Let $(v^1, (c_i^1 d_i^1), (\lambda_i^1)) = \phi^1(\hat{e}, \hat{Z})$ be the equilibrium observed at the second stage and suppose that this equilibrium is the one in which all investors enter the exchange ($\lambda_1 = 1$ for $i = a, b$). We can suppose without loss of generality that for any first stage choices (α, e, Z) in some sufficiently small neighborhood of $(\hat{\alpha}, \hat{e}, \hat{Z})$, $\phi^1(e, Z)$ is the equilibrium in which no investors enter the exchange. Clearly, any small deviation by the exchange owner from his equilibrium choice will cause a discontinuous drop in profits. Suppose, in fact, that the choice of $(\hat{\alpha}, \hat{e}, \hat{Z})$ uniquely maximizes the exchange owner's profits. Then it is possible to construct a continuum of full equilibria, each one corresponding to a different choice of the point of discontinuity in the equilibrium selection ϕ. Each choice of (α, e, Z) in a small neighborhood will constitute a local and hence a global maximum for profits for an appropriately constructed equilibrium selection. Simply associate (α, e, Z) with the equilibrium in which all investors enter the exchange and all other choices (α', e', Z') in some small neighborhood of (α, e, Z) with the equilibrium in which none of the investors enter the exchange. Then any deviation from (α, e, Z) leads to a discontinuous drop in profits. In this way, we see that any choice of (α, e, Z) in some small neighborhood of $(\hat{\alpha}, \hat{e}, \hat{Z})$ can be supported as a full equilibrium.

The concept of full equilibrium sketched above appears to be the right concept to use in these circumstances. With the appropriate adjustments for the competitive flavor of equilibrium at stage 1, it corresponds to the concept of subgame perfect equilibrium for an extensive form game. But while it gives us the right concept of non-cooperative equilibrium, the multiplicity of equilibria calls for some refinement. In section 8.4 we made use of one such refinement by allowing the exchange owner to choose the equilibrium that he liked best in the second stage. Such a refinement is not entirely without justification. Apart from theoretical arguments based on the notion of first mover advantage, there are institutional reasons for thinking the exchange owner may be in a position to choose the equilibrium. In stock exchanges which operate with specialist traders, one of the trader's most important functions—and one from which he is believed to make a great deal of money—is to choose the opening prices at the start of the day's trading. The choice of opening prices is analogous to the choice of an equilibrium and devolves to the specialist, as to our exchange owner, as a matter of institutional design.

8.6   The Impact of the Options Market on the Financial Decision of the Firm

So far we have assumed that firms do not make any decisions at all. We have shown that the choice of securities traded on the options exchange affects the value of firms. This suggests that when firms have non-trivial decisions to make there will be some interaction between the options market and the decisions of the firms.

In this section we introduce two extensions to the basic model. The first is to allow for the possibility that firms have issued debt and levered equity as well as unlevered equity in the past. We do this by making use of the equilibrium concepts developed in Allen and Gale (1988a). The second is to allow for asymmetric behavior on the part of firms and investors. Both of these extensions are necessary for an analysis of the interaction between the options market and the financial decisions of the firms.

Equilibrium is determined in three stages. At the first stage (stage 0), firms make financial decisions. At the second stage (stage 1), the exchange owner decides whether to open the exchange and if he does open the exchange, what fees should be charged and what derivative security should be traded. At the third stage (stage 2), investors decide whether to enter the exchange and then trade on the available markets.

Suppose to begin with that firms have made a decision about their financial structure at stage 0. A fraction μ of the firms have decided to issue equity only. The remaining $1 - \mu$ have decided to issue debt and levered equity. Let Z_2 and Z_3 denote the returns to the debt and levered equity respectively, where $Z_2 + Z_3 = Z_0$. Note that we are implicitly assuming that the firms that issue debt all issue the same amount of debt.

Let $Z = (Z_0, Z_1, Z_2, Z_3)$ denote the vector of securities that can be traded, let $v = (v_0, v_1, v_2, v_3)$ denote the vector of security prices and let $d = (d_0, d_1, d_2, d_3)$ denote a generic portfolio.

Suppose that the options exchange does not open ($\alpha = 0$). The budget set of an investor of type $i = a, b$ is denoted by $B_i^0(v, e)$ and defined by putting

$$B_i^0(v, e) = \{(c, d) \in \mathbb{R}^5 | c + v \cdot d \le 0, d_1 = 0 \text{ and } d_0, d_2, d_3 \ge 0\}. \tag{9}$$

Now suppose that the exchange has been opened ($\alpha = 1$). In the earlier definition, we assumed that either all investors of type i *entered the exchange or they all stayed out. Now we allow for the possibility of incomplete participation in the exchange. Let* λ_1 denote the fraction of investors of type $i = a, b$ who decide to pay the entry fee and enter the exchange. Their budget set is denoted by $B_i^1(v, e)$ and defined by putting

$$B_i^1(v, e) = \{(c, d) \in \mathbb{R}^5 | c + v \cdot d + e_i \leq 0, \text{ and } d_0, d_2, d_3 \geq 0\}. \tag{10}$$

Denote the investors of type $i = a, b$ who remain outside the exchange by $i = A, B$, respectively. The budget set for these investors is the same as when the exchange does not open. For example, $B_A^1(v, e) = B_a^0(v, e)$. With this notation, we can define an equilibrium at stage 2.

DEFINITION   Let (α, μ, Z, e) be given. Suppose that $\alpha = 0$. An equilibrium at stage 2 is an array $\{v, (c_i, d_i)\}$, consisting of a price vector v and a choice (c_i, d_i) for each type of investor $i = a, b$, that satisfies the following conditions:

(i) $(c_i, d_i) \in \underset{B_i^0(v, e)}{\arg\max} \; U_i(c_i, d_i \cdot Z)$ for $i = a, b$;

(ii) $\sum_i d_i = (\mu, 0, 1 - \mu, 1 - \mu)$.

If $\alpha = 1$, on the other hand, equilibrium at stage 2 is defined by an array $\{v, (c_i, d_i), (\lambda_i)\}$, consisting of a price vector v, a choice (c_i, d_i) for each type $i = a, b, A, B$, and a fraction λ_i for each type $i = a, b$, that satisfies the following conditions:

(i) $(c_i, d_i) \in \underset{B_i^1(v, e)}{\arg\max} \; U_i(c_i, d_i \cdot Z)$ for $i = a, b, A, B$;

(ii) $\sum_i \lambda_i d_i = (\mu, 0, 1 - \mu, 1 - \mu)$, where $\lambda_A = 1 - \lambda_a$ and $\lambda_B = 1 - \lambda_b$.

Condition (i) simply says that each investor is maximizing his utility subject to the appropriate budget constraint and to the available markets. Condition (ii) is the market-clearing condition. When $\alpha = 1$, the market-clearing condition has been changed to reflect the fact that investors inside and outside the exchange have different demands. In both cases, the market-clearing condition has been changed to reflect the fact that some firms issue equity only and some issue debt and levered equity.

Let $\Phi^\alpha(\mu, Z, e)$ denote the set of third-stage-equilibria relative to (α, μ, Z, e). Let $u_i^\alpha(v, e, Z)$ denote the maximum utility attainable when security prices are given by v and the stage 0 choices are given by (α, Z, e). That is,

$$u_i^\alpha(v, Z, e) = \underset{B_i^\alpha(v, e)}{\sup} \; U_i(c_i, d_i \cdot Z) \text{ for } i = a, b. \tag{11}$$

DEFINITION   A pre-equilibrium at stage 1 is defined by an array $\{(v^0, (c_i^0, d_i^0)), (v^1, (c_i^1, d_i^1), (\lambda_i^1)), \alpha, \mu, e, Z\}$ consisting of the third-stage-equilibria $(v^0, (c_i^0, d_i^0))$ and $(v^1, (c_i^1, d_i^1), (\lambda_i^1))$ corresponding to $\alpha = 0, 1$, the decision α whether to open the exchange, a fee structure $e = (e_a, e_b)$ and a choice of securities Z, that satisfies the following conditions:

(i) $\lambda_i \in \arg\max \lambda u_i^1(v^1, e, Z) + (1 - \lambda)u_i^0(v^1, e, Z)$ for $i = a, b$;

(ii) $(v^0, (c_i^0, d_i^0)) \in \Phi^0(\mu, e, Z)$ and $(v^1, (c_i^1, d_i^1), (\lambda_i^1)) \in \Phi^1(\mu, e, Z)$

(iii) (Z_0, Z_2, Z_3) and μ are given.

A pre-equilibrium in the second stage is called an equilibrium if there does not exist another pre-equilibrium that yields higher profits $\alpha(\sum_{i=a,b} \lambda_i e_i - \gamma)$.

The financial decisions of firms at stage 0 will be analyzed rather informally. Firms behave non-cooperatively so they take as given the decisions of the other firms. Furthermore, there is a continuum of firms so no one firm perceives that it has any impact on the subsequent equilibrium. As a result firms behave as price-takers. More precisely, they are equilibrium-takers, who take as given all the variables of the subsequent equilibrium. Let v^α denote the equilibrium prices when $\alpha = 0, 1$. The market value of the firm will be v_0^α if it issues equity only and $v_2^\alpha + v_0^\alpha$ if it issues debt and equity. Suppose there is no cost of issuing equity and a fixed cost γ_f of issuing debt. Then firms will choose their financial structure to maximize the value of the firm net of issuing costs. This means that μ must satisfy

$$\mu \in \arg\max \mu v_0^\alpha + (1 - \mu)(v_2^\alpha + v_3^\alpha - \gamma_f), \tag{12}$$

where v^α is taken as given.

What we have not considered yet is the firm's decision about the amount of debt to issue. In order for price-taking firms to decide how much debt to issue, they need to know the prices of securities that are not necessarily issued in equilibrium. In defining an equilibrium we have only quoted prices for the securities actually issued. In Allen and Gale (1988a), we have shown how other securities should be priced in equilibrium. The prices of unissued securities must be such that investors' demand and firms' supply are both zero so that markets clear. Let $p_i: S \to \mathbb{R}$ represent the shadow prices of consumption at date 2, measured in terms of consumption at date 1, for an investor of type $i = a, b, A, B$. In other words, $p_i(s)$ is investor i's marginal rate of substitution of present consumption for future consumption in state $s \in S$, for $i = a, b, A, B$. At the margin an investor of type i is willing to pay $p_i \cdot Z_j$ for a unit of the security Z_j, so the market value must be the $\max_i\{p_i \cdot Z_j\}$ where the maximum is taken over all types $i = a, b, A, B$. The market value of a firm that issues the securities (Z_2, Z_3) is equal to

$$MV(Z_2, Z_3) = \max_i\{p_i \cdot Z_2\} + \max_i\{p_i \cdot Z_3\}. \tag{13}$$

If only debt and equity can be issued, the firm chooses the face value D of the debt that it wishes to issue and then puts $Z_2 = \min\{D, Z_0\}$ and $Z_3 = \max\{Z_0 - D, 0\}$. D is chosen to maximize the market value $MV(Z_2, Z_3)$.

If $\lambda_i = 1$ the measure of investors outside the exchange is zero. Nevertheless, in valuing unissued securities the maximum valuation is taken over all four groups $i = a, b, A, B$. This is equivalent to taking the limit as $\lambda_i - 1$ and maintains continuity.

A full equilibrium of the extended institutional model consists of a choice of μ and (Z_2, Z_3), together with an equilibrium in the second stage, such that μ and (Z_2, Z_3) satisfy the two optimality conditions described above, given the equilibrium prices. This rather informal definition should be clarified in the example that follows.

A feature of the model that warrants further discussion is the assumption that investors cannot short sell corporate securities but can sell derivative securities. In Allen and Gale (1988a) we argued that, in practice, short sales of corporate securities are costly and are only rarely undertaken by investors. In contrast, selling options is, in practice, relatively cheap compared to short sales. Hence the assumption that corporate securities cannot be short sold while derivative securities can be does not involve an inconsistency.

In the context of this model it is possible to show the following result.

Proposition 5   An equilibrium exists in which some firms issue debt and levered equity and it is unprofitable for the exchange owner to set up the exchange. There also exists an equilibrium in which the exchange is set up. If the exchange is set up a Pareto superior allocation is feasible.

Proof   The proof is once again by example.

Example 3   The parameters of the example are similar to example 1(i). The differences are that the cost of setting up the exchange is assumed to be 0.001 and a firm can issue debt for a cost of 0.01.

Two full equilibria exist. In the first, the prices firms anticipate in the equilibrium at stage 2 are consistent with no exchange being set up at stage 1. Thus, at stage 0, a positive measure of firms issue debt and equity.

At stage 1, the exchange owner does not find it profitable to set up the options exchange. This is because the debt and equity issued by firms at stage 0 allows investors outside the exchange to smooth consumption across states fairly adequately so that the amounts that can be charged for entry to the exchange are limited. Firms' expectations about the prices they will receive for their securities at stage 2 therefore turn out to be correct.

The prices firms expect to hold at stage 2 correspond to the marginal rates of substitution, or in this context, the marginal utilities of consumption, for groups $i = a, b, A, B$ shown in table 8.3a. Suppose a firm were to issue debt with a face value of 1 so the debt has payoffs of $(1, 1)$ and the levered equity has payoffs $(0, 1)$ in the two states respectively. Investors of type b are more risk averse and so value the debt most. Hence the price of debt is $(0.5)(1)(0.35930) + (0.5)(1)(0.07473) = 0.21702$. Investors of type a value the levered equity the most so that its price is $(0.5)(1)(0.09473) = 0.04737$. Hence the gross value of a firm that issues debt with a face value of 1 is $0.21702 + 0.04737 = 0.26439$. It can easily be seen that this is in fact the optimal capital structure. If the face value on debt is increased above 1 the effect is to transfer consumption in state 2 from group a, who value it most, to group b, who value it least. For example, suppose the face value is 1.1. Then the debt has payoffs of $(1, 1.1)$ and is worth $(0.5)(1)(0.35930) + (0.5)(1.1)(0.07473) = 0.22075$ and the levered equity has payoffs of $(0, 0.9)$ and is worth $(0.5)(0.9)(0.09473) = 0.04246$ so the gross value of the firm is $0.22075 + 0.04246 = 0.26338$. Similarly, if the face value on debt is reduced below 1. For example, suppose the face value is 0.9. Then the debt has payoffs of $(0.9, 0.9)$ and is worth $(0.5)(0.9)(0.35930) + (0.5)(0.9)(0.07473) = 0.19531$ and the levered equity has payoffs of $(0.1, 1.1)$ and is worth $(0.5)(0.1)(0.31930) + (0.5)(1.1)(0.09474) = 0.06807$ so the gross value of the firm is $0.19531 + 0.06807 = 0.26338$.

The highest gross value a firm can obtain if it issues debt and levered equity is 0.26439. In contrast, the gross value of a firm that just issues unlevered equity is 0.25439. Since the cost of issuing debt is 0.01, this means that the firms' net values are the same so they are indifferent between issuing two securities and issuing one. The prices corresponding to the marginal utilities of consumption in table 8.3 a support a third-stage-equilibrium in which the measure of firms that issue debt and levered equity is 0.07333 and the measure that just issue unlevered equity is 1.92667.

Given that firms issue these securities at stage 0, what does the exchange owner do at stage 1? Taking the supply of firms' securities as given, he considers whether it is worthwhile opening an exchange. If he opens the exchange he must choose a derivative security, a proportion that enters the exchange and entry fees to maximize his profits. Since there are only two states the choice of derivative security is trivial; all options which are linearly independent of the existing securities allow entrants to the exchange to equate their marginal utilities of consumption. Our solution concept allows the exchange owner to choose the third-stage-equilibrium. The owner can choose the entry fees so that all investors are indifferent between being inside or outside the exchange, for any particular proportion of investors that enter the exchange. If he sets the entry fees high, only a small proportion of investors enter the exchange so that his total revenue is small. At the other extreme when all investors enter, the prices of debt and equity issued by the firms are the same as when markets are complete. In this case access to the options exchange does not improve investors' risk sharing possibilities so the amount that can be charged for entry to the exchange is zero and no revenue is raised. Hence the exchange owner's optimal strategy if he opens the exchange is to price entry so that only some portion of investors enter. In example 3 it can be shown the revenue-maximizing charges for types a and b are 0.00037 and 0.00721 respectively. In this case 47.1 percent of investors enter the exchange and the total receipts are 0.00051. The exchange owner is therefore unable to cover his costs of 0.001 and so does not find it worthwhile to open the exchange at stage 1. The third-stage-equilibrium is as shown in table 8.3a and firms' expectations about prices are fulfilled.

In the second full equilibrium, the prices firms anticipate in the equilibrium at stage 2 are consistent with the options exchange being set up at stage 1 and all investors entering. At stage 0, the measure of firms that issue debt and equity is zero since the anticipated existence of the options exchange means that markets are effectively complete. At stage 1, the exchange owner finds it profitable to set up the options exchange because investors outside the exchange are unable to smooth consumption across states adequately so that the amounts that can be charged for entry to the exchange are high. Firms' expectations about the third-stage-equilibrium therefore turn out to be correct.

The prices firms expect to hold in the third-stage-equilibrium correspond to the situation where everybody enters the exchange ($\lambda_i = 1$) and the marginal utilities of consumption for groups $i = a, b$ are the same as when markets are complete. These marginal utilities are shown in table 8.1(i)b. The marginal utilities of consumption of groups outside the exchange $i = A, B$ as $\lambda_i \to 1$ are used to price the securities. Table 8.3b shows these. It can be seen that the price of debt with payoffs $(1, 1)$ is $(0.5)(1)(0.35853) + (0.5)(1)(0.07434) = 0.21644$ and the price of levered equity with payoffs $(0, 1)$ is $(0.5)(1)(0.09434) = 0.04717$. Similarly for other possible capital structures. Given these prices, the supply of debt and levered equity is zero and the demand is also zero. The amounts that the exchange owner can charge are given by the differences between the utilities investors can obtain with access to the options market and the utilities that they can obtain using unlevered equity, debt and levered equity at the prices within that equilibrium. These charges are shown in table 8.3c. Notice that these charges differ from those in table 8.1(i)d. This is because in table 8.1(i)d the alternative if somebody did not enter the exchange is to use just unlevered equity.

Since the cost of setting up the exchange, 0.001, is less than the amount that can be charged for entry to the exchange, 0.00152, the owner is strictly better off setting up the exchange at stage 1. Moreover, the expectations of the firms that the prices in the third-stage-equilibrium are the complete markets prices are correct.

Thus two full equilibria are possible. Table 8.3d contains a comparison of these two full equilibria. It can be seen that both types of investor and the exchange owner are better off in the full equilibrium where the exchange is set up. Only the firms are better off in the full equilibrium with no options exchange. However, it is clearly possible to reallocate consumption to make everybody better off in the full equilibrium where the exchange is open. The essential reason such a reallocation is possible is that the cost of setting up the options exchange and sharing risk with options is less than the cost of some firms' issuing two securities and risk being shared with debt and levered equity.   ∎

Example 3 illustrates the interaction between firms' capital structure decisions and the exchange owner's decision. Given that two equilibria exist a question arises as to which is the more "plausible" one. Arguments can be made in favor of both. Firms are better off in the equilibrium where the exchange is not set up; since they move first it can be argued that the one where some firms issue both debt and levered equity and the exchange

Table 8.3a

The third-stage-equilibrium in example 3 where a positive measure of firms issue debt and equity

Group	Consumption		Marginal utility of consumption		Utility
	State 1	State 2	State 1	State 2	
A	1.14163	2.35658	0.31930	0.09474	4.49908
B	0.85837	1.64342	0.35930	0.07474	4.67587

The gross value of a one-security firm = 0.25439
The gross value of a two-security firm with optimal capital structure = 0.26439

Table 8.3b

The choices of groups A and B as $\lambda_i \to 1$ when an exchange opens in example 3

Group	Consumption		Marginal utility of consumption		Utility
	State 1	State 2	State 1	State 2	
A	1.14403	2.36083	0.31853	0.09434	4.50000
B	0.85944	1.64612	0.35853	0.07434	4.67653

The gross value of a one-security firm = 0.25361
The gross value of a two-security firm with optimal capital structure = 0.26361

Table 8.3c

Charges for access to the options exchange in example 3 when the exchange is set up

Utilities inside the exchange		Utilities outside the exchange		Charge for entry to the options exchange
a	4.50052	A	4.50000	0.00052
b	4.67754	B	4.67653	0.00101

The total charge for entry to the options exchange = 0.00153
The total profit from setting up the exchange = 0.00053

Table 8.3d

A comparison of the equilibrium where the exchange is set up and the equilibrium where the exchange is not set up in example 3

Utilities net of charges in the equilibrium with an exchange		Utilities in the equilibrium with no exchange		Difference in utilities
a	4.50000	A	4.49908	0.00092
b	4.67653	B	4.67587	0.00066
Firms	0.50720		0.50878	−0.00158
Exchange Owner	0.00053		0.00000	0.00053

The total surplus from the options exchange = 0.00053

is not set up is the more plausible one. On the other hand, it can be argued that the equilibrium in which the exchange is opened is more plausible since a reallocation exists which can make everybody better off than in the equilibrium in which the exchange is closed.

For different costs of setting up the exchange there may only exist one equilibrium in example 3. If the cost is above 0.00152, then the only equilibrium is where some firms issue debt and levered equity and no exchange is set up. If it is below 0.0051 then the only equilibrium is where the exchange is set up and no firms issue two securities.

In demonstrating proposition 5 we have assumed a particular sequence of events. In particular, we assumed that the firms move first and the exchange owner moves second. Another possibility is that the exchange owner moves first and the firms move second. Consider example 3 with this sequence. Since the exchange owner moves first he can set up the exchange and preempt firms from issuing debt and levered equity. He prefers to do this since his profits are maximized with the exchange open and no firms issuing two securities. In contrast to the case where firms move first and two equilibria exist, only one equilibrium exists. Another possibility is to model the exchange and firms as moving simultaneously. Both the equilibria described above are again possible.

In situations where the sequencing of moves does affect the equilibrium set, it is not clear which order of moves is more plausible. Firms must exist and therefore must have issued their securities before an exchange can issue derivative securities. On the other hand, firms continually change their capital structure after derivative securities have been issued. Thus it is possible to argue that all the different possibilities are of interest.

Proposition 5 was concerned with the case where an inefficient equilibrium could exist because firms' issuance of debt made it unprofitable for the exchange to let up. The reason this is inefficient is that, by issuing derivative securities, the exchange can provide risk sharing opportunities at lower cost than the firms can by issuing debt and levered equity. It is also possible to get an inefficient equilibrium where the opposite is true. In other words, the exchange may set up even though risk sharing opportunities could be provided more cheaply if firms issued debt and levered equity instead. For example, it can be shown this occurs in example 1(ii) if the cost of setting up exchange is 0.002 and the cost of issuing debt is 0.001.

8.7   Concluding Remarks

In this chapter we have considered the incentives of exchange owners to provide a socially efficient market structure. If firms and investors can be charged lump sum fees before the exchange is set up and if the agreement of all agents to pay these fees is required for the exchange to be established then the resulting market structure is socially efficient. These assumptions do not hold in practice. We therefore considered a model which is closer to institutional practice. In particular, it was assumed that the exchange was established before any fees were paid and only investors were charged fees. A number of examples were provided which suggest that the incentives of exchange owners are such that the equilibrium market structure obtained may not be socially efficient.

Markets for derivative securities are extensively regulated by the government. The rationale for this regulation and the form the regulations should take are currently not well understood. The models developed in this chapter pose a number of issues related to regulation and suggest that further research along these lines is warranted.

Note

We would like to thank the editor, Herakles Polemarchakis, and an anonymous referee for helpful comments and suggestions. Financial support from the NSF (Grant nos. SES-8813719 and SES-8720589 for the two authors respectively) is gratefully acknowledged.

References

Allen, F. and Gale, D. (1988a). "Optimal Security Design," *Review of Financial Studies* 1, 229–263.

Allen, F. and Gale, D. (1988b). "Arbitrage, Short Sales and Financial Innovation," Rodney L. White Center Working Paper 10-89, University of Pennsylvania.

Geanakoplos, J. and Polemarchakis, H. (1987). "Existence, Regularity, and Constrained Suboptimality of Competitive Portfolio Allocations when the Asset Market is Incomplete," in *Uncertainty, Information, and Communication: Essays in Honor of Kenneth J. Arrow*, Vol. 3. ed. by Walter Heller et al., Cambridge University Press, Cambridge, MA.

Green, R. C. and Jarrow, R. A. (1987). "Spanning and Completeness in Markets with Contingent Claims," *Journal of Economic Theory* 41, 202–210.

Green, R. C. and Spear, S. E. (1987). "Equilibria in Large Commodity Spaces with Incomplete Financial Markets," mimeo, Carnegie-Mellon University.

Hart, O. D. (1975). "On the Optimality of Equilibrium when Market Structure is Incomplete," *Journal of Economic Theory* 11, 418–433.

Newbery, D. M. G. and Stiglitz, J. E. (1984). "Pareto Inferior Trade," *Review of Economic Studies* 51, 1–12.

Ross, S. A. (1976). "Options and Efficiency," *Quarterly Journal of Economics* 90, 75–89.

9 The Efficient Design of Public Debt

Douglas Gale

9.1 Introduction

With a few notable exceptions, such as Fischer (1983), Peled (1985) and Bohn (1988a, b, c), the literature on public debt has concentrated on positive issues, such as the neutrality of the debt (Barro 1974; Tobin 1971). In this chapter I want to concentrate instead on welfare issues, in particular, the impact of debt policy on the efficiency of risk sharing.

As a prelude to the central part of the chapter, section 9.2 reviews the familiar issue of the neutrality of the debt. The classical Ricardian equivalence theorem assumes that markets are complete. Nonetheless, even if markets are incomplete, there is an analogue of the classical neutrality theorem. A theorem of this sort is proved in section 9.2 for a generic economy with incomplete markets. It shows that changes in the size and composition of the debt are neutral as long as the set of debt instruments issued by the government is unchanged. This result is similar to the Modigliani-Miller theorem of Wallace-Chamley-Polemarchakis (see Wallace 1981, and Chamley and Polemarchakis 1984). On the other hand, if markets are incomplete, it is clearly possible for the government to have an impact on the economy by introducing new securities that expand risk-sharing opportunities.

There is a tension between these two results. It seems that a tiny amount of a new security has a large impact while a large change in the amount of an existing security has no impact at all. The explanation for this asymmetry lies in the assumption that agents can take unlimited short positions. Introducing a small amount of a new security is like opening a new market. It can have a big impact on the economy simply because it allows a large open interest in the security. The discontinuity disappears as soon as short sales are constrained. It is well known, of course, that neutrality also disappears if short sales are constrained. Thus, at the theoretical level, we have to accept a discontinuity in the impact of public debt policy in order to have neutrality. This ought to give us pause for thought.

The core of the chapter begins in section 9.3, which studies the impact of particular financial innovations. For this purpose, I use a simple over-

This chapter originally appeared in *Public Debt Management: Theory and History*, edited by R. Dornbusch and M. Draghi, (1990) Cambridge, Cambridge University Press. Reprinted by permission.

lapping generations (OLG) model with identical generations that last two periods. There is a risky, constant returns to scale investment technology. The young can save for their retirement by investing in this risky technology, but that will mean that all the risk at any date is borne by only one of the two generations alive at that date. It is not hard to show that intergenerational risk-sharing can be improved by introducing "safe" securities that give the old a claim on the next young generation. (This kind of result has been obtained by Weiss, Fischer and Pagano.) By introducing a safe, short-dated security it is possible to allow each generation to transfer some risk from the second to the first period of its life. Under certain circumstances, this shift may be Pareto-improving ex post.

An even better allocation of risk can be achieved, however, if long-dated securities are used. If productivity shocks are positively serially correlated, bond prices will be low when returns to capital are high. This is because high returns to capital lead to expectations of future high returns which make bonds less attractive. Thus, the yield on long-dated securities will be negatively correlated with the return on capital, which makes long-dated securities an even better hedge against productivity shocks.

It is well known that in infinite-horizon economies with overlapping generations, competitive equilibrium may be inefficient, even if markets are complete. The failure of the First Theorem of Welfare Economics is partly responsible for the possibility of improving welfare through debt policy. It is known, however, that under some conditions the competitive equilibrium is efficient. In particular, if there exist durable assets producing positive returns at a zero interest rate, the competitive equilibrium is efficient when there are complete markets and no uncertainty. (This result, discovered by many for the steady-state case, has been proved in general by Scheinkman. His result, which remains unpublished, appears to be under-appreciated in the literature.) The question, then, is whether these conditions are sufficient to ensure efficient risk-sharing in the presence of uncertainty. If the answer is yes, then the possibility of improving risk-sharing through debt policy also disappears.

In section 9.4 I consider the efficiency of equilibrium when there are durable assets. It is shown that under certain conditions the equilibrium allocations cannot be Pareto-dominated by any stationary allocation. In particular, this means that debt policy cannot improve welfare in a stationary equilibrium. At first glance, this appears to undermine the analysis of the preceding section. However, the result is not quite as strong as it appears at first. Apart from the restriction to comparisons with stationary allocations, the result depends on the assumption that the returns to the durable asset are greater than the rate of growth with probability one. It also depends on the use of the ex post welfare criterion, which distinguishes individuals by the state in which they are born. There is still the possibility of obtaining a welfare improvement using the weaker ex ante criterion. (The ex ante criterion is used by Fischer 1983; also, in another context, by Gale, 1988.)

At the end of section 9.4 there is a discussion of the problem of characterizing an efficient, contingent debt policy. The problem can be broken into two parts. The first is the problem of choosing an efficient tax-transfer scheme. The second is the problem of implementing it via an appropriate public debt policy. In very simple models (e.g., Fischer 1983; Pagano 1988), there may be no essential difference between the tax-transfer scheme and the debt policy. One can simply reinterpret the one as the other. In general, this will not be the case. If the government can make efficient transfers directly, there is no reason to use security markets. If there is some reason to use security markets to implement efficient intergenerational risk-sharing, then the problem of choosing an efficient debt policy is inherently more difficult than simply choosing an efficient tax-transfer scheme. Relatively simple transfers may require complicated debt policies. It can be shown that within the general class of models studied in the second half of the chapter, an optimal debt policy will typically be unable to implement the allocation achieved by the optimal tax-transfer policy. To understand the force of this result it is helpful to restate it. In the optimal tax-transfer problem it is assumed that the government implements the entire allocation by fiat. In the very simple OLG models studied in the chapter, a debt policy is equivalent to making lump-sum, intergenerational transfers. So the optimal tax-transfer problem corresponds to finding the first-best allocation and the optimal debt policy problem corresponds to finding prices at which the first-best allocation can be supported as an allocation with lump-sum, intergenerational transfers. The additional constraint under the debt policy is that asset markets must be in equilibrium. In particular, agents must be willing to hold the durable asset at the prevailing prices. What the theorem says is that the first-best allocation achieved by a tax-transfer policy (including transfers of the asset) cannot be supported as an equilibrium with lump-sum transfers.

Once we have incomplete markets, it is not hard to obtain non-neutral effects from the debt and even to find scope for welfare-improving changes in the size or the structure of the debt. But an important question is begged as long as the market structure is taken as exogenous. Why should we assume that there is a role for the government as a financial innovator? If markets are missing they are presumably missing for a reason. The government may be able to replace these missing markets, but it does not necessarily have a cost advantage over the private sector. Is it clear that, if these costs were taken into account, it would be socially desirable to introduce the new securities?

A related question is why, assuming there is a role for the government to improve risk-sharing opportunities, it should choose to do so by introducing new securities (or altering the mix of existing securities) rather than making lump-sum transfers, for example. These issues are discussed in section 9.5.

Inevitably, some important issues have been left out. Perhaps the most important omission is the exclusion of any discussion of monetary issues. This is particularly unfortunate because a significant part of the risk of holding nominal government securities comes from uncertainty about the price level. Nonetheless, in what follows attention is restricted to real models. Although this approach is undoubtedly restrictive, I think one learns enough from it to justify the approximation. For an antidote to the present approach, the reader is directed to the excellent work on nominal debt by Henning Bohn. (See also the work on the role of money in intergenerational risk-sharing by Weiss 1979 and by Bhattacharya 1982.) A second omission is the exclusion of time-consistency issues (see Lucas and Stokey 1983). A third is the exclusion of the problems raised by distortionary taxation (see Barro 1979; Lucas and Stokey 1987). For all these, the excuse is simply the impossibility of including everything, in a coherent way, in a finite space.

9.2   Neutrality, Incomplete Markets and Financial Innovation

From the point of view of financial economics, the classical theorems on the neutrality of the debt are special cases of general results on linear spaces generated by sets of assets. They are part of a family that includes the familiar results on Arrow securities, the Modigliani-Miller theorem, the Black-Scholes option pricing theory and so forth. This perspective suggests that the classical neutrality theorems are very general. It also suggests some limitations. One of these is the need to allow unlimited short sales. An asset is redundant in these theories if it can be expressed as a linear combination of other assets. This notion of "spanning" assumes that it is possible to *sell* as well as to *buy* any amount of an asset at the prevailing price. For obvious reasons, however, there is an asymmetry between short and long positions. It is unrealistic to assume unlimited short sales and as we shall see, even if unlimited short sales are allowed there are purely theoretical problems that arise as a result of this unrealistic assumption. As we shall see in section 9.5, constraining short sales is not an insignificant change in the theory.

The essential ideas that lie behind debt neutrality are often obscured by the details of specific results. Re-expressing these arguments abstractly, with a minimum of unnecessary detail, makes clear the essential unity of all these results. In particular, it makes clear that the same arguments work whether markets are complete or incomplete. However, when markets are incomplete, there is a tension between the neutrality theorem, which holds when the set of securities is not changed, and the non-neutrality that results if new securities are introduced. In this section I first state a neutrality theorem and then discuss the importance of short sales in this context.

9.2.1 A Model of Incomplete Markets

Let X and Z be finite-dimensional Euclidean spaces. Call X the *commodity space* and Z the *security space*. An element of X represents a commodity bundle and an element of Z represents a trade in securities. The returns to trading securities are represented by a linear function $A: Z \to X$. A trade $z \in Z$ results in a vector of returns Az. Security prices are also represented by elements of Z. Let $\otimes$ be a bilinear function from $Z \times Z$ to Z. For any $(q, z) \in Z \times Z$, the value of (q, z) under $\otimes$ is denoted by $q \otimes z$. If q denotes the prices of securities and z denotes the security trade, then $q \otimes z$ is the value of the trade.

There is a finite number of agents indexed by $i = 1, 2, \ldots, n$. Each agent is defined by a consumption set $X_i \subset X$ and a utility function u_i on that set. The elements of X_i represent net consumption after the initial endowment has been subtracted.

There is also a government that consumes goods, levies taxes and trades in securities. The government's net consumption is denoted by $g \in X$, and its taxes are denoted by $H \in X$. Both are assumed to be exogenous. Let h_i denote the tax obligations of agent $i = 1, 2, \ldots, n$ where $H = \sum h_i$, and let $h = (h_1, \ldots, h_m)$.

Each agent $i = 1, 2, \ldots, m$ is assumed to choose a consumption bundle $x_i \in X_i$ and a security trade $z_i \in Z$ subject to the budget constraints $x_i + h_i + q \otimes z_i \leq Az_i$. Similarly, the government chooses a security trade $z_0 \in Z$ that satisfies the budget constraints $g - H + q \otimes z_0 \leq Az_0$.

Fix the government's expenditures $g \in X$ and taxes $h \in X$. An *equilibrium* relative to (g, h) is defined to be a price vector $q \in Z$ and an allocation $(z_0, (x_1, z_1), \ldots, (x_m, z_m))$ satisfying the following conditions:

(i) (x_i, z_i) is maximal with respect to u_i, in the set
$$\{(\xi, \zeta) \in X_i \times Z | x_i + h_i + q \otimes z_i \leq Az_i\} \text{ for } i = 1, 2, \ldots, m;$$

(ii) $z_0 \in Z$ satisfies $g - H + q \otimes z_0 \leq Az_0$;

(iii) $\sum_{i=1}^{m} x_i + g = 0$ and $\sum_{i=0}^{m} z_i = 0$.

9.2.2   The Neutrality Theorem

Let $\langle q, z_0, (x_1, z_1), \ldots, (x_m, z_m) \rangle$ be a fixed but artibrary equilibrium, relative to some policy (g, h). Suppose that the government decides to change its financial policy while keeping its expenditures g fixed. The new policy must satisfy the government's budget constraint. Let (g, h') denote the new policy. Then there exists a security trade $z_0' \in Z$ satisfying $g - H' + q \otimes z_0' = Az_0'$, where $H' \equiv \sum_i h_i'$. The policy change will be neutral if there is no redistribution of the tax burden among the individual agents. The change of policy will have no distribution effects if, for each $i = 1, 2, \ldots, m$, there is a security trade that agent i can make that will convert his new tax into the old one. More precisely, for each $i = 1, 2, \ldots, m$, there exists $\zeta \in Z$ so that $h_i' - h_i + q \otimes \zeta = A\zeta$. Then for each $i = 1, 2, \ldots, m$ there exists a security trade z_i' such that $x_i + h_i' + q \otimes z_i' = Az_i'$. Since the agents' budget sets have not changed, $(q, (z_0', (x_1, z_1'), \ldots, (x_m, z_m')))$ is an equilibrium relative to the new policy (g, h'). The allocation of goods is unchanged in the new equilibrium so the policy change is *neutral*.

THEOREM 2.1   A change in financial policy which leaves government expenditure unaltered and has no distributive effects is neutral.

This is all there is to the neutrality of the debt. I have deliberately used a rather roundabout argument in order to make explicit the role of securities. A more compact argument is possible if securities are eliminated.

Let $X(q)$ denote the set of commodity bundles that can be generated by security trades when the security prices are given by q. That is, $X(q) = \{\xi \in X | \xi \leq Az - q \otimes z, \exists z \in Z\}$. Then the budget constraints for the agents and the government can be written compactly as $x_i + h_i \in X(q)$ and $g - H \in X(q)$, respectively.

In this notation, an equilibrium is defined by an n-tuple of consumption bundles $(x_1, \ldots, x_m) \in X_1 \times \ldots \times X_m$ and a price vector $q \in Z$ satisfying the following conditions:

(i) x_i maximizes $u_i(x_i)$ subject to $x + h_i \in X(q) \cap X_i$, for $i = 1, 2, \ldots, m$;

(ii) $g - H \in X(q)$;

(iii) $\sum_{i=1}^{m} x_i + g = 0$.

Note that if these conditions are satisfied, there exists a security trade z_i for each $i = 1, 2, \ldots, m$ such that $x_i + h_i + q \otimes z_i \leq Az_i$. If we define $z_0 = \sum_{i=1}^{m} z_i$, then condition (iii) implies that $g = H + q \otimes z_0 \leq Az_0$. Thus, the definition of equilibrium is consistent with equilibrium in the securities markets.

Now consider a change in the government's financial policy. Government consumption is kept constant but its security trade and taxes may change. The budget constraint must be satisfied so $g - H' \in X(q)$, if h' denotes the new taxes. The new taxes are divided up among agents so that their individual shares of the tax burden are not changed. This is interpreted as the requirement that $x_i + h_i' \in X(q)$, for $i = 1, 2, \ldots, m$. Then, clearly, nothing has changed. If (x, q) is an equilibrium relative to the old pattern of taxes, it is an equilibrium relative to the new pattern.

9.2.3   Financial Innovation and Short Sales

The preceding argument does not depend in any way on the completeness or incompleteness of markets. However, it does depend on the fact that Z is fixed. If the government can change Z by introducing a new security, for example, then clearly it can have a real impact on the economy.

This fact, which is fairly obvious, is nonetheless somewhat puzzling on the surface. On the one hand, we have a neutrality theorem that says the quantity of government securities outstanding does not have any real effect as long as the set of traded securities does not change. On the other hand, the introduction of a small amount of a new security may have a large effect, by changing the dimension of the set of consumption bundles that can be reached by trading securities. There is a *discontinuity* in the effect of debt policy when financial innovation occurs.

The reason for this discontinuity is the implicit assumption that there are no constraints on short sales of securities. Agents are allowed to buy and sell as much of any security as they like. As soon as the government introduces a small amount of a new security, the volume of trade on the new market may explode. It is the volume of trade in the new security that matters, not the amount of the security that is issued by the government. On the other hand, if short sales were not allowed, the volume of trade would be restricted to the amount of the security issued by the government and there would be no discontinuity. However, as everyone knows, restricting short sales would destroy the neutrality of the debt. In order to undo the effects of the change in the government's debt policy, the private sector has to be able to short sell government securities.

Thus, one must either accept the existence of a discontinuity in the impact of government securities or abandon the neutrality theorem for incomplete markets.

9.3 Public Debt in an Infinite-Horizon Model

From the preceding discussion it is clear that the introduction of new securities can have an impact on the risk-sharing opportunities in the economy. But this theoretical possibility is not very interesting unless we can say something precise about the securities being introduced and the welfare effects of their introduction. A simple overlapping generations (OLG) framework provides the structure that is needed for this exercise.

Implicit in the OLG structure is the assumption that markets are incomplete. More precisely, there is *incomplete participation*. Each generation can only participate in the markets that are open during its lifetime. In the present context, this makes it impossible for an investor to write risk-sharing contracts with generations yet unborn. There is a role for long-lived institutions, of which the government is one, to act as intermediaries.

The idea that intergenerational risk-sharing could be facilitated by government-issued assets appears in Weiss (1979). (I am indebted to

Sudipto Bhattacharya for this reference.) Weiss characterized the optimal monetary policy in an OLG economy with a risky investment technology. He showed that, under certain conditions, an activist monetary policy that stabilized the value of money was welfare-increasing. The effect of this policy was to redistribute risk between the generations. The role of money in facilitating intergenerational risk sharing was studied further in Bhattacharya (1982). A particularly transparent example of intergenerational risk sharing with indexed debt was presented by Fischer (1983). He studied the efficiency properties of a pure exchange, OLG economy with two-period-lived agents. Fischer assumed that the aggregate endowment of the economy was constant but that the distribution between old and young was random. He showed that various arrangements, some of which could be interpreted as (indexed) debt, would lead to an ex ante increase in welfare. Peled (1985) studied a related set of issues in the context of a pure exchange, OLG economy with money. He showed that a stationary monetary equilibrium was ex post, stationary-efficient. That is, it was efficient when agents were distinguished by the state in which they are born and when the equilibrium allocation was compared only with other stationary allocations. He also argued that the introduction of indexed debt was destabilizing.

An *empirical* analysis of dynamic inefficiency is contained in Abel et al. (1989).

In this section we shall see that introducing public debt can lead to ex post increases in welfare. This result is stronger than Fischer's and appears to contradict Peled's. However, as we shall see in the next section, the introduction of durable assets, such as shares in firms or fiat money, changes the story somewhat.

9.3.1 A Model of an OLG Economy

There is an infinite sequence of dates indexed by $t \in T = \{1, 2, \ldots, \infty\}$. At each date $t \in T$, a random variable $\tilde{s}_t$ is observed. The stochastic process $\{\tilde{s}_t\}$ is assumed to be a finite Markov chain with a stationary transition probability matrix. Let $S = \{s_1, \ldots, s_n\}$ denote the values of the random variables $\{\tilde{s}_t\}$ and let $a_{ij} > 0$ denote the probability of a transition from state s_i to state s_j, for $i, j = 1, 2, \ldots, n$. At each date there is a single good that can be either consumed or invested. One unit of the good invested at date t produces $\tilde{R}_t$ units of the good at date $t + 1$. The return to the investment technology is assumed to be a function of the current state, that is, $\tilde{R}_t = R(\tilde{s}_{t+1})$.

Each generation consists of a single representative investor who lives for two periods. The generations have identical preferences that can be represented by a von Neumann–Morgenstern utility function $u(c_1, c_2)$, where c_τ denotes net consumption in the τth period of life.

In what follows, only stationary equilibria are considered. In a stationary equilibrium the stock of government securities is constant over time. Then the government's budget constraint requires that expenditure must be paid for out of current taxes, except possibly at the first date. In that case, we can assume without loss of generality that government expenditure is zero after the first period.

The government is assumed to issue (non-contingent) real bills of different maturities. Greater improvements in welfare could be achieved if the government were to issue more exotic securities. But endowing the government with the ability to create very complex securities may exaggerate the scope for improvements in risk-sharing. If the market has not produced certain kinds of securities, it may be because the costs outweigh the benefits. In that case, it is inefficient for the government to issue them, unless it has a cost advantage. By restricting attention to simple (non-contingent) securities we at least avoid the mistake of ascribing unrealistic powers to the public sector. Contingent securities will be considered in section 9.4. The question of the government's role as a financial innovator is considered in more detail in section 9.5.

A k-period bill issued at date t is a promise to deliver one unit of the consumption good at date $t + k$. Suppose that bills of maturities $k = 1, 2, \ldots, K$ have been issued. Then a price system is a function $v: S \to \mathbf{R}_+^K$. For any $s \in S$, $v(s)$ is the vector of security spot prices in terms of the Consumption good if slate s is observed.

Let B_k denote the stock of k-period bills outstanding at each date and let $B = (B_1, \ldots, B_K)$. A k-period bill issued at date t becomes a $(k-1)$-period bill at date $t + 1$. Thus, to maintain a constant stock of securities, the government has to issue $B_k - B_{k+1}$ new k-period bills each period. Alternatively, one can think of the government as retiring all bills after one period and issuing a new stock of B_k k-period bills. In either case the budget constraint is

$$B \cdot \hat{v}(s) - B \cdot v(s) = H(s) \tag{1}$$

where $H(s)$ denotes total tax revenue collected in state $s \in S$ and

$$\hat{v}(s) = (1, v_1(s), \ldots, v_{K-1}(s)) \tag{2}$$

is the resale value of the bills after one period in state $s \in S$. To avoid intergenerational transfers as a result of asymmetric tax treatment, it is assumed that all taxes are imposed on the young generation. The government's tax policy is represented by the function $h: S \to \mathbf{R}_+$, where $h(s)$ represents the tax levied on a young investor born in state $s \in S$.

In the first period of his life, a typical individual chooses an investment in the risky technology and a portfolio of securities to hold. His consumption at each date in each state is then determined by his budget constraint. Let $y: S \to \mathbf{R}_+$ denote an investor's investment choice and $b: S \to \mathbf{R}_+^K$ denote his portfolio choice. Then the investor's consumption is given by

$$c_1(s) = -v(s) \cdot b(s) - y(s) - h(s) \tag{3}$$

$$c_2(s, s') = R(s')y(s) + \hat{v}(s') \cdot b(s) \tag{4}$$

for any $(s, s') \in S \times S$. The investor chooses the functions c_1, c_2, y and b to maximize his expected utility conditional on the state in the first period.

An *equilibrium* for the OLG economy is an array $\langle y, b, h, B, v \rangle$ satisfying the following conditions:

(i) (b, y) maximizes $E[u(c_1(s), c_2(s, s'))|s]$ where c_1 and c_2 are defined by the budget constraints.

$$c_1(s) = -v(s) \cdot b(s) - y(s) - h(s), \quad \forall s \in S;$$

$$c_2(s, s') = R(s')y(s) + \hat{v}(s') \cdot b(s), \quad \forall (s, s') \in S \times S.$$

(ii) $B \cdot \hat{v}(s) - B \cdot v(s) = h(s)$, for any $s \in S$.

(iii) $b(s) = B$, for any $s \in S$.

The following assumptions are maintained throughout the remainder of this section.

(A.1) $u(c_1, c_2) = U(c_1) + V(c_2)$ for any $(c_1, c_2) \in \mathbf{R}^2$, where U and V are C^2, strictly increasing and strictly concave functions from $\mathbf{R}$ to $\mathbf{R}$;

(A.2) $U'(0) < V'(0) \sum_{j=1}^{n} a_{ij} R(s_j)$, for $i = 1, \ldots, n$.

THEOREM 3.1   Under the maintained assumptions, there exists an equilibrium of the OLG economy for any $B \geq 0$.

Note that consumption is unbounded below.

9.3.2   Intergenerational Risk-Sharing with Short-dated Securities

In order to understand the role of public debt in promoting more efficient
risk-sharing, it is useful to think of it as a kind of social security scheme.
Imagine an economy in which there were no government securities. Since
investors in different generations cannot issue securities to each other,
equilibrium is autarkic. The only way for investors to transfer wealth
between dates is to invest in the risky technology. Since R_t is random, their
first-period consumption will be certain but their second-period consumption will be risky. What each investor wants is to shift some of this risk
from the second period of his life to the first. The only way this can be
achieved is for the old to shift some of the risk to the young generation at
each date. One way to do this is by introducing a social security scheme.

Define a function y^* from S to $\mathbf{R}_+$ by putting

$$y^*(s_i) = \arg\max \sum_{j=1}^{n} a_{ij}[U(-y) + V(R(s_j)y)], \quad \text{for } i = 1,\ldots,n. \tag{5}$$

(A.1) implies that $y^*(s) > 0$ for all $s \in S$. y^* is the optimal investment policy
in the absence of government securities and social security. The question
is whether the introduction of social security would increase welfare. The
social security scheme requires each investor to pay a contribution σ when
young and promises to pay him a benefit σ when old. An increase in σ will
change the optimal y, but from the envelope theorem, the effect on utility
is negligible. Thus, the effect on expected utility of a small change in σ is
given by

$$\{-U'(-y^*(s_i)) + \sum_{j=1}^{n} a_{ij}V'(R(s_j)y^*(s_i))\}d\sigma + o(d\sigma). \tag{6}$$

If the term in braces is positive for each $s \in S$, then an increase in σ will
increase welfare for every $s \in S$. In other words, welfare increases even if we
distinguish investors by the state in which they are born.

PROPOSITION   If $U'(-y^*(s_i)) < \sum_{j=1}^{n} a_{ij}V'(R(s_j)y^*(s_i))$ for $i,\ldots,n$, a social
security scheme in which $\sigma = 0$ is dominated by one in which $\sigma > 0$.

Social security is like an asset with a zero rate of return. Although
capital has a higher expected return, an investor may be willing to invest
in the safe asset as a hedge. In fact, the inequality of the proposition will
always be satisfied if $\tilde{R}_t$ is random and the investor is sufficiently risk-
averse. Under the same conditions, there will be a demand for public debt.
Public debt operates like a social security scheme by offering the investor

a safe asset which is in fact a claim on the next generation. To see this, let $\langle b, y, h, B, v \rangle$ be a stationary equilibrium in which only 1-period bills are issued. That is, $B_k = 0$ for $k = 2, \ldots, K$. In the first period of his life, an investor pays a tax of $h(s) = (1 - v_1(s))B_1$ and buys bills worth $v_1(s)B_1$. His first-period consumption will be $c_1(s) = -y(s) - B_1$ and his second-period consumption will be $c_2(s, s') = R(s')y(s) + B_1$. Thus, putting $\sigma = B_1$ we see that his consumption will be exactly the same in an equilibrium with 1-period debt as it would be in an equilibrium with a social security scheme and no government securities. Conversely, if y is an optimal investment policy corresponding to a social security scheme σ, there is an equilibrium with government securities that implements the same consumption allocation. This equilibrium can be defined by putting $B_1 = \sigma$, $h(s) = (1 - v_1(s))B_1$, $\forall s \in S$, and choosing v to satisfy the first-order condition

$$U'(-y(s_i) - B_1)v_1(s_i) = \sum_{j=1}^{n} a_{ij}V'(y(s)R(s_j) + B_1). \tag{7}$$

THEOREM 3.2   Corresponding to any equilibrium with a social security scheme and no government securities, there exists an equilibrium with 1-period bills that has the same consumption and investment. Conversely, corresponding to any equilibrium with 1-period bills there is an equilibrium with a social security scheme and no government securities that has the same consumption and investment.

In a precise sense, public debt is equivalent to a social security scheme. Since (short-dated) public debt is riskless, it provides a hedge against the risky investment technology. Each generation is providing insurance to the preceding generation and, since there is an infinite horizon, they can all be better off. Thus, there is a role for public debt to improve risk-sharing in the economy even if there is no continuing need to finance government expenditure.

It is useful to compare this role for public debt to the one discovered by Diamond (1965). In Diamond's model there is no uncertainty and markets are complete. However, equilibrium may be inefficient because of over-accumulation of capital. In that case, an increase in public debt would crowd out part of the capital stock and so lead to a Pareto improvement. In the present case, in addition to an infinite horizon and an OLG structure, we have risk and incomplete markets. The expected rate of return on capital can be greater than zero, so there is no overaccumulation, yet there is still the possibility of an increase in welfare. The inefficiency arises not from overaccumulation but simply from unexploited opportunities for risk-sharing.

9.3.3   Intergenerational Risk-sharing with Long-dated Securities

The preceding analysis shows that the existence of public debt can improve risk-sharing in a simple, OLG economy. If short-term debt can improve welfare, is there a role for longer-dated securities? Under certain circumstances, as we shall see, lengthening the maturity structure of the debt can improve welfare even further.

Short-dated securities (1-period bills) offer a safe return. Longer-dated securities are inherently more "risky" because changes in the interest rate lead to random capital gains and losses. However, riskiness of this sort can be an advantage. Suppose that the observation of a high (low) value of R_t causes investors to expect high (low) future values of R_t and hence lowers (raises) the price of long-dated securities. If the price of bonds is high when the return to capital is low, then risky, long-dated securities will be an even better hedge against the risky investment technology than the safe, short-dated securities.

To make this argument precise, a general-equilibrium analysis is needed. Fix an equilibrium (y, b, h, B, v) and consider the effect of a small change in B. If $u^*(s_i)$ denotes the equilibrium expected utility of an investor born in state s_i, then the impact of the change in B is easily calculated to be

$$\frac{du^*(s_i)}{dB} = U'(c_1(s_i))\left\{-B\frac{dv(s_i)}{dB} - \frac{dh(s_i)}{dB}\right\}$$

$$+ \sum_{j=1}^{n} a_{ij} V'(c_2(s_i, s_j)) B \frac{d\hat{v}(s_j)}{bB} \tag{8}$$

where $\hat{v}(s) \equiv (1, v_1(s), \ldots, v_{K-1}(s))$.

One fact is immediately apparent from this formula. If there are no government securities in the initial equilibrium, then the welfare effect of introducing short-dated securities is determined entirely by the tax effect. Putting $B = 0$, the formula tells us that

$$\frac{du^*(s_i)}{dB} = -U'(c_1(s_i))\frac{dh(s_i)}{dB}. \tag{9}$$

This result can be explained as follows. The change in the equilibrium expected utility of an investor can be divided into three parts. First, there is the effect of the change in the investor's portfolio (y, b). Second, there is the wealth effect of the change in the prices v. Third, there is the effect of the change in taxes. The first of these effects vanishes by the Envelope Theorem. If $B = 0$, the second effect also vanishes. We are left with the tax effect. What the formula says is that welfare is increased if and only if taxes *fall* as a result of the introduction of short-dated securities.

At first glance, this may seem strange. Since taxes are used to pay the interest on the debt, an increase in debt would seem to require an increase in taxes. However, under the conditions of the proposition, the interest rate must be negative. Recall that an intergenerational transfer is like a safe asset with a zero rate of return. If there is a demand for this asset, the expected marginal utility of future consumption is greater than the marginal utility of present consumption. This is what the proposition assumes. Then in order for markets to clear when the supply of 1-period bills is zero, the price of these bills must be greater than unity, i.e., the interest rate is negative. Then the government can make a profit by issuing these bills: at each date the cost of redeeming last period's issue will be less than the revenue from the sale of this period's issue. To satisfy its budget constraint, the government will make transfers to investors. These transfers measure the increase in welfare.

The same argument can be used to analyze the welfare effects of introducing longer-dated securities. Suppose that $B = 0$ and a small quantity of k-period bills are introduced. If these bills are redeemed at maturity then, in a stationary equilibrium there must be bills of all maturities from 1 to k. More precisely, if the government issues $\varepsilon > 0$ k-period bills each period, the equilibrium stock must be

$$B_i = \begin{cases} \varepsilon & \text{if } i = 1, \ldots, k \\ 0 & \text{otherwise.} \end{cases} \tag{10}$$

The change in taxes will be approximately $(1 - v_k(s))\varepsilon$ in state $s \in S$, so from the earlier formula

$$\frac{du^*(s_i)}{dB} = -U'(c_1(s_i))(1 - v_k(s_i)). \tag{11}$$

As an illustration of what can happen when there is a positive stock of debt already in existence, suppose there is a positive quantity of 1-period bills outstanding and none of higher maturities. That is, $B_1 > 0$ and $B_k = 0$ for $k = 2, \ldots, K$. Now consider the effect of introducing a small amount of two-period debt. Note that what is held constant is the *flow* of newly issued 1-period bills. The *stock* of 1-period bills increases to accommodate the issue of 2-period bills. Thus, if the government issues ε units of 2-period bills at each date, the stock of 1-period bills will be $B_1 + \varepsilon$.

Let $\langle y, b, h, B, v \rangle$ be a fixed but arbitrary equilibrium. Substituting these assumptions into the formula, we see that the change in equilibrium expected utility is

$$\frac{du^*(s_i)}{dB_2} = -U'(c_1(s_i))\left\{-B_1\frac{dv_1(s_i)}{dB_2} - \frac{dh(s_i)}{dB_2}\right\}. \tag{12}$$

Imagine that the government's budget is divided into two parts, one devoted to servicing the existing one-period debt and one devoted to servicing the new two-period debt. Let h_k denote the tax payment from the young that is required to service the k-period debt. For any $s \in S$, $h_1(s) = (1 - v_1(s))B_1$. Holding the issue of 1-period bills constant, the change in h_1 is just offset by the change in the value of 1-period bills issued each period. In other words, the wealth effect and the tax effect cancel out for 1-period bills. Thus, the change in expected utility is determined by the change in h_2:

$$\frac{du^*(s_i)}{dB} = -U'(c_1(s_i))\frac{dh_2(s_i)}{dB_2}. \tag{13}$$

The introduction of long-date securities is welfare improving if and only if an increase in B_2, evaluated at the point $B_2 = 0$, reduces h_2. To determine the effect on taxes, simply differentiate the government's budget constraint:

$$\frac{dh_{12}}{dB_2} = \frac{d(1 - v_2)B_2}{dB_2} = (1 - v_2) \tag{14}$$

when $B_2 = 0$. So the introduction of long-dated securities will be welfare improving if and only if $1 < v_2$. A similar argument holds for k-period bills.

These results are summarized in the following theorem.

THEOREM 3.3   Let (y, b, h, B, v) be an equilibrium of the OLG economy. Issuing a small amount of k-period bills will increase the expected utility of every type of investor if $v_k(s) > 1$ for every $s \in S$ and either (i) $B = 0$ or (ii) $B_i = 0$ for $i = 2, \ldots, K$ and $k \geq 2$.

These results may suggest that a lengthening of the maturity of the debt is always beneficial. This is not the case. As a counterexample, consider the case of a perpetuity offering a constant coupon of one unit per period. To keep things simple, suppose that the security in existence is a one-period bill. Introduce a small amount of the perpetuity. The change in the price of 1-period bills is offset by the change in the taxes needed to redeem them. The change in the price of the perpetuity has no effect because the stock of perpetuities is zero. The introduction of the perpetuities affects welfare only through its effect on the taxes required to service them. In a stationary equilibrium, perpetuities are issued only once, at the first date. At each subsequent date, their existence must give rise to a positive demand for revenue. So taxes must rise, regardless of the price at which the perpetuities are sold initially.

9.4   The Efficient Design of Public Debt

Section 9.3 explored the role of public debt in facilitating intergenerational risk sharing. By issuing debt, the government acts as an intermediary between generations that cannot trade directly with each other. It appears that here the government can do something the market cannot do, but that is only because we have assumed that there are no other long-lived institutions besides the government. In fact, other institutions capable of creating long-lived securities do exist. For example, firms issue equity. It is not clear that public debt will have the same role to play when there exist alternative, long-lived securities.

There is an analogy here with the inefficiency of equilibrium in OLG economies with no uncertainty. It is well known that the equilibrium of an OLG economy can be inefficient even if markets are complete. This is true both for pure exchange models and for models with production subject to constant returns to scale. However, this inefficiency disappears if one introduces a scarce durable factor such as land or a firm that can earn positive profits at a zero interest rate.

9.4.1   The Efficiency of Equilibrium with Long-lived Assets

Consider a pure exchange economy with an OLG structure. Each generation consists of a single, representative agent who lives for two periods. Agents are identical and have preferences represented by a utility function

$U(c_1) + V(c_2)$ satisfying the usual properties. There is no production and the only security traded at each date is a 1-period bill. The only possible equilibrium allocation is the no-trade allocation. If $U'(0) < V'(0)$, the market-clearing interest rate must be less than zero and the equilibrium is inefficient. In fact, everyone can be made better off if each generation except the first transfers a small amount $\varepsilon > 0$ of the good to the preceding generation.

Now suppose there is a durable asset that produces a constant output of R units per period. The asset is initially owned by the first generation, but after receiving the output of the asset the first generation will sell it to the second and so on. In equilibrium, there will be no borrowing or lending. The only trade between generations will be the exchange of goods for the asset. Let q be the price of the asset in a stationary equilibrium. The first-order condition for an agent's optimum is

$$U'(-q)q = V'(R + q)(R + q). \tag{15}$$

Since $R > 0$, we must have $U'(-q) > V'(R + q)$. The interest rate is positive so efficiency follows by the Cass criterion (Cass 1972).

One way to understand the result is the following. The value of the asset is the present value of the stream of outputs it produces. If the interest rate gets too small, the value of the asset will become very large. But that means that each generation will have low first-period consumption and high second-period consumption, so the interest rate must be high in order to clear the market for bills. Thus, the interest rate cannot get "too low."

Stationarity is not needed to establish efficiency. Scheinkman (1980) has proved the result for the general case. The result was also discovered by Wallace. Weiss (1979) proves a similar result for the case of a monetary economy in steady-state equilibrium. The Scheinkman theorem is a powerful result. It says that if there are any long-lived assets, equilibrium will be efficient. However small the yield of the durable asset, the interest rate will adjust so that the value of the asset is adequate to support an efficient level of saving. Since there can never be an inadequate supply of long-lived securities, public debt cannot improve the allocation of resources (compare Diamond 1965).

Something similar happens when there is uncertainty. To illustrate the importance of durable assets, we can adapt the OLG framework from

section 9.3 as follows. As before, there is assumed to be an infinite sequence of dates. At each date, a single representative investor, who lives
for two periods, is born. There is a single good and investors have a zero
endowment of the good in each period of their lives. Their identical preferences are represented by the von Neumann–Morgenstern utility function
$U(c_1) + V(c_2)$ satisfying (A.1) and (A.2). Uncertainty is represented by the
finite Markov chain $\{s_t\}$ with stationary transition probabilities $\{a_{ij}\}$. So
far the model is identical with the one described in section 9.3. But here,
instead of assuming the existence of a constant returns to scale investment
technology, I assume there is a single unit of a perfectly durable and
non-reproducible asset. The asset produces a random output $\tilde{R}_t = R(\tilde{s}_t)$ at
each date $t = 1, 2, \ldots, \infty$. Let q_t denote the price of the asset at date t. In
a stationary equilibrium the asset price will be a function of the current
state: $q_t = q(\tilde{s}_t)$.

Let $y: S \to \mathbf{R}_+$ denote the investor's demand for the asset in each state.
Then consumption is given by

$$c_1(s) = -q(s)y(s), \quad \forall s \in S \tag{16}$$

$$c_2(s, s') = (R(s') + q(s'))y(s), \quad \forall (s, s') \in S \times S. \tag{17}$$

The investor chooses the functions c_1, c_2, and y to maximize his expected
utility conditional on the state in the first period.

An *equilibrium* for this OLG economy is an array $\langle y, q \rangle$ satisfying the
following conditions:

(i) y maximizes $E[u(c_1(s), c_2(s, s')|s]$ where c_1 and c_2 are defined by the
budget constraints

$$c_1(s) = -q(s)y(s), \quad \forall s \in S \tag{16}$$

$$c_2(s, s') = (R(s') + q(s'))y(s), \quad \forall (s, s') \in S \times S \tag{17}$$

(ii) $y(s) = 1, \quad \forall s \in S.$

Since markets are incomplete, equilibrium will not be Pareto-efficient. In
this sense, Scheinkman's result does not hold. However, it does not follow
that a simple, non-contingent debt policy of the kind studied in section 9.3
can make every one better off. In fact, even if the government pursues a
contingent debt policy, it cannot make every type of investor better off in
a stationary equilibrium. To see this, consider the more general problem

in which the government makes state contingent transfers between generations. Define a *stationary transfer scheme* to be a function $Q: S \to \mathbf{R}$ with
the interpretation that $Q(s)$ is the amount of the good transferred from the
young generation to the old in state $s \in S$ at any date. The government is
restricted to use a stationary transfer scheme. Assume without loss of
generality that the old consume the return to the asset at each date. Then
the consumption of the young and old generations are $c_1(s) = -Q(s)$ and
$c_2(s) = R(s) + Q(s)$, respectively, in state $s \in S$.

   To analyze the problem further it is convenient to have a slightly different notation. Let Q_i denote the transfer from the young generation to the
old generation in state s_i at each date and let $Q = (Q_1, \ldots, Q_n)$. Also, let
$R_i = R(s_i)$, and $q_i = q(s_i)$ for $i = 1, 2, \ldots, n$. Then the expected utility of an
investor in state s_i can be denoted by $u_i^*(Q)$, where

$$u_i^*(Q) = U(-Q_i) + \sum_{j=1}^{n} a_{ij} V(R_j + Q_j) \tag{18}$$

for $i = 1, \ldots, n$. In a stationary equilibrium the equilibrium price function
q is the transfer scheme, i.e., the net transfer from young to old in state
$s \in S$ is $q(s)$. The question is whether it is possible to make everyone better
off by choosing some other value of Q. A necessary condition for this to be
true is that $u_i^*(Q) \geq u_i^*(q)$, for $i = 1, \ldots, n$, and $Q \neq q^0$. (This condition is
not sufficient because it ignores the welfare of the first generation.)

   Let q^0 be an equilibrium price vector. From the definition of equilibrium q^0 must satisfy the condition

$$U'(-q_i^0)q_i^0 = \sum_{j=1}^{n} a_{ij} V'(R_j + q_j^0)(R_j + q_j^0) \quad \text{for } i = 1, \ldots, n. \tag{19}$$

The equilibrium conditions can be written in matrix form as

$$B_q^0 = CR \tag{20}$$

where $B = [b_{ij}]$ is an $n \times n$ matrix with elements

$$b_{ij} = \begin{cases} a_{ii} V'(R_i + q_i^0) - U'(-q_i^0) & \text{if } i = j \\ a_{ij} V(R_i + q_j^0) & \text{if } i \neq j \end{cases} \tag{21}$$

for $i, j = 1, \ldots, n$, and $C = [c_{ij}]$ is an $n \times n$ matrix with elements

$$c_{ij} = a_{ij} V'(R_j + q_j^0) \tag{22}$$

for $i, j = 1, \ldots, n$. Suppose there exists a Q such that $u_i^*(Q) \geq u_i^*(q^0)$ for
$i = 1, \ldots, n$ and $Q \neq q^0$. By the strict concavity of the utility function,

$$-U'(-q_i^0)\delta Q_i + \sum_{j=1}^n u_i^* a_{ij} V'(R_j + q_j^0)\delta Q_j > 0 \tag{23}$$

for $i = 1, \ldots, n$, where $\delta Q = Q - q^0$. These inequalities can be written in matrix form as

$$B\delta Q \gg 0. \tag{24}$$

Suppose that $R_i > 0$ for $i = 1, \ldots, n$. Then q^0 must be strictly positive. Since $b_{ij} > 0$ for $i \neq j$, the equilibrium conditions imply that B has negative diagonal and positive off-diagonal elements. In fact, the equilibrium conditions imply that B has a dominant diagonal. This in turn implies that δQ must be strictly negative. Then the first generation must be made worse off in each state. There cannot be a Pareto improvement.

To see that $\delta Q \ll 0$, write $\delta Q = \xi_i q_i^0$ for $i = 1, \ldots, n$ and assumes the numbers ξ_i are indexed so that $\xi_i \leq \xi_{i+1}$, for $i = 1, \ldots, n - 1$. Then the inequality

$$-U'(-q_n^0)\xi_n q_n^0 + \sum_{j=1}^n a_{nj} V'(R_j + q_j^0)\xi_j q_j^0 > 0 \tag{25}$$

implies that

$$-U'(-q_n^0)\xi_n q_n^0 + \sum_{j=1}^n a_{nj} V'(R_j + q_j^0)\xi_n q_j^0 > 0. \tag{26}$$

From the equilibrium condition, however,

$$-U'(-q_n^0)q_n^0 + \sum_{j=1}^n a_{nj} V'(R_j + q_j^0)q_j^0 < 0. \tag{27}$$

This can only be true if $\xi_n < 0$, in which case $\xi_i < 0$ for all $i = 1, \ldots, n$. This proves that $\delta Q \ll 0$ so there can be no Pareto improvement.

Note that if δQ_i were non-negative for some $i = 1, \ldots, n$ it would be possible to implement a (weak) Pareto improvement. One would simply begin the transfer scheme at the first date if $s = s_i$ and not otherwise.

THEOREM If $R_i > 0$, for every $i = 1, \ldots, n$, then it is impossible to make every type of investor better off using a stationary transfer scheme.

The theorem implies that it is impossible to use the kind of debt policy studied in section 9.3 to bring about an increase in welfare. To see this, one only has to examine the investor's budget constraints. Let B denote the stock of bills outstanding at each date. Then in equilibrium the consumption of a young investor in state $s \in S$ will be

$$c_1(s) = -q(s) - B \cdot v(s) - h(s)$$

$$= -q(s) - B \cdot v(s) + (B \cdot v(s) - B \cdot \hat{v}(s)) = -q(s) - B \cdot \hat{v}(s). \tag{28}$$

Similarly, the consumption of an old investor in state $s \in S$ will be

$$c_2(s) = R(s) + q(s) + B \cdot \hat{v}(s). \tag{29}$$

Putting $Q(s) = q(s) + B \cdot \hat{v}(s)$ for each $s \in S$, it is clear that any consumption allocation that can be supported as a stationary equilibrium with a constant stock of debt B can also be implemented by a stationary transfer scheme Q. The theorem implies that introducing debt cannot make every type of investor better off in a stationary equilibrium.

The sense in which equilibrium is shown to be efficient is a very weak one. Apart from the restrictions of stationarity, we have distinguished investors by the state in which they are born. It is not obvious that this is the right notion of Pareto efficiency to use. For example, Fischer (1983) uses the notion of ex ante efficiency (which Peled 1985 calls unconditional efficiency). The ex ante notion regards the investor born at date t as being the same individual, regardless of the state in which he is born. An increase in his expected utility, ex ante the realization of the state in which he is born, counts as an increase in welfare for him, even if he is worse off in some states. The theorem leaves open the possibility that debt policy can improve welfare according to this criterion.

A result analogous to theorem 3.3 is proved in Peled (1985). (See also Peled 1984.) In Peled's model, it is the existence of valued fiat money that ensures the efficiency of equilibrium. Both results suggest that the absence of durable assets may be a restrictive feature of the analysis in section 9.3, as also of Fischer (1983). However, the efficiency result is also special. It relies on the assumption that $R(s) > 0$ for all $s \in S$. If negative returns are possible, then an appropriate debt policy may lead to a welfare improvement. The following example makes this clear.

Example   Consider the special case of the model in which there are two states, $S = \{H, L\}$. The returns to the asset are R_H and R_L, respectively. Suppose that the states $\{s_t\}$ are i.i.d. and the high and low states have equal probability. In that case, the price of the asset is constant in a stationary equilibrium and the equilibrium conditions can be written as follows:

$$2U'(-q)q = V'(R_H + q)(R_H + q) + V'(R_L + q)(R_L + q). \tag{30}$$

For a sufficiently small but positive expected rate of return, the equilibrium must be inefficient. To see this consider the limiting case where $R_H + R_L = 0$. The equilibrium condition reduces to

$$[2U'(-q) - V'(R + q) - V'(-R + q)]q$$

$$= [-V'(R + q) - V'(-R + q)]R < 0 \qquad (31)$$

where $R = R_H = -R_L$. Then it is possible to make every generation better off simply by making a non-contingent transfer of $\varepsilon > 0$ units of the good from the young to the old at each date. By making the expected return sufficiently close to zero, the same result is obtained.

The source of the inefficiency is the same as the one exploited in section 9.3. It seems clear that it can be used in the presence of durable assets to derive results similar to those found in section 9.3.

The assumption that the return to the asset be negative with positive probability may seem quite strong. In a growing economy, the corresponding condition is that the returns be less than the rate of population growth with positive probability. This assumption seems much more acceptable.

Where does this leave us? The range of application of the results in section 9.3 is clearly limited by the existence of durable assets yielding positive returns. But that still leaves considerable scope for welfare-improving debt policies. If the asset returns are negative with positive probability, or if it is considered appropriate to use the ex ante welfare criterion, then debt policy may lead to a Pareto-improvement.

9.4.2 Characterization of Efficient, Contingent Debt Policies

Up to this point, only non-contingent debt instruments have been considered. If no restriction is placed on the government's ability to create new securities, the analysis becomes trivial. The government should simply replace all missing markets and implement the first best. This is not a plausible solution. Markets are missing for a reason, often because of transaction costs or lack of information. The government is subject to similar restraints and it is not sensible to assume it can costlessly issue any security it likes.

On the other hand, there may be circumstances in which the government has an advantage in providing insurance against some contingencies. One of these may be the provision of insurance against the business cycles. Since macroeconomic shocks tend to affect most asset returns in a similar way, it may be difficult for investors to hedge against the cycle by holding a diverse portfolio. The government, on the other hand, can provide insurance by arranging intergenerational risk-sharing. The idea is to exploit the

law of large numbers by spreading the risk of the cycle over many generations. In this context, contingent debt can be regarded as an extension of
traditional countercyclical policy. It may be interesting, then, to consider
briefly the problem of choosing an efficient, contingent debt policy.

To fix ideas, suppose the government issues a single, contingent bond.
The bond matures after one period and pays a return that depends on the
state at the redemption date. The bond is defined by a payoff function
$P: S \rightarrow \mathbf{R}$, where $P(s)$ is the payoff to one unit of the bond in state $s \in S$.
Without loss of generality it can be assumed that the government issues
one unit of the bond at each date. The young investor at each date chooses
a quantity of the bond and the durable asset to hold. As before, let $b(s)$ and
$y(s)$ denote the holdings of the bond and asset, respectively, in state $s \in S$
and let $v(s)$ and $q(s)$ denote the prices of the bond and asset, respectively,
in state $s \in S$. Then an *equilibrium* for the economy is defined to be an
array $\langle y, b, h, P, q, v \rangle$ satisfying the following conditions:

(i) (y, b) maximizes $E[u(c_1(s), c_2(s, s')) | s]$ where c_1 and c_2 are defined by the
budget constraints

$$c_1(s) = -q(s)y(s) - v(s)b(s) - h(s), \quad \forall s \in S;$$

$$c_2(s, s') = (R(s') + q(s'))y(s) + P(s')b(s), \quad \forall (s, s') \in S \times S;$$

(ii) $(y(s), b(s)) = (1, 1), \quad \forall s \in S.$

Notice that the kind of debt policy studied earlier is, in a certain sense, a
special case of the stationary, contingent debt policy defined here. The
portfolio B of non-contingent bills is equivalent to a single, contingent
bond. Simply put $P(s) = B \cdot \hat{v}(s)$ for every $s \in S$ and put the price of one
unit of the bond equal to $B \cdot v(s)$ in state $s \in S$. Then it is clear that a
stationary equilibrium with a stock of bills B can be replicated as a stationary equilibrium with a single contingent bond with payoff function P.

Note also that theorem 3.3 implies that it is impossible to improve
welfare by introducing contingent debt. If $\langle y, b, h, P, q, v \rangle$ is an equilibrium
with contingent debt, it is clear that the same consumption allocation can
be attained by making the lump-sum transfers $Q = q + P$. Even though it
is impossible to increase the expected utility of every type of investor, one
might still want to pursue a contingent debt policy if, for example, one
were willing to make distributional tradeoffs. In that case, one would need
to characterize the efficient, contingent debt policy.

We are used to thinking that an efficient allocation can be decentralized, that is, supported as an equilibrium with lump-sum transfers. We have seen that a contingent debt policy makes lump-sum transfers between generations. This suggests the following approach to characterizing an efficient, contingent debt policy. First, characterize an efficient allocation. Then show it can be supported as an equilibrium with a contingent debt policy. In fact, this approach does not work, because the first-best cannot be decentralized in this way. Nonetheless, it is interesting to see what goes wrong, because it shows that the problem of choosing an efficient debt policy is more complicated than merely choosing efficient lump-sum transfers.

Start by considering the efficient transfer policy. The problem is to choose a stationary transfer scheme $Q = (Q_1,\ldots,Q_n)$ that is maximal in the sense that it is impossible to make every type of investor better off by choosing some alternative transfer scheme. (The effect on the initial generation is ignored in what follows.) Since the utility functions are concave in Q, any choice of Q that is efficient in this sense must maximize a weighted sum of expected utilities. Let Q^* denote an efficient transfer scheme. A necessary and sufficient condition for efficiency is that, for some vector $\lambda = (\lambda_1,\ldots,\lambda_n) > 0$, Q^* is a maximum of $\sum_{i=1}^n \lambda_i u_i^*(Q)$, where

$$u_i^*(Q) \equiv U(-Q_i) + \sum_{j=1}^n a_{ij} V(R_j + Q_j) \tag{32}$$

for $i = 1,\ldots,n$. Note that this maximization problem can be thought of as the limiting case, as the discount factor $\delta \to 0$, of maximizing a weighted sum of all investors' expected utilities, where investors are distinguished only by birth state. The objective function in that case is

$$\sum_{t=1}^\infty \delta^{t-1} \sum_{i=1}^n \lambda_i u_i^*(Q) + \sum_{i=1}^n \lambda_i V(Q_i). \tag{33}$$

In any case, Q^* must satisfy the first-order conditions

$$\sum_{i=1}^n \lambda_i a_{ij} V'(R_j + Q_j) = \lambda_j U'(-Q_j) \tag{34}$$

for $j = 1,\ldots,n$. These conditions completely characterize the efficient transfer scheme Q^*.

The efficient transfer scheme always provides insurance against macroeconomic shocks. Other things being equal, an increase in $R(s)$ will be associated with a decrease in $Q(s)$. However, it is only in very special circumstances that the efficient policy provides the old with complete insurance against macroeconomic shocks. Suppose, for example, that the policy maximizes the expected utility of a representative investor. In that case, the weights λ are the invariant probability distribution of the stochastic process $\{\tilde{s}_t\}$ and hence satisfy the invariance condition

$$\sum_{i=1}^{n} \lambda_i a_{ij} = \lambda_j \tag{35}$$

for $j = 1, \ldots, n$. From the first-order condition it is clear that $U'(-Q_i) = V'(R_i + Q_i)$ for all $i = 1, \ldots, n$.

The problem of choosing an optimal transfer policy has been studied by Fischer (1983), by Pagano (1988) and, in a monetary context, by Bhattacharya (1982). Fischer (1983) discusses at length the problem of implementing efficient risk-sharing arrangements by means of debt policy. Because of the special structure of his model (pure exchange, no aggregate uncertainty) efficient solutions can be implemented by fairly simple institutional arrangements. Pagano (1988) studies the optimal transfer problem in a model that is very similar to Fischer's. He interprets the resulting transfer scheme as an optimal debt policy. Now, if the government can make transfers directly, there is no need to bother with security markets. On the other hand, if there is some reason to use security markets to implement efficient intergenerational risk-sharing, then the problem of choosing an efficient debt policy is inherently more difficult than simply choosing an efficient Q. These difficulties are studied by Bhattacharya, who stresses the informational asymmetries that may prevent the implementation of the first-best transfer scheme. Informational asymmetries are ignored here, but they must be important in explaining why the government would want to use financial markets rather than make lump-sum transfers directly. Even with complete information, however, implementing the optimal Q by an appropriate choice of contingent debt policy may not be possible, as we see below.

Once Q^* is determined, the next step is to see whether the same allocation can be supported as an equilibrium with contingent debt for some debt policy. Suppose that it can. Let $\langle y, b, h, P, q, v \rangle$ denote an equilibrium such that $Q^*(s) = q(s) + v(s)$ for $s \in S$. Letting $P(s_i) = P_i$, $q(s_i) = q_i$ and $v(s_i) = v_i$, for $i = 1, \ldots, n$, the conditions for equilibrium can be written

$$U'(-Q_i^*)q_i = \sum_{j=1}^{n} a_{ij} V'(R_j + Q_j^*)(R_j + q_j) \tag{36}$$

and

$$U'(-Q_i^*)v_i = \sum_{j=1}^{n} a_{ij} V'(R_j + Q_j^*)P_j \tag{37}$$

for $i = 1, \ldots, n$. The first set of equations must be used to define the equilibrium value of $q = (q_1, \ldots, q_n)$. P can be defined by the identity $Q^* = q + P$. Then the second set of equations can be used to define the equilibrium value of $v = (v_1, \ldots, v_n)$ Thus, the possibility of supporting the efficient allocation as an equilibrium is equivalent to the possibility of solving the equilibrium conditions for q.

Recall the first-order conditions for the solution of the efficient transfer problem:

$$\sum_{i=1}^{n} \lambda_i a_{ij} V'(R_j + Q_j) = \lambda_j U'(-Q_j) \quad (j = 1, \ldots, n) \tag{38}$$

and substitute them into the equilibrium conditions above:

$$U'(-Q_i^*)q_i = \sum_{j=1}^{n} a_{ij} U'(-Q_j^*)\lambda_j(R_j + q_j)/\sum_{k=1}^{n} a_{kj}\lambda_k. \tag{39}$$

Rewrite these equations in matrix form as

$$Bq = -CR \tag{40}$$

where $B = [b_{ij}]$ is an $n \times n$ matrix with elements

$$b_{ij} = \begin{cases} (a_{ii}\lambda_i/\sum_k a_{ki}\lambda_k - 1)U'(-Q_i^*) & \text{for } i = j \\ a_{ij}\lambda_j/\sum_k a_{kj}\lambda_k U'(-Q_j^*) & \text{for } i \neq j \end{cases} \tag{41}$$

for $i, j = 1, 2, \ldots, n$ and $C = [c_{ij}]$ is an $n \times n$ matrix with elements

$$c_{ij} = a_{ij}\lambda_j/\sum_k a_{kj}\lambda_k U'(-Q_j^*) \tag{42}$$

for $i, j = 1, \ldots, n$. To solve this equation generally requires B to be a non-singular matrix. Divide the j-th column of B by $U'(-Q_j^*)/\sum_k a_{kj}\lambda_k$, for $j = 1, \ldots, n$. Multiply the i-th row by λ_i, for $i = 1, \ldots, n$. These operations do not change the rank of the matrix. The columns of the resulting matrix sum to zero, proving that B is singular. Unless by accident $-CR$ lies in a linear subspace of dimension less than n, there will exist no q satisfying the equilibrium conditions. The efficient transfer scheme cannot be supported as an equilibrium with contingent debt.

It appears that the singularity is peculiar to the efficient allocation, so a small perturbation will remove it. Thus, it ought to be possible to implement an allocation that is very close to the efficient allocation. Yet even here there seem to be difficulties. It is worth pursuing this possibility because it reveals a little more of what goes wrong in the attempt to implement the efficient allocation. Consider the case mentioned earlier where

the efficient allocation maximizes the expected utility of the representative investor. In that case, $U'(-Q_i^*) - V'(Q_i^* + R_i)$ for every $i = 1, 2, \ldots, n$.
Suppose that Q is a transfer scheme very close to Q^* and let $u_i = U'(-Q_i)$,
$v_i = V'(Q_i + R_i)$ and $\varepsilon_i \equiv u_i - v_i$ for every $i = 1, 2, \ldots, n$. Substituting these
definitions into the equilibrium conditions for asset prices, we get

$$(v_i + \varepsilon_i)q_i = \sum_{j=1}^{n} a_{ij}v_j(R_j + q_j) \tag{43}$$

for $i = 1, 2, \ldots, n$. Multiplying by a_i and summing over i gives us

$$\sum_{i=1}^{n} a_i(v_i + \varepsilon_i)q_i = \sum_{i=1}^{n} a_i v_i(R_i + q_i) \tag{44}$$

or

$$\sum_{i=1}^{n} a_i \varepsilon_i q_i = \sum_{i=1}^{n} a_i v_i R_i. \tag{45}$$

Now suppose that $Q \to Q^*$. From the equation above it is clear that as
long as $\sum_{i=1}^{n} a_i v_i R_i$ is bounded away from zero, $q_i \to \infty$ for at least one i
and hence by the equilibrium conditions it must be so for all i. In order for
this behaviour of prices to be consistent with Q approaching Q^*, it must
be the case that $P_i \to -\infty$ for each i. Theoretically, this is possible but it
seems somewhat implausible. In practice, the volatility of prices and the
problems associated with negative face-value bonds would seem to rule
out this kind of scheme.

The result is in any case somewhat surprising since by issuing the contingent debt instrument (and adopting an appropriate tax policy to balance its budget), the government is effectively making lump-sum transfers
between generations. This is clear from the expression for the equilibrium
expected utility of a typical investor. Nonetheless, the fact that investors
are subject to additional risk in the form of capital gains and losses on
the durable asset puts the attainment of the first-best allocation beyond
the government's reach. In effect, the market frustrates the government's
attempt to achieve the best possible risk-sharing arrangement.

There is a family resemblance between this result and an example found
in Bhattacharya (1982). In Bhattacharya's setup, there is no durable capital good, only an investment technology. Generations live for two periods,
have an endowment of one unit in the first period and none in the second,
and have additively separable preferences. The government uses taxes and
transfers to maximize a weighted sum of utilities, in which the utility of
future generations is slightly discounted. Call this the first-best allocation.

Formally, the maximization problem is like that of an infinitely-lived individual with appropriately specified period utility functions. Bhattacharya asks whether this allocation can be implemented by injecting money in the form of transfers to the young. He shows that when agents have logarithmic utility functions, the answer is "no." In the context of Bhattacharya's example, some difficulties are clear even without uncertainty. Suppose that the return on invstment is a constant $R > 1$ and that the rate at which future generations' utility is discounted is small. Since the first-best problem is formally the same as a single, infinitely-lived individual's maximization problem, we know that the amount of capital invested must grow without bound. Then eventually there must be transfers from old to young. But this cannot be accomplished in a monetary equilibrium, where by definition goods are transferred only from young to old. Introducing uncertainty will not eliminate this problem.

Whether monetary policy fails in general to implement the first best and what the reasons for that failure might be, is not clear. In any case, the result is evidently rather different from the one derived above. In the model studied in this section, the debt policy is equivalent to a lump-sum transfer scheme. The result derived above can be interpreted as showing that a transfer scheme alone can do better than a transfer scheme operating in conjunction with a market for a durable capital good. Bhattacharya, on the other hand, compares the allocation implemented by a transfer scheme with the allocation implemented by a monetary policy, both operating in conjunction with an independent investment technology.

The question remains of what can be done by means of debt policy to improve risk-sharing. What follows is a sketch of the efficient debt problem. Suppose that in some open neighborhood of the efficient debt instrument P^* we can solve the equilibrium value of q as a C^1 function of P, say $q = \zeta(P)$. Then P^* must be a local solution to the constrained maximization problem

$$\text{Max} \sum_{i=1}^n \lambda_i \{ U(-q_i - P_i) + \sum_{j=1}^n a_{ij} V(R_j + q_j + P_j) \}$$

s.t. $q = \zeta(P)$.

The first-order conditions are

$$-\lambda_i U'(-q_i - P_i) + \sum_{j=1}^n \lambda_j a_{ij} V'(R_j + q_j + P_j) + \mu_i = 0 \qquad (46)$$

and

$$-\lambda_i U'(-q_i - P_i) + \sum_{j=1}^{n} \lambda_j a_{ji} V'(R_j + q_j + P_j) + \sum_{j=1}^{n} \mu_j \zeta_{ji}(P) = 0 \qquad (47)$$

where μ_i is the Lagrange multiplier attached to the i-th equilibrium condition and $\zeta_{ij}(P) \equiv \partial \zeta_i(P)/\partial P_j$, for $i,j = 1,\ldots,n$. Comparing these two equations, we see they imply that

$$\mu_i = \sum_{j=1}^{n} \mu_j \zeta_{ji}(P) \qquad (48)$$

for $i = 1,\ldots,n$. In matrix notation,

$$\mu(I - D\zeta) = 0 \qquad (49)$$

where $D\zeta = [\zeta_{ij}]$. Comparing the first-order conditions with those for the efficient transfer problem, we see that they differ only in the terms involving the multipliers μ. If μ were zero, the solutions would be identical. In a precise sense, μ measures the wedge between the efficient transfer outcome and the outcome of the efficient debt policy.

Pagano (1988) has suggested that the government should issue securities that are negatively correlated with the market portfolio. This proposal has a family resemblance to the contingent bonds described above. Pagano's argument is that since the negatively correlated securities can be sold at a higher price than safe securities, the government would make a profit that would allow it to retire the debt. The argument is essentially partial equilibrium in nature. As we have seen, the problem of achieving a genuine welfare improvement may be more complicated than the partial equilibrium argument suggests. In the first place, one has to pay attention to the government's budget constraint and its implications for different generations' tax liabilities. Second, one has to pay attention to the general-equilibrium effects of the debt policy on prices. When these effects are taken into account it is not clear that issuing a security which is negatively correlated with the market portfolio will be sufficient to ensure an increase in welfare. At the very least, the securities will have to be carefully designed and the informational requirements may be beyond the capacity of the government.

9.5   Privately Issued Debt

We have so far assumed that the private sector is only capable of developing a rather rudimentary capital market. As a result, the government has been the only source of long-dated securities. In this framework it has been relatively easy to show how public debt policy can have far-reaching consequences for the risk-sharing possibilities in the economy. Financial innovation by the public sector can make markets more complete and under certain circumstances lead to Pareto improvements.

The point of these exercises is not to suggest that financial innovation is the prerogative of the public sector. That is clearly not the case. On the other hand, it may be that there are gaps in the market that public debt instruments can fill. What makes the preceding exercises rather artificial is that we have not provided any reasons why the private capital market should be incomplete in the first place. By assuming that the private capital market is restricted to a single instrument, we have artificially provided a large role for the government as a financial innovator. If, instead, we had started by assuming the existence of a highly sophisticated financial market, providing perfect substitutes for most of the securities issued by government, the conclusion could have been quite different. To justify the analysis of the preceding sections, one should at least provide an explanation of why the private capital market might be incomplete in the first place. There are two types of arguments that might be used to justify a role for the public sector as a financial innovator. One is that the government has some kind of comparative advantage in providing certain kinds of securities to the market. In that case, even if the private sector can provide these securities, it may be efficient to let the public sector do the job. The second kind of argument is concerned with the incentives for innovation in the private sector. Even if the private sector has the capacity to issue certain securities, it may choose not to do so. In that case, there may be a case for government provision. The first kind of argument will not be pursued here. Instead, we concentrate on the private incentives for financial innovation.

In a series of papers (Allen and Gale 1988, 1989a and 1989b), Franklin Allen and I have investigated some of the issues concerning efficient financial innovation. Under certain conditions it appears that, in a competitive equilibrium, financial innovation is constrained efficient. What this means is that a planner, who was subject to the same technology, could not make everyone better off. However, the circumstances in which the equilibrium market structure will be efficient are restrictive. For example, it must be assumed that no short sales are allowed or that short sales are so costly that they are effectively bounded. If unlimited short sales are allowed, there are strong reasons for believing that the perfect competition assumption will not be satisfied. In Allen and Gale (1989a) it is shown that when unlimited short sales are allowed, the number who innovate in equilibrium may be small, even if the number of potential innovators is large. In order to give adequate incentives to innovate, it is necessary that the innovators have some monopoly power. But this implies that in equilibrium the number of securities is too small.

Part of the explanation of this inefficiency is that innovators create positive externalities. In a competitive equilibrium they may not be able to internalize these externalities and so they cannot extract all the rents from their innovation. One might think that a monopolist would have a better chance to introduce an efficient market structure. Allen and Gale (1989b) examine a situation where the innovator has a monopoly that allows him to extract all the rents from the innovation. Nonetheless, it turns out that in this situation as well, the equilibrium market structure may still be inefficient. The social value of the innovation is measured by the maximum amount the investors are willing to pay for the innovation before it occurs. The problem is that, since the innovation may have general-equilibrium effects, the surplus to be extracted after the innovation may be different from the surplus that existed ex ante. As a result, there may be too much or too little innovation.

There are some differences between the models described in Allen and Gale (1988, 1989a and 1989b) and the ones employed here. The former are restricted to two time-periods and trade only occurs in the first of these periods. Also, financial innovation consists of issuing securities with different patterns of returns across states of nature at the second date. In the present class of models, only non-contingent debt instruments are traded, but investors can adopt dynamic trading strategies which increase the possibilities of spanning states of nature. Because of these structural differences one must be careful about drawing analogies between the two classes of models. Nonetheless, it appears that similar arguments do apply in the present context.

A complete analysis of (private sector) financial innovation is out of place here. Instead, an extended example is analyzed to illustrate the sort of things that can happen. The point of this example is to show that even if the private sector can produce a socially desirable security, there may not be an incentive for any individual or institution to produce it. The example is constructed to demonstrate this point in the simplest possible way, but the same phenomenon will occur in more realistic contexts.

There are assumed to be three agents, two investors indexed $i = 1, 2$ and an entrepreneur indexed $i = 3$. The entrepreneur represents a large firm, say, General Motors, which has the capacity to issue securities with characteristics similar to public debt. There are three dates indexed $t = 1, 2, 3$. The entrepreneur's endowment can be interpreted as the firm's revenues. The entrepreneur has an endowment of goods at dates 2 and 3, but he only values consumption at the first date. Since the entrepreneur only values consumption at the first date, he will want to sell his future endowment in exchange for consumption at the first date. More precisely, he will sell securities which are claims against the future endowment.

Each agent $i = 1, 2, 3$ has a von Neumann–Morgenstern utility function $W_i(c_1, c_2, c_3)$, where c_t denotes consumption at date $t = 1, 2, 3$. By assuming that $W_i(c_1, c_2, c_3) = -\infty$ if $c_t < 0$ for some $t = 1, 2, 3$, we can restrict attention to the case where $(c_1, c_2, c_3) \in \mathbf{R}_+^3$. The three utility functions are assumed to satisfy:

$$W_1(c_1, c_2, c_3) = c_3 \tag{50}$$

$$W_2(c_1, c_2, c_3) = c_1 + u(c_3), \quad \text{where} \quad u'(1) = 1 \tag{51}$$

$$W_3(c_1, c_2, c_3) = c_1 \tag{52}$$

for any $(c_1, c_2, c_3) \in \mathbf{R}_+^3$. The function $u(\cdot)$ is assumed to satisfy all the usual neoclassical properties. The agents' endowments are given by:

$$e_1 = (1, 0, 0) \tag{53}$$

$$e_2 = (2, 0, 0) \tag{54}$$

$$e_3 = (0, 1, 1). \tag{55}$$

A single producer maximizes profits subject to the usual constant returns to scale investment technology. At date 1 the return to investment is assumed to be $R_1 = 0$. At date 2 the return to investment is random, taking the values $r_H = 1.5$ and $r_L = 0.5$ with equal probability. The producer earns zero profits in equilibrium.

There is assumed to be a market for one-period bills at each date. Investors can save (buy bills) but they cannot borrow (issue bills). Investors can also purchase securities issued by the entrepreneur but they cannot take short positions. The producer issues one-period bills in order to finance production.

The investors take prices as given and trade the available securities at each date in order to maximize expected utility. (Each of the investors represents a continuum of identical agents.) The entrepreneur, on the other hand, is a genuinely "big" agent.

To keep things simple, the entrepreneur is only given two options. The first is to sell equity only. One unit of equity entitles the holder to the endowment stream e_3. The other option is to split the endowment stream into two pieces, $(0, 1, 0)$ and $(0, 0, 1)$, and sell them separately. This option corresponds to issuing a one-period bill with face value of one unit and one unit of levered equity.

Suppose the entrepreneur chooses to issue two securities at the first date. Both securities sell for a price of one unit. Investor 1 buys all of the one-period bills and investor 2 buys all of the two-period bills. At date 2, investor 2 receives one unit of consumption. Since he does not value consumption at date 2 he will reinvest the entire amount and consume the proceeds at date 3. The supply of one-period bills at date 2 comes from the producer, so the price of one-period bills at date 2 is determined by the investment technology, i.e., the price is $1/R_2$. Investor 2 holds his security for the full two periods and consumes the dividend at date 2.

To see that this is an equilibrium, note first of all that the expected rate of return on both assets at date 1 is zero if they are held to maturity. Since investor 1 is risk-neutral his action is optimal at date 1. Investor 2 is also behaving optimally at date 1 since the marginal utility of consumption is one at dates 1 and 3. At date 2, it is optimal for investor 1 to reinvest everything and for investor 2 to hold on to his one-period bills. At date 3 they can only consume. The value of the firm in this equilibrium is $V = 2$.

Now suppose that there is only one security (equity). Both investors must now hold the same security at date 1. Furthermore, there is no opportunity to trade at date 2. As before, the dividends received at date 2 must be reinvested. The supply of one-period bills at date 2 must come from the producer so the price of one-period bills will be determined by the investment technology. Once the rate of return on investment is observed at date 2, the uncertainty has disappeared so there is no possibility of hedging. Each agent can only reinvest his dividend and hold on to the bills purchased at date 1. Without loss of generality, we can treat a unit of equity as a claim to $(1 + R_2)$ units of consumption at date 3, since we know the interim dividends will be reinvested at the rate R_2. If V is the price of equity at date 1 and E is the quantity held by investor 2, the first order condition that must be satisfied for an interior optimum is:

$$V = \{u'(2.5E)2.5 + u'(1.5E)1.5)\}/2. \tag{56}$$

Since investor 1 will use all of his first-period endowment to buy equity, the market-clearing condition is:

$$1 = V(1 - E). \tag{57}$$

It is easy to see that these two equations have a unique solution (V^*, E^*) with $0 < V^*$ and $0 < E^* < 1$. Furthermore, $V^* > 2$ if we assume that:

$$\{u'(1.25)2.5 + u'(0.75)1.5)\}/2 > 2 \tag{58}$$

which is consistent with $u'(1) = 1$. Thus, the value of the firm is higher when there is only one security.

The equilibrium with two securities is obviously Pareto-efficient because all the risk at date 3 is borne by the risk-neutral investor. In the equilibrium with one security, the risk-averse investor bears some risk at date 3. As a result that equilibrium is Pareto-inefficient. Thus, the entrepreneur has the ability to choose an effectively complete market structure that leads to an efficient equilibrium. But it is in his interest to choose an incomplete market structure that leads to an inefficient equilibrium. This is not to say that the two-security equilibrium Pareto-dominates the one-security equilibrium, since the entrepreneur is better off in the latter. However, a transfer at the first date could make everyone better off in the two-security equilibrium than he was in the one-security equilibrium. In this sense, the one-security equilibrium is not constrained efficient.

This brief discussion is obviously inadequate to settle any issues about the role of the government as a financial innovator. That important question must be left to future research. Another question that has not even been mentioned, is why the government would want to use debt policy to affect risk-sharing opportunities, rather than using lump-sum transfers. Bhattacharya (1982), in an intriguing and suggestive paper, has suggested that incomplete information may be the explanation. Asset markets may solve some of the incentive problems better than the available alternative institutions. This is an idea that should certainly be followed up. However, even if one finds the use of debt policy as a tool for achieving optimal risk-sharing fanciful, there is little doubt that the public debt does have an impact on risk-sharing opportunities. Understanding this mechanism would seem to be important for the formulation of sound policy.

Note

An earlier version of this chapter was presented at a seminar at the Wharton School. I am grateful to the participants for their comments. The discussants at the Castelgandolfo conference, Olivier Blanchard and Sudipto Bhattacharya, also made helpful comments.

References

Abel, A., G. Mankiw, L. Summers and R. Zeckhauser (1989). "Assessing Dynamic Efficiency," *Review of Economic Studies* 56, 1–20.

Allen, F. and D. Gale (1988). "Optimal Security Design," *Review of Financial Studies* 1, 229–263.

————. (1989a). "Arbitrage, Short Sales and Financial Innovation," Rodney L. White, Center for Financial Research, University of Pennsylvania, Working Paper.

————. (1989b). "Incomplete Markets and the Incentives to Set Up an Options Exchange." *Geneva Papers on Risk and Insurance*, forthcoming.

Barro, R. (1974). "Are Bonds Net Wealth?," *Journal of Political Economy* 82, 1095–118.

————. (1979). "On the Determination of Public Debt," *Journal of Political Economy* 87, 940–71.

Bhattacharya, S. (1982). "Aspects of Monetary and Banking Theory and Moral Hazard," *Journal of Finance* 37, 371–84.

Bohn, H. (1988a). "A Positive Theory of Foreign Currency Debt," Rodney L. White, Center for Financial Research, University of Pennsylvania, Working Paper 19–88.

————. (1988b). "Tax Smoothing with Financial Instruments," Rodney L. White, Center for Financial Research, University of Pennsylvania, Working Paper 27–88.

————. (1988c). "Time Consistency of Monetary Policy in the Open Economy," Rodney L. White, Center for Financial Research, University of Pennsylvania, Working Paper 33–88.

Cass, D. (1972). "On Capital Overaccumulation in the Aggregative, Neoclassical Model of Economic Growth: A Complete Characterization," *Journal of Economic Theory* 4, 200–23.

Chamley, G. and H. Polemarchakis (1984). "Asset Markets, General Equilibrium and the Neutrality of Money," *The Review of Economic Studies* 51, 129–38.

Diamond, P. (1965). "National Debt in a Neoclassical Growth Model," *American Economic Review* 55, 1125–50.

Fischer, S. (1983). "Welfare Aspects of Government Issue of Indexed Bonds," in R. Dornbusch and M. Simonsen (eds.), *Inflation, Debt and Indexation*, Cambridge MA: MIT Press, 223–46.

Gale, D. (1988). "Underinvestment and the Demand for Liquid Assets," University of Pittsburgh, mimeo.

Lucas, R. and N. Stokey (1983). "Optimal Fiscal and Monetary Policy in an Economy without Capital," *Journal of Monetary Economics* 12, 55–93.

————. (1987). "Money and Interest in a Cash-in-Advance Economy," *Econometrica* 55, 491–514.

Pagano, M. (1988). "The Management of Public Debt and Financial Markets," in F. Giavazzi and L. Spaventa (eds.), *High Public Debt: the Italian Experience*, Cambridge: Cambridge University Press, 135–66.

————. (1984). "Stationary Pareto Optimality of Stochastic Equilibria with Overlapping Generations," *Journal of Economic Theory* 34, 396–403.

————. (1985). "Stochastic Inflation and Government Provision of Indexed Bonds," *Journal of Monetary Economics* 15, 291–308.

Scheinkman, J. (1980). "Notes on Asset Trading in an Overlapping Generations Model," University of Chicago, mimeo.

Tobin, J. (1971). "An Essay on the Principles of Debt Management," In *Essays in Economics*, Vol. 1, Chicago: Markham.

Wallace, N. (1981). "A Modigliani-Miller Theorem for Open Market Operations," *American Economic Review* 71, 267–74.

Weiss, L. (1979). "The Effects of Money Supply on Economic Welfare in the Steady State," *Econometrica* 48, 565–76.

10 Standard Securities

Douglas Gale

10.1 Introduction

When firms raise external capital by issuing securities, they almost always use one of a small number of financial instruments: debt, equity, convertible debt, preferred shares, warrants, etc. There are undoubtedly many explanations for this stylized fact, but they all suggest that the firm reaps some private gains from standardization. In this chapter, I want to investigate one source of private gains from standardization, the informational costs of learning about new securities. Buying a new security involves uncertainty in the same way that buying any new product involves uncertainty. This uncertainty may reduce the price that investors are willing to pay for the security. In other words, investors charge an "uncertainty premium" for holding the unfamiliar security. By issuing standard securities, with which investors are already familiar, firms avoid paying this uncertainty premium. As a result, the value of the firm is higher if it issues standard securities.

The existence of private gains from standardization raises the possibility of coordination failure: there may be too much standardization. The argument is simple. Consider an equilibrium in which all firms are issuing standard securities. Suppose that a single firm wants to issue a "non-standard" security. Without further information, investors will not be willing to pay a price that will induce the deviant firm to issue the security. The question then is whether it is worthwhile for the investors to become informed. It may not be. If an investor makes a large investment in the new security, he is taking on a large amount of the idiosyncratic risk associated with that particular firm. On the other hand, if he buys a small amount of the new security, his surplus from the transaction will not compensate him for the cost of becoming informed. Thus, he may not wish to become informed. As a result, the price of the security remains low and the firm, anticipating this, decides not to issue the non-standard security. Thus, only standard securities are issued in equilibrium.

Another story can be told, however. Suppose that a large number of firms decided to issue the "non-standard" securities. Then it might be

This chapter originally appeared in *Review of Economic Studies* 59 (1992) 731–755. © 1992 The Review of Economic Studies Limited. Reprinted by permission.

worthwhile for the investors to become informed. They could avoid the idiosyncratic risk attached to individual firms by diversifying and at the same time recoup the cost of becoming informed by purchasing a large number of the new securities. Then the price of the non-standard securities will be higher and the firms will find it worthwhile to issue them. We have found a second equilibrium in which all firms issue the "non-standard" securities, i.e., the "non-standard" securities become the standard ones.

What these arguments suggest and what turns out to be the case is that there may be multiple equilibria and that some of these equilibria may be unattractive from a welfare point of view.

Although the arguments sketched above are quite simple, perhaps deceptively so, in attempting to make them precise one encounters technical and conceptual difficulties. In particular, the modeling of uncertainty requires some care. We need a framework in which information creates an externality and prices do not reveal all the relevant information. The model described in the chapter is one way of resolving these difficulties and making precise the ideas outlined above; there are undoubtedly other ways.

The analysis of the chapter is carried out in a standard competitive framework. Three main results are proved.

(I)   There always exists a competitive equilibrium and furthermore at least one of the equilibria is constrained efficient.

(II)   If the costs of acquiring information are zero (or, equivalently, investors have complete information or there is no information to be had) then every competitive equilibrium is constrained efficient.

(III)   When information costs are non-zero, there may exist competitive equilibria which are not constrained efficient. In fact, there may exist Pareto-ranked equilibria.

The message is that uncertainty about innovative securities matters. The cost of acquiring information about new securities produces private gains from standardization that in turn may lead to coordination failure.

Although the chapter focusses on theoretical issues, it may be helpful to give a couple of examples to illustrate the empirical relevance of these ideas. The first example is the introduction of *original issue discount* (*OID*) bonds.[1] These bonds were issued in large numbers by firms in the early 1980s. At that time, the tax code allowed interest to be amortized on a straight-line basis that took no account of compounding. When interest rates rose substantially, this provision created an extremely profitable opportunity for tax arbitrage.[2] The tax code was altered by *TEFRA* in 1982 and firms stopped issuing the OID bonds. However, even after the removal of the tax-arbitrage opportunity, there was a demand for the bonds and investment banks supplied the market by stripping the interest from conventional bonds.[3] Evidently the experience gained by the market had created a demand for a previously unfamiliar asset. The "technology" of OID bonds was known prior to 1980, but it took the unusually large tax-arbitrage incentive to spur their introduction. However, once introduced, the experience gained by the market eliminated the uncertainty premium and demand remained.

The second example suggests that even a "standard" (old) security may have an uncertainty premium attached to it. Hirshleifer (1988) has analysed a model of futures markets in which investors have to pay a fixed setup cost to operate in the market. He interprets this fixed cost as representing the unfamiliarity of some investors with commodity futures. In equilibrium, the fixed cost causes residual risk to be priced.[4] The pricing of residual risk is related to the hedging positions of commodity producers. In a recent paper, Bessembinder (1990) has verified empirically that there is a significant relationship between residual risk and hedging positions and commodity risk premia. This evidence supports the hypothesis of market segmentation, which can be explained by the information costs of trading unfamiliar securities.[5]

The focus of the present chapter is on the problem of security design in the context of corporate finance. But as suggested above, the ideas developed in the chapter may have a wider application. In particular, the tremendous amount of financial innovation that has occurred in recent years raises questions about the possibility of coordination failure in alternative institutional settings. Do different institutional settings imply different incentives to innovate? Is it possible that innovations in other institutional settings may be a substitute for the failure of firms to innovate? These issues are discussed further at the end of the chapter. Although they are interesting and somewhat related to the subject of this chapter, they go far beyond its limited scope. Throughout most of the chapter, then, the focus will be on the narrower question of why firms use a limited set of securities despite the apparent gains from tailoring securities to the tastes of individual investors.

Security Design in a Model of Incomplete Markets

The analysis begins with a simple security design problem. In order to finance their operations, firms can issue a variety of securities. In a competitive market, they will choose the securities that maximize the value of the firm. The problem for the firm is to find the financial structure that will maximize its market value. As a paradigm of this kind of decision, consider the case of an entrepreneur who owns 100 percent of the equity in a firm. For some reason, the entrepreneur wants to sell the firm. If markets are complete, the firm will have a unique market value that is independent of its financial structure. It will not matter whether the entrepreneur issues equity alone or issues some combination of debt and levered equity. The amount that is realized from the sale of the firm will be the same in either case.

If markets are incomplete, however, the value of the firm may depend on the form in which it is sold. More precisely, it may be possible to increase the value of the firm by issuing different claims against the future revenues of the firm. Because markets are incomplete, different investors may value the same securities differently at the margin.[6] By "splitting" the firm and marketing each piece to the "clientele" that values it most, the market value may be greater than if the firm were sold in one piece. For example, by selling debt to one group and levered equity to another, the entrepreneur may realize a higher value than if he sold unlevered equity to one group only.

This kind of security design problem is studied by Allen and Gale (1988) in a general-equilibrium model with incomplete markets. There is assumed to be a large number of firms and investors. Each firm is owned by a single entrepreneur who wants to liquidate his assets in order to maximize current consumption. To do this he issues securities (claims against the future income of the firm). The securities are bought by the investors to provide for future consumption. Markets are competitive and information is complete. The only non-standard assumption is that firms can choose the number and kind of securities to issue. Allen and Gale show that, under certain conditions, the security-design decisions of firms are constrained efficient and that it is optimal for firms to issue "extremal" securities,[7] a form of securities that we do not see in practice. One of the motivations for the present chapter is to explain why firms may not use these securities.

The main innovation in the present model is that the assumption of complete information is dropped. Instead, it is assumed that investors can become informed about the properties of securities before they purchase them. The information that agents acquire is of a special kind. Since this process of information acquisition is at the heart of the model, I will try to motivate the ideas in a general way before getting down to the details of the model.

Product Uncertainty and Information Acquisition

When an investor purchases a familiar security, he is uncertain what the return will be. This uncertainty can be attributed mainly to the randomness of the return to the underlying asset. For example, even if he holds debt which promises a certain return, the randomness of the firm's revenues implies there is a positive probability of bankruptcy. When the investor purchases a new security, however, there is an additional source of uncertainty which is not traceable to the randomness of the underlying asset returns. Unlike the case of a risky but familiar security, the investor buying a genuinely novel security is uncertain exactly what he is buying. This kind of uncertainty will be referred to as *product uncertainty*.[8]

I assume that, in order to reduce uncertainty about new financial products, investors may acquire costly information. I shall be interested in cases where this information has two special features. The first is that the information acquired by the investors is *non-transferable*. It is either hard to communicate to other investors or is irrelevant to them. The second feature is that the information is *generic*: it concerns entire classes of securities rather than the particular security issued by a single entrepreneur. A few examples will make these ideas clear.

Consider first an example of information that is relevant only to a single individual. Suppose that an entrepreneur issues a new claim whose return is contingent on some macroeconomic variable, such as an exchange rate or an interest rate. If the investor does not know how these macroeconomic variables are correlated with his own income, say, he will be unable to evaluate the riskiness of the claim correctly. More precisely, there will be an additional source of riskiness in holding the security, arising from uncertainty about the impact of the new contingency. This extra risk can be reduced if the investor acquires information about the correlation between the macroeconomic variable and his income. But this information may not be of any interest to another investor.

Product uncertainty may also arise because a new type of claim requires general knowledge in order to be fully understood. Suppose, for example, that an entrepreneur issues a new security whose return is contingent on accounting data about the firm. An investor who is unfamiliar with accounting systems will have difficulty evaluating the riskiness of this asset. Although he may know a great deal about the firm, he does not know the implications of the contingencies that define the security.

Another example is a security involving unfamiliar legal provisions. These may be difficult for an investor to evaluate, either because they have not been tested in the courts or because the investor, having no experience of how these provisions work in practice, is unable to work out their implications in circumstances that he can foresee. In order to cope with these unfamiliar provisions, it may be necessary for an investor to acquire information about the legal system, what the relevant laws are, how the courts work and how they are likely to react to these provisions.[9] General knowledge of this kind is not easy to transfer from one person to another. In fact, without some initial knowledge of this kind, it may be impossible to understand what a more expert investor knows.

The fact that information is *generic* is important because it means that, in acquiring information about the claims issued by one entrepreneur, an investor is becoming informed about the claims issued by any other entrepreneur who chooses the same general kind of security. For example, if an investor acquires some knowledge of accounting systems, this knowledge will help him evaluate any claim whose payoff depends on the accounting data of the firm. Likewise, acquiring knowledge of the legal system will help the investor to evaluate any security which involves unfamiliar legal provisions.

The fact that the information is *non-transferable* means that each investor must acquire it for himself.[10] For example, if a claim is contingent on a macroeconomic variable, an investor must find out the correlation between his income and the macroeconomic variable on which the claim is contingent. This information is of no use to another investor whose income is uncorrelated with that of the first. There is little scope for delegation and the information cannot be revealed by prices.

The characteristics of genericity and non-transferability are crucial in generating the coordination failures discussed below.

The rest of the chapter is organized as follows. The basic modeling ideas are introduced informally in section 10.2 and illustrated with an example of coordination failure. A formal model is described in section 10.3. Section 10.4 describes financial equilibrium. The main efficiency results are stated in section 10.5. In section 10.6, alternative approaches and connections with the relevant literature are discussed. Proofs are found in the appendix.

10.2   Coordination Failure

In order to introduce the basic ideas, I start with a sketch of the model and an extended example. A more formal treatment begins in the next section. (Some readers may prefer to read the formal treatment first and then come back to the example.)

The Model

Time is divided into two periods, the present and the future. There is a single consumption good, which serves as the numeraire.

There is a large (countable) number of firms indexed by $n = 1, 2, \ldots$. Each firm generates a random income in the future but has no income in the present. The (future) income of firm n is represented by a random variable Z_n.

Each firm is owned by a single entrepreneur, who wants to liquidate his assets to maximize his present consumption. Obviously, the entrepreneur will want to maximize the market value of his firm. The entrepreneur "sells" the firm by issuing claims against its future income. In general, a claim is any promise to make a future payment, contingent on the state of nature. For present purposes, it is sufficient to consider claims that are functions of the firm's income: a claim is a function f that promises $f(z)$ units of consumption if the firm's income is $Z_n = Z$. The set of claims issued by the entrepreneur is called a financial structure. Let F denote the financial structure of the firm.[11]

To illustrate these ideas, consider a few examples. Suppose that the entrepreneur wants to issue unlevered equity only. Then he chooses a financial structure $F = \{f_0\}$ consisting of the single claim f_0 defined by putting

$$f_0(z) = z \quad \forall z.$$

If, on the other hand, he wanted to issue debt and levered equity, he would have to choose a financial structure $F = \{f_1, f_2\}$ containing two claims. Suppose that f_1 is debt with a face value of R and f_2 is equity. Then the claims are defined by putting

$$f_1(z) = \min\{z, R\} \quad \forall z$$

and

$$f_2(z) = \max\{z - R, 0\} \quad \forall z.$$

Investors have incomplete information about the claims issued by the entrepreneurs, but the information they lack is of a special kind. It is generic and non-transferable (cf. the discussion in the introduction). Incompleteness of information can be modeled in a variety of ways. A particular tractable way for present purposes is to model it as uncertainty about the investors' own characteristics. Modeling uncertainty in this way is really a metaphor for some deeper lack of knowledge on the part of investors. (See section 10.6 for a discussion of alternative approaches.)

Suppose that each investor has a random source of future income. The distribution of this future income is determined by the investor's type. If the investor does not know his own type, this creates an additional source of uncertainty about the value of a new claim. Suppose there is a finite set K of types of investors. Each investor of type k receives a random future income of Y_k. Uncertainty about k implies uncertainty about the distribution of Y_k and this in turn implies uncertainty about the investor's induced preferences over portfolios. Obviously, information about an investor's type is of value to him; but it is not of value to anyone else (it is non-transferable). Also, it affects his preferences for all securities (it is generic).

For simplicity, all investors are assumed to have the same von Neumann–Morgenstern utility function $U(c_1, c_2)$, where c_1 is present consumption and c_2 is future consumption.

Investors can purchase information about their types. Since information is costly, their incentives to acquire information will depend on the securities that are available.

A competitive equilibrium for this economy is defined in the usual way. All agents take the prices of all securities as given. Entrepreneurs choose the financial structure that will maximize the market value of their firms and hence maximize their current consumption. Investors decide what information to purchase and then demand those securities that will maximize their expected utility, conditional on their information about preferences, subject to their budget constraints. At the prevailing prices, all markets clear.

The one non-standard aspect of equilibrium is the treatment of markets. Each claim issued by a firm is, strictly speaking, a unique commodity, because it contains idiosyncratic risk. But here, it is convenient to treat securities that are the same except for an i.i.d. component as identical and have them traded on the same market. The reason is that, in equilibrium, investors will want to diversify completely across such securities, which in the limit means that they will hold an infinitesimal amount of each. It is therefore convenient to describe their portfolios in terms of total demand for such securities. Note that the attractiveness of any type of security will depend on the number of independent entrepreneurs issuing it. This will turn out to be a crucial feature of the model. Although there is assumed to be a market-clearing price for all securities, i.e., all markets are open, if firms choose not to issue a security the investor conjectures correctly that there is no possibility of diversifying the idiosyncratic risk.[12]

To illustrate these ideas, I now describe an extended example.

An Example

There are two macroeconomic states $s = 1, 2$, occurring with equal probability. These states should be thought of as economy-wide shocks that affect the distribution of incomes for firms and investors. There are two types of firms, $j = 1, 2$, and half the firms are of each type. A firm's type is common knowledge. Firm n's future income is represented by the random variable Z_n. The family of random variables $\{Z_n\}$ is assumed to be independently distributed conditional on the macroeconomic state s. If firm n is of type j, then Z_n has the distribution

$$Z_n = \begin{cases} 3 & \text{w. pr. } 1/2 \text{ if } s = j; \\ 1 & \text{w. pr. } 1/2 \text{ if } s = j; \\ 1 & \text{w. pr. } 1 \text{ if } s \neq j. \end{cases}$$

Note each firm has higher expected income in one state than in the other and that there is idiosyncratic risk in the firm's income in the high state. The incomes of the two types of firms are negatively correlated so there is no aggregate uncertainty. For example, in state 1, firms of type 2 have one unit of income each while firms of type 1 have expected incomes of two units. Since there is a large number of firms of each type, the law of large numbers ensures that the income per firm in state 1 is 1.5. The same calculation can be made in state 2, with the types reversed, so income per firm is independent of the macroeconomic state.

There are two financial structures, one consisting of unlevered equity and the other consisting of debt and levered equity. Formally, the financial structures are denoted by $F_1 = \{f_0\}$ and $F_2 = \{f_1, f_2\}$, where

$$f_0(z) = z \quad \forall z;$$

$$f_1(z) = \min\{1, z\} \quad \forall z;$$

$$f_2(z) = z - f_1(z) \quad \forall z.$$

These securities are all quite standard nowadays. The reader should use his imagination to see them as stand-ins for something more exotic. (The trouble is that in such a simple example all the claims one can think of (warrants, preferred stock, convertible debt, etc.) tend to look pretty much the same. Nonetheless, these securities illustrate the basic idea perfectly well.)

There are three types of investors, indexed by $k = 0, 1, 2$. Investors' risk preferences are represented by a von Neumann–Morgenstern utility function

$$U(c_1, c_2) = c_1 + V(c_2)$$

where V has the usual properties.[13] Each investor is assumed to have a sufficiently large first-period income so that, in equilibrium, his first-period consumption is strictly positive. Each type of investor has a different distribution of future income. Type 0 investors have no future income. Type 1 investors have an income of 0 if $s = 1$ and 2 if $s = 2$. Type 2 investors have an income of 2 if $s = 1$ and 0 if $s = 2$.

The stochastic structure of the example is summarized in table 10.1.

It is clear from the data in table 1 that investors of type 0 may be expected to have a preference for debt and that investors of type $k = 1, 2$ may have a preference for levered equity issued by firms of type $j = k$.

Let v_k denote the proportion of investors of type k. It is assumed that $v = (v_0, v_1, v_2) = (\frac{1}{2}, \frac{1}{4}, \frac{1}{4})$, that is, $\frac{1}{2}$ are of type 0, $\frac{1}{4}$ are of type 1 and $\frac{1}{4}$ are of type 2. Investors of type 0 are assumed to know their type. Investors of types 1 and 2 are initially ignorant of their types; they assign equal probability to being type 1 or type 2. By incurring a small cost $c > 0$, they can learn their types with certainty.

There are two types of equilibrium in this example. In the first, all firms choose the financial structure F_2 and all investors of types $k = 1, 2$

Table 10.1
Incomes of firms and investors

	States	
	$s = 1$	$s = 2$
Types of firms		
$j = 1$	$\begin{cases} 3 \text{ w. pr. } 1/2 \\ 1 \text{ w. pr. } 1/2 \end{cases}$	1
$j = 2$	1	$\begin{cases} 3 \text{ w. pr. } 1/2 \\ 1 \text{ w. pr. } 1/2 \end{cases}$
Types of Investors		
$k = 0$	0	0
$k = 1$	0	2
$k = 2$	2	0

choose to become informed. In the second, all firms choose F_1 and none of the investors becomes informed. The first equilibrium will be shown to Pareto-dominate the second.

An Efficient Equilibrium

Suppose that all entrepreneurs choose the financial structure F_2 for their firms. A unit of f_1 promises one unit of consumption whatever the state. A unit of f_2 issued by a firm of type j promises nothing in state $s \neq j$ and two units with probability $\frac{1}{2}$ in state $s = j$. However, by diversifying across firms of the same type, an investor can eliminate idiosyncratic risk and be sure of getting 0 in state $s \neq j$ and 1 in state $s = j$. So there are effectively three securities, riskless debt and two Arrow securities.

   Suppose that all investors who know they belong to type 1 or type 2 decide to learn their true types. Suppose further that all the debt is purchased by investors of type 0 and that all the levered equity issued by firms of type j is purchased by investors of type $k = j$. In order for the market for each type of security to clear, each investor must purchase two units of his preferred security (diversified across all the firms issuing it). Then each type of investor will have a future consumption of 2 units for certain. Since this allocation is clearly Pareto-efficient and since investors' utility is linear in first-period consumption, we can find prices at which it is optimal for them to choose these portfolios. Let $P = (p_0, p_1, p_2)$, where p_i is the price of the claim f_i. Then put

$$p_0 = \tfrac{3}{2}V'(2), \qquad p_1 = V'(2) \quad \text{and} \quad p_2 = \tfrac{1}{2}V'(2).$$

Note that, since all investors have the same future consumption, they all have the same marginal valuation for these securities. Also, since their consumption is certain, they will value the securities at the margin as if they were risk-neutral. It is clear, then, that at these prices the first-order conditions for an optimum are satisfied.

At the prevailing prices, the market value of a firm is independent of its financial structure. So it is optimal for entrepreneurs to choose F_2 as assumed. There is no advantage in choosing the more complex financial structure because the example has been rigged to produce efficient risk sharing. Typically, we should expect that risk sharing is incomplete, in which case the financial structure will have some effect on the value of the firm.

Finally, we need to check that it is optimal for the investors to become informed. To do this, we first need to calculate the optimal portfolio for an investor of type 1, say, who does not become informed. Since all securities are priced as if investors were risk neutral, an uninformed investor cannot do better than to buy riskless debt. Then his problem is to choose the quantity of debt d_1 to maximize

$$\tfrac{1}{2}V(d_1) + \tfrac{1}{2}V(2 + d_1) - p_1 d_1.$$

Suppose that

$$p_1 = \tfrac{1}{2}[V'(1) + V'(3)].^{14} \tag{*}$$

Then it is clear that the optimal value of d_1 is 1. Let u^* denote the investor's surplus when he is informed and let u^{**} denote his surplus when he is uninformed, that is,

$$u^* = V(2) - 2p_2$$

and

$$u^{**} = \tfrac{1}{2}[V(1) + V(3)] - p_1.$$

Then the investor's decision is optimal if and only if

$$u^* - c \geq u^{**}.$$

Since V is strictly concave, $u^* > u^{**}$. The inequality will be satisfied for any $c > 0$ sufficiently small.

Since the equilibrium achieves efficient risk sharing, it seems likely that it is, in some sense, constrained efficient. This is indeed the case, but the proof is non-trivial. (See section 10.5.)

An Inefficient Equilibrium

Now suppose that all entrepreneurs choose a financial structure F_1 for their firms and that no investors choose to become informed. The only security issued is unlevered equity. By diversifying across firms of both types, all risk can be eliminated and a unit of (diversified) equity f_0 pays a sure return of $\frac{3}{2}$.

Suppose that the equilibrium prices are the same as in the previous equilibrium. The investors of type 0 will demand $\frac{4}{3}$ units of diversified unlevered equity and their future consumption will be 2 with certainty. In order to have market-clearing, each of the uninformed investors will have to demand $\frac{2}{3}$ units of f_0, which will give them a future income of 1 in their low state and 3 in their high state. The first-order condition that must be satisfied by an optimal portfolio is

$$p_0 = \tfrac{1}{2}[V'(1) + V'(3)]\tfrac{3}{2}.$$

But this is equivalent to (∗), so the market for unlevered equity will clear. Also, it will be optimal for these investors to demand none of the other securities f_1 and f_2. f_1 is identical to f_0 in a completely diversified portfolio; f_2 is risky but uncorrelated with the (uninformed) investors' income, so the appropriate first-order condition is

$$p_2 = \tfrac{1}{2}[V'(1) + V'(3)]\tfrac{1}{2}$$

and this is implied by the earlier assumption (∗). It also follows that the expected utility of uninformed investors is the same in the two equilibria.

It remains to show that the investors of types 1 and 2 could not be made better off by becoming informed. Suppose that an investor of type 1, say, learns his type. He is in the same position as an investor of his type in the efficient equilibrium, *except* that since there is not an infinite number of firms issuing levered equity he cannot obtain an Arrow security. In fact, the number of firms issuing f_2 is zero (or negligible) so there is some difficulty defining the returns to this security. Suppose that we assume that there is always at least one firm issuing any security. This is consistent with optimal behavior for almost all firms. Then the investor will demand d_1 units of riskless debt and d_2 units of levered equity, where the portfolio is chosen to maximize

$$\tfrac{1}{2}V(2 + d_1) + \tfrac{1}{4}V(d_1) + \tfrac{1}{4}V(d_1 + 2d_2) - p_1 d_1 - p_2 d_2.$$

Call the value of his surplus u^{***}. The crucial point is that the prices faced by the investor are the same as in the efficient equilibrium but, because of the presence of the idiosyncratic risk, he cannot do as well here as in the other equilibrium. That is, $u^* > u^{***}$. Then we can choose c so that

$$u^* - c > u^{**} > u^{***} - c.$$

With this assumption it is optimal for the uninformed investors to remain uninformed.

At the assumed prices, entrepreneurs are indifferent between the two financial structures.

Comparing the two equilibria, we see that the expected utilities of the entrepreneurs and of the investors of type 0 are the same. However, investors of types 1 and 2 are better off in the first equilibrium, since $u^* - c > u^{**}$. Note that because of the symmetry of the example, the two equilibria can be Pareto-ranked whether we make the welfare comparison on an ex ante or an ex post basis, i.e., before or after we know an investor's type.

10.3   The Model

This section begins the development of the formal theory with a description of the model and the assumptions needed for the subsequent analysis. The example discussed in the preceding section is not, strictly speaking, a special case of this model. The basic ideas, however, are the same.

There are two *dates*, indexed by $t = 1, 2$. At each date there is a single consumption good which serves as numeraire. Economic agents are either *entrepreneurs* or *investors*.

Each entrepreneur owns an asset which yields a random return, measured in terms of the consumption good, at the second date. There is a countable number of entrepreneurs indexed by $n = 1, 2, \ldots$. The return to asset n is represented by the random variable Z_n.

The definition of claims is somewhat more general than that allowed in the previous section. The payoff to a claim can depend on contingencies other than the return to the underlying asset. These contingencies might include macroeconomic variables such as interest rates, energy costs or exchange rates. The reason for including such contingencies is clear: they might be correlated with other risks against which investors want to hedge. Suppose that these contingencies are represented by a random vector X with values in $\mathbb{R}^m_+$. Then a claim is a function of the return to the underlying asset and the contingencies associated with the financial structure. Formally, a *claim* is a measurable function $f: \mathbb{R}_+ \times \mathbb{R}^m_+ \to \mathbb{R}_+$. If an entrepreneur issues a claim f against the income Z_n, then the payoff will be given by $f(Z_n, X)$.

There is a finite set of *financial structures* $\mathscr{F} = \{F_i: i \in I\}$. The contingencies associated with financial structure F_i are represented by the random vector X_i. Each financial structure F_i consists of a finite set of claims and the claims exhaust the return to the underlying asset, i.e. $\sum_{f \in F_i} f(Z_n, X_i) = Z_n$.

Issuing claims may be costly. Let C_i denote the cost of the financial structure F_i. Although it is not necessary for the theory, we assume there is a zero-cost financial structure that corresponds to the status quo. For example, this could be the structure consisting only of equity.

It is assumed that entrepreneurs are only interested in consumption at the first date. They maximize their current consumption by issuing claims against their future income.

There is a countable number of investors and a finite set K of investor *types*. Initially, investors are ignorant of their type. In fact, they are ex ante identical. They have a common prior distribution over types denoted by $v \in M(K)$.[15] Types are assumed to be independently distributed across investors. Then the law of large numbers ensures that the cross-sectional distribution of types is almost surely equal to v. Investors' preferences are represented by a von Neumann–Morgenstern utility function $U: \mathbb{R}^2_+ \to \mathbb{R}$. Each investor receives an income of $Y_0 > 0$ units of the consumption good at date 1. At the second date, an investor of type k receives a random income Y_k. To simplify the notation, it is assumed that investors of the same type have identical incomes, but this is not strictly necessary for the results.

Investors acquire information about their types by purchasing an *information structure*. Each information structure is a partitition of the set of types K. If an investor purchases the information structure H he learns the cell in which his true type lies. For example, in the preceding section, types 1 and 2 were uncertain about their type. The information structure available to them was $H = \{\{1\}, \{2\}\}$. By purchasing this information structure, they learned their true type. Not all information structures will reveal this much information. In general, an investor purchasing H learns that his true type belongs to some set $h \in H$. There is a finite set of information structures $\mathscr{H} = \{H_j: j \in J\}$. The cost of purchasing H_j is denoted by C_j.

Without loss of generality, we can assume that each investor purchases at most one information structure. By a suitable relabeling, each combination of structures can be treated as an information structure in its own right. With this convention, there must exist a null structure that gives no information and a maximal structure that is finer than every other structure.

All random variables are assumed to be defined on some underlying probability space $(\Omega, \mathcal{B}, \mu)$.[16] The first assumption says that asset returns are determined by a combination of macroeconomic and idiosyncratic shocks.

Assumption 1 There exists a random variable Z_∞ such that $\{X_i : i \in I\}$ and $\{Y_k \in K\}$ are Z_∞-measurable. Furthermore, there exists a family of random variables $\{\varepsilon_n : n \in N\}$ and a measurable function ζ, such that $\{\varepsilon_n\}$ are i.i.d. and independent of Z_∞ and $Z_\infty(\omega) = \zeta(\varepsilon_n(\omega), Z_\infty(\omega))$ for every ω in Ω and n in $\mathbb{N}$.

The random variable Z_∞ represents the macroeconomic or economy-wide shocks while the random variables ε_n represent the idiosyncratic shocks. The returns to each asset are functions of an idiosyncratic shock and an economy-wide shock. If a large number of entrepreneurs choose the same financial structure, the idiosyncratic risk can be eliminated through diversification. Suppose that an infinite number of entrepreneurs choose the structure F_i. The return to a well-diversified unit of security $a \in A_i$ will be given by

$$R_a = \lim_{N \to \infty} \frac{1}{N} \sum_{n=1}^{\infty} f_a(\zeta(\varepsilon_n, Z_\infty), X_i) = E[f_a(\zeta(\varepsilon_n, Z_\infty), X_i)|Z_\infty].$$

In deriving this formula, we can assume without loss of generality that all the entrepreneurs choose the same financial structure. The return R_a is obviously a function of Z_∞ in the limit.

Assumption 1 imposes a symmetry condition on the joint probability distribution of asset returns: although the assets are not necessarily perfect substitutes, they all make similar contributions to a well-diversified portfolio. Note that the example in section 10.2 did not satisfy assumption 1.[17]

The next two assumptions are in the nature of regularity conditions and are self-explanatory.

Assumption 2 U is defined on an open set containing $\mathbb{R}_+ \times \mathbb{R}_+$. It is continuously differentiable, concave and strictly increasing.

Assumption 3 For every n in $\mathbb{N}$, Z_n has a positive expected value and takes values in the interval $[0, \bar{z}]$ with probability one. For every k in K, Y_k has values in the interval $[0, \bar{y}]$ with probability one.

10.4 Financial Equilibrium

The equilibrium concept used in this section is essentially the familiar Walrasian competitive equilibrium. However, the definition of markets and commodities requires some care. At the first date, consumption and securities are traded (there is no need for trade at the second date). Securities are distinguished by their payoff functions and by the financial structures to which they belong, but not by the entrepreneur who issues them. Thus the set of securities can be indexed by $A = \{(f, i) \in F \times I \mid f \in F_i\}$. The various claims denoted by $a \in A$ need not be perfect substitutes: they may involve risk that is idiosyncratic to the issuer. For this reason, the investor who purchases securities of type a will be interested in the number of entrepreneurs who issue them, because he wants to diversify his holdings to eliminate this idiosyncratic risk. Thus, the number of entrepreneurs issuing security a in equilibrium is a key variable. Investors take this number as given, along with prices.

A difficulty arises when no entrepreneur issues a security of some type. How are investors to form their demands? One option is to treat the corresponding market as closed: no trade in that security is allowed at any price. But without a market-clearing price, how can entrepreneurs decide whether to issue the security? An alternative approach is adopted here. It is assumed that every financial structure is chosen by some entrepreneur. Then every market is open and every security has a market-clearing price. Since a finite set of entrepreneurs is negligible in this economy, this assumption is consistent with optimal behavior for "almost every" entrepreneur.[18]

Entrepreneurs' Behavior

For the reasons given above, we must distinguish between the *number* of entrepreneurs who choose a particular structure and the *proportion* who do so. Let $\alpha \in \Delta(I)$ denote the (normalized) cross-sectional distribution of financial structures, so that α_i is the proportion who chose F_i. Let $\alpha^* \in \Delta^*(I)$ denote the frequency distribution of financial structures, so that

α_i^* is the number of entrepreneurs who chose F_i in equilibrium. (α, α^*) is consistent if and only if $\alpha_i^* < \infty$ implies that $\alpha_i = 0$.[19]

A price system is a function $p\colon A \to \mathbb{R}_+$, with the interpretation that $p(a)$ is the price of one unit of security a in terms of consumption at date 1. Let P denote the set of price systems. Since entrepreneurs are only interested in consumption at date 1, they will choose a financial structure to maximize their first-period wealth net of issuing costs. Let $MV_i(p) = \sum_{f \in F_i} p(f, i)$ denote the market value of the claims associated with market structure F_i when the equilibrium prices are given by p. The entrepreneur seeks to maximize $MV_i(p) - C_i$ with respect to the choice of F_i. In equilibrium $\alpha_i > 0$ only if $MV_i(p) - C_i$ is a maximum. The cross-sectional distribution α is said to be *optimal* for entrepreneurs if and only if $\alpha \in \operatorname{Arg\,Max} \sum_{i \in I} (MV_i(p) - C_i)\alpha_i$.

Investors' Behavior

An investor chooses a portfolio of securities to maximize his expected utility. A portfolio is any function $d\colon A \to \mathbb{R}_+$. The interpretation of a portfolio requires some care: $d(a)$ is the total amount of securities of type a demanded from all entrepreneurs. Under the symmetry assumptions imposed in section 10.3, it is optimal for an investor to spread his demand for security a uniformly among the entrepreneurs selling it. Thus, if there are two entrepreneurs issuing security a, the investor will demand $d(a)/2$ units of the security from each of them. In what follows, it will always be assumed that investors spread their demand for a security evenly among the entrepreneurs supplying it. Let D denote the set of portfolios.

Let $W(d; \alpha^*)$ denote the total payoff to a portfolio $d \in D$ when the frequency distribution of financial structures is $\alpha^* \in \Delta^*(I)$. Obviously, $W(d; \alpha^*)$ is a random variable. It depends on α^* because the investor's total demand for a security $a \in A_i$ is spread across all the entrepreneurs offering that security. That is, he buys $d(a)/\alpha_i^*$ from each one.[20]

Next define an indirect utility function on $\mathbb{R}_+ \times D \times \Delta^*(I) \times K$ by putting

$$u(c, d; \alpha^*, k) = E[U(c, W(d, \alpha^*) + Y_k)]$$

$$\forall (c, d, \alpha^*, k) \in \mathbb{R}_+ \times D \times \Delta^*(I) \times K.$$

$u(c, d; \alpha^*, k)$ is the expected utility of an investor of type k who chooses a first-period consumption c and a portfolio d, taking as given the frequency distribution α^*. Let H denote the set of subsets of K. For any h in H, let

$$u(c, d; \alpha^*, h) = \sum_{k \in h} u(c, d; \alpha^*, h)v(k)/v(h)$$

denote the expected utility conditional on h.

The description of an investor's behavior is somewhat complicated by the fact that his choice of portfolio and current consumption depend on his information, which is random and depends on his choice of information structure. It is helpful to think of his decisions as being made sequentially. First, he chooses an information structure; then he observes an information set; then he chooses his portfolio and current consumption.

Since investors are ex ante identical, it is convenient to develop notation to describe the behavior of all investors simultaneously. Let β_j denote the proportion of investors who choose the information structure H_j and let $\beta = (\beta_j)_{j \in J}$ describe the choices of all investors. An *information set* is an ordered pair (h, j), with the interpretation that an investor observes (h, j) if he has chosen the information structure H_j and his type belongs to the set $h \in H_j$. The set of all information sets is denoted by $B = \{(h, j) \in H \times J \mid h \in H_j\}$. The set of information sets that can be observed after the choice of H_j is denoted by $B_j = \{b \in B \mid b = (h, j)\}$, for every j in J.

We have to specify a choice of portfolio and current consumption for every information set an investor could possibly observe. Let $\gamma(b)$ denote the choice of consumption level and let $\delta(b)$ denote the (unique) choice of portfolio at the information set b.

The investors' equilibrium choices can be represented by the functions $\gamma: B \to \mathbb{R}_+$, $\delta: B \to D$ and $\beta \in \Delta(J)$. The choice of (β, γ, δ) is *optimal* if it maximizes ex ante expected utility subject to the budget constraint, that is,

$$(\beta, \gamma, \delta) \in \arg\max \sum_{j \in J} \sum_{b \in B_j} u(\gamma(b), \delta(b); \alpha^*, \mathbb{H}(b))v((\mathbb{H}(b))\beta_j$$

$$\text{s.t.} \sum_{b \in B_j} v(\mathbb{H}(b))(\gamma(b) + p \cdot \delta(b) + C_j \leq Y_0 \quad \forall j \in J,$$

where $\mathbb{H}(b) \equiv \mathbb{H}((h, j)) \equiv h$ for any $b = (h, j) \in B$. Note the form of the budget constraint, which requires the investor to balance his budget across the information sets associated with each information structure.[21]

Market Clearing

The mean supply of a security $a = (f, i)$ is α_i. The mean demand for the security is $\sum_{j \in J} \beta_j \sum_{b \in B_j} \delta(a, b)v(\mathbb{H}(b))$. Markets clear if mean demand equals mean supply, that is, for each structure i in I,

$\alpha_i = \sum_{j \in J} \beta_j \sum_{b \in B_j} \delta(a, b) v(\mathbb{H}(b)) \quad \forall a \in A_i,$

where $A_i = F_i \times \{i\}$ denotes the set of securities associated with F_i. The array (α, β, δ) is said to be *feasible* if and only if (α, β, δ) satisfies the market-clearing condition.

Equilibrium

In equilibrium, entrepreneurs choose a financial structure to maximize current consumption, investors choose an information structure and portfolio to maximize expected utility and markets clear.

DEFINITION   A symmetric equilibrium is defined to be an array $\langle \alpha, \alpha^*, \beta, \gamma, \delta, p \rangle \in \Delta(I) \times \Delta^*(I) \times \Delta(J) \times \mathbb{R}_+^B \times D^B \times P$ satisfying the following equilibrium conditions:

(i) (β, δ) is optimal for investors, that is,

$$(\beta, \gamma, \delta) \in \arg\max \sum_{j \in J} \sum_{b \in B_j} u(\gamma(b), \delta(b); \alpha^*, \mathbb{H}(b)) v(\mathbb{H}(b)) \beta_j$$

$$\text{s.t.} \sum_{b \in B_j} v(\mathbb{H}(b))(\gamma(b) + p \cdot \delta(b) + C_j) \leq Y_0 \quad \forall j \in J;$$

(ii) (α, α^*) is consistent and α is optimal for entrepreneurs, that is,

$$\alpha \in \arg\max \sum_{i \in I} (MV_i(p) - C_i)\alpha(i);$$

(iii) (α, β, δ) is feasible, that is,

$$\alpha_i = \sum_{j \in J} \beta_j \sum_{b \in B_j} \delta(a, b) v(\mathbb{H}(b)) \quad \forall a \in A_i.$$

Note that in this definition, the only constraint on α^* is that it be consistent with α. In particular, if $\alpha_i = 0$, the only equilibrium condition is that α_i^* be finite. In a large economy, any finite number is negligible, but the number of entrepreneurs choosing to issue a particular type of claim does affect the returns to a diversified unit of that claim and hence the equilibrium price. In what follows, we focus on the extreme cases, $\alpha_i^* = 1$ and $\alpha_i^* = \infty$.

10.5   Efficiency

Since markets are incomplete, there is no reason to expect that equilibrium will be Pareto-efficient. On the other hand, the Pareto criterion may not be the relevant measure of efficiency because it assumes that resources can be reallocated without cost. If markets are incomplete, it is presumably because of the costs of making certain kinds of trades. Any alternative institutions will also be subject to some costs and this fact must be taken into account in framing an appropriate definition of efficiency. In this section a concept of constrained efficiency is used. Roughly speaking, an equilibrium is said to be constrained efficient if a planner could not do better using the same transactions technology, that is, subject to the same costs of information and the same costs of issuing claims.

An *allocation* is an array $\langle \alpha, \alpha^*, \beta, \gamma, \delta \rangle$ in $\Delta(I) \times \Delta^*(I) \times \Delta(J) \times \mathbb{R}_+^B \times D^B$. An allocation is said to be *attainable* if (α, β, δ) is feasible and (α, α^*) is consistent. A symmetric equilibrium $\langle \alpha, \alpha^*, \beta, \gamma, \delta, p \rangle$ is said to be *constrained efficient* if there does not exist an attainable allocation $\langle \hat{\alpha}, \hat{\alpha}^*, \hat{\beta}, \hat{\gamma}, \hat{\delta} \rangle$ satisfying the following conditions:

(i) $\sum_{b \in B_j} u(\hat{\gamma}(b), \hat{\delta}(b); \hat{\alpha}^*, \mathsf{H}(b)) v(\mathsf{H}(b))$

$$> \text{Max}_{j \in J} \sum_{b \in B_j} u(\gamma(b), \delta(b); \alpha^*, \mathsf{H}(b)) v(\mathsf{H}(b)) \quad (\forall j \in J, \hat{\beta}_j > 0)$$

and

(ii) $\sum_{j \in J} \hat{\beta}_j C_j + \sum_{i \in I} \hat{\alpha}_i C_i + \sum_{j \in J} \hat{\beta}_j \sum_{b \in B_j} \hat{\gamma}(b) v(\mathsf{H}(b))$

$$< \sum_{j \in J} \beta_j C_j + \sum_{i \in I} \alpha_i C_i + \sum_{j \in J} \beta_j \sum_{b \in B_j} \gamma(b) v(\mathsf{H}(b)).$$

The first inequality ensures that every investor is better off under the alternative allocation than he was in equilibrium. The second inequality ensures that the investors absorb fewer resources in toto under the alternative allocation than in equilibrium. Then it is possible, by some appropriate redistribution, to make every entrepreneur better off than he was in equilibrium.

Note that this concept of efficiency compares agents' welfare on an *ex ante* basis. That is, it compares the expected utility of investors after they have selected an information structure but before they have received their information. In equilibrium, all investors receive the same expected utility in this sense. An alternative notion of efficiency would make comparisons on an *ex post* basis. That is, it would calculate expected utilities conditional on the information set observed by the investor. The ex post efficiency concept is strictly weaker than the ex ante efficiency concept: an equilibrium is ex post constrained efficient if it is ex ante constrained efficient but the converse does not necessarily hold. Another alternative would be to compare utilities before the choice of information structure has been made; but in the present context, this apparently stronger notion is identical with the definition given above.

THEOREM 1   For any economy $\mathscr{E}$ satisfying the maintained assumptions, there exists a constrained efficient equilibrium.

The strategy of the proof is the following. Assume that $\alpha_i^* = \infty$ for every i in I. Then standard arguments can be used to show the existence of an equilibrium, relative to the assumed value of α^*. Note that for any financial structure F_i, if $\alpha_i = 0$ in equilibrium then any finite value of α_i^* can be substituted for $\alpha_i^* = \infty$. If demand is zero when a $\alpha_i^* = \infty$ then demand will remain zero when $\alpha_i^* < \infty$. Once this equilibrium has been found, it is easy to show that it is efficient.

THEOREM 2   Suppose that $\mathscr{E}$ is an economy satisfying the maintained assumptions. If $C_j = 0$ for every j in J, then any equilibrium of $\mathscr{E}$ is constrained efficient.

The equilibrium price of a security that is in zero supply must be high enough to make demand equal to zero. When there are no (fixed) costs of information, the market-clearing price must equal the value of a marginal unit to investors. Since investors are approximately risk-neutral for small risks the value of the security is independent of the number of entrepreneurs who issue it. This is enough to ensure that prices give the right signals to entrepreneurs.

Finally, it can be shown that a strong form of coordination failure is possible.

THEOREM 3   There exists an economy, satisfying the maintained assumptions, that has two Pareto-ranked equilibria.

Since the example of Section 2 does not satisfy some of the structural assumptions of the formal model, an alternative example of coordination failure is given in the appendix.

10.6   Discussion

Modeling Issues

The model analyzed in the chapter is similar to an Arrow–Debreu model in which the commodities traded consist of current consumption and securities. Constrained efficiency of the original model corresponds to Pareto-efficiency of the Arrow–Debreu model. Since markets are in some sense complete. the inefficiency of equilibrium is initially puzzling. The explanation involves the peculiar structure of markets in this model.

In the standard Arrow–Debreu model, all markets are *open*. That is, for every conceivable commodity, there is a price at which agents can buy and sell as much as they want. There may be no trade on some of these markets, but nonetheless there is a market-clearing price for each commodity. The situation is quite different in a market that is *closed*. If a market for some commodity is closed, there is no price at which that commodity can be bought or sold.

Because of the idiosyncratic risk in firms' incomes, claims with the same payoff functions issued by two different firms are really different commodities. We treat them as if they were the same, because in a well-diversified portfolio they will be the same. But they are not the same if the portfolio is not well-diversified. If claims were distinguished by the firm that issued them as well as by their other characteristics, we would have to say that some markets were *closed* and some were *open*. If a firm does not issue a particular type of security, there is no price at which investors can buy that security from *that* firm. Conversely, if markets for all claims, so defined, were assumed to be open, regardless of the decisions of the firms, then all equilibria would be efficient. The reason is simply that in equilibrium residual risk will not be priced.[22]

A comparison with the inefficiency results of Hart (1980) and Makowski (1980) is revealing. Hart and Makowski showed that, even in a large economy characterized by price-taking behavior, firms may not have the right incentives to introduce new commodities. The essential idea can be illustrated by a simple example. Suppose that nuts and bolts can only be produced by separate firms. Suppose further that neither commodity has any value without the other. Then there will exist an equilibrium in which neither nuts nor bolts are produced. Each firm perceives that if it produces a positive amount of its product, the equilibrium price will be zero because the complementary product is not produced. Since firms do not coordinate their actions, it is an equilibrium for each firm to produce nothing.

Two assumptions are crucial for the Hart–Makowski result. The first is that markets are *closed* if a good is not produced. For example, if nuts are not produced then consumers cannot buy nuts at any price. In the equilibrium described above, firms anticipate a zero price for their product. But if consumers thought that they could buy as much as they wanted at these prices, the equilibrium would be destroyed.

The second crucial assumption is that marginal utility is discontinuous on the boundary of the consumption set. In the present model, by contrast, preferences are assumed to be "well-behaved." As a result, we obtain efficiency when there are no information costs (theorem 2 above). Information costs are crucial in generating coordination failure.

In many economic settings, the order in which agents make their moves may be important in determining the outcome. In a perfectly competitive model, such as the one studied in this chapter, the order of moves does not matter. All that agents care about is the prices at which they can trade. Since these prices are treated as parameters by the agents and are known with certainty, it does not matter when the agents decide which action to take. It is worth thinking about the timing of moves because there are plenty of examples from game theory where the order of moves makes a big difference. For example, think of a dynamic game in which a finite number of entrepreneurs move in a fixed sequence. If everyone but the last entrepreneur has chosen F_2, then it will be optimal for the last to choose F_2 as well. Then by backward induction, one could show that all will do so. This kind of reasoning depends crucially on having a last period, a finite number of entrepreneurs and a fixed order. Without these assumptions, the coordination problem would be just as severe as in the competitive model. Whether one deals with competitive models (where the order of moves does not matter) or strategic models (where it does) the coordination problem seems to be robust.

Another issue that deserves comment is the treatment of investors' uncertainty about the nature of securities. In the model, I have followed the usual reductionist approach of modeling "uncertainty" as if it were "risk." This approach has the advantage that there is no need to introduce nonstandard assumptions and the model is easily compared to the existing literature. On the other hand, some of the flavour of the ideas discussed in the Introduction is lost. Bewley (1989) has taken a different approach and used an alternative decision-theoretic framework to study innovation. In Bewley's theory, an agent's beliefs are characterized by a *set* of probability distributions. The agent will choose a given alternative to the *status quo* only if it yields higher expected utility evaluated according to each of these distributions. This implies a rather extreme incompleteness of preferences and places a lot of weight on the *status quo*. As a result, the theory has limited predictive power and behavior is strongly history-dependent. Bewley's distinction between risk and uncertainty is extremely interesting in its own right but the incompleteness of agents' preferences would make the analysis of the present chapter difficult. That is one of the costs of abandoning the standard framework.

Product Uncertainty and Financial Innovation

There has been a tremendous amount of financial innovation in recent years. Most of this innovation has been carried out by commercial and investment banks or by organized financial exchanges, rather than by firms issuing new securities.[23] It is natural to ask whether the lessons of the present analysis have any relevance to these quite different institutional settings.

The first point to note is that the incentives to innovate are quite different in different institutional settings. A couple of examples will make this clear. In the model described in this chapter, a firm's incentive to issue different securities comes from their effect on the value of the firm. The incentive to set up an exchange for the trading of a new stock option or futures contract comes from the commissions that will be collected on every trade. These incentives are quite different and lead to different behavior. The firm that issues a new security may not be able to capture all the rents that are generated by the introduction of the new security. This will be a source of inefficiency (Allen and Gale 1991). A commodity exchange may or may not be able to capture all the rents from the introduction of a new option or futures contract (Allen and Gale 1990; Duffie and Jackson 1989). Furthermore, the presence of imperfect competition may lead to inefficient innovation, either too much or too little. In any case, it is clear that each institutional setting leads to its own problems and requires its own modelling strategy.

What I think is robust is the notion that product uncertainty is a factor in determining the incentives to innovate in a variety of settings, whether the innovation is undertaken by "firms" or financial institutions. Ross (1989), for example, has emphasized the importance of marketing in determining not only the extent but the form of financial innovation. The function of marketing is to reduce the uncertainty premium on a new security. The work of Hirshleifer and Bessembinder, referred to earlier, suggests there may be uncertainty premia even in markets for "old" securities.

Other Examples of Coordination Failure

There is a large class of economic and social phenomena that involve some sort of "critical mass" behavior (see Schelling 1978 for a wide-ranging survey). These all have a family resemblance, to each other and to the model described in the present chapter; but they differ widely in the exact nature of the externality that leads to the coordination failure. It is the differences that are interesting. One of the major differences between the model described in this chapter and many of the models found in the literature is that here the behavior of the mass has no direct impact on the preferences of an individual agent. We are dealing with a purely pecuniary externality. Nonetheless, some parallels are worth mentioning.

The macroeconomic literature has produced a number of examples of coordination failure.[24] These models typically produce multiple, Pareto-ranked equilibria. In these cases the source of the coordination failure is either imperfect competition or search externalities.

There is a burgeoning literature on coordination failure in models with strategic interaction. As Milgrom and Roberts (1990) have shown, these models have a common game-theoretic structure, based on the notion of "strategic complementarity." The example that is closest to the present work is the problem of "network externalities." Katz and Shapiro (1985, 1986) and Farrell and Saloner (1985, 1986) have studied the adoption of new technologies when there are network externalities. They show that Pareto-superior technologies may not be adopted if the value of the technology depends on how many individuals adopt it.

The conclusions of Katz–Shapiro and Farrell–Saloner are similar to the ones reached in this chapter. The differences lie in the models used. A competitive market is studied instead of a non-cooperative game. Rather than assuming the existence of a physical externality, the gains from standardization are modeled as a purely pecuniary externality. The value of this approach is that one sees exactly what assumptions on preferences, technologies etc. are necessary to produce the externality. Finally, the source of the externality is different: there is no counterpart to information costs or the diversification motive in the network-externality models.

Appendix

Before proving the theorems, we note some properties of the indirect utility function. Fix k and α^* and let R_a denote the return to a (diversified) unit of security a, Then $W(d, \alpha^*) = \sum_{a \in A} d(a) R_a$. Let $V(c, d, R) = U(c, W(d, \alpha^*) + Y_k) = U(c, \sum_{a \in A} d(a) R_a + Y_k)$ for any c, d and R in some compact interval, $\hat{K}$, where $R = \{R_a : a \in A\}$. By the maintained assumptions the derivative of V with respect to (c, d), denoted by $(D_1 V(c, d, R), D_2 V(c, d, R))$ is continuous on $\hat{K}$. Then the derivative of $u(\cdot; \alpha^*, k)$ exists and is given by

$$D_1 u(c, d; \alpha^*, k) = \int_{\hat{K}} D_2 V(c, d; R) F(dR)$$

$$D_2 u(c, d; \alpha^*, k) = \int_{\hat{K}} D_2 V(c, d; R) F(dR),$$

where F denotes the joint c.d.f. of the random variables $\{R_a\}$. In fact, the derivatives $D_1 u$ and $D_2 u$ must be continuous.

Obviously $u(\cdot; \alpha^*, k)$ is concave. Without loss of generality we can assume that $E[f(Z_n, X_i)] > 0$ for every $(f, i) \in A$. Then $u(\cdot; \alpha^*, k)$ is strictly increasing also.

Proof of theorem 1   Fix α^* by putting $\alpha_i^* = \infty$ for all $i \in I$. Reference to α^* will be suppressed as long as α^* has this fixed value.

Part (a) Existence   For any positive integer q, let $P^q = \{p \in P | 1/q \leq p(a) \leq q, \forall a \in A\}$. For any p in P^q, let $\psi(p)$ denote the set of optimal choices (β, γ, δ) for investors and let $\varphi(p)$ denote the set of optimal choices α for entrepreneurs. By a standard fixed point argument there exists an array $(\alpha^q, \beta^q, \gamma^q, \delta^q, p^q)$ in $\Delta(I) \times \Delta(J) \times \mathbb{R}_+^B \times D^B \times P^q$ with the following properties:

(i) $\alpha^q \in \varphi(p^q)$;

(ii) $(\beta^q, \gamma^q, \delta^q) \in \psi(p^q)$;

(iii) $p \cdot z^q \leq p^q \cdot z^q, \forall p \in P^q$;

where $z^q : A \to \mathbb{R}$ is defined by

$$z^q(a) = \sum_{j \in J} \beta_j^q \sum_{b \in B_j} \delta(b, a) v(\mathbb{H}(b)) - \alpha_i$$

for every a in A_i and every i in I.

Let $\{(\alpha^q, \beta^q, \gamma^q, \delta^q, p^q)\}_{q=1}^{\infty}$ be a sequence of such fixed points. Note the following facts.

Fact (1) $p^q \cdot z^q$ is bounded.

In fact, $p^q \cdot z^q \leqq Y_0$.

Fact (2) $p^q(a)$ is bounded away from zero for any a in A.

If not, then for some a and some subsequence, $p^q(a) \to 0$ and $z^q(a) \to \infty$. But for q sufficiently large it must be possible to choose $p \in P^q$ so that $p \cdot z^q > Y_0$, contradicting fact (1).

Fact (3) p^q is bounded above.

If not, there is some security a and some subsequence along which $p^q(a) \to \infty$, α_i^q is bounded away from zero and $\sum_{j \in J} \beta_j^q \sum_{b \in B_j} \delta(a, b) v(\mathbb{H}(b)) \to 0$. Then $\limsup z^q(a) < 0$, which implies that $p^q(a) = 1/q$ for q sufficiently large.

Fact (4)   From facts (2) and (3) it follows that $\{p^q\}$ has a convergent subsequence, $p^q \to p^\infty$, say. Then $\{z^q\}$ has a convergent subsequence $z^q \to 0$, say.

Fact (5)   Since $p^\infty \gg 0$, $\{(\alpha^q, \beta^q, \gamma^q, \delta^q)\}$ is bounded and therefore has a convergent subsequence $(\alpha^q, \beta^q, \gamma^q, \delta^q) \to (\alpha^\infty, \beta^\infty, \gamma^\infty, \delta^\infty)$.

By simple continuity arguments it can be shown that $\alpha^\infty \in \varphi(p^\infty)$ and $(\beta^\infty, \gamma^\infty, \delta^\infty) \psi(p^\infty)$. So $(\alpha^\infty, \beta^\infty, \gamma^\infty, \delta^\infty p^\infty)$ is an equilibrium.

Part (b) Efficiency   To establish that this equilibrium is constrained efficient it is not necessary to consider any other value of α^* than the one fixed at the outset. To see this, consider an alternative value $\hat{\alpha}^*$. Since $\alpha_i^* = \infty$ for each i, $R_a = E[f(Z_n, X)|Z_\infty]$ is Z_∞-measurable. Then Jensen's inequality implies that

$$E[U(c, W(d; \alpha^*) + Y_k)|Z_\infty] = U(c, E[W(d; \alpha^*) + Y_k|Z_\infty])$$

$$\geqq E[U(c, W(d; \hat{\alpha}^*) + Y_k)|Z_\infty]$$

since $W(d; \alpha^*)$ is Z_∞-measurable and U is concave. Integrating with respect to Z_∞ gives the result that

$$E[U(c, W(d; \alpha^*) + Y_k)] \geqq E[U(c, W(d; \hat{\alpha}^*) + Y_k)]$$

for any (c, d) in $\mathbb{R}_+ \times D$ and k in K.

To show that the equilibrium $((\alpha^\infty, \beta^\infty, \gamma^\infty, \delta^\infty p^\infty)$ is constrained efficient we assume the contrary and obtain a contradiction. Let $(\alpha, \beta, \gamma, \delta)$ be the alternative attainable and Pareto-preferred allocation. By revealed prefer-ence, for any j such that, $\beta_j > 0$,

$$\sum_{b \in B_j} v(\mathbb{H}(b))(\gamma(b) + p^\infty \cdot \delta(b) + C_j) > Y_0.$$

For any j such that $\beta_j^\infty > 0$,

$$\sum_{b \in B_j} v(\mathbb{H}b))(\gamma^\infty(b) + p^\infty \cdot \delta^\infty(b) + C_j) = Y_0$$

so

$$\sum_{j \in J} \beta_j \sum_{b \in B_j} v(\mathbb{H}(b))(\gamma(b) + p^\infty \cdot \delta(b) + C_j)$$
$$> \sum_{j \in J} \beta_j^\infty \sum_{b \in B_j} v(\mathbb{H}(b))(\gamma^\infty(b) + p^\infty \cdot \delta^\infty(b) + C_j).$$

The profit-maximization condition implies that

$$\sum_{j \in J} \beta_j \sum_{b \in B_j} v(\mathbb{H}(b))(\gamma(b) + C_j) + \sum_{i \in I} \alpha_i C_i$$
$$> \sum_{j \in J} \beta_j^\infty \sum_{b \in B_j} v(\mathbb{H}(b))(\gamma^\infty(b) + C_j) + \sum_{i \in I} \alpha_i^\infty C_i,$$

contradicting the required condition for entrepreneurs to be made better off.   ∎

Proof of theorem 2   Let $(\alpha, \alpha^*, \beta, \delta, p)$ be a fixed but arbitrary equilib-rium of an economy $\mathscr{E}$ in which $C_j = 0$ for every j in J. The strategy of the proof is to show that we can substitute the frequency distribution $\hat{\alpha}^*$ sat-isfying $\hat{\alpha}_i^* = \infty$ for all i in I, without disturbing the equilibrium. The con-strained efficiency of equilibrium follows immediately from the second half of the proof of theorem 1.

Suppose that an investor chooses the information structure H_j in equi-librium and learns that his type belongs to the set h in H_j. He has to solve the following decision problem:

$\text{Max}\, u(c, d; \alpha^*, h)$ subject to $c \geq 0, d \geq 0, c + p \cdot d \leq Y_0$.

The utility function $u(\cdot; \alpha^*, h)$ is defined and C^1 on an open set containing $\mathbb{R}_+ \times \mathbb{R}_+^4$. It is also concave on $\mathbb{R}_+ \times \mathbb{R}_+^4$. The set of feasible choices has a non-empty interior, so the "constraint qualification" is satisfied. Then the Kuhn–Tucker Theorem provides necessary and sufficient conditions for the solution of this problem: $\nabla u(c, d; \alpha^*, h) \leq \lambda(1, p)$ plus the usual comple-mentary slackness conditions.

The Kuhn–Tucker conditions will be satisfied for every h in H_j, for every structure H_j such that $\beta_j > 0$. Suppose that these conditions continue to hold when $\hat{\alpha}^*$ is substituted for α^*. Then I claim that $(\alpha, \hat{\alpha}^*, \beta, \gamma, \delta, p)$ is an equilibrium. To prove this it is sufficient to show that (β, γ, δ) remains an optimal choice for investors. It is clear that (γ, δ) remains optimal for every structure H_j such that $\beta_j > 0$. Also, the investors' expected utility, conditional on the choice of a structure H_j such that $\beta_j > 0$, remains unchanged. The reason for this is that returns are altered only for claims f in F_i for which $\alpha_i^* < \infty$, that is, $\alpha_i = 0$. But for these claims, market-clearing implies that $\delta(a, b) = 0$ for $a \in A_i$ and $b \in B_j$. Thus, to show that (β, γ, δ) is optimal, it only remains to show that he cannot get a higher expected utility by choosing some structure H_j such that $\beta_j = 0$. Let H_0 denote the information structure that is finer than any other information structure. Without loss of generality, we can assume that $\beta_0 > 0$, since any choices that are feasible for H_j are feasible for H_0 and by the definition of equilibrium must be optimal for H_0 if they are optimal for H_j and $\beta_j > 0$. Now if (γ, δ) is optimal for H_0 when $\hat{\alpha}^*$ is substituted for $\hat{\alpha}$, an investor cannot do better by choosing any other structure. Thus, (β, γ, δ) is optimal for investors when $\hat{\alpha}^*$ is substituted for α^*.

It remains to show that the Kuhn–Tucker conditions are satisfied for every financial structure H_j such that $\beta_j > 0$. Choose a structure H_j such that $\beta_j > 0$ and fix $b = (h, j)$ in B_j. Let R_a denote the return to the claim a when the frequency distribution is α^* and let $\hat{R}_a$ denote the corresponding return when the frequency distribution is $\hat{\alpha}^*$. Recall that $\alpha_i^* < \infty$ implies $\delta(a, b) = 0$ for any $a \in A_i$. It is immediate that

$$\frac{\partial u(\gamma(b), \delta(b); \alpha^*, k)}{\partial c} = \frac{\partial u(\gamma(b), \delta(b); \hat{\alpha}^*, k)}{\partial c}$$

and

$$\frac{\partial u(\gamma(b), \delta(b); \alpha^*, k)}{\partial d(a)} = \frac{\partial u(\gamma(b), \delta(b); \hat{\alpha}^*, k)}{\partial d(a)}$$

for any a in A_i and any i in I such that $\alpha_i > 0$ and any k in h. For any a in A,

$$\frac{\partial u(\gamma(b), \delta(b); \alpha^*, k)}{\partial d(a)} = E[D_2 U(\gamma(b), W(\delta(b), \alpha^*) + Y_k) R_a].$$

If $\delta(a, b) = 0$ then independence conditional on Z_∞ implies that

$$E[D_2 U(\gamma(b), W(\delta(b), \alpha^*) + Y_k)R_a|Z_\infty]$$

$$= E[D_2 U(\gamma(b), W(\delta(b), \alpha^*) + Y_k)|Z_\infty]E[R_a|Z_\infty]$$

$$= E[D_2 U(\gamma(b), W(\delta(b), \hat{\alpha}^*) + Y_k)|Z_\infty]E[\hat{R}_a|Z_\infty]$$

$$= E[D_2 U(\gamma(b), W(\delta(b), \hat{\alpha}^*) + Y_k)\hat{R}_a|z_\infty].$$

Then

$$\frac{\partial u(\gamma(b), \delta(b); \alpha^*, k)}{\partial d(a)} = \frac{\partial u(\gamma(b), \delta(b); \hat{\alpha}^*, k)}{\partial d(a)}$$

for any a in A_i if $\alpha_i = 0$. From this it follows immediately that the Kuhn–Tucker conditions continue to hold when α^* is replaced by $\hat{\alpha}^*$. ∎

Proof of theorem 3 The random variables $\{Z_n\}$ are i.i.d., taking the values 0 and 1 with equal probability. There are two financial structures, $F_0 = \{f\}$, consisting of unlevered equity and $F_1 = \{f_A, f_B\}$. There is a contingency X taking the values A and B with probability 1/2. The claims in F_2 are defined by putting

$$f_A(Z_n, X) = \begin{cases} Z_n & \text{if } X = B \\ 0 & \text{otherwise} \end{cases}$$

and $f_B(Z_n, X) = Z_n - f_A(Z_n, X)$. Both financial structures are assumed to be costless, i.e., $C_i = 0$ for $i = 1, 2$.

There are two types of investors, indexed by $k = A, B$. Investors' incomes are:

$$Y_A = \begin{cases} 1 & \text{if } X = A \\ 0 & \text{otherwise} \end{cases}$$

and $Y_B = 1 - Y_A$. The utility function is assumed to be quadratic over the relevant range:

$$U(c_1, c_2) = c_1 + ac_2 - \frac{b}{2}(c_2)^2 \quad \text{(with } a > 2b > 0\text{)}.$$

There are two information structures, $H_0 = \{\{A, B\}\}$ and $H_1 = \{\{A\}, \{B\}\}$. The costs of choosing H_0 and H_1 are zero and $C > 0$, respectively. Each investor has a prior probability of $\frac{1}{2}$ of belonging to either type, i.e. $v_k = \frac{1}{2}$ for $k = A, B$.

We can assume that Y_0 is sufficiently large so that consumption is always positive at the first date. Other constraints on parameters will be added as the analysis proceeds.

To prove the theorem we must construct two financial equilibria that are Pareto-ranked. In the first, all investors choose H_1 and all entrepreneurs (except one) choose F_2. Investors of type A buy only claims of type A and investors of type B buy only claims of type B. Since there is an equal proportion of investors of each type, markets clear if each investor buys two units of the preferred claim. For example, an investor of type A holds a (diversified) portfolio of two units of claim A which pays 1 when $X = B$ and 0 when $X = A$. The investor's income Y_A is 1 when $X = A$ and 0 when $X = B$, i.e., it is perfectly negatively correlated with the portfolio return. Holding this portfolio, each investor of type A will achieve a constant level of consumption, equal to one unit, in each state.

Let p_A and p_B denote the prices of the claims A and B, respectively. Put $p_A = p_B = \frac{1}{4}u'(1)$, where $u'(c) \equiv a - bc$. Then it is easy to check that, at these prices, it is optimal for each investor to demand two units of the preferred claim if he becomes informed.

Letting $p = \frac{1}{2}u'(1)$ denote the price of a unit of unlevered equity, it is obvious that an entrepreneur is indifferent between the two financial structures. Then it is (weakly) optimal for entrepreneurs to choose F_1.

To show that we have an equilibrium, it only remains to prove that no investor would be better off choosing the trivial information structure. Suppose that an investor chose H_0 and purchased d units of equity. A (diversified) unit of equity pays $\frac{1}{2}$ almost surely, so the investor's expected utility is

$$Y_0 - pd + \tfrac{1}{2}u(\tfrac{1}{2}d) + \tfrac{1}{2}u(1 + \tfrac{1}{2}d).$$

The first-order condition for a maximum is

$$\tfrac{1}{2}(u'(\tfrac{1}{2}d) + u'(1 + \tfrac{1}{2}d)) = p = \tfrac{1}{2}u'(1).$$

Using the linearity of marginal utility one can solve this equation to find that $d = 1$. (At this point one should check the first-order conditions to make sure that the investor does not want to hold any of claims A and B.) Since $d = 1$, the investor who chose H_0 pays the same amount for his portfolio as the investor who chose H_1 does for his. Thus, the difference in expected utility is accounted for by the cost of information and the difference in second-period consumption. The investor will strictly prefer to be informed if and only if

$$\frac{1}{2}u(\frac{1}{2}) + \frac{1}{2}u(\frac{3}{2}) < u(1) - C. \tag{1}$$

This inequality will be assumed to hold.

To construct the second equilibrium, suppose that all investors choose H_0 and all entrepreneurs (except one) choose F_1. The price system is assumed to be the same as in the full-innovation equilibrium, that is $p_A = p_B = p/2 = u'(1)/4$. At these prices, entrepreneurs are obviously indifferent between the two financial structures. Also, by the argument given above, an uninformed investor will choose to hold one unit of unlevered equity and none of the other claims. This implies that markets clear. To show that this is an equilibrium, then, it is necessary and sufficient to show that an investor does not want to become informed.

Suppose that the investor who becomes informed discovers he is of type A (the other case is exactly symmetrical). He chooses a portfolio (d, d_A, d_B), where d is the amount of unlevered equity and d_A and d_B are the amounts of claims A and B, respectively. Recalling that the securities A and B are issued by a single entrepreneur, the expected utility associated with this portfolio is

$$Y_0 - pd - p_A d_A - p_B d_B + \frac{1}{4}(u(\frac{1}{2}d) + u(\frac{1}{2}d + d_A) + u(1 + \frac{1}{2}d)$$
$$+ u(1 + \frac{1}{2}d + d_B)).$$

The necessary and sufficient conditions for an optimum are:

$$\frac{1}{4}(u'(\frac{1}{2}d) + u'(\frac{1}{2}d + d_A) + u'(1 + \frac{1}{2}d) + u'(1 + \frac{1}{2}d + d_B))\frac{1}{2} \leqq p$$

$$\frac{1}{4}u'(\frac{1}{2}d + d_A) \leqq p_A$$

$$\frac{1}{4}u'(\frac{1}{2}d + 1 + d_B) \leqq p_B,$$

together with the usual complementary slackness conditions. Using the linearity of marginal utility, these conditions can be solved to yield the solution $d = d_A = \frac{2}{3}$ and $d_B = 0$. Expected utility is easily calculated to be

$$Y_0 - p - C + \frac{1}{4}(u(\frac{1}{3}) + u(1) + 2u(\frac{4}{3})).$$

Note that the informed investor's portfolio costs exactly as much as the uninformed investor's portfolio. Thus, an investor will strictly prefer to be uninformed if and only if

$$\tfrac{1}{4}(u(\tfrac{1}{3}) + u(1) + 2u(\tfrac{4}{3})) - C < \tfrac{1}{2}(u(\tfrac{1}{2}) + u(\tfrac{3}{2})). \tag{2}$$

Thus there exists an equilibrium with no innovation ($\alpha_1 = 0$) if (2) is satisfied.

Since u is strictly concave,

$$u(1) > \tfrac{1}{2}(u(\tfrac{1}{2}) + u(\tfrac{3}{2}))$$

and

$$u(1) > \tfrac{1}{4}(u(\tfrac{1}{3}) + u(1) + 2u(\tfrac{4}{3})).$$

Then it is clear by inspection that there exists a value of C that simultaneously satisfies inequalities (1) and (2). This completes the demonstration that the economy has two equilibria. By construction, the first equilibrium dominates the second. In fact, these equilibria are Pareto-ranked ex post, that is, after agents know their types.   ∎

Acknowledgments

An earlier version of this chapter was presented at the Sloan School and the London School of Economics. I am grateful for the comments of the seminar participants. I also received helpful advice from Franklin Allen and David Hirshleifer on empirical matters. John Moore and two anonymous referees made helpful suggestions on the exposition. Financial support from the NSF under grant no. SES 8720589 is gratefully acknowledged.

Notes

1. I am grateful to Franklin Allen for suggesting this episode as an example of an "uncertainty premium" at work.

2. The interest on an OID bond is represented by the discount, i.e., the difference between the face value of the bond and its issue price. For tax purposes, this amount was amortized over the life of the bond using a straight-line formula. Since the formula ignored compounding, it allowed interest to be deducted from income faster than it was implicitly being paid, thus yielding an enormous profit to the issuer. See Finnerty (1988) for details and further references.

3. Banks would buy bonds and then sell the income stream derived from the coupons separately from the principal amount that would be paid at maturity

4. Through diversification, investors are assumed to eliminate the purely idiosyncratic or "residual" risk associated with any security. Consequently, the price of the security does not reflect the presence of such risk. With setup costs, investors require an additional incentive to trade the securities and this takes the form of a reward for bearing residual risk.

5. I am grateful to David Hirshleifer for pointing out the relevance of his own and Bessembinder's work to me.

6. The assumption that investors are not allowed to make short sales or that their short positions are constrained is crucial here. See Allen and Gale (1991).

7. In each state of nature, one unit of an extremal security entitles the holder either to the entire return to the underlying asset or to nothing. For example, if there are three states of nature and the returns of the firm are 5, 9, and 13 in the three states respectively, then the firm might issue two extremal securities with returns of (5, 0, 13) and (0, 9, 0).

8. The importance of product uncertainty has been emphasized by Ross (1989). He has argued that one of the major forces guiding the direction of financial innovation is the cost of marketing different types of claims. Among the various costs of marketing new securities, the need to explain the nature of the new security is clearly a major factor (Ross 1989, p. 550). In the present chapter, the information acquisition process is explicitly modeled.

9. See the discussion of the changing nature of debt and equity in Normandin (1990). He makes it clear that the property rights embodied even in familiar securities depend on judicial interpretation and may be quite uncertain in new circumstances.

10. In particular, this kind of information cannot be revealed by prices. Thus, even in a rational expectations equilibrium, each investor may have a motive to become informed.

11. In what follows a financial structure is assumed to consist of a finite number of claims. Also, the claims are assumed to exhaust the firm's revenues, that is, $\sum_{f \in F} f(z) = z$ for any z.

12. The distinction between open and closed markets is discussed in more detail in section 10.6.

13. U is a twice continuously differentiable, real-valued function defined on an open set containing $\mathbb{R}_+ \times \mathbb{R}_+$. V satisfies $V'(c) > 0$ and $V''(c) < 0$ for any $c \geqq 0$.

14. This condition will automatically be satisfied if V is quadratic, since V' is affine and $p_0 = 3V'(2)/2$.

15. $M(K)$ denotes the set of probability measures on K. For any subset $S \subseteq K$, $v(S)$ is the probability that the investor's type belongs to the set S.

16. It is assumed that Ω is a metric space, $\mathscr{B}$ is the family of Borel subsets of Ω and μ is a probability measure on $(\Omega, \mathscr{B})$.

17. In the example, the state s played the role of the random variable Z_∞. The random incomes of a given type of firm satisfy assumption 1 because they are independently and identically distributed conditionally on s. But assumption 1 requires all firms to be of the same type, a condition the example obviously fails to satisfy.

18. This approach is consistent with the open market/closed market framework if equilibrium is achieved in two stages. Imagine that entrepreneurs make their choices first and that market-clearing prices for the securities that exist in positive quantities are determined ex post, once the supplies are given. This type of structure is exploited in Hart (1979, 1980). If an entrepreneur changes his financial structure and issues previously non-existent securities, the resulting equilibrium differs only to the extent that it must include prices for the new securities. The resulting allocation is unaffected since the entrepreneur is negligible and can only supply a negligible amount of any security. This equilibrium concept gives essentially the same results as the one used in the chapter, where everything is compressed into a single instant.

19. Let $\mathbb{N}^* = \mathbb{N} \cup \{\infty\}$ and let $\Delta^*(I)$ denote the set of functions from I to $\mathbb{N}^*$ with the property that $\sum \alpha_i^* = \infty$ for any α^* in $\Delta^*(I)$. Suppose that $\{i_n : n \in \mathbb{N}\}$ is an assignment of optimal structures to entrepreneurs. Then $\alpha_i^* = \#\{n \in \mathbb{N} | i_n = i\}$ and $\alpha_i = \lim_{N \to \infty} \#\{0 \leqq n \leqq N | i_n = i\}/N$. An ordered pair (α, α^*) in $\Delta(I) \times \Delta^*(I)$ is consistent if it can be derived in this way from some sequence $\{i_n\}$. Implicit in the definition of frequency distributions is the assumption that every financial structure is chosen by some entrepreneur, that is, $\alpha_i^* \geqq 1$ for every i.

20. For any $\alpha^* \in \Delta^*(I)$, consider some particular assignment $\{i_n : n \in \mathbb{N}\}$ that has this distribution. Suppose that an investor has chosen a portfolio d. Then $W(d; \alpha^*)$ is defined by putting

$$W(d; \alpha^*) = \lim_{N \to \infty} N^{-1} \sum_{i \in I} \sum_{f \in F_i} \sum_{n \in S_i^N} (d(f, i)/\# S_i^N) f(Z_n, X_i),$$

where for each N, S_i^N denotes the set of entrepreneurs $n = 1, \ldots, N$ who choose financial structure i. Because of the symmetry of the distribution of returns, this definition is clearly independent of any particular assignment of financial structures to entrepreneurs. It depends only on the portfolio d and on the frequency distribution α^*. To see this, it is sufficient to consider the return to a typical claim $f(Z_n, X_i)$. Since Z_n is a function of ε_n and Z_∞ and X_1 is Z_∞-measurable, the return to the claim will be a function of ε_n and Z_∞. Since the ε_n are i.i.d. we can permute the financial structures among entrepreneurs without changing the distribution of returns to the portfolio.

21. Implicitly, we are allowing the investor to purchase insurance against the outcome of the information process. The reason for doing this is simply to rule out one source of inefficiency: if investors could not purchase this insurance, a planner could make everyone better off by reallocating goods at the first date. This kind of inefficiency is clearly irrelevant to the issues that are the focus of this chapter, so I have simply chosen to assume them away. Alternatively, one could alter the definition of constrained efficiency, but this is messier and no more convincing.

22. Because an investor perceives that in equilibrium he can purchase every type of claim, where each claim is *distinguished by the firm that issues it*, he can eliminate the idosyncratic risk associated with any type of claim through diversification. Thus, the claim must be priced as if this idiosyncratic risk did not exist. This will be true regardless of the set of claims actually traded in equilibrium.

23. See the survey by Finnerty (1988).

24. In the macoeconomic literature, "strategic complementarities" have been studied by Diamond (1982), Cooper and John (1988) and Heller (1986). Their results have a family resemblence to the ones obtained here. In particular, they obtain multiple, Pareto-ranked equilibria.

References

Allen, F. and Gale, D. (1988), "Optimal Security Design," *Review of Financial Studies*, 1, 229–263.

Allen, F. and Gale, D. (1990), "Incomplete Markets and the Incentives to Set Up an Options Exchange," *The Geneva Papers on Risk and Insurance Theory*, 15, 17–46.

Allen, F. and Gale, D. (1991), "Arbitrage, Short Sales and Financial Innovation," *Econometrica*, 59, 1041–1069.

Bessembinder, H. (1990), "An Empirical Analysis of Risk Premia in Future Markets" (University of Arizona, mimeo).

Bewley, T. (1989), "Market Innovation and Entrepreneurship: a Knightian View" (Cowles Foundation Discussion Paper No. 905, Yale University).

Cooper, R. and John, A. (1988), "Coordinating Coordination Failures in Keynesian Models," *Quarterly Journal of Economics*, 103, 441–163.

Diamond, P. (1982), "Aggregate Demand Management in Search Equilibrium," *Journal of Political Economy*, 90, 881–894.

Duffie, D. and Jackson, M. (1988), "Optimal Innovation in Futures Contracts," *Review of Financial Studies*, 2, 275–296.

Farrell, J. and Saloner, G. (1985), "Standardization, Compatibility and Innovation," *Rand Journal of Economics*, 16, 70–83.

Farrell, J. and Saloner, G. (1986), "Installed Base and Compatibility: Innovation, Product Preannouncements and Predation," *American Economic Review*, 76, 940–955.

Finnerty, J. (1988), "Financial Engineering in Corporate Finance: An Overview," *Financial Management*, Winter, 14–33.

Hart, O. (1979), "On Shareholder Unanimity in Large Stock Market Economies," *Econometrica*, 47, 1057–1084.

Hart, O. (1980), "Perfect Competiton and Optimal Product Differentiation," *Journal of Economic Theory*, 22, 279–312.

Heller, W. (1986), "Coordination Failure Under Complete Markets with Applications to Effective Demand," in Heller, W., Starr, R., and Starrett, D. (eds.), *Equilibrium Analysis: Essays in Honor of Kenneth J. Arrow* (Cambridge: Cambridge University Press).

Hirshleifer, D. (1988), "Residual Risk, Trading Costs and Commodity Futures Risk Premia," *Review of Financial Studies*, 1, 173–193.

Katz, M. and Shapiro, C. (1985), "Network Externalities, Competition and Compatibility," *American Economic Review*, 75, 424–440.

Katz, M. and Shapiro, C. (1986), "Technology Adoption in the Presence of Network Externalities," *Journal of Political Economy*, 94, 822–841.

Makowski, L. (1980), "Perfect Competition, the Profit Criterion and the Organization of Economic Activity," *Journal of Economic Theory*, 22, 222–242.

Milgrom, P. and Roberts, J. (1990), "Rationalizability, Learning and Equilibrium in Games with Strategic Complementarities," *Econometrica*, 58, 1255–1278.

Normandin, C. (1990), "The changing Nature of Debt and Equity: A Legal perspective," in Kopcke, R. and Rosengren, E. (eds.), *Are the Distinctions between Debt and Equity Disappearing*? Conference Series No. 33, (Boston: Federal Reserve Bank of Boston), 49–66.

Ross, S. (1989), "Institutional Markets, Financial Marketing and Financial Innovation," *The Journal of Finance*, 44, 541–556.

Schelling, T. (1978) *Micromotives and Macrobehavior* (New York: Norton).

11 The Changing Nature of Debt and Equity: A Financial Perspective

Franklin Allen

Historically, corporations have mainly financed their activities with two securities, debt and equity. The stockholders have responsibility for the operation of the firm through the election of the board of directors; the dividends they receive in return for their subscription of capital are not guaranteed and are paid at the discretion of the board of directors. In contrast, debtholders are promised a particular rate of return; they have no rights of control unless payments by the firm are omitted, in which case they have the right to foreclose on assets or, in some cases, force bankruptcy. Dewing (1934, pp. 236–37) ascribes these differences in rights between debtholders and equityholders to the historical distinction in Anglo-Saxon law between debtors and creditors.

As a result of the importance of debt and equity, the focus of inquiry into firms' choice of capital structure has traditionally been "What is the optimal debt-equity ratio?" Modigliani and Miller (1958) and subsequent authors[1] showed that if capital markets are perfect and complete and no taxes are in effect, a firm's debt-equity ratio has no effect on its value because investors' opportunity sets are not affected by its capital structure. If a corporate income tax is in effect, with interest deductibility, Modigliani and Miller (1963) used the same logic to show firms should use entirely debt finance since this allows corporate taxes to be avoided.

This prediction of the theory did not square well with empirical evidence; despite interest deductibility and a corporate tax rate of almost 50 percent at that time, firms typically used only moderate amounts of debt. This led a number of authors[2] to point to the capital market imperfection of bankruptcy and liquidation costs. They suggested that a firm balances these costs against the tax advantage of debt and it is this trade-off that determines the optimal debt-equity ratio.

The trade-off theory has been criticized on a number of grounds. Evidence on the direct costs of bankruptcy, such as lawyers' fees, suggested they were small (Warner 1977). Direct measurement of the indirect costs of bankruptcy, such as the difficulties of running a firm while it is in bankruptcy court, are difficult to obtain; proponents of the trade-off the-

This chapter originally appeared in *Are the Differences between Equity and Debt Disappearing?*, edited by R. W. Kopcke and E. S. Rosengren, Conference Series No. 33, 1989, Federal Reserve Bank of Boston, 12–38. Reprinted by permission.

ory suggest they are significant while detractors suggest they are small relative to the tax advantage of debt. It is widely agreed that liquidation costs, which are the costs of breaking up a firm and selling it off piecemeal, are sufficiently large to explain firms' observed debt ratios if included with bankruptcy costs. However, Haugen and Senbet (1978) argued that liquidation costs should not be included with bankruptcy costs since liquidation was not implied by bankruptcy; if the firm was worth more as a going concern it would not be liquidated. In addition, they argued that if bankruptcy was costly it could be avoided by firms' buying back their debt just before it became due. These arguments depend on perfect markets; a number of recent papers have investigated why bankruptcy and liquidation may be linked and why bankruptcy may be difficult to avoid by repurchasing securities when markets are imperfect.[3]

The deficiencies of the trade-off theory resulted in the development of a number of alternative theories. Miller (1977) pointed to the importance of personal taxes. He argued that personal taxes on equity were lower than on debt and presented a model where this personal tax disadvantage of debt entirely offset its corporate tax advantage so that in equilibrium each firm was indifferent between the use of equity and debt. DeAngelo and Masulis (1980) and subsequent authors[4] developed this model to allow for bankruptcy costs and other factors; in this case again a trade-off exists between the use of debt and equity and firms have an interior optimal capital structure.

Some of the alternative theories that did not rely on the inclusion of personal taxes were based on asymmetric information. Agency theories started from the premise that managers' actions could not be fully contractually specified because they were unobservable and would be influenced by capital structure choices (Jensen and Meckling 1976; Myers 1977; and Green 1984). Signaling theories were based on the idea that firms' capital structure choices could convey information about their prospects to investors (Ross 1977; Myers and Majluf 1984; and Brennan and Kraus 1987). More recently, it has been suggested that imperfectly competitive markets for outputs and inputs and opportunities for product innovation may influence firms' choice of capital structure.[5]

The deficiencies of these theories in explaining the use of debt and equity by firms are well documented by Myers (1984). He gives the following succinct summary of the literature (p. 575): "'How do firms choose their capital structures?' ... the answer is 'We don't know.'"

Financial Innovation

The notion that firms finance their activities with debt and equity is a simplification; corporations have issued securities other than standard debt and equity for many centuries. Dewing (1934, p. 135) recounts that multiple classes of stock with certain preferences or disabilities were issued by some of the first English companies in the middle of the sixteenth century. He also gives examples (pp. 377–78) of a number of English firms that issued convertible securities in the seventeenth and eighteenth centuries.

In the United States, corporations also have a long history of use of securities other than debt and equity. Since the late 1880s, firms have issued significant amounts of preferred stock. This form of stock combines many of the features of equity with those of debt; in particular, a level of payments is specified, as with debt, but unlike debtholders, investors in preferred stock cannot force bankruptcy if the firm omits these payments. Firms have also issued income bonds at various times since 1848. Like preferred stock, income bonds have a number of features of debt and equity. Unlike preferred stock, the specified payments are not at the discretion of the board of directors but depend on the level of accounting earnings. If they are omitted, however, the securityholders cannot force bankruptcy. Still other types of securities such as convertible bonds and warrants have also been issued by corporations for many decades. Dewing (1934) gives a full account of the early history of these securities.

Financial innovation is, therefore, not a recent phenomenon. However, Miller (1986) suggests that financial innovation has proceeded at a particularly fast pace during the last twenty years. Not only have corporations started to issue new securities such as zero coupon bonds and adjustable rate bonds, but also entirely new markets such as the Chicago Board Options Exchange have been established.[6]

Miller argues that much of this recent innovation is in response to features of the tax code and to regulation. A classic example of innovation in response to the tax code is zero coupon bonds. Before the Tax Equity and Fiscal Responsibility Act of 1982 (TEFRA), the tax liability on zero coupon bonds was allocated on a straight line basis; that is, the annual interest deduction was the amount to be repaid at the due date less the issue price, divided by the number of years until repayment. This rule ignored the effect of compounding of interest and created an opportunity for corporations to avoid taxes by issuing long-term zero coupon bonds to tax-exempt investors. When interest rates were high in the early 1980s, the potential tax benefits from this type of security became large and corporations issued a large amount of these bonds. Although TEFRA closed this loophole, the market for zero coupon bonds continued but now was mainly supplied by investment banks "stripping" government securities into principal and interest (Kanemasu, Litzenberger, and Rolfo 1986).

An alternative rationale for financial innovation, stressed by Van Horne (1985), is that new securities may make markets more complete in the sense that they increase opportunities for risk sharing between investors. In a categorization of the primary factors responsible for the introduction of sixty-eight new types of security, Finnerty (1988) lists tax and regulatory advantages in twenty-seven cases and risk reallocation in fifty-three cases. (More than one factor is possible for each type of security.)

In addition to taxes and regulation and risk reallocation, another important class of security innovation has resulted from attempts by incumbent managements to discourage takeovers. Examples of these "poison pill" defenses are preferred stock plans, flip-over plans, back-end plans and voting plans. The securities associated with these plans all have the common feature that on the occurrence of a takeover attempt not approved by the board of directors, certain rights accrue to the securityholders. For example, target shareholders may be given the right to buy the stock of the bidder at a substantial discount on completion of the takeover.[7]

Tufano (1988) has constructed a data base of fifty-eight financial innovations introduced by investment banks between 1974 and 1987. These innovations, often bonds, equities or preferred stocks with novel features, can cost substantial amounts to develop. Tufano finds that the banks that create these products almost immediately face competition from rivals offering imitative products. During the brief period of monopoly before imitation, originators do not charge high prices to recoup their development costs. Moreover, once the imitative products appear, they charge a lower rather than a higher price than the imitators. The main difference between the originating bank and imitators is that the originating bank obtains a larger share of the market. Tufano gives a number of reasons why market share may allow originators to recoup the costs of developing the products. Sunk costs may be involved in entering the underwriting business. These may deter entry and allow positive profits; price competition may be limited by the type of noncooperative collusion considered by the threat of reverting to the single-period equilibrium. Another possibility is that the bank may make profits on related business so that it can recapture the costs in this way.

The fact that debt and equity are not the only securities that firms use to finance their activities, and the constant introduction of new forms of securities, suggest that a more fundamental issue than "What is the optimal debt equity ratio?" is "What are the optimal securities that should be issued?" Many recent studies of capital structure have taken this perspective. These studies provide some insight into the changing nature of debt and equity.

This literature has two branches. The first has been concerned with trying to identify the circumstances in which debt and equity are optimal. This will be considered in the next section of this chapter. The second branch has been concerned with the optimal securities that a firm should issue. The succeeding section considers this, followed by a summary and conclusions.

When Are Debt and Equity Optimal?

A number of papers have identified situations where debt contracts are optimal. Townsend (1979) considers the optimal contract between a risk-averse agent and a risk-neutral principal. In one version of the model, the agent requires funds at the beginning of the period to produce a random income at the end. The principal can observe the realization of the agent's income only if bankruptcy is declared and the agent's income is transferred to the principal. This bankruptcy process is costly. Among the class of deterministic strategies, where the principal observes the agent's income with probability either one or zero, Townsend shows that debt is an optimal contract. This requires the agent to pay a constant amount to the principal; if the agent's income is insufficient to pay this amount, then bankruptcy is declared and the agent's income is transferred to the principal.

This basic idea has been used by a number of authors to consider the role of debt contracts in various contexts. For example, Diamond (1984) used a similar framework to explain the use of debt contracts by financial intermediaries such as banks. Gale and Hellwig (1985) consider the case where the agent's investment is mutually observable in order to show that underinvestment can occur.

Allocation of Cash Flows

An important issue is whether this type of analysis can be applied to corporate securities. If the agent is interpreted to be the insiders that operate the firm, and the principal the outside investors that supply capital, then the optimal security for the firm to issue is debt. The question is whether equityholders correspond to the insiders that run the firm or the outside investors. For privately held firms, the equityholders correspond to the insiders that run the firm. For publicly traded corporations, however, most equityholders are outside investors with access to the same information as bondholders; in this case it is not immediately evident that Townsend's type of analysis can be used to justify the existence of debt and equity.

Williams (1989) develops a model to consider this issue. He assumes markets are complete in the sense that everybody is effectively risk neutral with respect to aggregate-state prices. However, asymmetric information about the earnings of individual firms in any particular ·period can only be observed by the managers or insiders that run the firms; as a result securities cannot be made contingent on earnings in a manner similar to Townsend's type of analysis. In addition, Williams introduces "ex ante monitoring," such as accounting controls, which prevents the managers from simply expropriating a firm's assets. It is also assumed that an agency problem exists between managers and outside investors. It is shown that it is optimal for the firm to issue debt or stock or both to outside investors, with the precise mix of securities depending on the nature of the agency problem.

An important issue is how general the assumptions of the model are and, in particular, the circumstances in which markets are complete in the sense that managers are effectively risk neutral with respect to aggregate-state prices. One possibility is that the managers are risk neutral; if they are risk averse, the fact that they cannot trade securities state by state that are contingent on the firm's earnings will presumably prevent markets from being effectively complete.

In addition to the applicability of this type of analysis to corporations, another issue to be considered is the assumption by Townsend that strategies are deterministic, so that income is observed by declaring bankruptcy with probability one or zero. Mookherjee and Png (1989) show that if random strategies are possible, then the optimal contract involves randomization. To see why it is possible to do better with random strategies, consider the optimal deterministic contract, which is a debt contract. Suppose that the agent is now made to announce his income, and bankruptcy occurs with probability one whenever the announced income is less than the required payment. During bankruptcy, the true value of the agent's income is revealed. By rewarding the agent when he has correctly announced his income level, it is possible to provide a strict incentive to tell the truth. This means it is no longer necessary to force bankruptcy all the time. Since the agent is risk averse and the principal is risk neutral, this change allows a Pareto improvement. The important issue here is whether randomization is possible. If a device exists that both parties know is truly random, then Townsend's type of analysis is unable to provide a rationale for debt contracts, but if such randomization devices do not exist, it can.

Allocation of Control Rights

The papers considered above are primarily concerned with the allocation of cash flows. In a recent paper, Aghion and Bolton (1988) take a different approach by looking at the allocation of control rights among different securityholders in closely held firms. They consider a model with the sequence of events shown in figure 11.1. An entrepreneur has insufficient resources of his own to finance a project he wishes to undertake. The project involves an outlay at time 0 and yields revenues at time 1 and time 2. The entrepreneur can finance the investment by issuing securities at time 0 to an outside investor who receives a portion of the firm's profits at time 1 and time 2. Both the entrepreneur and the investor are assumed

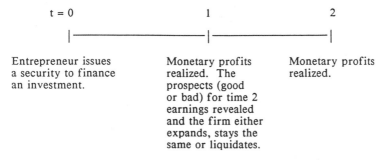

Figure 11.1
The sequence of events in the Aghion and Bolton (1988) model

to be risk neutral, so that risk-sharing issues are not considered in the model.

At time 1, the firm's monetary profits and its prospects for future earnings, which can be either good or bad, are determined. After receiving this information, the party in control of the firm decides on which of three possible courses of action to undertake: expand the firm, continue as before, or liquidate. If the time 1 prospects for future earnings are good, expansion leads to the highest expected profits, continuing as before the next highest, and liquidating the least. If the prospects are bad, the reverse is true. The private costs to the entrepreneur of the three courses are different, with liquidation being the most costly, expansion the next most costly, and keeping operations the same the least costly. The magnitudes of the expected monetary profits and private costs to the entrepreneur are such that in the first-best world where all states can be contracted on, it is optimal for the firm to continue operations as before in the state where prospects are good, and liquidate in the state where prospects are bad.

The critical assumption that Aghion and Bolton make is that contracting possibilities are incomplete. In particular, the earnings prospects cannot be contracted upon; the only variable that can be contracted on is monetary profits. This creates two problems. The first occurs if the entrepreneur uses securities that cede control of the firm to the investor and the good state is realized. In this case, the investor would like the firm to expand since this maximizes expected monetary profits. However, this is not optimal since it imposes large costs on the entrepreneur; when these costs are taken into account, continuing the current level of operations is optimal.

The second problem occurs if the entrepreneur retains control. Now if prospects are good the efficient action of continuing operations will be chosen; however, if prospects are bad the entrepreneur may not have the correct incentives to liquidate. The entrepreneur bears high private costs with liquidation; unless he also receives a high proportion of the monetary profits so that most of the marginal benefits of liquidation are obtained, it will be not be worth doing. The problem is that since it is not possible to distinguish between states where earnings prospects are good and states where they are bad, it is also necessary to give the entrepreneur most of the monetary profits in the good state. The overall payoff to the investor is then insufficient to make financing the project worthwhile. Hence, a drawback also exists if the entrepreneur retains control.

These arguments imply that giving the control entirely to either the investor or the entrepreneur may mean the first-best contract cannot be implemented: if the investor has control, the entrepreneur may be forced to expand, which has high private costs; but if the entrepreneur has control, he may be unwilling to liquidate because of the high private costs associated with that. Ideally, what is required is a mechanism that grants control to the entrepreneur when earnings prospects are good and to the investor when they are bad. Aghion and Bolton argue that the use of debt by the entrepreneur and the institution of bankruptcy can achieve this outcome, if monetary profits and the prospects for future earnings are positively correlated at time 1: for example, in the case where they are perfectly correlated, when earnings prospects are good, monetary profits are high and the entrepreneur retains control. When earnings prospects are bad, monetary profits are low, and if the level of debt issued initially has been correctly chosen, the firm will go bankrupt and control will be transferred to the outside investor.

Zender (1989) also develops a model based on the allocation of control rights where the use of debt and equity is optimal for closely held firms. Once again, all agents are risk neutral so that risk-sharing considerations are not considered in the model. The sequence of events is illustrated in figure 11.2. At time 0, an entrepreneur designs and sells securities to two identical investors to finance a project. Individually, neither investor has the funds to finance the project so both must contribute money if the project is to be undertaken. The investor who is assigned control then hires a manager who undertakes an effort choice at time 1. No agency

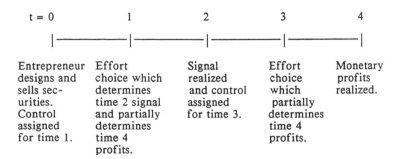

t = 0	1	2	3	4

| Entrepreneur designs and sells securities. Control assigned for time 1. | Effort choice which determines time 2 signal and partially determines time 4 profits. | Signal realized and control assigned for time 3. | Effort choice which partially determines time 4 profits. | Monetary profits realized. |

Figure 11.2
The sequence of events in the Zender (1989) model

problem exists between the manager and the investor, so the manager acts as the investor specifies. The time 1 effort choice determines the level of a signal at time 2 and partially determines the level of profits at time 4. In addition to the signal that is observed at time 2, control is allocated for time 3. At time 3, the party in control again specifies an effort choice for the manager. This, together with the effort choice at time 1, determines the expected monetary profits realized at time 4.

The problem in the model is to provide the correct incentives for the effort choices at times 1 and 3. A single investor with sufficient funds to finance the entire project would obtain the full marginal benefits of the effort choices and so would be prepared to undertake the efficient level. However, because neither investor has sufficient funds to finance the entire project, the securities must be such that both have a chance of obtaining part of the time 4 payoffs. This means that the investor in control does not get the full marginal benefit of the effort choice at times 1 and 3.

Zender shows that the optimal contract involves making control at time 3 and the allocation of payoffs at time 4 contingent on the time 2 signal. If a good signal is observed at time 2, the investor in control at time 1 remains in control and retains the residual of the payoffs less a constant amount at time 4. If a bad signal is observed, then control is switched to the second investor who obtains the payoffs at time 4. This optimal contract is interpreted as the investor in control initially having equity and the other investor having debt; it ensures that the investor who is delegated control is made the residual claimant and so has incentives to make the proper decisions.

Another paper that is related to Aghion and Bolton (1988) is Hart and Moore (1989). They also consider a model of an entrepreneur who wishes to raise funds to undertake a project when contracting possibilities are incomplete. The focus of their analysis, however, is the problem of providing an incentive for the entrepreneur to repay the borrowed funds. It is the ability of the creditor to seize the entrepreneur's assets that provides this incentive.

The sequence of events in the simplest version of their model is shown in figure 11.3. A risk-neutral entrepreneur raises funds from a risk-neutral outside investor to purchase assets that can realize payoffs at times 1 and 2. If the entrepreneur does not fulfill the contract at time 1, the outside investor can renegotiate or can seize some proportion of the assets and liquidate them. Liquidation is socially inefficient, however, because the

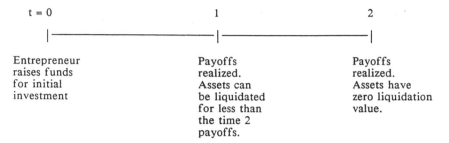

t = 0   1   2

Entrepreneur   Payoffs   Payoffs
raises funds   realized.   realized.
for initial   Assets can   Assets have
investment   be liquidated   zero liquidation
                      for less than   value.
                      the time 2
                      payoffs.

Figure 11.3
The sequence of events in the Hart and Moore (1989) model

liquidation value of the assets at time 1 is less than the present value of the time 2 payoffs. Although both the entrepreneur and the outside investor have symmetric information, third parties such as the courts cannot observe the asset payoffs so these cannot be contracted upon. The entrepreneur can appropriate the cash flows from the assets for his own use, so the problem is to design a contract that provides incentives for the entrepreneur to repay the loan.

It is shown that the optimal contract is a debt contract and the incentives to repay are provided by the threat of liquidation. Since the present value of the time 2 payoffs of the assets is above their liquidation value, the entrepreneur will always want to hold on to as high a proportion of the assets as possible and will be prepared to pay up to the assets' present value. In low payoff states, the entrepreneur will have insufficient cash to make the required payment; the outside investor therefore renegotiates the loan and liquidates a certain proportion of the assets to make the payment up to the required amount. Although this liquidation is inefficient relative to an ideal world, it is necessary because the entrepreneur cannot commit to pay any of the time 2 payoffs to the investor. The threat of liquidation also ensures that the entrepreneur pays the required amount in high output states.

One interesting implication of the analysis is that reducing the amount borrowed is not always desirable. If the time 1 payoffs or time 2 liquidation values are uncertain, it may be better for the entrepreneur to borrow more than strictly the initial cost of the assets. This allows him to make a higher payment in low output states at time 1, so that a smaller proportion of the assets is liquidated.

A version of the model where the assets pay off at time 3 is also considered. It is shown that the use of short-term or long-term debt depends on when information arrives and the pattern of payoffs. Short-term debt gives the outside investor a high degree of control early on since the entrepreneur has to renew the loan. This has the advantage that the size of the debt can be kept low, which avoids the inefficiencies associated with liquidation. However, it has the disadvantage that the outside investor may liquidate projects early on even though this is inefficient from a social point of view. For example, if information arrives at time 1 that a project will have high time 2 payoffs and low time 3 payoffs, the outside investor may force liquidation at time 1, anticipating that it will not be possible to extract any payment at time 2. This type of inefficiency can be avoided with long-term debt.

The papers by Aghion and Bolton (1988), Zender (1989), and Hart and Moore (1989) provide rationales for the use of debt and equity by closely held firms. Their analyses raise at least two issues that remain to be fully resolved. The first is which results depend on risk neutrality and which are robust to the introduction of risk aversion. The second is that it is not immediately evident how this type of theory can be applied to justify the use of debt and equity by large corporations. The problem is how to identify the interests of managers with those of outside equityholders, given the latter are in a similar position to outside bondholders. These are important topics for future research.

Allocation of Voting Rights

Another strand of the literature has considered the question of control in terms of the way in which voting rights should be assigned to securities. The aspect of equity that has been of particular concern is the use of one vote per share and majority voting as the decision rule. A number of papers have identified the circumstances where these provisions are optimal.

Grossman and Hart (1988) argue that the voting structure of securities is important primarily because of its impact on the market for corporate control. When securities are widely held, a free-rider problem exists: individual shareholders do not have an incentive to carefully monitor management and vote them out when they perform badly. Monitoring of management is likely to be important when a single individual or group has a large enough ownership share to make the free-rider problem insignificant. A prime example of the type of situation where this occurs is the case of a takeover bid. Grossman and Hart therefore consider a model where the allocation of voting rights and dividends to securities is determined by its effect on allowing rivals to obtain control from an incumbent management.

Initially, the firm is owned by an entrepreneur who wishes to draw up a corporate charter that maximizes the value of the firm. Grossman and Hart are interested in schemes that are privately optimal for the entrepreneur. A number of different classes of shares can be created and the share of votes and the share of dividends accruing to each can be varied. The entrepreneur anticipates that these securities will be widely held and that the firm will be run by an incumbent management. At some date in the future, a rival team, which may or may not be able to manage the firm better than the incumbent team, may attempt to acquire control by bidding for the securities to which control rights are attached. The incumbent team makes a counteroffer and holders of the securities decide which offer to accept.

The critical assumption of the model is that management teams can obtain private benefits from controlling the firm; the optimal allocation of voting rights and dividends depends on the absolute and relative sizes of the private benefits accruing to the incumbent management team and the rival team. If private benefits are negligible, then the allocation of control is unimportant and one share, one vote is as good as any other allocation.

Grossman and Hart first consider the case where all securities of a particular class must be treated equally, so that the whole class must be purchased if the votes of that class are necessary for control. Suppose that the private benefits of control are one-sided; for example, suppose the incumbent team has no private benefits of control but the rival team does. In this case one share, one vote is optimal because it maximizes the amount the rival must pay to obtain control. If a firm has a voting structure that allows the rival to obtain control by buying securities with only a small proportion of dividends attached, then he can obtain control and the associated benefits it provides to him at a small price. This may even be worth doing when the rival cannot generate as high a dividend stream as the incumbent. In order to make sure the rival pays as much as possible for control and its associated private benefits, and in particular at least as much as the value of the dividend stream provided by the incumbent, votes must be spread as widely as possible. This implies one share, one vote. A similar argument holds if the incumbent team has one-sided private benefits of control.

If private benefits are two-sided so that both teams value control, one share, one vote is no longer optimal. The reason is that by separating votes from dividends it is possible to get the incumbent and rival to compete for control and pay for the associated private benefits they obtain. Grossman and Hart argue that this case is of little interest empirically for large publicly owned corporations, since the extent to which management can extract benefits is limited by corporate law, which gives a corporation's directors a fiduciary duty to all shareholders. It then follows that their theory is consistent with the widespread use of one share, one vote among publicly owned corporations.

Finally, Grossman and Hart consider the case where it is not necessary to treat all holders of a particular class of securities equally, it is only necessary for the rival to obtain the proportion of votes specified in the charter to obtain control. This prespecified proportion is assumed to be between 50 and 100 percent. Ignoring the case where both incumbent and rival have private benefits of control for the reasons mentioned above, the analysis of the optimal proportion is similar to before. The main difference occurs when the incumbent has one-sided benefits of control. In this case, it is optimal to set the proportion at the lowest value of 50 percent, since this minimizes the chance of the incumbent team maintaining control. Their paper thus provides some rationale for the use of a single class of equity with control requiring a majority of the votes.

Harris and Raviv (1988a) also consider the optimal allocation of voting rights and dividends to securities. Although the details differ somewhat, the framework is similar. One of the main differences between the papers is in the focus of the analysis. Grossman and Hart consider arrangements that are privately optimal as far as the original entrepreneur who designs the charter is concerned; they do not consider a criterion of social optimality, which includes the private benefits accruing to the incumbent and rival management teams. In contrast Harris and Raviv do explicitly distinguish between private and social optimality.

Harris and Raviv show that one-share, one-vote majority rule is socially optimal since it ensures that the management team that generates the greatest total amount (including payouts to shareholders and private benefits to managers) controls the firm. This is because the arrangement allows the team that can pay the most to gain control; any deviation gives an advantage to the incumbent or rival that may allow them to gain control even though they generate a lower total amount. The arrangement that is privately optimal for the original owner involves issuing two extreme classes of security, one with all the voting rights and one with all the dividends. The reason this is optimal is that it allows the securityholders to extract as much of the benefits of control from the management teams as possible because it forces them to compete for them. Thus, in general, the rules that are privately and socially optimal are not the same.

Grossman and Hart obtain one-share, one-vote majority rule as privately optimal, whereas Harris and Raviv obtain issuing extreme securities as privately optimal, because of differences in their assumptions. Among other things, the two papers are concerned with different parameters for the benefits of control the incumbent and rival can capture. Grossman and Hart argue that the case where both have benefits of control is of little empirical interest, whereas Harris and Raviv do not make this restriction. If the private benefits for both incumbent and rival are high, concentrating votes among a small class of equity is optimal in the Grossman and Hart model.

In the cases where only the rival or only the incumbent obtains benefits of control, both one-share, one-vote majority rule and extreme securities are optimal arrangements in the Harris and Raviv model. Extreme securities are optimal in these circumstances in their model but not in Grossman and Hart's, because Harris and Raviv assume that each investor can construct an optimal portfolio containing both of the extreme securities and that each investor's tender decision can be pivotal. This means that investors take into account the effect of tendering their votes on the value of their nonvoting shares. In contrast, Grossman and Hart assume each investor ignores any effects his actions may have on the outcome of the tender.

These differences between the assumptions and results of the two papers raise a number of issues. The private optimality of firms issuing equity with one share, one vote apparently depends critically on the assumption that the private benefits of control of the incumbent and the rival are asymmetric. If both have significant benefits, then concentration of votes appears to be (privately) desirable. If this type of theory is to explain the predominance of one share, one vote, it is necessary to provide some theoretical or empirical justification for why asymmetric private benefits of control is a plausible assumption. A priori, one might expect private benefits would be symmetric, since the limitations on the amounts managers can capture are set by corporate law and other factors that are the same for both incumbents and rivals. The main private benefit that can differ is, perhaps, the psychic satisfaction of control. An important question empirically is, therefore, how much this does differ between incumbents and rivals. Another issue is the best way to model shareholders' decisions; in particular, in close contests do they in practice regard themselves as unimportant in influencing the outcome, or pivotal?

Blair, Golbe, and Gerard (1989) consider a model similar to that of Harris and Raviv (1988a) in that they are concerned with social optimality and both the rival and incumbent have private benefits of control, but these authors obtain rather different results. They are able to show that, in the absence of taxes, one-share, one-vote majority rule and extreme securities that unbundle voting rights and cash flows are equivalent and both lead to social optimality. In contrast, Harris und Raviv show that only one-share, one-vote majority rule is socially optimal; extreme securities can lead to suboptimal outcomes. The reason for this difference is that Blair, Golbe, and Gerard assume the rival and incumbent bid simultaneously, whereas Harris and Raviv assume they bid sequentially. Again, this difference in approaches and its effect on the results raises the question of which is the most appropriate way of modeling the situation.

The main concern of Blair, Golbe, and Gerard is to consider the effect of capital gains taxes on the allocation of voting rights and cash flows. If capital gains taxes are in effect, then welfare is improved if extreme securities are used. This is because a lock-in effect means capital gains taxes may prevent a superior rival from winning if there is one-share, one-vote majority rule; tax liabilities may be higher when the rival wins than when the incumbent wins. Allowing separate trading of votes alleviates this effect.

Taking the security structure of voting equity and debt as exogenous, Harris und Raviv (1988b) stress the importance of capital structure for takeover contests, because high leverage allows a controlling interest to be acquired for a low outlay. Harris and Raviv (1989) combine this idea with the approaches in Grossman and Hart (1988) and Harris and Raviv (1988a) by considering the allocation of voting rights and cash flows when the firm is not restricted to issuing just equity. They use a similar model to that of Grossman and Hart. In particular they focus on privately optimal securities, only the incumbent (or the rival) is assumed to have private benefits of control, and each investor ignores any effect his actions may have on the outcome of the tender.

The problem of the entrepreneur who owns the firm initially is to design securities that prevent the incumbent management that has private benefits from maintaining control when a superior rival appears. This means that the cost of resisting takeovers must be maximized. As in the papers focusing only on equity, one share, one vote among voting securities is an important component of this, since it means that control cannot be acquired cheaply by the party with private benefits. In addition, they show that nonvoting risky securities should not be sold to outside investors; if nonvoting securities are sold to outside investors, they should be risk-free debt. The reason is again that these maximize the cost of obtaining control and so tend to favor the superior rival.

The private optimality of one share, one vote in Harris and Raviv (1989) again appears to depend on the assumption of asymmetric benefits of control between the incumbent and rival. If both had private benefits of control, extreme securities of some sort might be optimal as in Harris and Raviv (1988a). An interesting issue is whether debt and equity remain optimal in this case.

The models to analyze the design of equity that have been considered above are all concerned with the effect of voting when an incumbent management team is challenged by a rival team. Bagwell and Judd (1989) take a different approach by considering the optimality of majority rule where control is concerned with payout and investment decisions.

The sequence of events in their model is shown in figure 11.4. Initially all investors are identical; they design corporate charters and issue securities to finance firms' investments. At time 1 investors discover whether they are type A or B. Type As value consumption at time 1 and time 2 and require a minimum level of consumption at time 1. Type Bs only value consumption at time 2 and are less risk averse than type As at that time. Just after investors' types are discovered, firms decide on how much of the cash generated by the initial investment to pay out to shareholders and whether to invest the retained earnings in a safe or a risky project. If investors have any cash remaining at time 1 they can invest it in new firms. At time 2, the final payoffs from firms' investments are realized and paid out to shareholders.

A crucial feature of Bagwell and Judd's model is the existence of transaction costs for trading securities at time 1 after investors have discovered

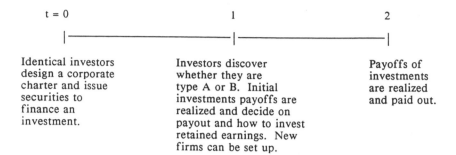

Figure 11.4
The sequence of events in the Bagwell and Judd (1989) model

their type. The particular cost that is modeled is the capital gains tax. In the absence of this cost, investors would simply reallocate their portfolios. Type A investors would choose firms that pay out their required consumption at time 1 and invest in relatively safe projects and type B investors would choose firms that invest all their time 1 earnings in risky projects. When this type of rebalancing is prohibitively costly, each firm will have shareholders with different views about its optimal policy and control will be important. For example, suppose there is majority rule and type As are just in the majority. In this case they will prefer dividends to share repurchase even though the former strategy involves a higher tax burden, because this allows them to maintain control and implement the investment choice they prefer.

Bagwell and Judd show that the optimal decision rule in the corporate charter depends on the level of these transaction costs for rebalancing at time 1. For small transaction costs, majority rule is optimal because investors can rebalance at low cost and not much shareholder diversity is found among firms. However, for transaction costs that are so high that no rebalancing occurs, majority rule is not optimal. In this case the corporate charter should specify that the firm's policy is chosen to maximize a welfare function where the weights assigned to each type correspond to their representation in the firm at time 1. This maximizes investors' welfare initially since they only know the probability of being a particular type.

Bagwell and Judd's model illustrates that control may be important in situations other than takeovers. They focus on a particular situation of this type. One issue is in what other circumstances control matters. Another is how important empirically each of these possible scenarios is in influencing the design of corporate charters.

Overall, the papers considered in this section indicate circumstances do exist where debt and equity are optimal. However, these circumstances appear to be rather special relative to the wide set of circumstances in which debt and equity are used in practice. Thus the contribution of the literature to date is to provide some insights into why debt and equity are used, rather than a single comprehensive theory. The literature has also succeeded in identifying a number of important issues and has provided paradigms within which to consider these issues.

What Are the Optimal Securities?

As mentioned above, the circumstances so far identified where debt and equity are optimal are fairly restricted. In particular, most of the papers mentioned require that the firm or its investors or both be risk neutral. Since it has traditionally been argued that one of the main roles of the stock market is to allow risk to be shared, this assumption is fairly restrictive. Moreover, the long history and extent of financial innovation suggest that firms' financing needs are not satisfied by debt and equity.

Rather than ask "What are the circumstances where debt and equity are optimal?" another branch of the literature has been concerned with the question "What are the optimal securities to issue?" The Modigliani and Miller result, that capital structure is irrelevant when markets are complete, suggests that the form of securities issued is also irrelevant in these circumstances. In order to develop a theory of optimal securities, it is necessary that markets be incomplete. One possible reason for incompleteness that is often suggested is transaction costs. Allen and Gale (1988, 1989) have considered the implications of the transaction costs of issuing securities.

Allen and Gale (1988) develop a simple model of financial innovation with two dates and a finite set of states of nature. Information is symmetric; the state is unknown to everybody at the first date and revealed to all at the second. A single good exists at both dates, along with a finite number of investor and firm types with a continuum of each type. Instead of assuming that firms are restricted to issuing debt and equity, however, Allen and Gale assume that firms choose the securities that they issue and this determines the transaction costs they incur. This means the market structure is endogenous and it is possible to consider the theoretical issues raised by financial innovation.

The equilibrium concept used is based on that of Hart (1979) and is essentially Walrasian. Markets are perfectly competitive since there is a continuum of firms and consumers. Prices are quoted to both firms and investors for every possible security. This includes all those securities that are issued in equilibrium as in Hart's model. It also includes all those securities that could be issued but in equilibrium are not (that is, demand and supply are both zero). This contrasts with Hart's approach where markets for these unissued securities are closed to investors and prices are quoted only to firms.

The first result obtained is that under standard assumptions equilibrium exists provided short sales are not possible. If securities can be costlessly sold short, then equilibrium may not exist because shortsellers are effectively able to expand the supply of firms' securities more cheaply than firms can. For example, suppose a firm can issue two securities rather than one for some additional cost. In order for the firm to be willing to do this, its gross value with two securities must be larger than with one to allow it to recoup this additional cost. However, if costless short sales are possible this implies an arbitrage opportunity is available, since by going short in a two-security firm and long in a one-security firm, an investor can earn the difference between the two. An equilibrium where all firms issue one security may not be feasible because at the prevailing prices issuing two securities may be profitable. Thus equilibrium may not exist unless short sales are ruled out.

The short sales constraint means that with incomplete markets distinct types of investor value securities differently on the margin. The price of a security, whether issued or unissued, is determined by the group that values it most. In equilibrium, the firm issues the securities that maximize its value and sells them to the groups or clienteles that value them the most.

The second result obtained is that every equilibrium is constrained efficient. In other words, a planner subject to the same transaction costs for issuing securities and able to make transfers between investors at the first date cannot make everybody better off than in the market allocation. This result arises because of the assumption that the prices of unissued securities are quoted to both firms and investors. If prices are only quoted to

firms, then inefficient equilibria may exist because of a pecuniary externality. To see this, suppose there are two types of firm, each of which
produces output in one state only. Investors have Cobb-Douglas utility
functions so that consumption in one state will not have value unless
consumption is positive in the other. If markets for unissued securities are
closed to investors, an equilibrium exists where the firms do not issue any
securities because the price quoted to them for all securities is zero. This
cannot be an equilibrium if prices are quoted to investors as well, because
at zero prices they would demand securities that allow them to consume
in both states.

A third result is that debt and equity are not optimal but that the
optimal securities do have a particularly simple form. To see this, suppose
there are two types of investor, one type of firm and two states. When
firms issue only equity, the more risk-averse investors have a lower marginal utility of consumption in the high-output state than the less risk-
averse investors; in the low-output state, the reverse is true. If a firm issues
debt and levered equity, the more risk-averse group will pay a premium
for the debt since it allows them to smooth consumption; the levered
equity will be held by the less risk-averse group since they value consumption most in the high-output state. This split is not optimal, however,
because the debt allocates payoffs in the good state to the more risk-averse
group that values consumption the least. The firm could obtain more for
its securities by allocating all the payoffs in the good state to the security
that is held by the less risk-averse group, which values consumption most
in this state. In general, it can be seen that optimal securities involve
allocating all the firm's output in a particular state to the security held by
the group that values consumption most in that state.

The critical assumption for all these results is the one ruling out short
sales. In practice, short selling of corporate securities is costly and only a
limited amount is undertaken (Pollack 1986). This suggests that in some
circumstances it may be appropriate to rule out short sales. However,
markets for stock options and index futures may represent a low-cost
substitute for short sales. This suggests that the case of unlimited short
sales is also of interest. In addition, the fact that unlimited short sales is a
crucial assumption of many models in financial economics means this case
is important theoretically.

Allen and Gale (1989) develop a model where unlimited short sales are
possible. The main differences between this model and the one in Allen

and Gale (1988) are that the number of agents is finite and the sequence of events is as shown in figure 11.5. Firms first choose the securities to issue, these securities are then traded on competitive markets, and finally the securities' payoffs are realized. When choosing securities initially, firms play a noncooperative game; they take into account the effect of their actions on the equilibrium of the securities market at the next stage.

In contrast to the model of Allen and Gale (1988), firms are not price-takers; if a firm issues a new security it changes the security market equilibrium. Nevertheless it can be shown that if short sales are ruled out, then as the number of agents approaches infinity the equilibrium is essentially equivalent to that in Allen and Gale (1988); each firm's actions have a negligible impact on the equilibrium at the second stage.

If short sales are *not* ruled out, the equilibrium of the model may differ significantly from that in Allen and Gale (1988). Even if the value of a two-security firm is the same as that of an identical one-security firm, so that no arbitrage opportunity exists in the second-stage equilibrium, a firm may nevertheless have an incentive to issue a costly security initially. A new security may increase the value of the firm in the second-stage equilibrium relative to the equilibrium that would occur if no innovation were made. Thus there can be an ex ante incentive to innovate even when there is no ex post incentive. This is true even as the number of agents approaches infinity. Now a single firm can affect the security-market equilibrium even though it is negligible, because the existence of short sales means that the open interest in the security may be large.

The fact that firms are no longer price-takers ensures that the existence of equilibrium is not a problem even though short sales are possible. However, the equilibrium is no longer constrained efficient. An example is given of too little innovation; the change in firm value across security-

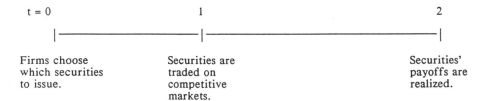

Figure 11.5
The sequence of events in the Allen and Gale (1989) model

market equilibria is such that firms fail to issue a security even though everybody could be made better off if such a security were issued and appropriate initial transfers were made. An example is also given of too much innovation; in this case firms issue securities even though everybody could be made better off if fewer securities were issued. In the context of this model, therefore, the endogenous incomplete market structure that arises from profit-maximizing behavior is not necessarily efficient. Another aspect of this result is that the equilibrium with short sales ruled out may be superior to the equilibrium where short sales are not ruled out. For a given set of securities, allowing short sales improves possibilities for risk sharing. However, allowing short sales reduces the incentives to innovate, so overall risk-sharing opportunities may be reduced.

As far as the form of optimal securities is concerned, an example is given where debt and equity are optimal. This example is clearly a special case, however, and in general the optimal securities have a complex form that cannot be characterized simply.

This section has considered models of financial innovation where corporations issue securities. However, in addition to corporations a number of other types of institution such as futures and options exchanges issue securities. Duffie and Jackson (1989 and the references therein) consider innovation by futures exchanges; Allen and Gale (1990) consider innovation by options exchanges. The implications of incomplete markets for the design of government securities are considered in Gale (1989).

As with the literature on the optimality of debt and equity, the literature on optimal securities is still at a very early stage. The results in Allen and Gale (1988), showing that optimal securities involve allocating all the firm's payoffs in a particular state to the security held by the group that values consumption the most, provide some insight into the option-like form of many new securities. However, the literature to date does not provide much insight into the actual path of most financial innovations. Its main contribution is again in identifying the theoretical issues and in providing models to analyze these issues.

Summary and Conclusions

The traditional approach to understanding firms' choice of capital structure has been to consider firms' optimal debt-equity ratios. This approach has not been very successful in terms of providing an understanding of the capital structures firms choose in practice. The introduction of many new securities in recent years suggests the alternative approach of considering the optimal form of securities that firms should issue. The literature based on this approach has been the subject of this chapter.

The first branch of this literature has considered the circumstances in which debt and equity are optimal. A number of situations where debt is optimal have been identified. These typically involve a principal-agent relationship where an investor (the principal) lends money to an entrepreneur (the agent) to allow him to undertake an investment project. A debt contract is optimal in these models because it ensures that the entrepreneur takes a particular action. Although these theories are suggestive of why a public corporation may want to issue debt and equity, they cannot be directly applied in this case. Williams (1989) has extended this type of analysis to public corporations by assuming ex ante monitoring that prevents managers from expropriating firms' assets.

The assumptions of all these models are fairly restrictive. It is usually critical that either one or both parties is risk neutral and/or the earnings from the investment or actions of the entrepreneur are difficult for the outside investor to observe and so cannot be contracted upon. If earnings or anything else related to the management's performance can be observed at all, and the management is risk averse, the results of Holmstrom (1979) suggest that the optimal payments to the bondholder should be conditioned on this information. In practice, even though typically the parties are risk averse and some information on earnings is available, payments on debt contracts are fixed and do not vary with the available information. An exception is provided by income bonds but these are rarely used.

Another part of the literature has looked at the question of why public corporations typically have equity securities with one vote per share and majority rule. Most of these papers are concerned with the effect of voting on the market for corporate control. Again, the circumstances where these results hold are rather special. Moreover, they critically depend on the magnitude of the private benefits of control and the distribution of these between incumbents and rivals.

Overall, the literature on the optimality of debt and equity suggests that the circumstances in which these commonly used securities are the best are fairly restrictive. This is difficult to reconcile with the fact that debt and equity are so widely used. However, the literature has identified a number of important issues and identified ways to think about these issues. A similar argument can be made concerning the literature on the form of optimal securities.

The results to date do suggest a number of important questions to be investigated in future research. Debt and equity have been used in numerous diverse situations. Why is it that they are so robust? What are the incentives for firms to issue securities other than debt and equity, and what are the general principles underlying the design of these securities, Finally, even though the securities that are issued may be optimal privately, the results of Harris and Raviv (1988a) and Allen and Gale (1989) suggest that no particular reason exists to believe that they are optimal from a social point of view. In other words, as far as the issue of securities is concerned, it is not immediately obvious that the "invisible hand" operates and ensures that market structure is efficient. A critical issue is, therefore, under what circumstances the market structure that arises is socially desirable and under what circumstances government intervention is justified.

The papers considered above all assume discrete time. The use of continuous time models to price derivative securities has not been discussed. As Hakansson (1979) has pointed out in the context of option securities, these models rely on the fact that dynamic trading strategies make markets effectively complete. This makes the analysis of financial innovation using continuous time techniques difficult. However, Merton (1989) has made progress in this direction by considering a world where individuals face transaction costs but intermediaries do not so that continuous time techniques can still be used. The relationship between financial innovation and dynamic trading strategies is an important topic for future research.

In conclusion, the theoretical literature has just begun to look at the question "What are the optimal securities for firms to issue?" Recent research has shed some light on the changing nature of debt and equity by identifying some of the important issues in this area.

Notes

The author is grateful to Jaime Zender and to his discussants, Oliver Hart and Robert Merton, for helpful comments. financial support from the National Science Foundation (Grant No. SES-8813719) is acknowledged.

1. See, for example, Hellwig (1981) and the references therein.

2. See, for example, Kim (1978) and the reference therein.

3. See, for example, Titman (1984); Allen (1987); Webb (1987); Giammarino (1989); and Mooradian (1989).

4. See Kim (1989) for a survey of this literature.

5. See Ravid (1988) for a survey and also Baldwin (1983a, 1983b, and 1988).

6. For a full account of recent innovation see Finnerty (1988).

7. See Malatesta and Walkling (1988) for a more complete description of actual poison pills.

References

Aghion, Philippe and Patrick Bolton. 1988. "An 'Incomplete Contract' Approach to Bankruptcy and the Financial Structure of the Firm." Technical Report 536, IMSSS, Stanford University.

Allen, Franklin. 1987. "Capital Structure and Imperfect Competition in Product Markets." Working paper 11-87, Rodney L. White Center, University of Pennsylvania.

Allen, Franklin and Douglas Gale. 1988. "Optimal Security Design." *Review of Financial Studies*, vol. 1, pp. 229–263.

———. 1989. "Arbitrage, Short Sales and Financial Innovation." Working paper 10-89, Rodney L. White Center, University of Pennsylvania.

———. 1990. "Incomplete Markets and Incentives to Set Up an Options Exchange." *Geneva Papers on Risk and Insurance*, special issue on "The Allocation of Risk with Incomplete Asset Markets," edited by Herakles Polemarchakis, vol. 15, pp. 15–44.

Bagwell, Laurie Simon and Kenneth L. Judd. 1989. "Transactions Costs and Corporate Control." Working paper 67, Kellogg Graduate School of Management, Northwestern University.

Baldwin, Carliss Y. 1983a. "Productivity and Labor Unions: An Application of the Theory of Self-Enforcing Contracts." *Journal of Business*, vol. 56. pp. 155–185.

———. 1983b. "Innovation and the Vertical Structure of Industry." Working paper, Harvard Business School.

———. 1988. "Time Inconsistency in Capital Budgeting." Working paper, Harvard Business School.

Blair, Douglas H., Devra L. Golbe and James M. Gerard. 1989. "Unbundling the Voting Rights and Profit Claims of Common Shares." *Journal of Political Economy*, vol. 97, pp. 420–443.

Brennan, Michael and Alan Kraus. 1987. "Efficient Financing under Asymmetric Information." *Journal of Finance*, vol. 42, pp. 1225–1243.

DeAngelo, Harry and Ronald W. Masulis. 1980. "Optimal Capital Structure under Corporate and Personal Taxation." *Journal of Financial Economics*, vol. 8, pp. 3–30.

Dewing, Arthur S. 1934. *A Study of Corporation Securities: Their Nature and Uses in Finance.* Ronald Press Company: New York.

Diamond, Douglas W. 1984. "Financial Intermediation and Delegated Monitoring." *Review of Economic Studies*, vol. 51, pp. 393–414.

Duffie, Darrell and Matthew O. Jackson. 1989. "Optimal Innovation of Futures Contracts." *Review of Financial Studies*, vol. 2, pp. 275–296.

Finnerty, John D. 1988. "Financial Engineering in Corporate Finance: An Overview." *Financial Management*, vol. 17, pp. 14–33.

Gale, Douglas. 1989. "Notes on Efficient Public Debt." Working paper, University of Pittsburgh.

Gale, Douglas and Martin Hellwig. 1985. "Incentive-Compatible Debt Contracts: The One-Period Problem." *Review of Economic Studies*, vol. 52, pp. 647–663.

Giammarino, Ronald M. 1989. "The Resolution of Financial Distress." *Review of Financial Studies*, vol. 2, pp. 25–47.

Green, Richard C. 1984. "Investment Incentives, Debt and Warrants." *Journal of Financial Economics.* vol. 13, pp. 115–136.

Grossman, Sanford J. and Oliver D. Hart. 1988. "One Share/One Vote and the Market for Corporate Control." *Journal of Financial Economics*, vol. 20, pp. 175–202.

Hakansson, Nils H. 1979. "The Fantastic World of Finance: Progress and the Free Lunch." *Journal of Financial and Quantitative Analysis*, vol. 14, pp. 717–734.

Harris, Milton and Artur Raviv. 1988a. "Corporate Governance: Voting Rights and Majority Rule." *Journal of Financial Economics*, vol. 20, pp. 203–235.

––––––. 1988b. "Corporate Control Contests and Capital Structure." *Journal of Financial Economics*, vol. 20, pp. 55–86.

––––––. 1989. "The Design of Securities." Working paper, Graduate School of Business, University of Chicago.

Hart, Oliver D. 1979. "On Shareholder Unanimity in Large Stock Market Economies." *Econometrica*, vol. 47, pp. 1057–1084.

Hart, Oliver D. and John Moore. 1989. "Default and Renegotiation: A Dynamic Model of Debt," Working paper 89-069, Harvard Business School.

Haugen, Robert A. and Lemma W. Senbet. 1978. "The Insignificance of Bankruptcy Costs to the Theory of Optimal Capital Structure." *Journal of Finance*, vol. 33, pp. 383–393.

Hellwig, Martin F. 1981. "Bankruptcy, Limited Liability and the Modigliani-Miller Theorem." *The American Economic Review*, vol. 71, pp. 155–170.

Holmstrom, Bengt. 1979. "Moral Hazard and Observability." *Bell Journal of Economics*, vol. 10, pp. 74–91.

Jensen, Michael C. and William H. Meckling. 1976. "Theory of the Firm: Managerial Behavior, Agency Costs and Ownership Structure." *Journal of Financial Economics*, vol. 3, pp. 305–360.

Kanemasu, Hiromitsu, Robert H. Litzenberger and Jacques Rolfo. 1986. "Financial Innovation in an Incomplete Market: An Empirical Study of Stripped Government Securities." Working paper 26-86, Rodney L. White Center, University of Pennsylvania.

Kim, E. Han. 1978. "A Mean-Variance Theory of Optimal Capital Structure and Optimal Debt Capacity." *Journal of Finance*, vol. 33, pp. 45–63.

––––––. 1989. "Optimal Capital Structure in Miller's Equilibrium." In *Financial Markets and Incomplete Information: Frontiers of Modern Financial Theory*, Volume 2, edited by Sudipto Bhattacharya and George M. Constantinides. Totowa, N.J.: Rowman and Littlefield.

Malatesta, Paul H. and Ralph A. Walkling. 1988. "Poison Pill Securities: Stockholder Wealth, Profitability and Ownership Structure." *Journal of Financial Economics*, vol. 20, pp. 347–376.

Merton, Robert C. 1989. "On the Application of the Continuous-Time Theory of Finance to Financial Intermediation and Insurance." *Geneva Papers on Risk and Insurance*, vol. 14, pp. 225–261.

Miller, Merton H. 1977. "Debt and Taxes." *Journal of Finance*, vol. 32, May, pp. 261–275.

———. 1986. "Financial Innovation: The Last Twenty Years and the Next." *Journal Financial and Quantitative Analysis*, vol. 21, pp. 459–471.

Modigliani, Franco and Merton H. Miller. 1958. "The Cost of Capital, Corporation Finance and the Theory of Investment." *The American Economic Review*, vol. 48, pp. 261–297.

———. 1963. "Corporate Income Taxes and the Cost of Capital: A Correction." *The American Economic Review*, vol. 53, pp. 433–443.

Mookherjee, Dilip and Ivan Png. 1989. "Optimal Auditing, Insurance and Redistribution." *Quarterly Journal of Economics*, vol. 104, pp. 399–416.

Mooradian, Robert M. 1989. "Recapitalizations and the Free-Rider Problem: Bankruptcy and the Theory of Capital Structure." Working paper 89-3, Graduate School of Business, University of Florida.

Myers, Stewart C. 1977. "Determinants of Corporate Borrowing." *Journal of Financial Economics*, vol. 5, November, pp. 147–175.

———. 1984. "The Capital Structure Puzzle." *Journal of Finance*, vol. 39, pp. 575–592.

Myers, Stewart C. and Nicholas S. Majluf. 1984. "Corporate Financing and Investment Decisions When Firms Have Information That Investors Do Not Have." *Journal of Financial Economics*, vol. 13, pp. 187–221.

Pollack, Irving M. 1986. "Short-Sale Regulation of NASDAQ Securities." NASDAQ pamphlet.

Ravid, S. Abraham 1988. "On Interactions of Production and Financial Decisions." *Financial Management*, vol. 17, pp. 87–99.

Ross, Stephen A. 1977. "The Determination of Financial Structure: The Incentive Signaling Approach." *Bell Journal of Economics*, vol. 8, pp. 23–40.

Titman, Sheridan. 1984. "The Effect of Capital Structure on a Firm's Liquidation Decision." *Journal of Financial Economics*, vol. 13, pp. 137–152.

Townsend, Robert M. 1979. "Optimal Contracts and Competitive Markets with Costly State Verification." *Journal of Economic Theory*, vol. 22, pp. 265–293.

Tufano, Peter. 1988. "Financial Innovation and First-Mover Advantages: An Empirical Analysis." Working paper, Harvard Business School.

Van Horne, James C. 1985. "Of Financial Innovation and Excesses." *Journal of Finance*, vol. 40, pp. 621–631.

Warner, Jerold B. 1977. "Bankruptcy Costs: Some Evidence." *Journal of Finance*, vol. 32, pp. 337–347.

Webb, David C. 1987. "The Importance of Incomplete Information in Explaining the Existence of Costly Bankruptcy." *Economica*, vol. 54, pp. 279–288.

Williams, Joseph. 1989. "Ex-Ante Monitoring, Ex-Post Asymmetry, and Optimal Securities." Working paper, University of British Columbia.

Zender, Jaime F. 1989. "Optimal Financial Instruments." Working paper, University of Utah.

Index